WI

THE WORLD'S CLASS

THE REC

AND

GEORGE FARQUHAR was bo
Dublin, and left without a d
the career of playwright aft
travelled to London, and at 2
in this volume he wrote three
Wildair, and *The Inconstant*, as well as an afterpiece, *The Stage-Coach* (with
Peter Motteux). He had mixed success. One of his mistresses was a talented
and successful actress, but he was tricked into marriage by an impecunious
widow. His plays were alternately wildly successful and unhappy failures. He
joined the army, but resigned his commission and failed to get another. He
seems to have been companionable, and to have enjoyed the friendship of
people from many different social backgrounds (though he disliked academ-
ics), but he ended his life alone, except for his faithful friend the actor Robert
Wilks. He wrote his last play as he lay dying poverty-stricken in a garret. He
was 29.

WILLIAM MYERS is Professor of English Literature at the University of
Leicester. He was born in Dublin in 1939 and brought up in England. A
university teacher since 1964, he has written books on Milton, Dryden,
George Eliot, and Evelyn Waugh, and has taught in the United States as well
as in Britain.

MICHAEL CORDNER is a Senior Lecturer in the Department of English and
Related Literature at the University of York. He has edited George
Farquhar's *The Beaux' Stratagem*, the *Complete Plays* of Sir George Etherege,
Four Comedies of Sir John Vanbrugh, and, for the World's Classics series,
Four Restoration Marriage Comedies. He has also co-edited *English Comedy*
(Cambridge, 1994) and is completing a book on *The Comedy of Marriage
1660–1737*.

PETER HOLLAND is Judith E. Wilson University Lecturer in Drama in the
Faculty of English at the University of Cambridge.

MARTIN WIGGINS is a Fellow of the Shakespeare Institute and Lecturer in
English at the University of Birmingham.

DRAMA IN WORLD'S CLASSICS

J. M. Barrie
Peter Pan and Other Plays

Aphra Behn
The Rover and Other Plays

George Farquhar
The Recruiting Officer and Other Plays

John Ford
'Tis Pity She's a Whore and Other Plays

Ben Jonson
The Alchemist and Other Plays

Christopher Marlowe
Doctor Faustus and Other Plays

Arthur Wing Pinero
Trelawny of the 'Wells' and Other Plays

J. M. Synge
The Playboy of the Western World and Other Plays

Oscar Wilde
The Importance of Being Earnest and Other Plays

Campion, Carew, Chapman, Daniel, Davenant, Jonson, Townshend
Court Masques

Chapman, Kyd, Middleton, Tourneur
Four Revenge Tragedies

Coyne, Fitzball, Jones, Lewes, Sims
The Lights o' London and Other Plays

Dryden, Lee, Otway, Southerne
Four Restoration Marriage Comedies

THE WORLD'S CLASSICS

====

GEORGE FARQUHAR

The Constant Couple
The Twin Rivals
The Recruiting Officer
The Beaux' Stratagem

====

Edited with an Introduction by
WILLIAM MYERS

General Editor
MICHAEL CORDNER

Associate General Editors
PETER HOLLAND   MARTIN WIGGINS

Oxford   New York
OXFORD UNIVERSITY PRESS
1995

Oxford University Press, Walton Street, Oxford OX2 6DP

Oxford New York
Athens Auckland Bangkok Bombay
Calcutta Cape Town Dar es Salaam Delhi
Florence Hong Kong Istanbul Karachi
Kuala Lumpur Madras Madrid Melbourne
Mexico City Nairobi Paris Singapore
Taipei Tokyo Toronto
and associated companies in
Berlin Ibadan

Oxford is a trade mark of Oxford University Press

First published as a World's Classics paperback 1995

British Library Cataloguing in Publication Data
Data available

Library of Congress Cataloging in Publication Data
Farquhar, George, 1677?–1707.
The recruiting officer, and other plays / George Farquhar; edited with
an introduction by William Myers; general editor, Michael Cordner;
associate general editors, Peter Holland, Martin Wiggins.
I. Myers, William, 1939– . II. Title. III. Series.
PR3436.M94 1995 822'.4—dc20   95–2971
ISBN 0–19–282249–7

1 3 5 7 9 10 8 6 4 2

Typeset by Pure Tech India Ltd, Pondicherry, India
Printed in Great Britain
by Biddles Ltd.
Guildford and King's Lynn

CONTENTS

ACKNOWLEDGEMENTS

THE four plays in this volume have been edited in the light of the distinguished work of earlier editors, especially William Archer, Louis Strauss, Charles Stonehill, Michael Shugrue, Norman Jeffares, John Ross, Michael Cordner, Charles Fifer, Peter Dixon, and Shirley Strum Kenny. Almost every decision about text or notes has been directly or indirectly influenced by their example, and they have been invaluable in bringing secondary sources to my attention. My thanks are also due to Dr Frank Felsenstein who kindly let me see an extract from his forthcoming study of anti-Semitism in eighteenth-century England, to Professor Gordon Campbell who advised a tone-deaf editor on matters musical, and to Mrs Rose Bakker who helped me with Farquhar's erratic Flemish. I am particularly grateful to M. J. Kidnie, who had the unenviable task of collating my draft typescript of the text.

W.M.

INTRODUCTION

BORN in 1677 or 1678, the son of a parson with seven children and £150 a year, George Farquhar was brought up among the beleaguered Protestant planters of Ulster;[1] his widow was to claim that her late husband's family had been burned out of house and home[2] when the Catholic James II invaded Ireland in 1689 in an attempt to recover the kingdoms he had lost the previous year. Farquhar celebrated King James's defeat in 1690 by composing a Pindaric ode on the death of one of the generals of the victorious William of Orange; later he produced an elegy on the death of William's wife, Mary. Of William he was to write, he 'first asserted our Liberties at home against Popery and Thraldom, headed our Armies abroad with bravery and success, gave Peace to Europe, and security to our Religion.'[3]

Farquhar entered Trinity College, Dublin, in 1694, but was unhappy and rebellious as a student, and left after two years to go on the stage, where he became friends with the brilliant young actor Robert Wilks. He was unimpressive in performance and after wounding a fellow player with a sword, he set off for London at about the age of 20, possibly with a draft of his first play in his portmanteau. *Love and a Bottle* is a licentious piece about a young man from Ireland, 'of a wild roving temper; newly come to London',[4] pursued by two women, Drudge, his whore and the mother of his child whom he treats abominably, and the virtuous, wealthy Leanthe, disguised as a young man, whom he eventually marries. (Drudge bore him twins, but 'Heaven was pleased to lessen [his] affliction, by taking away the she Brat.'[5]) The play was produced successfully in December 1698, in spite of the campaign against indecency launched by the Jacobite Jeremy Collier the previous March.

[1] I rely on Eric Rothstein, *George Farquhar* (1977), 13-29, for much of the biographical data in this Introduction.

[2] J. R. Sutherland, 'New Light on George Farquhar', *Times Literary Supplement*, 6 Mar. 1937, 171.

[3] Dedication, *Sir Harry Wildair*, *The Works of George Farquhar*, ed. Shirley Strum Kenny (2 vols.; 1988), i. 252. All quotations from Farquhar's works, other than those in this volume, are from this edition.

[4] *Love and a Bottle*, Dramatis Personae.

[5] *Love and a Bottle*, 1.1.241-2.

Although he probably had no thoughts then of becoming a soldier, Farquhar, the committed Williamite, aligns himself with the military in this first play, and these sentiments reappear in his second, *The Constant Couple* (1699), in which Wilks played Sir Harry Wildair, and which was hugely successful. Success, however, was not easily sustained. Playwrights were being driven towards respectable, sentimental comedy, and the theatrical profession was demoralized by bad management, inter-house rivalry, and the new, expensive Italian opera. The ferociously anti-Catholic *Sir Harry Wildair* (1701), produced after a visit to Holland, was not revived after its first season for thirty-six years, and Farquhar's next two plays (if we exclude his farcical afterpiece written with Peter Motteux, *The Stage-Coach*, the date of which is uncertain) were equally disappointing. *The Inconstant* (1702) was heckled on its first night. *The Twin Rivals* (1703) was attacked before it was staged and was thinly attended during its first run. Farquhar supplemented his income with other writing. He followed *Love and a Bottle* with the anonymous romance *The Adventures of Covent Garden* (1699) which contained material he was to reuse in *The Constant Couple*. (In the same way Archer's flirtation with Cherry is recycled in *Love's Catechism* (1707).) He contributed to miscellanies, and published 'a Collection of Occasionary Verse, and Epistolary Prose' under the title *Love and Business* (1701) including love letters to two women, Anne Oldfield, an actress whom he was reputed to have discovered, and Margaret Pemell, a widow with three children, ten years his senior, who apparently tricked him into marriage in 1703 by pretending to have an income of £700 a year.

In 1704 he was in the army, serving as a recruiting officer in Shrewsbury before going to Ireland—he had obtained his commission through the patronage either of the Earl of Orrery or of the Duke of Ormonde (the latter certainly claimed as much in 1709).[6] But he was in debt, possibly because of expenses incurred recruiting. He wrote a poem on the relief of Barcelona in 1705, but the Earl of Peterborough, to whom the poem was dedicated, was disgraced shortly thereafter and the poem was not published until after Farquhar's death. Apparently with Ormonde's support—he was Lord Lieutenant of Ireland—Farquhar returned to the stage in a benefit performance of *The Constant Couple* in Dublin. He was in England again in the late summer of 1705, possibly recruiting near Lichfield. *The Recruiting Officer* was written by the following February. But in spite of receipts

---

[6] Kenny (ed.), *Works*, ii. 601.

from his benefit in Dublin and his latest play's success, his money problems persisted and he sold his commission, it seems at Ormonde's suggestion. But the Duke failed to present him with the captaincy he expected, and he became destitute. Early in 1707 Wilks discovered him ill in a garret and encouraged him to write his last play, *The Beaux' Stratagem*. It opened on 8 March; Farquhar was buried on 23 May.

This is not the record of the kind of young man Farquhar depicted in his plays, of a Wildair, a Plume, or an Archer. He describes his mind as 'generally drest like my Person, in Black' and his 'Constitution [as] very Splenatick and yet very Amorous',[7] qualities he endeavoured to hide. This 'Picture' of himself may be tongue-in-cheek, but the facts are clear. He had some success as a playwright, but as a student, actor, client of the great, recruiting officer, and family man who left a widow and two daughters in poverty when he died at 29, he knew little but defeat and virtual dishonour. His career and personality are thus in marked contrast to those of William Congreve, also an alumnus of Trinity College, Dublin, and also in his twenties the writer of a series of celebrated plays. For Congreve was a gentleman, the friend of Dryden, Swift, Steele, and Pope, a sinecurist, the father of the Duchess of Marlborough's daughter. His carefully composed comedies struggle vainly but with high intelligence to sustain traditional conceptions of humane worldliness in an age of cynically pragmatic politics and power based on contractual not traditional relations. When the contradictions of this programme became clear to him, he could afford to fall silent. But Farquhar had no such programme, nor the standing or skills of a man of the world. He was socially on the margins.

Imaginatively, however, he was not on the margins at all but in touch with themes, attitudes, and comic modes which became 'canonical' after his death, so that one gets the curious sense from his plays that he was as influenced by later as by earlier writers. In *The Twin Rivals* we not only hear echoes of Shakespeare's villains in Young Wouldbe, notably Gloucester in *Richard III* and Edmund in *King Lear*, but also of Dickens's Mrs Gamp (and a long line of pantomime dames also, for the part was originally played by a man) in the hard-drinking midwife, Mrs Mandrake. *The Recruiting Officer* is more traditional, recalling the recruiting scenes in Shakespeare's *1 Henry IV*, and the conjuring scenes in Jonson's *The Alchemist*. Brazen

---

[7] *Love and Business*, ibid. ii. 351.

reworks Bobadil in *Every Man in his Humour*, and Sylvia numerous heroines in earlier comedy from Shakespeare to Farquhar's immediate predecessors. In *The Beaux' Stratagem*, however, the treatment of criminals anticipates John Gay's *The Beggar's Opera* and the general setting and situation anticipate Goldsmith's *She Stoops to Conquer*, while in both the last two plays the action moves out of the enclosed 'world' of London into the socially more mixed, less pressured territory of country towns, inns, and country houses—the setting 'canonized' by numerous eighteenth- and nineteenth-century novels.

Farquhar's work thus slots easily into the tradition and has accordingly proved very adaptable to the shifting values of different generations. *The Twin Rivals* is the only play in this volume to have proved intermittently troublesome. One reason may have been the tradition of giving the part of Mrs Mandrake to a man. Another was the fact that the taboos surrounding childbirth were stricter than those surrounding promiscuity. In Bath in 1812, the line, 'Only a poor gentlewoman in labour' (5.2.34), provoked violent hissing and the performance had to be halted.[8] Nevertheless the play was revived ten times in London before 1778, and was, in Shirley Strum Kenny's words, 'a dependable staple of eighteenth-century repertory theatre'.[9] No such problems checked the stage-history of the other three plays reprinted here. They had successful first runs, and subsequently escaped the radical censorship which in 1766 led David Garrick to rewrite Wycherley's *The Country Wife* as *The Country Girl*. Even in 1823, when Lamb declared the 'artificial Comedy, or Comedy of manners . . . quite extinct on our stage',[10] he made a partial exception of Congreve and Farquhar. In 1840 Leigh Hunt declared Farquhar to be far and away the most popular of the Restoration dramatists 'in the number of editions'[11] and performances of his plays.

Lamb's description of Restoration Comedies as constituting 'a world of themselves almost as much as fairy-land . . . [without] reference to the world that is . . . a Utopia of gallantry',[12] defines very well the spirit in which Farquhar was acted in the early years of this century. Following her brilliant performance as Millamant in the 1924

---

[8] *The Complete Works of George Farquhar*, ed. Charles Stonehill (2 vols.; 1930), i. 284.

[9] Kenny (ed.), *Works*, 468.

[10] 'On the Artificial Comedy of the Last Age', in *The Works in Prose and Verse of Charles and Mary Lamb*, ed. Thomas Hutchinson (2 vols.; 1909), i. 648.

[11] *The Dramatic Works of Wycherley, Congreve, Vanbrugh, and Farquhar*, ed. Leigh Hunt (1840), p. xxviii.

[12] Hutchinson (ed.), *Lamb*, i. 650.

production of *The Way of the World*, Edith Evans played Mrs Sullen in Nigel Playfair's production of *The Beaux' Stratagem* in 1927. In these and subsequent productions of Restoration Comedy, historical reference went no deeper than costume, gesture, and accent. In 1955, however, Bertolt Brecht's adaptation of *The Recruiting Officer*, *Pauken und Trompeten* (*Drums and Trumpets*), set in America during the Civil War, disclosed a potently subversive Farquhar, by no means tethered safely to the mannered frivolity with which early eighteenth-century England had come, mistakenly, to be associated. And in 1965 William Gaskill directed the recruiting and court scenes at the National Theatre in a style which put on savage display the complacency with which the rich oppress the poor in all societies. Of course, if we accept Timberlake Wertenbaker's play, *Our Country's Good*, based on a novel by Thomas Keneally,[13] Farquhar had already spoken in these terms to the eighteenth-century convicts whose version of *The Recruiting Officer* was the first production of a play to be acted in Australia, but it was Brecht and Gaskill who showed how such claims could be made for Farquhar's work as a whole. In *The Beaux' Stratagem*, for example, the lower classes are thoroughly in the know: the gentlemanly thieves astutely 'smoke' the thieving gentlemen and in the end are only outwitted by one of their own—the clever and passionate Cherry.

Wertenbaker's play focuses particularly sharply on the uncomfortable truths of sexual politics in *The Recruiting Officer*, truths of which Farquhar was by no means unconscious. Parallels in *The Constant Couple*, for example, between the language of the brothel and the marriage market bear tellingly on Angelica's complaints about the 'strict confinement' (3.2.3) of feminine utterance as well as of feminine behaviour. This presumably is why, even before she puts on her dead brother's clothes, Silvia, in *The Recruiting Officer*, emancipates herself verbally. Talking to the linguistically inhibited Melinda, she recalls how 'the sharp air from the Welsh mountains made our noses drop in a cold morning at the boarding school' (1.2.23–5), and resorts to an obscene pun ('shoot flying') to indicate one of the things her father can do and she cannot. She wants her man's life and thoughts to be equally unconfined—she approves of Plume's fathering a bastard on Molly at the Castle. More sombrely, in *The Beaux' Stratagem*, Mrs Sullen's verbal fluency implies a vigorous sexuality

---

[13] Timberlake Wertenbaker, *Our Country's Good* (1989); see also Max Stafford-Clark, *Letters to George: The Account of a Rehearsal* (1989).

frustrated by a silent, sexless husband who 'comes flounce into bed, dead as a salmon in a fishmonger's basket' (2.1.60–1). Her emancipation only begins when Dorinda is aroused for the first time and so becomes 'conversable in the subjects of the sex' (3.1.4). The oppression experienced by women is thus internalized more deeply in Farquhar's world than the oppression of the poor—at least the lower orders are not shamed into shallow gentility of speech.

In fact the two forms of oppression were connected. Collier's was a political as well as a moral campaign—he was contending on behalf of his party for the strategic position identified as 'virtue' which the societies for the reformation of manners were seeking to appropriate on behalf of his bitterest political enemies. Routinely, the Court too issued proclamations against vice. Respectability was becoming ideologically more important, double standards applying as much to the poor as to women. The social control which this facilitated is plainly illustrated in the dialogue in *The Twin Rivals* (5.3.56–96) between Richmore and Trueman, disguised as a constable who has tricked a young woman into bed with a false promise of marriage, and in *The Recruiting Officer* (5.5.26–180), when the justices condone the licentiousness of the soldiery, but conscript the father of five children, send his wife to the house of correction (the couple's enthusiasm for family life threatens the parish finances and the supply of game on local estates), illegally enlist a miner, and give his companion the option of becoming a camp-follower or drowning herself. They thus happily embrace the ethos of Kite's famous song, 'Over the hills and far away', with all its cheerfully proclaimed contradictions. The same anarchic spirit of lust and rebellion with which it entices young men to accept the brutalities of army discipline is censoriously punished in civilians with impressment and the house of correction.

Yet for two hundred and fifty years these elements in Farquhar's texts passed virtually unnoticed. Only the Collierists were prepared to see the implications of his plays. Arthur Bedford vociferously complained about *The Recruiting Officer* in 1706:

In this Play the *Officers* confess, that they greatly abuse the new listed *Soldiers*; Debauchery of the Country Wenches is represented as a main Part of the Service; all the private Centinals are guilty of stealing . . . and the *Captain* desires, that he may have but one honest Man in the Company for the Novelty's sake.[14]

---

[14] Arthur Bedford, *Evil & Danger of Stage Plays, Shewing their Natural Tendency to Destroy Religion & Introduce a General Corruption of Manners* (1706), 152.

Pope, on the other hand, only noted Farquhar's 'pert, low dialogue',[15] a lack of linguistic polish which Theophilus Cibber attributed to Farquhar's failure to associate 'with persons of rank'.[16] Somewhat later Mrs Inchbald,[17] and to a lesser extent Leigh Hunt,[18] worried about his libertinism, while the main interest which scholars took in his work was in identifying local Shropshire worthies in *The Recruiting Officer*, and in following up Lyrick's assertion in *Love and a Bottle* that 'the Hero in Comedy is always the Poet's Character . . . [a] Compound of practical Rake, and speculative Gentleman'.[19] Farquhar did frequently represent himself as youthful, unacademic and unliterary, easy with country gentlemen and confident in his address to his patrons, a companionable soldierly rakehell. Biographical readings of the plays, however, ignore the extent to which their heroes are unlike each other; nor would any of them have allowed themselves to be tricked into marrying a poor widow, as Farquhar apparently was, and then remained loyal to her. The 'spark' of the Prologue to *The Constant Couple* and the 'author' of the dedications, prefaces, prologues, and epilogues, even when he is dying, is a mask, a self-conscious attempt by a young outsider to find a place for himself in the fashionable world. When he died, however, it was easy enough to compose from actual and putative references to himself in his writings a safe notion of the man and so to read his plays as the work of 'a happy-go-lucky Celt who entered the world of warring conventions without prejudice as to forms of discipline, but with a mighty propensity for free living and the enjoyment of life'.[20]

By a somewhat similar process, Sir Harry Wildair in *The Constant Couple* became a 'breeches' part in numerous eighteenth-century productions. The role as created by the handsome Wilks is that of a

---

[15] Alexander Pope, 'Imitations of Horace', II. i. 288. Pope does not attack Farquhar in this often quoted line, but cites him, along with Congreve and Vanbrugh, as evidence of 'how seldom ev'n the best succeed' (II. i. 28). As several commentators have pointed out, he is indebted to Farquhar for some famous lines. See Explanatory Notes *CC* 5.1.113–14 (rev. text) and *Sir Harry Wildair*, 1.1.20–2: 'A fine Lady can laugh at the death of her Husband, and cry for the loss of a Lap Dog.' Cf. *The Rape of the Lock*, iii. 158.

[16] Theophilus Cibber, *The Lives of the Poets of Great Britain and Ireland* (5 vols.; 1753), iii. 137–8.

[17] See *The British Theatre; or, A Collection of Plays, which are Acted at the Theatres Royal Drury Lane, Covent Garden, & Haymarket . . . by Mrs Inchbald* (25 vols.; 1808), viii. 3–4.

[18] See Hunt (ed.), *Dramatic Works*, pp. lxii–lxiii.   [19]*Love and a Bottle*, 4.2.47–51.

[20] *A Discourse upon Comedy, The Recruiting Officer and The Beaux' Stratagem by George Farquhar*, ed. Louis A. Strauss (1914), xiii.

sexual predator, supremely civilized without being in the least restrained by civilization. As an unmasking of the true masculine ideal underlying the sexual ethos of the age, however, Sir Harry could hardly be assimilated into the genteel decencies of the reformed theatre; anxiety about his moral standing persists in William Archer's description of him as 'a reprobate, a son of chaos, inadmissable into any moral order'.[21] But when the part was given to a woman, as it regularly was at least until 1820, the threat posed by his sexual energy and freedom was cleverly deflected. The mild titillation of watching a woman dressed as a man enabled productions of the play to sustain an air of daring without giving the male members of the audience real grounds for envy or the female for comparison.

Nor did the critics and players falsify Farquhar's achievement by thus making it safe. There is a vein of complacency and conservatism in the plays as ingrained as their implicit radicalism, and a consequence, perhaps, of the social and professional insecurity Farquhar evidently experienced. In the first version of *The Constant Couple*, for example, the *éclaircissement* scene between Sir Harry and Angelica is deformed by Sir Harry's lapsing unconvincingly into the sentimental rhetoric of Romance. In the revised version, rhetoric of just this kind is mocked; Sir Harry incontinently boasts of his inches only to be humiliated by the reading of Vizard's letter, and is forced by the relentless Lady Darling into marrying her daughter, thus nicely reinforcing the parallel in the play between mothers and madams. In *The Twin Rivals*, however, Farquhar resorts to the very rhetoric he had thus tried and found wanting in the earlier play.

The Twin Rivals is a difficult and disturbing work. Young Wouldbe, Richmore, Subtleman, the Clearaccounts, and Mandrake are savagely vigorous—the black farce by which Lord Wouldbe's last words are forced out of his corpse is breathtaking. On the other hand, the deformity of Young Wouldbe is only one instance of the play's discreditable reliance on stereotypes, sentimentality, and conventional rhetoric. The attitudes of Elder Wouldbe and the sanctimonious and superfluous goldsmith, Fairbank, in Act 3 unhappily anticipate Steele's tendentious comedy, *The Conscious Lovers*, which lavishly celebrates the City of London and its purported values. In each play, the hero even returns from his European travels with his chastity intact. Farquhar has evidently decided to flatter the very people who had hitherto been the butt of theatrical jokes. But he abandoned his

---

[21] George Farquhar, [*Four Plays*], ed. with an introduction and notes by William Archer, Mermaid Books edn. (1959), 19.

new line almost at once. When the play failed, he wrote a Preface jeering at the very people the figure of Fairbank attempted to please. At the same time, he undermined the sententious moral of the subplot by announcing that Richmore went back on his promise to marry the pregnant Clelia the moment he quit the stage. Farquhar was evidently a theatrical opportunist. He assumed the moral high ground (and vacated it) whenever it was advantageous to do so, and flattered his audience as shamelessly as he flattered his noble patrons, though not always consistently or with success in either case.

Nor are the problems of instability of viewpoint and facile social conformism confined to the early plays. The upshot of the fifth act of *The Recruiting Officer* is the triumph of Worthy and Justice Balance, that is of precisely those Friends Round the Wrekin, young and old, to whom the play is dedicated. We are even invited to agree that Worthy ought to have 'made . . . better use' (5.3.31) of the chance he had to exploit Melinda before she came into her money, and to enjoy Balance's taking charge in the fifth act, checking out Plume's good faith before giving his daughter and her fortune to a man who may now do what before was deemed dishonourable, that is 'quit the service' (2.1.40) in order to become a 'plain country gentleman' (2.1.32) like his future father-in-law. For his part, the newly enriched Plume is not above selling the recruits he has tricked and forced into the army to Captain Brazen, who presumably takes Molly and her little bastard off his hands as well. Brazen for all his silliness remains an officer and a gentleman and has therefore to be rescued from marriage to a servant. Lucy is accordingly punished for an intrigue in which Melinda was also involved, and Rose conveniently provided for. In the end, Farquhar is eager to respect the conventions: even Melinda and Silvia's dripping noses become ladylike chilblains in all editions of the play after the first.

Similar conclusions may be drawn from *The Beaux' Stratagem*. One sign of this is the contrast between Teague in *The Twin Rivals* and Foigard. Behind Teague's stage Irishry lurks a potential satirist. Of his starving and abused country, he remarks that sleeping instead of eating is 'the fashion in Ireland' (*TR* 3.2.99); he checks our laughter by demonstrating the sense in an 'Irishism' (*TR* 3.2.103), corrects Elder Wouldbe's failure to count him as a friend (*TR* 4.3.49), and announces he is making a joke directly to the audience (*TR* 5.3.23–4). Foigard is simply nasty and dull. Cordner[22] has shown that he was

---

[22] George Farquhar, *The Beaux' Stratagem*, ed. Michael Cordner (1990), p. xviii.

educated at a famous school in Kilkenny, so he must have changed his religion to get an education, but the example of bright, honest Protestant boys has no effect on his irremediable native stupidity, and he returns shiftily to his Catholic allegiance. (How Archer learns so much about him is not disclosed.) More troubling is the treatment of Cherry. Her interrogation of Archer after he has patronizingly cate-chized her (2.2) is astute and sensitive. She seems to be clearly his intellectual and moral superior, but he can only weigh up the chances of her dying once he has spent her handsome (if stolen) dowry. His disposal of her as Dorinda's maid is trivially convenient and singularly insensitive. (Poor Gypsy is discarded, presumably as punishment for being seduced by Foigard.) Farquhar clearly did not feel the need to take the personal lives of servants at all seriously. Jessica Munns points out that in the first edition of *The Recruiting Officer*, Rose's virginity 'is treated as a negotiable commodity'[23] by both Plume and Silvia (4.1.52–66). The revision of the text is probably due to the ineffective-ness of the original French. Admittedly Archer and Scrub note the sad lot of servants under the Pressing Act (*BS* 3.3.50–8), but the satire may be at the expense of servants dunning their masters, not masters cheating their servants, while the countrywoman who seeks Lady Bountiful's help (4.1) is made into a cruel figure of fun. Even Lady Bountiful—if Kenny is right in connecting her with Mercy's sister, Bountiful, in *Pilgrims Progress: The Second Part*[24]—may be an object of derision: Bunyan was regarded as a killjoy in theatrical circles.

A related problem is represented by Count Bellair. The jokes at his expense are as bad as those at Foigard's—it is inconceivable that a man of his standing would not know the difference in value between the *livre* and the pound (5.4.250). But Foigard has at least a part in the plot—he conducts Archer to Mrs Sullen's bedroom in place of the count—whereas Bellair's contribution to the action is nugatory. The role was savagely cut after the play's first performance. Such poor joinery is common in Farquhar's plays. In *The Recruiting Officer*, Melinda's signature is obtained by a trick (4.3) and Worthy is misled into thinking she has agreed to marry Brazen; but Brazen has already had two letters supposedly from Melinda in Lucy's hand—and so a genuine signature would have alerted him to the deception.[25] There

[23] Jessica Munns, 'The Recruiting Officer. By George Farquhar. Edited by Peter Dixon' (review), *Modern Language Review*, 84 (1959), 130.

[24] Kenny (ed.), *Works*, ii. 558.

[25] See Robert L. Hough, 'An Error in "The Recruiting Officer"', *Notes and Queries*, 198 (1953), 340–1, and 199 (1954), 474.

are also difficulties about the location of the last scene: if Balance's entry with a napkin in his hand is a continuation of 5.6, he must have risen from table on the news of Silvia's disappearance to walk in the Fields, with servants in attendance; but if a fresh scene, in Balance's house, begins at this point, the later entry of Rose and Bullock becomes absurd. A comparable slackness is evident in *The Twin Rivals*, 5.2, when Teague leads Trueman in the wrong direction and so saves Aurelia from Richmore.

A partial explanation for these inconsistencies, however, may be found in this last example. Having taken Mandrake prisoner, Teague finds the pregnant Clelia's letter to Richmore, and Trueman soliloquizes on his lucky escape from marriage in terms which draw unashamed attention to the play's reliance on coincidence (5.3.36–41). Virtue (or its rough male equivalent) triumphs not as a consequence of the wit and address of the good characters, nor—whatever the Elder Wouldbe may profess to believe (3.2.123–5)—of Providence, but solely by chance as embodied in Teague. This highlights, for a modern audience at least, the moral confusion in Trueman's speech. Poor Clelia is instantly transformed form delicious bride to repellant whore; Richmore's real offence has been against Trueman, not Clelia; and while Richmore is coerced into marrying the latter, we know from the Preface what value attaches to that promise. Nor is this the only instance of a 'happy ending' arising by chance in Farquhar's plays. Chance rules in *The Constant Couple* and *The Beaux' Stratagem* also. Neither wit nor virtue ever brings success to Farquhar's protagonists. Justice Balance takes control at the end of *The Recruiting Officer*, as no father could in earlier Restoration Comedy; the Elder Wouldbe is pathetically dependent on Trueman and luck; and while there is the token moral conversion of Aimwell and Dorinda in *The Beaux' Stratagem*, Archer remains eager to exploit Mrs Sullen's separation, and the outcome of the evening depends on the fortuitous death of an elder brother and the seizure of Sullen's papers. Farquhar's happy endings are thus produced out of the hat by legerdemain. His favourite metaphor is a symbol of the social and personal pretences on which the lives of his characters are based.

It seems, then, that unlike the world of Etherege and Wycherley in which wit is tested, or that of Congreve in which its weakness is concealed, Farquhar's is a world in which all understandings, values, and principles, even the self-assurance of a wit on the make, are nakedly provisional. His first plain dealer is the Hobbesean Young Wouldbe, who begins *The Twin Rivals* with a possible allusion to the opening lines of Rochester's 'Satire against Mankind' and later (2.5.64–75) soliloquizes his 'atheism' in terms which reflect the obsession with paternal authority and the state of nature in the social thinking of the age—he enters into insolent debate with Sir William Temple, John Locke,[26] and others. We might dismiss his views merely as those of a villain if the forces lined against him offered more than luck and platitudes in reply. Still, coming from Young Wouldbe such sentiments are formally disowned. Farquhar's second plain dealer, however, Sergeant Kite, is instructed in the life skills of 'canting, lying, impudence, pimping, bullying, swearing, whoring [and] drinking' (*RO* 3.1.117–18) by every class in society from the nobility to the gypsies, and is also motivated by the Hobbesean passions of hunger and ambition. Farquhar's is thus a world in which there is no stance which is self-evidently sensible. This, paradoxically, is why even Peter Dixon's dislike of the 'Brechtian shadows'[27] which fell on the play after 1955 is as legitimate as carefully explicated modifications of them in productions by William Gaskill in 1971, and Max Stafford-Clark in 1988. Farquhar eludes definitive performance.

One sign of this scepticism in his writing is the way he revised it and even (in the case of Richmore's repentance) repudiated it. Farquhar is a dramatist for whom it is simply misleading to print a definitive text. We need rather to catch his writing on the move, to discover in his decisions to abandon Sir Harry's heroics or the pert low dialogue and dialect forms of *The Recruiting Officer* the essence of his achievement, which was simply to please an audience. (This view is at the heart of 'A Discourse upon Comedy' in *Love and Business*.) In the Prologue to *Sir Harry Wildair*, he tells the audience that they themselves 'are the Rules by which he writes his plays' (l. 12); his texts are the pliant instruments of their theatrical pleasure. This is why he has proved so attractive to generations of actors, who like him have livings to make. This flexibility is inseparable from the energy of his characterizations and the informality of his style. He had a poor ear for metre, and in the early plays too often lapses into pseudo-blank verse—any sort of writing was worth a try. His dialogue is occasionally ungrammatical, and his sentences run on, accumulating abundant subordinate clauses and parentheses, but rarely losing their way.

[26] See Sir William Temple, *An Essay upon the Original and Nature of Government* (1680); and John Locke, *An Essay Concerning the True Original Extent, and End of Civil Government* (1713), esp. sections vi 'Of Paternal Power' and vii 'Of Political and Civil Society'.

[27] George Farquhar, *The Recruiting Officer*, ed. Peter Dixon (1986), 32.

Again the contrast with Congreve is notable. But it was with this linguistic precipitancy that Farquhar was able to catch from his audience the rules by which he wrote his plays, and so to reflect, in the very disorder of his writing, contemporary realities to which his critics, and perhaps even Pope, were blind.

The Revolution of 1688 was followed by a period of 'political chaos . . . when ministers and ministries, from left, right and centre, toppled and changed like a kaleidoscope tossed by a gale' and 'England seemed to have escaped the danger of arbitrary government only to succumb to political anarchy.'[28] The succession remained in doubt: and a newly enlarged electorate generated new levels of virulent political debate, culminating in the Sacheverell Riots of 1710.

All the hate and blood lust spawned by the civil war *manqué* of 1688 and 1689, the terrible division of allegiance between Jacobites and Williamites in the nineties, the almost continuous fear of treason, assassination and rebellion, plus two dragging, lacerating wars in twenty years, had poisoned men's minds and pens.[29]

Farquhar's swift passage from Ulster parsonage, to university, the stage, London, mistresses, marriage, the army, a garret, and the grave; his natural stage-sense; the precipitancy of his style; his adaptability, opportunism, and lack of a fixed attitude to life; all these, taken together, allowed this poison to infiltrate the shapely, self-assured, hedonistic conventions of comedy to remarkable effect.

In particular, his sceptical determinism excused him (as Congreve could never have been excused) from respecting the demands not just of formal coherence but of virtue, or at any rate of moral consistency. No serious constraint is imposed on the libidinal energies of his women or his men. Even his low-life characters are uncensoriously assumed to be getting away with what they can—the criminals in *The Beaux' Stratagem* are on level benches with the rakes. But the effect of these relaxed attitudes towards gallantry is the opposite of utopian because Farquhar's linguistic openness also permits us, particularly in the last two plays, to glimpse a surprisingly wide range of contemporary unpleasantness—the whipping of prostitutes (*CC* 2.4.31); public hangings (*CC* 5.2.48–51); the corruption of the legal process in *The Twin Rivals*—both government and opposition had cynically relied on

---

[28] J. A. Plumb, *The Growth of Political Stability in England 1675–1725*, Peregrine Books edn. (1969), 32.

[29] J. P. Kenyon, *The Stuarts: A Study in English Kingship*, Fontana Books edn., (1970), 197.

perjured witnesses in political trials at least since the time of the
Exclusionist crisis in the late 1670s; ten thousand soldiers dead on
the Grenadiers' 'Bed of Honour' (*RO* 1.1.30); the drab lives of
camp-followers (*RO* 1.1.99–113); soldiers making their wills before
the slaughter of Blenheim—recalled by Plume in response to a
frivolous obscenity of Silvia's (*RO* 2.1.59–60); the improvised
amputation of an officer's leg shattered by a great shot (*RO*
4.2.153); the 'horsing' (*RO* 5.5.137–8) and flogging of soldiers (*BS*
2.2.132); convict labour, fevered troops, and prostitution in the
West Indies (*RO* 4.1.70–1; *BS* 3.2.82–8)

The significance of such allusions is that they are not satirical, like
the imagery of disease and rotten fruit in a play such as Etherege's
Man of Mode, but casually humorous, war and politics being simply
an easy metaphoric resource for Farquhar's precipitate pen. A passionate supporter of William of Orange and Marlborough, he was
none the less no party man when it came to making political allusions.
The Whig cry of 'liberty and property' falls subversively from the lips
first of Tom Errand in Newgate gaol ('We're all gentlemen here . . .
Newgate's a commonwealth'—*CC* 5.2.58–9), then of Trueman disguised as the two-timing constable ('I am for liberty and property. I
vote for parliament-men. I pay taxes, and truly I don't think
matrimony consistent with the liberty of the subject'—*TR* 5.3.80–2).
Admittedly Young Wouldbe presses his suit with Constance in terms
of extreme royalist theory, and Constance defends herself by appeals
to overtly Williamite constitutionalism (*TR* 5.4.9–32), but 'liberty of
conscience' is astutely perceived by the lower classes of Lichfield as a
privilege of recruiting officers and their men (*RO* 2.3.115–16). Sexual
relations are conventionally presented in images of war, but
Farquhar's references to battles, sieges, and negotiated surrenders or
capitulations (*CC* 2.4.100; *TR* 2.4.41–2) are historically specific,
technically exact, and casually aggressive. Male lovers, like soldiers or
sportsmen, 'shoot flying' (*RO* 1.2.32; 5.5.60–1). At one point Plume
seems to imply that Worthy's best policy with Melinda—when she
came into her money and 'capitulations' were no longer practicable—
would have been to have 'taken the town by storm, or died upon the
breach' (*RO* 1.1.188), an action—if the actor chooses to make it sound
so—amounting to rape interrupted by premature ejaculation. A
similar set of images, notably in the Prologues to *The Twin Rivals* and
The Recruiting Officer, the Epilogue to *The Recruiting Officer*, and the
bizarre dialogue between Brazen and Plume about privateers and
theatres (*RO* 5.4.19–36), refers to the war between the theatres, and

the relations between actors and audience in terms which remarkably declare the roughness of the acting trade. Perhaps the omnipresence of war in Farquhar's imaginative world is most clearly signified in Sergeant Kite's fantastic inclusion of allied victories among the signs of the zodiac (*RO* 4.2.33–5).

The results are not at all gloomy, but a change in the ethos of classical comedy is none the less effected. Farquhar's protagonists are former or would-be soldiers, but in neoclassical theory a soldier is never a wit, and though the military stereotypes demanded by this convention are represented in the plays by the stiffly honourable Standard in *The Constant Couple* and the absurd old boaster Brazen in *The Recruiting Officer*, in Plume, and even in Sir Harry who fought at Landen (*CC* 1.1.156–7) and in Archer and Aimwell who are perilously near to joining the ranks, Farquhar introduces a new kind of hero to the stage, men whose status is reinforced yet qualified by their soldierly qualities. They are undoubtedly wits (even Standard engages in an intrigue), but they never finally control the comic arena as Wycherley's Horner and Congreve's Mirabel do. As soldiers, however, their masculine standing does not depend on their being successful intriguers. Nor, as soldiers, are they ever wholly absorbed into the comic, that is the conventional social, world. Admittedly Standard and Plume leave the army, and Aimwell inherits a peerage and marries Dorinda; but Standard remains the military type, and for every Plume there is a Kite, for every Aimwell an Archer. The devil-may-care fatalism of the soldier—and between 1688 and 1714 that attitude was not a mere theatrical notion—together with the persistence of brutality and fear at the end of the plays, if only in the background, fundamentally changes the ethos of classical comedy.

We may conclude, therefore, that Farquhar's effectiveness as a dramatist is a consequence of his carelessness, his lack of seriousness. But this is a patronizing way of putting it. He was obviously a writer of passionate allegiances and of vigorous, sexually charged sympathies. His strength, from which his marginalized social status cannot be dissociated, is that he never tried to make these attachments add up. His lack of a programme, for society, for comedy, for himself, was an honest and intelligent response to a world that had so abused principle and intellectual good faith as to have virtually lost the capacity for belief. His contemporaries justly prided themselves on their manners, their architecture, and on styles of speech and writing which eschewed the pertness and lowness of ordinary conversation, but their religious and philosophical discourse was shallow, and their notions of personal, social, and political morality sentimental and dishonest. The realities of their world were after all what Farquhar shows them to be—money (the sums mentioned in his plays are enormous), the conspicuous consumption and display about which Dorinda fantasizes so shamelessly and Mrs Sullen weeps so disturbingly in *The Beaux' Stratagem* (4.1.412–22), and war.

The clearest sign of the uncertainties of this world are disclosed in Farquhar's treatment of marriage. Famously, he quotes Milton's divorce pamphlets in *The Beaux' Stratagem*,[30] but unlike Milton he has no positive view of marriage to construct. As the by-no-means entirely fanciful bigamies of Sergeant Kite and the extraordinary marriage ritual of Sylvia and Rose (*RO* 5.2.46–9) illustrate, he represents marriage as a mirage and a fraud, or at any rate 'so odd a thing, that hardly any two people under the sun agree in the ceremony; some make it a sacrament, others a convenience, and others make it a jest' (*RO* 5.2.42–5). Yet marriage, as the foundation of the rights of fathers and husbands, was the institution on which contemporary English society founded its social theory and based the transmission of its ever-increasing wealth. The relation of Farquhar's plays to society's professed beliefs and practices is exactly expressed in the purely symbolic ritual of divorce between the Sullens at the end of *The Beaux' Stratagem*, a ritual which provides a mirror-image of the 'wedding' of Silvia and Rose in the earlier play, with the upper-classes in effect imitating their inferiors. Farquhar's former mistress, Anne Oldfield, 'thought he had dealt too freely . . . in giving [Mrs Sullen] to Archer without a proper Divorce, which was not a Security for her Honour'.[31] But the implicit moral of the play is that any such security would be hypocrisy and an illusion.

In seeking to make his living by writing for the theatre in such a society, Farquhar had thus the imaginative resources and flexibility of attitude to give his audiences what they wanted frankly and unpretentiously. In doing so, however, he had available a vocabulary and a body of experience which encompassed aspects of his society that few of his contemporaries could face with equanimity, so that in giving them no more than they wanted he could nevertheless represent to them a remarkably complete and casually truthful reflection of their world. But he also gave them something in addition, a festive restlessness not only in his heroes and heroines, but also in his low

---

[30] See Martin A. Larson, 'The Influence of Milton's Divorce Tracts on Farquhar's *Beaux' Stratagem*', *PMLA* 39 (1924), 174–8.

[31] W. R. Chetwood, *A General History of the Stage* (1749), 151.

characters and his villains—the lustful, cross-dressing Smuggler, the hard-drinking Mandrake, the happily cynical Kite, and the weathered villainous Gibbet. Thackeray detected 'a grand diabolical fire in him',[32] and paradoxically it is precisely this fire, irresponsible, anti-social, spendthrift, and individualistic, which (if Empson's theory of mock pastoral is sound)[33] binds players and audience in the theatre into a particularly fierce kind of social unity, which is never trivial, gross, or dull, and which makes Farquhar a great playwright.

[32] *The Letters and Private Papers of William Makepeace Thackeray* (4 vols.; 1945–6), iii. 38.

[33] See '*The Beggar's Opera*. Mock Pastoral as the Cult of Independence', in *Some Versions of Pastoral: A Study of the Pastoral Form in Literature*, Penguin Books edn. (1966), 157–200.

NOTE ON THE TEXTS

ONE of the aims of this edition is to represent the textual evolution of Farquhar's four most important plays. The text of each play is therefore based on the first edition, subsequently revised scenes in *The Constant Couple*, *The Recruiting Officer*, and *The Beaux' Stratagem* being printed alongside the main text. In his edition of *The Recruiting Officer* (1986) Peter Dixon has argued persuasively that the second quarto edition of the play must have been a manuscript, the ultimate source of which was Farquhar's papers. Similarly, in her edition of the *Works* (1988), Shirley Strum Kenny argues that the text of *The Twin Rivals* in the 1728 edition of the *Works* was corrected from the original promptbook. These findings reinforce my belief that Farquhar is best interpreted as a striking example of the multiple drafts model of literary meaning and my decision not to incorporate them in my main text should not be interpreted as indicating disagreement with two such distinguished predecessors. I do, however, rely on later editions to correct what seem to me to be obvious misprints in the first, all such changes being recorded in the Explanatory Notes. The Notes also record substantive emendations in later editions. In the case of *The Recruiting Officer*, however, I only give a sample of the changes to the dialect speeches of the rustic characters.

I have silently translated all Latin stage directions except '*Exit*' and '*Exeunt*', and have moved stage directions to the point in the text where the reader will find them most helpful. In particular '(*aside*)' now appears in front of the words so designated. The end of an aside is indicated either by a dash (—), or by [*Aloud*]. All stage directions not in the copy texts are in square brackets, with the following exceptions: I have changed '*Re-enter*' to '*Enter*'; I have spelt out the names of characters fully in all stage directions; and I have changed the designation of some characters to the name by which they are most commonly referred to in the text.

In seeking to respect the punctuation of the original texts, as the best available guide to the run and cadence of Farquhar's dialogue, I have made more liberal use of the comma and the dash, and have avoided the full-stop more frequently than modern practice usually allows. Sometimes I have compromised by using a semi-colon where

I would have preferred a comma. Like Charles Fifer in his edition of *The Beaux' Stratagem* (1978), 'I have tried to retain the movement of Farquhar's brisk and often racy prose.'

SELECT BIBLIOGRAPHY

All of Farquhar's plays, apart from *The Twin Rivals*, were printed in at least two quarto editions (see Chronology for details). Editions of *The Comedies* appeared in 1707, the *Works* in 1711, and (more authoritatively) in 1728. A Dublin edition of the *Works* in 1775 included a Life by Thomas Wilkes. The most important nineteenth-century editions were by Leigh Hunt (1840) and A. C. Ewald (1892). There have been two modern editions of the *Works*, by Charles Stonehill (1930) and Shirley Strum Kenny (1988). The most influential selections of Farquhar's work have been William Archer's edition of the four plays in this volume (1906; repr. 1959) and *A Discourse upon Comedy, The Recruiting Officer and The Beaux' Stratagem*, edited by Louis A. Strauss (1914). There have also been important editions of *The Recruiting Officer* by Michael Shugrue (1966), A. Norman Jeffares (1972), John Ross (1973; rev. 1991), and Peter Dixon (1986); and of *The Beaux' Stratagem* by Vincent G. Hopper and Gerald B. Lahey (1963), A. Norman Jeffares (1972), Michael Cordner (1976; rev. 1990), and Charles Fifer (1978).

The first modern full-length study of Farquhar was D. Schmid's *George Farquhar, Sein Leben und Seine Original-Dramen* (1904). *Young George Farquhar: The Restoration Drama at Twilight* (1949) by Willard Connely is a speculative biography. *George Farquhar* (1966) by A. J. Farmer; Eric Rothstein's definitive *George Farquhar* (1967); and Eugene Nelson James's *The Development of George Farquhar* (1972) are mainly or entirely critical.

The latter contains a survey of Farquhar criticism since 1700, a relatively full selection of which is collected in *Farquhar, The Recruiting Officer and The Beaux' Stratagem: A Casebook*, ed. Raymond A. Anselment (1977). Significant criticism of Farquhar, not discussed or included in either of these two volumes, is to be found in Louise Imogen Guiney, *A Little English Gallery* (1894); William Archer, *The Old Drama and the New* (1923); J. W. Krutch, *Comedy and Conscience after the Restoration* (1924); H. Ten Eyck Perry, *The Comic Spirit of Restoration Drama* (1925); Kathleen M. Lynch, *The Social Mode of Restoration Comedy* (1926); Peter Kavanagh, *The Irish Theatre* (1946); John Harrington Smith, *The Gay Couple in Restoration Comedy* (1948); T. H. Fujimara, *The Restoration Comedy of Wit* (1952); Allardyce Nicoll, *A History of Early Eighteenth Century Drama 1700–1750*, vols. i and ii, rev. edn. (1952); Frederick S. Boas, *An Introduction to Eighteenth-Century Drama 1700–1780* (1953); John Loftis, *Comedy and Society from Congreve to Fielding* (1959); *The London Stage 1660–1800*, ed. William Van Lennep *et al.* (11 vols.; 1960–8); R. C. Sharma, *Themes and Conventions of the Comedy of Manners* (1965); Ben Ross Schneider, Jr., *The Ethos of Restoration Comedy* (1971); Robert D. Hume, *The Development of English Drama in the Late Seventeenth Century*

(1976); J. Loftis *et al.*, *The Revels History of Drama in English*, v. *1660–1750* (1976); and Laura Brown, *English Dramatic Form, 1660–1760* (1981).

Articles on Farquhar (again excluding work covered by James and Anselment) include M. A. Larson, 'The Influence of Milton's Divorce Tracts on Farquhar's *Beaux' Stratagem*', *PMLA* 39 (1924); James Sutherland, 'New Light on George Farquhar' (letter), *TLS*, 6 Mar. 1937; Peter Kavanagh, 'George Farquhar', *TLS*, 10 Feb. 1945; Robert L. Hough, 'An Error in "The Recruiting Officer" ', *Notes and Queries*, 198 (1953), and 199 (1954); K. Spinner, 'George Farquhar als Dramatiker', *Schweizer Anglistische Arbeiten*, Berne, 1956; Fitzroy Pyle, 'George Farquhar (1677–1707)', *Hermathena*, 92 (1958); J. P. W. Rogers, 'The Dramatist vs. the Dunce: George Farquhar and John Oldmixon', *Restoration and Eighteenth-Century Theatre Research*, 10 (1971); Jack Gravitt Garland, 'A Primer for Pleasure: Neo-Epicureanism in Farquhar's *Beaux' Stratagem*', *Thoth*, 12 (1972); R. J. Jordan, 'George Farquhar's Military Career', *Huntingdon Library Quarterly*, 27 (1974); Robert D. Hume, 'Marital Discord in English Comedy from Dryden to Fielding', *Modern Philology*, 74 (1976–7); Peter Lewis, '*The Beaux' Stratagem* and *The Beggar's Opera*', *Notes and Queries*, NS 18 (1981); J. C. Ross, 'Some Notes on the Recruiting Officer', *Notes and Queries*, NS 18 (1981); and John McVeagh, 'George Farquhar and Commercial England', *Studies on Voltaire and the Eighteenth Century*', 217 (1983).

The following provide information about the stage history of Farquhar's plays: William Egerton, *Some Memoirs of Mrs Anne Oldfield* (1731); Daniel O'Bryan, *Authentic Memoirs; or, the Life and Character of . . . Mr. Robert Wilkes* (1732); Edmund Curll, *The Life of that Eminent Comedian Robert Wilkes, Esq.* (1733); Colley Cibber, *An Apology for the Life of Mr. Colley Cibber, Comedian . . . Written by Himself* (1740); W. R. Chetwood, *A General History of the Stage* (1749); Shirley Strum Kenny, 'Theatrical Warfare, 1695–1710', *Theatre Notebook*, 27 (1973); Judith Milhous and Robert D. Hume, *Producible Interpretation: Eight English Plays 1665–1707* (1985); Joanne Lafler, *The Celebrated Mrs. Oldfield: The Life and Art of an Augustan Actress* (1989); John Genest, *An Account of the English Stage* (10 vols.; 1832); Barry N. Olsen, '*The Beaux' Stratagem* on the Nineteenth Century London Stage', *Theatre Notebook*, 28 (1974); Kenneth Tynan (ed.), *The Recruiting Officer: The National Theatre Production* (1965); William L. Sharp, 'Restoration Comedy: An Approach to Modern Production', *Drama Survey*, 7 (1968–9); William Gaskill, 'Finding a Style for Farquhar', *Theatre Quarterly*, 1 (1971); Albert Wertheim, 'Berthold Brecht and George Farquhar's *The Recruiting Officer*', *Comparative Drama*, 7 (1973); Sybil Rosenfeld, 'Notes on *The Recruiting Officer*', *Theatre Notebook*, 18 (1981); and Max Stafford-Clark, *Letters to George* (1989). This last describes Stafford-Clark's production of *The Recruiting Officer* at The Royal Court, London, in 1988, which played concurrently and with the same cast as *Our Country's Good* (1989), Timberlake Wertenbaker's adaptation of Thomas Kenneally's novel *The Playmaker* (1987), about a production of *The Recruiting Officer* (with a convict cast) in eighteenth-century Australia.

A CHRONOLOGY OF
GEORGE FARQUHAR

Haymarket, October the 15th, 1706' and the Prologue to Centi-livre's *The Platonick Lady*.

1707   *The Beaux' Stratagem* performed; first and second quarto editions of *The Beaux' Stratagem*; Farquhar dies; *Love's Catechism* published; fourth quarto edition of *The Recruiting Officer*.

1707?/8?   Second quarto edition of *Love and a Bottle*.

1708   *The Comedies*, first edition.

1709   Farquhar's widow petitions Queen Anne; third and fourth octavo editions of *The Stage-Coach*.

1710   *Barcellona* published by Margaret Farquhar.

1711   *The Comedies*. 'Second edition'.

1714   *The Comedies*. 'Third Edition'.

1718   *The Works*. 'Fourth Edition'.

1728   *The Works*. 'Sixth edition'.

THE CONSTANT COUPLE

or

A Trip to the Jubilee

A Comedy

Sive favore tuli, sive hanc ego carmine famam
Jure tibi grates, candide lector, ago.°

(Ovid, *Tristia* iv. 10)

DRAMATIS PERSONAE

The play was first staged at the Theatre Royal, Drury Lane, in late November 1699, with the following cast:

[MEN]

Sir Harry Wildair, *an airy gentleman affecting humorous gaiety and freedom in his behaviour*	Mr Wilks
Standard, *a disbanded° colonel, brave and generous*	Mr Powell
Vizard,° *outwardly pious, otherwise a great debauchee, and villainous*	Mr Mills
Smuggler,° *an old merchant*	Mr Johnson
Clincher° Senior, *a pert London 'prentice turned beau, and affecting travel*	Mr Pinkethman
Clincher Junior, *his brother, educated in the country*	Mr Bullock
Dicky, *his man*	Mr Norris
Tom Errand, *a porter*	Mr Haines

[WOMEN]

Lurewell, *a lady of a jilting temper proceeding from a resentment of her wrongs from men*	Mrs Verbruggen
Lady Darling, *an old lady, mother to Angelica*	Mrs Powell
Angelica, *a woman of honour*	Mrs Rogers
Parly, *maid to Lurewell*	Mrs More

Constable, mob, porter's wife, servants, etc.

SCENE

London

To the Honourable Sir Roger Mostyn° Baronet, of Mostyn Hall in Flintshire

Sir,

'Tis no small reflection on pieces of this nature, that panegryic is so much improved, and that dedication is grown more an art than poetry; that authors, to make their patrons more than men, make themselves less; and that persons of honour are forced to decline patronising wit, because their modesty cannot bear the gross strokes of adulation. 5

But give me leave to say, Sir, that I am too young an author° to have learnt the art of flattery; and, I hope, the same modesty which recommended this play to the world, will also reconcile my addresses to you, of whom I can say nothing but what your merits may warrant, 10 and all that have the honour of your acquaintance will be proud to vindicate.

The greatest panegyric upon you, Sir, is the unprejudiced and bare truth of your character—the fire of youth, with the sedateness of a senator,° and the modern gaiety of a fine English gentleman, with the 15 noble solidity of the ancient Briton.°

This is the character, Sir, which all men, but yourself, are proud to publish of you, and which more celebrated pens than mine should transmit to posterity.

The play has had some noble appearances to honour its repre- 20 sentation;° and to complete the success, I have presumed to prefix so noble a name to usher it into the world. A stately frontispiece is the beauty of a building. But here I must transverse Ovid:
Materia superabit Opus.°

I am, 25
Honourable Sir,
Your most devoted, and humble servant,
Geo. Farquhar.

3

PREFACE TO THE READER

An affected modesty is very often the greatest vanity, and authors are sometimes prouder of their blushes than of the praises that occasioned them. I shan't therefore, like a foolish virgin, fly to be pursued, and deny what I chiefly wish for. I am very willing to acknowledge the beauties of this play, especially those of the third night,° which not to be proud of were the height of impudence. Who is ashamed to value himself upon such favours, undervalues those who conferred them.

As I freely submit to the criticisms of the judicious, so I cannot call this an ill play, since the Town° has allowed it such success. When they have pardoned my faults, 'twere very ill manners to condemn their indulgence. Some may think (my acquaintance in Town being too slender to make a party for the play°) that the success must be derived from the pure merits of the cause. I am of another opinion. I have not been long enough in Town to raise enemies against me; and the English are still kind to strangers. I am below the envy of great wits, and above the malice of little ones. I have not displeased the ladies, nor offended the clergy; both which are now pleased to say, that a comedy may be diverting without smut and profaneness.°

Next to these advantages, the beauties of action° gave the greatest life to the play, of which the Town is so sensible, that all will join with me in commendation of the actors, and allow (without detracting from the merit of others) that the Theatre Royal affords an excellent and complete set of comedians. Mr Wilks's° performance has set him so far above competition in the part of Wildair, that none can pretend to envy the praise due to his merit. That he made the part will appear from hence, that whenever the stage has the misfortune to lose him, Sir Harry Wildair may go to the Jubilee.°

A great many quarrel at the *Trip to the Jubilee* for a misnomer.° I must tell them that perhaps there are greater trips in the play;° and when I find that more exact plays have had better success, I'll talk with the critics about decorums, etc. However, if I ever commit another fault of this nature, I'll endeavour to make it more excusable.

Prologue
by a Friend°

Poets will think nothing so checks their fury
As wits, cits, beaux, and women for their jury.
Our spark's half dead to think what medley's come,°
With blended judgments to pronounce his doom.
'Tis all false fear; for in a mingled pit,   5
Why, what your grave don thinks but dully writ,
His neighbour i'th' great wig may take for wit.°
Some authors court the few, the wise, if any;
Our youth's content, if he can reach the many,
Who go with much like ends to church and play,   10
Not to observe what priests or poets say—
No! no! your thoughts, like theirs, lie quite another way.
The ladies safe may smile, for here's no slander,
No smut, no lewd-tongued beau, no *double entendre*.°
'Tis true he has a spark just come from France,°   15
But then so far from beau, why he talks sense!
Like coin oft carried out, but—seldom brought from thence.°
There's yet a gang to whom our spark submits,°
Your elbow-shaking fool that lives by's wits,°
That's only witty though, just as he lives, by fits;   20
Who lion-like through bailiffs scours a way,°
Hunts in the face a dinner all the day,
At night with empty bowels grumbles o'er the play.
And now the modish prentice he implores,°
Who with his master's cash stol'n out of doors,   25
Employs it on a brace of—honourable whores;
While their good bulky 'mother', pleased, sits by,°
Bawd regent of the bubble gallery.°
Next to our mounted friends we humbly move,°
Who all your side-box tricks are much above,°   30
And never fail to pay us—with your love.°
Ah friends! Poor Dorset Garden House is gone—°
Our merry meetings there are all undone,
Quite lost to us: sure, for some strange misdeeds
That strong dog Samson's pulled it o'er our heads,°   35
Snaps rope like thread, but when his fortune's told him,

He'll hear perhaps of rope will one day hold him.°
At least I hope that our good-natured Town
Will find a way to pull his prizes down.°
   Well, that's all! Now, gentlemen, for the play—   40
On second thoughts, I've but two words to say;
Such as it is for your delight designed,
Hear it, read, try, judge, and speak as you find.

A New Prologue°

In answer to my very good friend, Mr Oldmixon; who, having two
plays damned at the old house, had a mind to curry favour to have a
third damned at the new.°

'Tis hard the author of this play in view
Should be condemned, purely for pleasing you:
Charged with a crime, which you, his judges, own
Was only this, that he has pleased the Town.
He touch'd no poet's verse, nor doctor's bills;   5
No foe to B——re, yet a friend to Will's;
No reputation stabbed by sour debate;°
Nor had a hand in bankrupt Brisco's fate.°
And, as an ease to's tender conscience, vows
He's none of those that broke the t'other house.°   10
In perfect pity to their wretched cheer,
Because his play was bad—he brought it here.
The dreadful sin of murder cries aloud;
And sure these poets ne'er can hope for good,
Who dipped their barbarous pens in that poor house's blood.   15
'Twas malice all: no malice like to theirs,
To write good plays, purpose to starve the players.°
To starve by's wit is still the poet's due,
But here are men whose wit is matched by few;
Their wit both starves themselves, and others too.   20
Our plays are farce, because our house is crammed;°
Their plays all good; for what?—because they're damned.
Because we pleasure you, you call us tools;°
And 'cause you please yourselves, they call you fools.
By their good nature, they are wits, true blue,°   25

And, men of breeding, by their respects to you.°
To engage the fair, all other means being lost,
They fright the boxes with old Shakespeare's ghost;°
The ladies of such spectres should take heed;
For 'twas the Devil did raise that ghost indeed.   30
Their case is hard, that such despair can show;
They've disobliged all powers above, they know,
And now must have recourse to powers below.
Let Shakespeare then lie still—ghosts do no good;
The fair are better pleased with flesh and blood.   35
What is't to them, to mind the ancients' taste?
But the poor folks are mad, and I'm in haste.
      Runs off

1.[1]

Scene, the Park°

Enter Vizard with a letter, servant following

VIZARD Angelica send it back unopened, say you?

SERVANT As you see, sir.

VIZARD The pride of these virtuous women is more insufferable than the immodesty of prostitutes. After all my encouragement to slight me thus!   5

SERVANT She said, sir, that imagining your morals sincere, she gave you access to her conversation;° but that your late behaviour in her company has convinced her, that your love and religion are both hypocrisy, and that she believes your letter like yourself, fair on the outside, foul within; so sent it back unopened.   10

VIZARD May obstinacy guard her beauty till wrinkles bury it, then may desire prevail to make her curse that untimely pride her disappointed age repents: I'll be revenged the very first opportunity. Saw you the old Lady Darling, her mother?

SERVANT Yes, sir, and she was pleased to say much in your   15
commendation.

VIZARD That's my cue. An esteem grafted in old age is hardly rooted out—years stiffen their opinions with their bodies, and old zeal is only to be cozened by young hypocrisy. Run to the Lady Lurewell's, and know of her maid whether her ladyship will be at home   20
this evening—her beauty is sufficient cure for Angelica's scorn.

>   *Exit Servant. Vizard pulls out a book, reads, and walks about.*
>   *Enter Smuggler*

SMUGGLER Ay, there's a pattern for the young men o'th' times—at his meditation so early: some book of pious ejaculations,° I'm sure.

VIZARD (*aside*) This Hobbes° is an excellent fellow!—O uncle Smuggler! To find you in this end o'th' Town is a miracle.   25

SMUGGLER I have seen a miracle this morning indeed, cousin Vizard.

VIZARD What was it, pray sir?

SMUGGLER A man at his devotion so near the Court. I'm very glad boy, that you keep your sanctity untainted in this infectious place; the very air of this park is heathenish, and every man's breath I   30
meet scents of atheism.

VIZARD Surely sir, some great concern must bring you to this unsanctified end of the Town.

SMUGGLER A very unsanctified concern, truly cousin.

VIZARD What is't?   35

SMUGGLER A lawsuit, boy. Shall I tell you? My ship, the Swan, is
newly arrived from St Sebastian's,° laden with Portugal wines.
Now the impudent rogue of a tide-waiter has the face to affirm 'tis
French wines in Spanish casks, and has indicted me upon the
statute.° O conscience, conscience! These tide-waiters and sur-   40
veyors plague us more with their French wines, than the war
did° with French privateers.°

    Enter Standard [*in army officer's uniform*]

Ay, there's another plague of the nation—a red coat and feather.°

VIZARD Colonel Standard, I'm your humble servant.

STANDARD Maybe not, sir.   45

VIZARD Why so!

STANDARD Because—I'm disbanded.

VIZARD How? broke!°

STANDARD This very morning, in Hyde Park, my brave regiment,
a thousand men that looked like lions yesterday were scattered,   50
and looked as poor and simple as the herd of deer that grazed°
beside 'em.

SMUGGLER (*singing*) Tal, al, deral. I'll have a bonfire this night as
high as the Monument.°

STANDARD A bonfire! thou dry, withered, ill nature, had not these   55
brave fellows' swords defended you, your house had been a bonfire
ere this about your ears. Did not we venture our lives, sir?

SMUGGLER And did not we pay you for your lives, sir? Venture your
lives! I'm sure we ventured our money, and that's life and soul to
me. Sir, we'll maintain you no longer.   60

STANDARD Then your wives shall, old Actaeon.° There are five and
thirty strapping officers gone this morning to live upon free
quarter° in the City.

SMUGGLER O Lord! O Lord! I shall have a son within these nine
months born with a leading-staff in his hand. Sir, you are—   65

STANDARD What, sir?

SMUGGLER Sir, I say that you are—

STANDARD What sir?

SMUGGLER Disbanded sir, that's all. I see my lawyer yonder.

    Exit [*Smuggler*]

VIZARD Sir, I'm very sorry for your misfortune.   70

STANDARD Why so? I don't come to borrow money of you; if you're
my friend, meet me this evening at the Rummer°—I'll pay my

9

way, drink a health to my king, prosperity to my country, and
away for Hungary° tomorrow morning.

VIZARD What! you won't leave us? 75

STANDARD What! a soldier stay here! to look like an old pair of
colours in Westminster Hall,° ragged and rusty! No, no. I met
yesterday a broken lieutenant—he was ashamed to own that he
wanted a dinner, but begged eighteen pence of me to buy a new
sheath for his sword. 80

VIZARD O, but you have good friends, Colonel!

STANDARD O very good friends! my father's a lord, and my elder
brother a beau.

VIZARD But your country may perhaps want your sword again.

STANDARD Nay for that matter, let but a single drum beat up for 85
volunteers between Ludgate and Charing Cross,° and I shall
undoubtedly hear it at the walls of Buda.°

VIZARD Come, come, Colonel, there are ways of making your fortune
at home. Make your addresses to the fair—you're a man of honour
and courage. 90

STANDARD Ay, my courage is like to do me wondrous service
with the fair. This pretty cross-cut over my eye will attract a
duchess. I warrant 'twill be a mighty grace to my ogling. Had I used
the stratagem of a certain brother colonel of mine, I might succeed.

VIZARD What was it, pray? 95

STANDARD Why to save his pretty face for the women, he always turned
his back upon the enemy. He was a man of honour—for the ladies.

VIZARD Come, come, the loves of Mars and Venus° will never
fail—you must get a mistress.

STANDARD Prithee, no more on 't. You have awakened a thought, 100
from which, and the kingdom, I would have stolen away at once.
To be plain, I have a mistress.

VIZARD And she's cruel?

STANDARD No.

VIZARD Her parents prevent your happiness. 105

STANDARD Nor that.

VIZARD Then she has no fortune.

STANDARD A large one, beauty to tempt all mankind, and virtue to
beat off their assaults. O Vizard! such a creature! [*Looking off-stage*]
Hey-day! who the Devil have we here? 110

VIZARD The joy of the playhouse, and life of the Park.

*Enter Sir Harry Wildair; crosses the stage singing, [and exit [s]]
with footmen after him*

Sir Harry Wildair newly come from Paris.

STANDARD Sir Harry Wildair! Did not he make a campaign in Flanders° some three or four years ago?

VIZARD The same.

STANDARD Why, he behaved himself very bravely.°

VIZARD Why not? Dost think bravery and gaiety are inconsistent? He's a gentleman of most happy circumstances, born to a plentiful estate, has had a genteel and easy education, free from the rigidness of teachers, and pedantry of schools. His florid constitution being never ruffled by misfortune, nor stinted in its pleasures, has rendered him entertaining to others and easy to himself, turning all passion into gaiety of humour, by which he chooses rather to rejoice his friends than be hated by any—as you shall see.

Enter Sir Harry [with footmen]

SIR HARRY Ha Vizard!

VIZARD Sir Harry!

SIR HARRY Who thought to find you out of the rubric° so long? I thought thy hypocrisy had been wedded to a pulpit-cushion long ago.—Sir, if I mistake not your face, your name is Standard.

STANDARD Sir Harry, I'm your humble servant.

SIR HARRY Come, gentlemen, the news, the news o'th' Town; for I'm just arrived.

VIZARD Why, in the City end o'th' Town we're playing the knave to get estates.

STANDARD And in the Court end playing the fool in spending 'em.

SIR HARRY Just so in Paris; I'm glad we're grown so modish.

VIZARD We are all so reformed,° that gallantry is taken for vice.

STANDARD And hypocrisy for religion.

SIR HARRY À la mode de Paris,° again.

VIZARD Not one whore between Ludgate and Aldgate.°

STANDARD But ten times more cuckolds than ever.

VIZARD Nothing like an oath in the City.

STANDARD That's a mistake; for my major swore a hundred and fifty last night to a merchant's wife in her bedchamber.

SIR HARRY Pshaw, this is trifling—tell me news, gentlemen. What lord has lately broke his fortune at the Groom-porter's?° or his heart at Newmarket,° for the loss of a race? What wife has been lately suing in Doctors' Commons° for alimony? or what daughter run away with her father's valet? What beau gave the noblest ball at the Bath,° or had the finest coach° in the Ring?° I want news, gentlemen.

STANDARD Faith, sir, these are no news at all.

VIZARD But pray, Sir Harry, tell us some news of your travels.

SIR HARRY With all my heart. You must know then, I went over to
Amsterdam in a Dutch ship; I there had a Dutch whore for five   155
stivers. I went from thence to Landen,° where I was heartily drubbed
in the battle with the butt-end of a Swiss musket.° I thence went to
Paris, where I had half a dozen intrigues, bought half a dozen new
suits, fought a couple of duels, and here I am again *in statu quo*.°

VIZARD But we heard that you designed to make the tour of Italy;   160
what brought you back so soon?

SIR HARRY That which brought you into the world, and may perhaps
carry you out of it—a woman.

STANDARD What! Quit the pleasures of travel for a woman!

SIR HARRY Ay, Colonel, for such a woman! I had rather see her *ruelle*   165
than the palace of *Louis le Grand*.° There's more glory in her smile
than in the Jubilee at Rome; and I would rather kiss her hand than
the Pope's toe.

VIZARD You, Colonel, have been very lavish in the beauty and virtue
of your mistress; and Sir Harry here has been no less eloquent in   170
the praise of his. Now will I lay you both ten guineas apiece, that
neither of them is so pretty, so witty, or so virtuous as mine.

STANDARD 'Tis done.

SIR HARRY I'll double the stakes. But, gentlemen, now I think on't, how
shall we be resolved? for I know not where my mistress may be found.   175
She left Paris about a month before me, and I had an account—

STANDARD How, sir! left Paris about a month before you!

SIR HARRY Yes, sir, and I had an account that she lodged somewhere
in St James's.°

VIZARD How is that, sir? Somewhere in St James's, say you?°   180

SIR HARRY Ay, but I know not where, and perhaps mayn't find her
this fortnight.

STANDARD Her name, pray, Sir Harry.

VIZARD Ay, ay, her name—perhaps we know her.

SIR HARRY Her name! Ay—she has the softest, whitest hand that   185
ever was made of flesh and blood, her lips so balmy sweet!

STANDARD But her name, sir.

SIR HARRY Then her neck and breast!° (*Singing*) '*Her breast do so
heave, so heave.*'

VIZARD But her name, sir, her quality?°   190

SIR HARRY Then her shape, Colonel!

STANDARD But her name I want, sir.

12

SIR HARRY Then her eyes, Vizard!

STANDARD Pshaw, Sir Harry, her name, or nothing.

SIR HARRY Then if you must have it, she's called the Lady—but   195
then her foot, gentlemen, she dances to a miracle. Vizard, you have
certainly lost your wager.

VIZARD Why you have lost your senses; we shall never discover the
picture unless you subscribe the name.

SIR HARRY Then her name is Lurewell.   200

STANDARD (*aside*) 'Sdeath, my mistress!

VIZARD (*aside*) My mistress by Jupiter!

SIR HARRY Do you know her, gentlemen?

STANDARD I have seen her, sir.

SIR HARRY Canst tell where she lodges? Tell me, dear Colonel.   205

STANDARD Your humble servant, sir.

    Exit Standard

SIR HARRY Nay, hold, Colonel, I'll follow you, and will know.
    [*Sir Harry*] *runs out.* [*Footmen follow*]

VIZARD The Lady Lurewell his mistress! He loves her. But she loves
me—but he's a baronet, and I plain Vizard; he has coach-and-six,
and I walk afoot; I was bred in London, and he in Paris. That very   210
circumstance has murdered me. Then some stratagem must be laid
to divert his pretensions.
    Enter Sir Harry [*and footmen*]

SIR HARRY Prithee, Dick, what makes the colonel so out of humour?

VIZARD Because he's out of pay, I suppose.

SIR HARRY 'Slife, that's true—I was beginning to mistrust some   215
rivalship in the case.

VIZARD And suppose there were, you know the colonel can fight, Sir
Harry.

SIR HARRY Fight! Pshaw! but he can't dance, ha! We contend for a
woman, Vizard! 'Slife man, if ladies were to be gained by sword   220
and pistol only, what the Devil should all the beaux do?

VIZARD (*aside*) I'll try him further.—But would not you, Sir Harry,
fight for this woman you so admire?

SIR HARRY Fight! Let me consider. I love her, that's true—but then
I love honest Sir Harry Wildair better. The Lady Lurewell is   225
divinely charming—right—but then a thrust i' th' guts, or a
Middlesex jury,° is as ugly as the Devil.

VIZARD Ay, Sir Harry, 'twere a dangerous cast° for a beau baronet
to be tried by a parcel of greasy, grumbling, bartering boobies, who
would hang you purely because you're a gentleman.   230

SIR HARRY Ay, but on t'other hand, I have money enough to bribe
the rogues with. So upon mature deliberation, I would fight for
her. But no more of her. Prithee, Vizard, can't you recommend a
friend to a pretty mistress by the by, till I can find my own? You
have store I'm sure; you cunning poaching dogs make surer game   235
than we that hunt open and fair. Prithee now, good Vizard!

VIZARD Let me consider a little. (*Aside*) Now love and revenge
inspire my politics.

[*Vizard*] *pauses, whilst Sir Harry walks singing*

SIR HARRY Pshaw! thou'rt as long studying for a new mistress, as a
drawer is piercing a new pipe.°   240

VIZARD I design a new pipe for you and wholesome wine; you'll
therefore bear a little expectation.

SIR HARRY Ha! sayest thou, dear Vizard?

VIZARD A girl of sixteen, Sir Harry.

SIR HARRY Now sixteen thousand blessings light on thee!   245

VIZARD Pretty and witty.

SIR HARRY Ay, ay, but her name, Vizard?

VIZARD Her name! Yes—she has the softest whitest hand that ever
was made of flesh and blood, her lips so balmy sweet.

SIR HARRY Well, well, but where shall I find her, man?   250

VIZARD Find her—but then her foot, Sir Harry: she dances to a
miracle.

SIR HARRY Prithee don't distract me.

VIZARD Well then, you must know, that this lady is the curiosity and
ambition of the Town; her name's Angelica. She that passes for   255
her mother is a private bawd, and called the Lady Darling—she
goes for a baronet's lady (no disparagement to your honour,° Sir
Harry) I assure you.

SIR HARRY Pshaw, hang my honour; but what street, what house?

VIZARD Not so fast, Sir Harry—you must have my passport for your   260
admittance, and you'll find my recommendation in a line or two
will procure you very civil entertainment; I suppose twenty or
thirty pieces° handsomely placed will gain the point; I'll ensure her
sound.°

SIR HARRY Thou dearest friend to a man in necessity. (*To his*   265
servant) Here sirrah, order my coach about to St James's; I'll walk
across the Park.

[*Exit footman.*] *Enter Clincher Senior*

CLINCHER SENIOR [*to servant off-stage*] Here sirrah, order my coach
about to St James's, I'll walk across the Park too.° Mr Vizard, your

most devoted. [*To Sir Harry*] Sir, I admire the mode of your   270
shoulder-knot—methinks it hangs very emphatically, and carries
an air of travel in it; your sword-knot too is most ornamentally
modish, and bears a foreign mien. Gentlemen, my brother is just
arrived in Town, so that being upon the wing to kiss his hands, I
hope you'll pardon this abrupt departure of, gentlemen, your most   275
devoted, and most faithful humble servant.

> *Exit* [*Clincher Senior*]

SIR HARRY Prithee, dost know him?

VIZARD Know him! Why, 'tis Clincher who was apprentice to my
uncle Smuggler, the merchant in the City.

SIR HARRY What makes him so gay?   280

VIZARD Why, he's in mourning for his father—the kind old man in
Hertfordshire t'other day broke his neck a-fox-hunting; the son upon
the news has broke his indentures, whipped from behind the counter
into the side-box, forswearing merchandise, where he must live by
cheating, and usurps gentility, where he may die by raking. He keeps   285
his coach, and liveries, brace of geldings, leash of mistresses, talks of
nothing but wines, intrigues, plays, fashions, and going to the Jubilee.

SIR HARRY Ha, ha, ha, how many pound of pulvil must the fellow
use in sweetening himself from the smell of hops and tobacco,
faugh. I' my conscience methought, like Olivia's lover, he stunk of   290
Thames Street.° But now for Angelica—that's her name? We'll to
the Princess's chocolate-house,° where you shall write my passport. *Allons.*°

> *Exeunt.*

[1.2]

Scene, Lady Lurewell's lodgings

Lady Lurewell, and her maid, Parly

LADY LUREWELL Parly, my pocket-book. Let me see [*leafing through
the pages*]—Madrid, Venice, Paris, London—ay, London! They
may talk what they will of the hot countries, but I find love most
fruitful under this climate. In a month's space have I gained . . .
let me see . . . *imprimis*, Colonel Standard.   5

PARLY And how will your ladyship manage him?

LADY LUREWELL As all soldiers should be managed, he shall serve
me till I gain my ends, then I disband him.

PARLY But he loves you, madam.

LADY LUREWELL Therefore I scorn him; I hate all that don't love   10
me, and slight all that do. Would his whole deluding sex admired
me, thus would I slight them all. My virgin and unwary innocence
was wronged by faithless man, but now glance eyes, plot brain,
dissemble face, lie tongue, and be a second Eve° to tempt, seduce,
and damn the treacherous kind. Let me survey my captives. The   15
colonel leads the van; next Mr Vizard—he courts me out of *The
Practice of Piety*,° therefore is a hypocrite. Then Clincher—he
adores me with orangery, and is consequently a fool; then my old
merchant, Alderman Smuggler—he's a compound of both; out of
which medley of lovers, if I don't make good diversion! What d'ye   20
think, Parly?

PARLY I think, madam, I'm like to be very virtuous in your
service, if you teach me all those tricks that you use to your
lovers.

LADY LUREWELL You're a fool, child; observe this, that though a   25
woman swear, forswear, lie, dissemble, backbite, be proud, vain,
malicious, anything, if she secures the main chance,° she's still
virtuous—that's a maxim.

PARLY I can't be persuaded though, madam, but that you really
loved Sir Harry Wildair in Paris.   30

LADY LUREWELL Of all the lovers I ever had, he was my greatest
plague, for I could never make him uneasy; I left him involved in
a duel upon my account—I long to know whether the fop be killed
or not.

Enter Standard

O Lord, no sooner talk of killing, but the soldier is conjured up.   35
You're upon hard duty, Colonel, to serve your king, your country,
and a mistress too.

STANDARD The latter, I must confess, is the hardest; for in war,
madam, we can be relieved in our duty; but in love who would
take our post° is our enemy; emulation in glory is transporting, but   40
rivals here intolerable.

LADY LUREWELL Those that bear away the prize in the field should
boast the same success in the bedchamber; and I think, considering
the weakness of our sex, we should make those our companions
who can be our champions.   45

STANDARD I once, madam, hoped the honour of defending you from
all injuries through a title to your lovely person, but now my love
must attend my fortune. This commission,° madam, was my

passport to the fair; adding a nobleness to my passion, it stamped
a value on my love; 'twas once the life of honour, but now its   50
hearse, and with it must my love be buried.

PARLY What! Disbanded, Colonel?

STANDARD Yes, Mrs Parly.

PARLY (*aside*) Faugh, the nauseous fellow, he stinks of poverty already.

LADY LUREWELL (*aside*) His misfortune troubles me, 'cause it may   55
prevent my designs.

STANDARD I'll choose, madam, rather to destroy my passion by
absence abroad, than have it starved at home.

LADY LUREWELL I'm sorry, sir, you have so mean an opinion of my
affection, as to imagine it founded upon your fortune. And to   60
convince you of your mistake, here I vow by all that's sacred, I
own the same affection now as before. Let it suffice, my fortune is
considerable.

STANDARD No, madam, no, I'll never be a charge to her I love. The
man that sells himself for gold is the worst of prostitutes.   65

LADY LUREWELL (*aside*) Now were he any other creature but a man,
I could love him.

STANDARD This only last request I make, that no title recommend a
fool, office introduce a knave, nor coat a coward° to my place in
your affections; so farewell my country, and adieu my love.   70
    Exit [*Standard*]

LADY LUREWELL Now the Devil take thee for being so honourable.
Here, Parly, call him back, I shall lose half my diversion else.
    [*Exit Parly*]
 - Now for a trial of skill.
    Enter Standard [*with Parly*]
Sir, I hope you'll pardon my curiosity. When do you take your
journey?   75

STANDARD Tomorrow morning early, madam.

LADY LUREWELL So suddenly! Which way are you designed to
travel?

STANDARD That I can't yet resolve on.

LADY LUREWELL Pray, sir, tell me, pray sir, I entreat you, why are   80
you so obstinate?

STANDARD Why are you so curious, madam?

LADY LUREWELL Because—

STANDARD What?

LADY LUREWELL Because, I, I—   85

STANDARD Because! what, madam? Pray tell me.

LADY LUREWELL (*crying*) Because I design—to follow you.

STANDARD Follow me! by all that's great! I ne'er was proud before, but love from such a creature might swell the vanity of the proudest prince. Follow me! By Heavens thou shalt not. What! 90 expose thee to the hazards of a camp! Rather I'll stay, and here bear the contempt of fools, and worst of fortune.

LADY LUREWELL You need not, shall not—my estate for both is sufficient.

STANDARD Thy estate! no, I'll turn a knave and purchase one myself; 95 I'll cringe to that proud man I undermine, and fawn on him that I would bite to death; I'll tip my tongue with flattery, and smooth my face with smiles; I'll turn pimp, informer, office-broker,° nay coward, to be great; and sacrifice it all to thee, my generous fair.

LADY LUREWELL And I'll dissemble, lie, swear, jilt, anything but I'd 100 reward thy love, and recompense thy noble passion.

STANDARD Sir Harry, ha, ha, ha, poor Sir Harry, ha, ha, ha. Rather kiss her hand than the Pope's toe, ha, ha, ha.

LADY LUREWELL What Sir Harry? Colonel, what Sir Harry?

STANDARD Sir Harry Wildair, madam— 105

LADY LUREWELL What! is he come over?

STANDARD Ay, and he told me—but I don't believe a syllable on't.

LADY LUREWELL What did he tell you?

STANDARD Only called you his mistress, and pretending to be extravagant in your commendation, would vainly insinuate the 110 praise of his own judgment and good fortune in a choice—

LADY LUREWELL How easily is the vanity of fops tickled by our sex!

STANDARD Why, your sex is the vanity of fops.

LADY LUREWELL O' my conscience I believe so; this gentleman, because he danced well, I pitched on for a partner at a ball in Paris, 115 and ever since he has so persecuted me with letters, songs, dances, serenading, flattery, foppery, and noise, that I was forced to fly the kingdom. And I warrant he made you jealous.

STANDARD Faith, madam, I was a little uneasy.

LADY LUREWELL You shall have a plentiful revenge—I'll send him 120 back all his foolish letters, songs and verses, and you yourself shall carry 'em; 'twill afford you opportunity of triumphing, and free me from his further impertinence; for of all men he's my aversion. I'll run and fetch them instantly.

STANDARD Dear Madam, a rare project. How I shall bait him like 125 Actaeon with his own dogs.

Exit Lady Lurewell

Well, Mrs Parly, 'tis ordered by Act of Parliament,° that you receive no more pieces, Mrs Parley.

PARLY 'Tis provided by the same Act, that you send no more messages by me, good Colonel; you must not pretend to send any more letters, unless you can pay the postage.   130

STANDARD Come, come! don't be mercenary—take example by your lady; be honourable.

PARLY Alack-a-day, sir, it shows as ridiculous and haughty for us to imitate our betters in their honour, as in their finery; leave honour to nobility that can support it. We poor folks, Colonel, have no pretence to't; and truly, I think, sir, that your honour should be cashiered with your leading-staff.   135

STANDARD 'Tis one of the greatest curses of poverty, to be the jest of chambermaids!   140

    Enter Lady Lurewell

LADY LUREWELL Here's the packet, Colonel, the whole magazine of love's artillery.

    Gives him the packet

STANDARD Which since I have gained, I will turn upon the enemy. Madam, I'll bring you the news of my victory this evening. Poor Sir Harry! ha, ha, ha.   145

    Exit [Standard]

LADY LUREWELL To the right about! As you were! march, Colonel! ha, ha, ha.

    Vain man, who boasts of studied parts and wiles,
    Nature in us your deepest art beguiles,
    Stamping deep cunning in our frowns and smiles.   150
    You toil for art, your intellects you trace;
    Woman without a thought, bears policy in her face.
    Exeunt

2.[1]

Scene, Clincher Junior's lodgings

Enter Clincher Junior opening a letter, servant [Dicky] following

CLINCHER JUNIOR (*reads*) 'Dear Brother; I will see you presently; I have sent this lad to wait on you, he can instruct you in the fashions of the Town. I am your affectionate brother, Clincher.' Very well, and what's your name, sir?

DICKY My name is Dicky, sir.   5

CLINCHER JUNIOR Dicky!

DICKY Ay, Dicky, sir.

CLINCHER JUNIOR Very well, a pretty name! and what can you do Mr Dicky?

DICKY Why sir I can powder a wig, and pick up a whore.   10

CLINCHER JUNIOR O Lord! O Lord! a whore! Why are there many whores in this town?

DICKY Ha, ha, ha, many whores! there's a question indeed; why sir, there are above five hundred surgeons° in Town. [*Pointing*°] Hark'ee sir, do you see that woman there in the velvet scarf, and   15
red knots?

CLINCHER JUNIOR Ay sir, what then?

DICKY Why she shall be at your service in three minutes, as I'm a pimp.

CLINCHER JUNIOR O Jupiter Ammon!° why she's a gentlewoman.   20

DICKY A gentlewoman! why so are all the whores in Town, sir.°

Enter Clincher Senior

CLINCHER SENIOR Brother, you're welcome to London!

CLINCHER JUNIOR I thought, brother, you owed so much to the memory of my father, as to wear mourning for his death.

CLINCHER SENIOR Why so I do fool, I wear this because I have the   25
estate, and you wear that because you have not the estate. You have cause to mourn indeed, brother. Well brother, I'm glad to see you, fare you well. (*Going*)

CLINCHER JUNIOR Stay, stay brother, where are you going?

CLINCHER SENIOR How natural 'tis for a country booby to ask   30
impertinent° questions. Hark'ee sir, is not my father dead?

CLINCHER JUNIOR Ay, ay, to my sorrow.

CLINCHER SENIOR No matter for that, he is dead, and am not I a young powdered extravagant° English heir?

CLINCHER JUNIOR Very right sir.   35

CLINCHER SENIOR Why then sir, you may be sure that I am going to the Jubilee, sir.

CLINCHER JUNIOR Jubilee! what's that?

CLINCHER SENIOR Jubilee! why, the Jubilee is—faith I don't know what it is.   40

DICKY Why the Jubilee is the same thing with our Lord Mayor's day in the City;° there will be pageants, and squibs, and raree-shows, and all that, sir.

CLINCHER JUNIOR And must you go so soon brother?

CLINCHER SENIOR Yes, sir, for I must stay a month in Amsterdam,   45
to study poetry.°

CLINCHER JUNIOR Then I suppose brother, you travel through Muscovy to learn fashions,° don't you, brother?

CLINCHER SENIOR 'Brother!' Prithee, Robin, don't call me 'brother'; 'sir' will do every jot as well.   50

CLINCHER JUNIOR O Jupiter Ammon! why so?

CLINCHER SENIOR Because people will imagine that you have a spite at me. But have you seen your cousin Angelica yet, and her mother the Lady Darling?

CLINCHER JUNIOR No, my dancing-master has not been with me   55
yet. How shall I salute them, brother?

CLINCHER SENIOR Pshaw! that's easy, [*demonstrating*] 'tis only two scrapes, a kiss, and 'Your humble servant'. I'll tell you more when I come from the Jubilee. Come along.

    Exeunt

2.[2]

    Scene, Lady Darling's house

    Enter Sir Harry with a letter

SIR HARRY Like light and heat incorporate we lay;
    We blessed the night, and cursed the coming day.°
Well, if this paper-kite° flies sure, I'm secure of my game.—
Humph! the prettiest bordel I have seen, a very stately genteel one.

    Footmen cross the stage

Hey-day! Equipage too! Now for a bawd by the courtesy,° and a   5
whore with a coat of arms. 'Sdeath, I'm afraid I've mistaken the house.

Enter Lady Darling

No, this must be the bawd by her bulk.

LADY DARLING Your business, pray sir?

SIR HARRY Pleasure, madam.   10

LADY DARLING Then, sir, you have no business here.

SIR HARRY This letter, madam, will inform you further; Mr Vizard
sent it, with his humble service to your ladyship.

LADY DARLING How does my cousin, sir?

SIR HARRY [*aside*] Ay, her 'cousin' too—that's right procuress   15
again.°

LADY DARLING (*reads*) 'Madam . . . earnest inclination to serve . . .
Sir Harry . . . madam . . . court my cousin . . . gentleman . . . fortune . . . Your ladyship's most humble servant, Vizard.' Sir, your
fortune and quality are sufficient to recommend you anywhere; but   20
what goes further with me, is the recommendation of so sober and
pious a young gentleman as cousin Vizard.

SIR HARRY [*aside*] A right sanctified bawd, o' my word.

LADY DARLING Sir Harry, your conversation with Mr Vizard argues
you a gentleman, free from the loose and vicious carriage of the   25
Town; I'll therefore call my daughter.°

Exit [Lady Darling]

SIR HARRY Now go thy way for an illustrious bawd of Babylon.° She
dresses up a sin so religiously, that the Devil would hardly know
it of his making.

Enter Lady Darling with Angelica

LADY DARLING [*aside to Angelica*] Pray, daughter, use him civilly—   30
such matches won't offer every day.

Exit [Lady Darling]

SIR HARRY [*aside*] O all ye powers of love! an angel! 'Sdeath, what
money have I got in my pocket? I can't offer her less than twenty
guineas—and by Jupiter she's worth a hundred.

ANGELICA [*aside*] 'Tis he! the very same! and his person as agreeable 35
as his character of° good humour. Pray Heaven his silence proceed
from respect.

SIR HARRY [*aside*] How innocent she looks! How would that modesty
adorn virtue, when it makes even vice look so charming! By
Heaven, there is such a commanding innocence in her looks, that   40
I dare not ask the question.

ANGELICA [*aside*] Now all the charms of real love and feigned
indifference assist me to engage his heart, for mine is lost
already.

SIR HARRY Madam—I, I—[*aside*] Zoons! I cannot speak to her. But   45
she's a whore, and I will. [*Aloud*] Madam, in short I, I—[*aside*] O
hypocrisy! hypocrisy! What a charming sin art thou!

ANGELICA [*aside*] He is caught; now to secure my conquest. [*Aloud*]
I thought sir, you had business to impart?

SIR HARRY [*aside*] Business to impart!° how nicely she words it! [*Aloud*]   50
Yes madam; don't you, don't you love singing birds, madam?

ANGELICA [*aside*] That's an odd question for a lover. [*Aloud*] Yes, sir.

SIR HARRY [*showing her a purse*] Why then madam, here is a nest of
the prettiest goldfinches that ever chirped in a cage;° twenty young
ones, I assure you madam.   55

ANGELICA Twenty young ones! What then, sir?°

SIR HARRY Why then madam, there are twenty young ones. 'Slife, I
think twenty is pretty fair.

ANGELICA [*aside*] He's mad sure.—Sir Harry, when you have learned
more wit and manners, you shall be welcome here again.   60
        Exit Angelica

SIR HARRY Wit and manners! Egad now I conceive there is a great
deal of wit and manners in twenty guineas—I'm sure 'tis all the
wit and manners I have about me at present. What shall I do?
        Enter Clincher Junior and Dicky
What the Devil's here? Another 'cousin' I warrant ye! Hark'ee sir,
can you lend me ten or a dozen guineas instantly? I'll pay you   65
fifteen for them in three hours upon my honour.

CLINCHER JUNIOR These London sparks are plaguy impudent!
This fellow by his wig and assurance can be no less than a courtier.

DICKY He's rather a courtier by his borrowing.

CLINCHER JUNIOR Faith sir, I han't above five guineas about me.   70

SIR HARRY What business have you here then sir?—for to my
knowledge twenty won't be sufficient.

CLINCHER JUNIOR Sufficient! For what sir?

SIR HARRY What sir? Why, for that sir—what the Devil should it be,
sir? I know your business notwithstanding all your gravity, sir.   75

CLINCHER JUNIOR My business! why my cousin lives here.

SIR HARRY I know your 'cousin' does live there, and Vizard's
'cousin', and my 'cousin', and everybody's 'cousin'. Hark'ee sir, I
shall return immediately, and if you offer to touch her till I come
back, I shall cut your throat, rascal.   80
        Exit [Sir Harry]

CLINCHER JUNIOR Why the man's mad sure.

DICKY Mad, sir—ay, why, he's a beau.

CLINCHER JUNIOR A beau! what's that? Are all madmen beaux?

DICKY No sir, but most beaux are madmen. But now for your cousin; remember your three scrapes, a kiss, and 'Your humble servant'.   85

Exeunt, as into the house°

2.[3]

Scene, the street

Enter Sir Harry, Standard following

STANDARD Sir Harry, Sir Harry.

SIR HARRY I'm in haste, Colonel; besides, if you're in no better humour than when I parted with you in the Park this morning, your company won't be very agreeable.

STANDARD You're a happy man, Sir Harry, who are never out of   5
humour. Can nothing move your gall, Sir Harry?

SIR HARRY Nothing but impossibilities, which are the same as nothing.

STANDARD What impossibilities?

SIR HARRY The resurrection of my father to disinherit me, or an Act of Parliament against wenching. A man of eight thousand pound   10
per annum to be vexed! No, no—anger and spleen are companions for younger brothers.

STANDARD Suppose one called you son of a whore behind your back.

SIR HARRY Why then would I call him rascal behind his back, and so we're even.   15

STANDARD But suppose you had lost a mistress?

SIR HARRY Why then I would get another.

STANDARD But suppose you were discarded by the woman you love—that would surely trouble you.

SIR HARRY You're mistaken, Colonel—my love is neither romantically   20
honourable, nor meanly mercenary; 'tis only a pitch of gratitude. While she loves me, I love her; when she desists, the obligation's void.

STANDARD But to be mistaken in your opinion, sir; if the Lady Lurewell (only suppose it) had discarded you—I say only suppose it—and had sent your discharge by me.   25

SIR HARRY Pshaw! that's another impossibility.

STANDARD Are you sure of that?

SIR HARRY Why 'twere a solecism in nature—we're finger and thumb, sir. She dances with me, sings with me, plays with me, swears with me, lies with me.   30

24

STANDARD How sir?

SIR HARRY I mean in an honourable way, that is, she lies for me.°
In short, we are as like one another as a couple of guineas.

STANDARD Now that I have raised you to the highest pinnacle of
vanity, will I give you so mortifying a fall, as shall dash your hopes   35
to pieces.

    Gives him the packet

I`pray your honour to peruse these papers.

SIR HARRY What is't, the muster-roll of your regiment, Colonel?

STANDARD No, no, 'tis a list of your forces in your last love
campaign; and for your comfort all disbanded.   40

SIR HARRY Prithee, good metaphorical Colonel, what d'ye mean?

STANDARD Read, sir, read—these are the Sibyl's Leaves° that will
unfold your destiny.

SIR HARRY So it be not a false deed to cheat me of my estate, what
care I? (*Opening the packet*) Humph! my hand! 'To the Lady   45
Lurewell', 'To the Lady Lurewell', 'To the Lady Lurewell'. What
devil hast thou been tampering with to conjure up these spirits?

STANDARD A certain familiar of your acquaintance, sir.

SIR HARRY [*reading*] 'Madam, my passion . . . so natural . . . your
beauty contending . . . force of charms . . . mankind . . . eternal   50
admirer, Wildair!' I never was ashamed of my name before.

STANDARD What, Sir Harry Wildair out of humour, ha, ha, ha! Poor
Sir Harry. More glory in her smile than in the Jubilee at Rome,
ha, ha, ha! But then her foot, Sir Harry, she dances to a miracle!
ha, ha, ha! Fie Sir Harry, a man of your parts write letters not   55
worth a-keeping! What say'st thou, my dear knight errant? ha, ha,
ha; you may go seek adventures now indeed.

SIR HARRY [*sings*] *'Let her wander',&c.*°

STANDARD You are jilted to some tune, sir, blown up with false
music, that's all.°   60

SIR HARRY Now why should I be angry that a woman is a woman?
Since inconstancy and falsehood are grounded in their natures,
how can they help it?

STANDARD Then they must be grounded in your nature; for you and
she are finger and thumb, sir.   65

SIR HARRY Here's a copy of verses too—I must turn poet in the
Devil's name. [*Aside*] Stay—'sdeath, what's here? This is her hand.
O the charming characters! (*Reading*) 'My dear Wildair'—that's
I—'this huff-bluff colonel'—that's he—'is the rarest fool in
nature'—the Devil he is!—'and as such have I used him'—with all   70

my heart faith—'I had no better way of letting you know that I
lodge in Pall Mall° near the Holy Lamb.'° [*Aloud*] Colonel, I'm
your most humble servant.

STANDARD Hold, sir, you shan't go yet, I han't delivered half my
message.   75

SIR HARRY Upon my faith but you have, Colonel.

STANDARD Well, well, own your spleen, out with it, I know you're
like to burst.

SIR HARRY I am so, by Gad, ha, ha, ha.

STANDARD Ay, with all my heart, ha, ha.   80
        [*They*] *laugh, and point at one another*
Well, well, that's all forced, Sir Harry.

SIR HARRY I was never better pleased in all my life, by Jupiter.

STANDARD Well, Sir Harry, 'tis prudence to hide your concern, when
there's no help for't. But to be serious now, the lady has sent you
back all your papers there—I was so just as not to look upon 'em.   85

SIR HARRY I'm glad on't, sir; for there were some things that I would
not have you see.

STANDARD All this she has done for my sake, and I desire you would
decline any further pretensions for your own sake. So, honest,
good-natured Sir Harry, I'm your humble servant.   90
        Exit [*Standard*]

SIR HARRY Ha, ha, ha, poor Colonel! O the delight of an ingenious
mistress! What a life and briskness° it adds to an amour, like the
loves of mighty Jove, still suing in different shapes.° A legerdemain
mistress, who—'Presto', pass—and she's vanished, then—'Hey'—
in an instant in your arms again.° (*Going*)   95
        Enter Vizard

VIZARD Well met, Sir Harry—what news from the Island of Love?

SIR HARRY Faith we made but a broken voyage by your card;° but now
I am bound for another port. I told you the colonel was my rival.

VIZARD [*aside*] The colonel! cursed misfortune! another!

SIR HARRY But the civillest in the world—he brought me word   100
where my mistress lodges; the story's too long to tell you now, for
I must fly.

VIZARD What! have you given over all thoughts of Angelica?

SIR HARRY No, no, I'll think of her some other time. But now for
the Lady Lurewell; wit and beauty calls.   105
That mistress ne'er can pall her lover's joys,
Whose wit can whet whene'er her beauty cloys.
Her little amorous frauds all truths excel,

And make us happy, being deceived so well.

    Exit [Sir Harry]

VIZARD [*alone*] The colonel my rival too! how shall I manage? There is   110
but one way—him and the knight will I set a-tilting, where one cuts
t'other's throat, and the survivor's hanged. So there will be two rivals
pretty decently disposed of. Since honour may oblige them to play
the fool, why should not necessity engage me to play the knave?

    Exit

2.[4]

Scene, Lady Lurewell's lodgings

Lady Lurewell and Parly

LADY LUREWELL Has my servant brought me the money from my
merchant?

PARLY No, madam, he met Alderman Smuggler at Charing Cross,
who has promised to wait on you himself immediately.

LADY LUREWELL 'Tis odd, that this old rogue should pretend° to   5
love me, and at the same time cheat me of my money.

PARLY 'Tis well, madam, if he don't cheat you of your estate; for
you say the writings° are in his hands.

LADY LUREWELL But what satisfaction can I get of him?

    Enter Smuggler

Mr Alderman, your servant—have you brought me any money, sir?   10

SMUGGLER Faith, madam, trading is very dead; what with paying the
taxes, raising the customs, losses at sea abroad, and maintaining
our wives at home, the bank is reduced very low.°

LADY LUREWELL Come, come, sir, these evasions won't serve your
turn—I must have money, sir. I hope you don't design to cheat me.   15

SMUGGLER Cheat you, madam! have a care what you say. I'm an
alderman, madam—cheat you, madam! I have been an honest
citizen these five and thirty years!

LADY LUREWELL [*aside to Parly*] An honest citizen! bear witness,
Parly! I shall trap him in more lies presently.—Come, sir, though   20
I'm a woman, I can take a course.°

SMUGGLER What course, madam? You'll go to law, will ye? I can
maintain a suit of law, be it right or wrong, these forty years, I'm
sure of that, thanks to the honest practice of the courts.

LADY LUREWELL Sir, I'll blast your reputation, and so ruin your credit.   25

SMUGGLER Blast my reputation! he, he, he. Why I'm a religious man, madam, I have been very instrumental in the reformation of manners. Ruin my credit! ah, poor woman! There is but one way, madam—you have a sweet leering eye.

LADY LUREWELL You instrumental in the reformation! How?   30

SMUGGLER I whipped all the whores, cut and long tail,° out of the parish.—Ah, that leering eye!—Then I voted for pulling down the playhouse.°—Ah, that ogle, that ogle!—Then my own pious example.—Ah, that lip, that lip!

LADY LUREWELL [aside] Here's a religious rogue for you now! As I   35 hope to be saved, I have a good mind to beat the old monster.

SMUGGLER Madam, I have brought you about a hundred and fifty guineas (a great deal of money as times go) and—

LADY LUREWELL Come, give it me.

SMUGGLER Ah, that hand, that hand, that pretty, soft, white—I have   40 brought it you see, but the condition of the obligation is such, that whereas that leering eye, that pouting lip, that pretty soft hand, that—you understand me, you understand I'm sure you do, you little rogue.

LADY LUREWELL [aside] Here's a villain now, so covetous that he   45 won't wench upon his own cost, but would bribe me with my own money. I will be revenged—Upon my word, Mr Alderman, you make me blush—what do you mean, pray?

SMUGGLER See here, madam.
        Puts a piece of money in his mouth
        Buss and guinea,° buss and guinea, buss and guinea.   50

LADY LUREWELL Well, Mr Alderman, you have such pretty yellow teeth, and green gums, that I will, ha, ha, ha, ha.

SMUGGLER Will you indeed, he, he, he, my little cocket? and when, and where, and how?

LADY LUREWELL 'Twill be a difficult point, sir, to secure both our   55 honours—you must therefore be disguised, Mr Alderman.

SMUGGLER Pshaw! no matter, I am an old fornicator—I'm not half so religious as I seem to be. You little rogue, why I'm disguised as I am—our sanctity is all outside, all hypocrisy.

LADY LUREWELL No man is seen to come into this house after nightfall;   60 you must therefore sneak in, when 'tis dark, in woman's clothes.

SMUGGLER Egad so, cod so°—I have a suit o' purpose, my little cocket—I love to be disguised; ecod I make a very handsome woman, ecod I do.
        Enter servant, [who] whispers [to] Lady Lurewell. [Exit servant]

LADY LUREWELL O! Mr Alderman, shall I beg you to walk into the   65
next room?°—here are some strangers coming up.

SMUGGLER Buss and guinea first, ah my little cocket.

     Exit [Smuggler]. Enter Sir Harry

SIR HARRY My life, my soul, my all that heaven can give . . .

LADY LUREWELL Death's life with thee, without thee death to live.°
Welcome, my dear Sir Harry—I see you got my directions.   70

SIR HARRY Directions! In the most charming manner, thou dear
Machiavel° of intrigue.

LADY LUREWELL Still brisk and airy I find, Sir Harry.

SIR HARRY The sight of you, Madam, exalts my air, and makes joy
lighten in my face.   75

LADY LUREWELL I have a thousand questions to ask you, Sir Harry.
How d'ye like France?

SIR HARRY *Ah! c'est le plus beau pays du monde.*°

LADY LUREWELL Then what made you leave it so soon?

SIR HARRY *Madame, vous voyez que je vous suis partout.*°   80

LADY LUREWELL *O monsieur, je vous suis fort obligée.*° But where's
the Court now?

SIR HARRY At Marli, madam.°

LADY LUREWELL And where my Count Le Valier?

SIR HARRY His body's in the church of *Notre Dame*°—I don't know   85
where his soul is.

LADY LUREWELL What disease did he die of?

SIR HARRY A duel, madam—I was his doctor.

LADY LUREWELL How d'ye mean?

SIR HARRY As most doctors do, I killed him.   90

LADY LUREWELL *En cavalier,*° my dear knight-errant. Well, and
how? And how, what intrigues, what gallantries are carrying on in
the *beau monde*?°

SIR HARRY I should ask you that question, madam, since your
ladyship makes the *beau monde* wherever you come.   95

LADY LUREWELL Ah! Sir Harry, I've been almost ruined, pestered
to death here by the incessant attacks of a mighty colonel—he has
besieged me as close as our army did Namur.°

SIR HARRY I hope your ladyship did not surrender though.

LADY LUREWELL No, no, but was forced to capitulate;° but since   100
you are come to raise the siege, we'll dance, and sing, and laugh.

SIR HARRY And love and kiss. *Montrez-moi votre chambre.*°

LADY LUREWELL *Attende, attende, un peu.*° I remember, Sir Harry, you
promised me in Paris never to ask that impertinent question again.

SIR HARRY Pshaw, madam, that was above two months ago; besides,   105
madam, treaties made in France are never kept.°

LADY LUREWELL Would you marry me, Sir Harry?

SIR HARRY O! *Le mariage est un grand mal*°—but I will marry you.

LADY LUREWELL Your word, sir, is not to be relied on: if a
gentleman will forfeit his honour in dealings of business, we may   110
reasonably suspect his fidelity in an amour.

SIR HARRY My honour in dealings of business! Why, madam, I never
had any business in all my life.

LADY LUREWELL Yes, Sir Harry, I have heard a very odd story, and
am sorry that a gentleman of your figure should undergo the   115
scandal.

SIR HARRY Out with it, madam.

LADY LUREWELL Why the merchant, sir, that transmitted your bills
of exchange° to you in France, complains of some indirect and
dishonourable dealings.   120

SIR HARRY Who? old Smuggler!

LADY LUREWELL Ay, ay, you know him I find.

SIR HARRY I have no less than reason, I think; why the rogue has
cheated me of above five hundred pound within these three years.

LADY LUREWELL 'Tis your business then to acquit yourself public-   125
ly, for he spreads the scandal everywhere.

SIR HARRY Acquit myself publicly! [*To servant*] Here sirrah, my
coach—I'll drive instantly into the City, and cane the old villain
round the Royal Exchange;° he shall run the gauntlet° through a
thousand brushed beavers and formal cravats.°   130

LADY LUREWELL Why he's in the house now, sir.

SIR HARRY What, in this house?

LADY LUREWELL Ay, in the next room.

SIR HARRY [*to servant*] Then, sirrah, lend me your cudgel.

LADY LUREWELL Sir Harry, you won't raise a disturbance in my   135
house?

SIR HARRY Disturbance, madam—no, no, I'll beat him with the
temper of a philosopher; here, Mrs Parly, show me the gentleman.
        Exit [*Sir Harry*] *with Parly* [*and servant*]

LADY LUREWELL Now shall I get the old monster well beaten, and
Sir Harry pestered next term with bloodsheds, batteries, costs and   140
damages, solicitors and attorneys;° and if they don't tease him out
of his good humour, I'll never plot again.
        Exit

2.[5]

Scene changes to another room in the same house°

Enter Smuggler [reading a document]

SMUGGLER O this damned tide-waiter! A ship and cargo worth five thousand pound! why, 'tis richly worth five hundred perjuries.

Enter Sir Harry [carrying a cudgel]

SIR HARRY Dear Mr Alderman, I'm your most devoted and humble servant.

SMUGGLER My best friend, Sir Harry, you're welcome to England.   5

SIR HARRY I'll assure you sir, there's not a man in the king's dominions I'm gladder to meet.

SMUGGLER O Lord, sir, you travellers have the most obliging ways with you.

SIR HARRY There is a business, Mr Alderman, fallen out, which you   10
may oblige me infinitely by—I am very sorry that I'm forced to be troublesome; but necessity, Mr Alderman.

SMUGGLER Ay, sir, as you say, necessity. But upon my word, sir, I am very short of money at present, but—

SIR HARRY That's not the matter, sir—I'm above an obligation that   15
way—but the business is, I am reduced to an indispensable necessity of being obliged to you for a beating. Here take this cudgel.

SMUGGLER A beating, Sir Harry! ha, ha, ha, I beat a knight baronet! an alderman turn cudgel-player, ha, ha, ha.

SIR HARRY Upon my word, sir, you must beat me, or I cudgel   20
you—take your choice.

SMUGGLER Pshaw, pshaw, you jest.

SIR HARRY Nay, 'tis as sure as fate; so, Alderman, I hope you'll pardon my curiosity.

SMUGGLER Curiosity! Deuce take your curiosity, sir, what d'ye mean?   25

SIR HARRY Nothing at all, I'm but in jest, sir.

SMUGGLER O, I can take anything in jest, but a man might imagine by the smartness of the stroke, that you were in downright earnest.

SIR HARRY Not in the least, sir, (*strikes him*) not in the least indeed sir.

SMUGGLER Pray good sir, no more of your jests, for they are the   30
bluntest jests that I ever knew.

SIR HARRY [*strikes*] I heartily beg your pardon with all my heart, sir.

SMUGGLER Pardon sir—well sir, that is satisfaction enough from a gentleman;° but seriously now if you pass any more of your jests upon me, I shall grow angry.   35

SIR HARRY I humbly beg your permission (*striking him*) to break one
or two more.

SMUGGLER O Lord, sir, you'll break my bones. Are you mad, sir?
Murder, felony, manslaughter!

   Sir Harry knocks him down

SIR HARRY Sir, I beg you ten thousand pardons; but I am absolutely   40
compelled to't upon my honour, sir. (*Striking him all this while*)
Nothing can be more averse to my inclinations, than to jest with
my honest, dear, loving, obliging friend, the alderman.

   *Smuggler tumbles over and over, and shakes out his pocket-book
   on the floor; Lady Lurewell enters [and] takes it up*

LADY LUREWELL [*aside*] The old rogue's pocket-book; this may be
of use.—O Lord, Sir Harry's murdering the poor old man.   45

SMUGGLER O dear, madam, I was beaten in jest till I am murdered
in good earnest.

LADY LUREWELL Well, well, I'll bring you off *Signor*.° [*To Sir
Harry*] *Frappez, frappez.*°

SMUGGLER O for charity's sake, madam, rescue a poor citizen.   50

LADY LUREWELL O you barbarous man, hold, hold.—*Frappez plus
rudement, frappez.*°—I wonder you are not ashamed (*holding Sir
Harry*). A poor reverend honest Elder.

   Helps up Smuggler

It makes me weep to see him in this condition, poor man! Now
the Devil take you, Sir Harry. [*Whispering*] Fear not beating him   55
harder. [*To Smuggler*] Well, my dear, you shall come at night, and
I'll make you amends!

   Here Sir Harry takes snush

SMUGGLER Madam, I will have amends before I leave the place. Sir,
how durst you use me thus?

SIR HARRY Sir?   60

SMUGGLER Sir, I say that I will have satisfaction.

SIR HARRY With all my heart.

   Throws snush in his eyes

SMUGGLER O, murder, blindness, fire. O madam, madam, get me
some water, water, fire, fire, water.

   Exit [Smuggler] with Lady Lurewell

SIR HARRY How pleasant is resenting an injury without passion; 'tis   65
the beauty of revenge.

   Let statesmen plot, and under business groan,
   And settling public quiet lose their own;
   Let soldiers drudge and fight for pay or fame,

For when they're shot, I think 'tis much the same.   70
Let scholars vex their brains with mood and tense,
And mad with strength of reason, fools commence—°
Losing their wits in searching after sense;
Their *summum bonum* they must toil to gain,°
And seeking pleasure, spend their life in pain.   75
I make the most of life, no hour misspend;
Pleasure's the means, and pleasure is my end.
No spleen, no trouble, shall my time destroy;
Life's but a span; I'll every inch enjoy.
    Exit

3.[1]

Scene, the street

Enter Standard and Vizard

STANDARD I bring him word where she lodged! I the civillest rival in the world!—'tis impossible.

VIZARD I shall urge it no further, sir; I only thought sir, that my character in the world might add authority to my words without so many repetitions.

STANDARD Pardon me, dear Vizard—our belief struggles hard, before it can be brought to yield to the disadvantage of what we love; 'tis so great an abuse to our judgment, that it makes the faults of our choice our own failing. But what said Sir Harry?

VIZARD He pitied the poor credulous colonel, laughed heartily, flew away with all the raptures of a bridegroom, repeating these lines:

'A mistress ne'er can pall her lover's joys,

Whose wit can whet whene'er her beauty cloys.'

STANDARD 'A mistress ne'er can pall!' By all my wrongs he whores her! and I'm made their property.° Vengeance! Vizard, you must carry a note from me to Sir Harry.

VIZARD What! a challenge! I hope you don't design to fight?

STANDARD What! wear the livery of my King and pocket an affront—'twere an abuse to his Sacred Majesty. A soldier's sword, Vizard, should start of itself to redress its master's wrong.

VIZARD However, sir, I think it not proper for me to carry any such message between friends.

STANDARD I have ne'er a servant here—what shall I do?

VIZARD [*pointing off-stage*] There's Tom Errand, the porter, that plies at the Blue Posts,° and who knows Sir Harry and his haunts very well—you may send a note by him.

STANDARD [*calls*] Here, you, friend.

VIZARD I have now some business, and must take my leave; I would advise you nevertheless against this affair.

STANDARD No whispering now, nor telling of friends to prevent us.° He that disappoints a man of an honourable revenge, may love him foolishly like a wife, but never value him as a friend.

VIZARD Nay, the Devil take him that parts you, say I!

Exit [Vizard]. Enter Tom Errand running

TOM ERRAND Did your honour call a porter?

STANDARD Is your name Tom Errand?   35

TOM ERRAND People call me so,° an't like your worship.

STANDARD D'ye know Sir Harry Wildair?

TOM ERRAND Ay, very well sir—he's one of my masters; many a
   round half-crown have I had of his worship; he's newly come home
   from France, sir.   40

STANDARD Go to the next coffee-house, and wait for me.
        Exit [Tom Errand]
   O woman, woman,
   How blest is man, when favour'd by your smiles,
   And how accursed when all those smiles are found
   But wanton baits to soothe us to destruction.   45
   Thus our chief joys with base alloys are curst,
   And our best things, when once corrupted, worst.
        Exit [Standard]. Enter Sir Harry, and Clincher Senior following

CLINCHER SENIOR Sir, sir, sir, having some business of importance
   to communicate to you, I would beg your attention to a trifling
   affair that I would impart to you.   50

SIR HARRY What is your trifling business of importance pray sweet
   sir?

CLINCHER SENIOR Pray sir, are the roads deep between this and
   Paris?

SIR HARRY Why that question, sir?   55

CLINCHER SENIOR Because I design to go to the Jubilee, sir. I
   understand that you are a traveller, sir; there is an air of travel in
   the tie of your cravat, sir, there is indeed, sir—I suppose, sir, you
   bought this lace in Flanders.

SIR HARRY No, sir, this lace was made in Norway.   60

CLINCHER SENIOR Norway, sir!

SIR HARRY Yes, sir, of the shavings of deal boards.°

CLINCHER SENIOR That's very strange now, faith—lace made of the
   shavings of deal boards; egad sir, you travellers see very strange
   things abroad, very incredible things abroad, indeed. Well, I'll   65
   have a cravat of that very same lace before I come home.

SIR HARRY But, sir, what preparations have you made for your
   journey?

CLINCHER SENIOR A case of pocket-pistols for the bravoes—and a
   swimming girdle.°   70

SIR HARRY Why these, sir?

CLINCHER SENIOR O Lord, sir, I'll tell you. Suppose us in Rome
   now; away goes me, I,° to some ball—for I'll be a mighty beau.

Then as I said, I go to some ball, or some bear-baiting,° 'tis all one
you know—then comes a fine Italian *bona roba*,° and plucks me by   75
the sleeve. '*Seigniour Angle. Seigniour Angle*'—she's a very fine
lady, observe that—'*Seigniour Angle*,' says she. '*Seigniora*,'° says I,
and trips after her to the corner of a street—suppose it Russell
Street° here, or any other street; then you know I must invite her
to the tavern, I can do no less. There up comes her *bravo*,° the   80
Italian grows saucy, and I give him an English douse of the face.
I can box, sir, box tightly—was a 'prentice, sir—but then, sir, he
whips out his stiletto, and I whips out my bull-dog°—slaps him
through, trips down stairs, turns the corner of Russell Street again,
and whips me into the ambassador's train, and there I'm safe as a   85
beau behind the scenes.°

SIR HARRY Was your pistol charged, sir?

CLINCHER SENIOR Only a brace of bullets, that's all, sir. I design to
shoot seven Italians a week,° sir.

SIR HARRY Sir, you won't have provocation.   90

CLINCHER SENIOR Provocation, sir! Zauns,° sir, I'll kill any man for
treading upon my corn, and there will be a devilish throng of
people there; they say that all the princes in Italy will be there.

SIR HARRY And all the fops and fiddlers in Europe. But the use of
your swimming-girdle, pray, sir?   95

CLINCHER SENIOR O Lord, sir, that's easy. Suppose the ship cast
away;° now, whilst other foolish people are busy at their prayers,
I whips° on my swimming girdle, claps a month's provision into
my pockets, and sails me away like an egg in a duck's belly. And
hark'ee, sir, I have a new project in my head. Where d'ye think   100
my swimming girdle shall carry me upon this occasion? 'Tis a new
project.

SIR HARRY Where, sir?

CLINCHER SENIOR To Civita Vecchia,° faith and troth, and so save
the charges of my passage! Well, sir, you must pardon me   105
now—I'm going to see my mistress.

　　　　Exit [Clincher Senior]

SIR HARRY This fellow's an accomplished ass before he goes abroad.°
Well! this Angelica has got into my heart, and I can't get her out
of my head. I must pay her t'other visit.

　　　　Exit

3.[2]

Scene, Lady Darling's house

Angelica alone

ANGELICA Unhappy state of woman! whose chief virtue is but ceremony, and our much boasted modesty but a slavish restraint. The strict confinement on our words makes our thoughts ramble more; and what preserves our outward fame, destroys our inward quiet. 'Tis hard that love should be denied the privilege of hatred; 5 that scandal and detraction should be° so much indulged, yet sacred love and truth debarred our conversation.°

Enter Lady Darling, Clincher Junior and Dicky

LADY DARLING This is my daughter, cousin.

DICKY Now, sir, remember your three scrapes.

CLINCHER JUNIOR (*saluting Angelica*) One, two, three, (*kisses her*) 10 your humble servant. Was not that right, Dicky?

DICKY Ay faith, sir, but why don't you speak to her?

CLINCHER JUNIOR I beg your pardon, Dicky. I know my distance— would you have me speak to a lady at the first sight?

DICKY Ay, sir, by all means, the first aim is the surest. 15

CLINCHER JUNIOR Now for a good jest, to make her laugh heartily. By Jupiter Ammon, I'll go give her a kiss.

Goes towards her. Enter Sir Harry, interposing

SIR HARRY 'Tis all to no purpose, I told you so before—your pitiful five guineas will never do. You may march, sir,° for as far as five hundred pounds will go, I'll outbid you. 20

CLINCHER JUNIOR What the Devil! the madman's here again.

LADY DARLING [*to Clincher Junior*] Bless me, cousin! what d'ye mean? Affront a gentleman of his quality in my house!

CLINCHER JUNIOR Quality! Why, Madam, I don't know what you mean by your madmen, and your beaux, and your quality. They're 25 all alike, I believe.

LADY DARLING Pray, sir, walk with me into the next room.

Exit Lady Darling leading Clincher Junior. Dicky follows

ANGELICA Sir, if your conversation be no more agreeable than 'twas the last time, I would advise you to make it as short as you can. 30

SIR HARRY The offences of my last visit, madam, bore their punish- ment in the commission; and have made me as uneasy till I receive pardon, as your ladyship can be till I sue for it.

ANGELICA Sir Harry, I did not well understand the offence, and must therefore proportion it to the greatness of your apology; if 35 you would therefore have me think it light, take no great pains in an excuse.

SIR HARRY How sweet must be the lips that guard that tongue! Then, madam, no more of past offences—let us prepare for joys to come; let this seal my pardon. 40

Kisses her hand

And this ([*kisses*] *again*) initiate me to further happiness.

ANGELICA Hold, sir—one question, Sir Harry, and pray answer plainly: d'ye love me?

SIR HARRY Love you! Does fire ascend? Do hypocrites dissemble? Usurers love gold, or great men flattery? Doubt these, then 45 question that I love.

ANGELICA This shows your gallantry,° sir, but not your love.

SIR HARRY View your own charms, madam, then judge my passion; your beauty ravishes my eye, your voice my ear, and your touch has thrilled my melting soul. 50

ANGELICA If your words be real, 'tis in your power to raise an equal flame in me.

SIR HARRY Nay, then—I seize—

ANGELICA Hold, sir, 'tis also possible to make me detest and scorn you worse than the most profligate of your deceiving sex. 55

SIR HARRY Ha! A very odd turn this. I hope, madam, you only affect anger, because you know your frowns are becoming.

ANGELICA Sir Harry, you being the best judge of your own designs, can best understand whether my anger should be real or dissembled—think what strict modesty should bear, then judge of my 60 resentments.

SIR HARRY Strict modesty should bear! Why faith madam, I believe the strictest modesty may bear fifty guineas, and I don't believe 'twill bear one farthing more.

ANGELICA What d'mean, sir? 65

SIR HARRY Nay, madam, what do you mean? If you go to that, I think now fifty guineas is a very fine offer for your strict modesty, as you call it.

ANGELICA 'Tis more charitable, Sir Harry, to charge the impertinence of a man of your figure on his defect in understanding than 70 on his want of manners—I'm afraid you're mad, sir.

SIR HARRY Why, madam, you're enough to make any man mad. 'Sdeath, are not you a—

ANGELICA What, sir?

SIR HARRY Why, a lady of—strict modesty, if you will have it so.   75

ANGELICA I shall never hereafter trust common report, which represented you, sir, a man of honour, wit, and breeding; for I find you very deficient in them all.

    Exit [Angelica]

SIR HARRY (*alone*) Now I find that the strict pretences which the ladies of pleasure make to strict modesty, is the reason why those   80 of quality are ashamed to wear it.

    Enter Vizard

VIZARD Ah, Sir Harry, have I caught you? Well, and what success?

SIR HARRY Success! 'tis a shame for you young fellows in Town here, to let the wenches grow so saucy. I offered her fifty guineas, and she was in her airs presently. I could have had two countesses   85 in Paris for half the money, and '*Je vous remercie*'° into the bargain.

VIZARD Gone in her airs, say you? And did not you follow her?

SIR HARRY Whither should I follow her?

VIZARD Into her bedchamber, man. She went on purpose; you a man of gallantry, and not understand that a lady's best pleased when   90 she puts on her airs, as you call it.

SIR HARRY She talked to me of strict modesty, and stuff.

VIZARD Certainly most women magnify their modesty, for the same reason that cowards boast their courage, because they have least on't. Come, come, Sir Harry, when you make your next assault,   95 encourage your spirits with brisk burgundy—if you succeed, 'tis well; if not, you have a fair excuse for your rudeness. I'll go in, and make your peace for what's past. O, I had almost forgot— Colonel Standard wants to speak with you about some business.

SIR HARRY I'll wait upon him presently—d'ye know where he may   100 be found?

VIZARD In the Piazza of Covent Garden,° about an hour hence, I promised to see him, and there you may meet him; (*aside*) to have your throat cut. [*Aloud*] I'll go in and intercede for you.

SIR HARRY But no foul play with the lady, Vizard.   105

    [*Exit Sir Harry*]

VIZARD No fair play I can assure you.°

    Exit

3.[3]

Scene, the street before Lady Lurewell's lodgings

Clincher Senior and Lady Lurewell coquetting in the balcony°
Enter Standard

STANDARD How weak is reason in disputes of love—that daring reason which so oft pretends to question works of high omnipotence, yet poorly truckles to our weakest passions, and yields implicit faith to foolish love, paying blind zeal to faithless woman's eyes!° I've heard her falsehood with such pressing proofs, that I no longer should   5
distrust it. Yet still my love would baffle demonstration.

Looks up

Ha! that fool too! What stoop so low as that animal! 'Tis true, women once fallen, like cowards in despair, will stick at nothing, there's no medium in their actions. They must be bright as angels, or black as friends. But now for my revenge—I'll kick her cully before her face,   10
call her a whore, curse the whole sex, and so leave her.

*[Standard] goes in [the house]. Lady Lurewell comes down with
Clincher Senior°*

3.[4]

The scene changes to a dining-room°

LADY LUREWELL O Lord, sir, 'tis my husband. What will become of you?

CLINCHER SENIOR Eh! Your husband! O, I shall be murdered. What shall I do? Where shall I run? I'll creep into an oven; I'll climb up the chimney; I'll fly; I'll swim. I wish to the Lord I were at the   5
Jubilee now.

LADY LUREWELL Can't you think of anything, sir?

Enter Tom Errand

What do you want, sir?

TOM ERRAND Madam, I am looking for Sir Harry Wildair; I saw him come in here this morning; and did imagine he might be here still.   10

LADY LUREWELL A lucky hit! Here friend, change clothes with this gentleman quickly. Strip.

CLINCHER SENIOR Ay, ay, quickly strip. I'll give you half-a-crown. Come here: so.

They change clothes

LADY LUREWELL (*to Clincher Senior*) Now slip you downstairs, and   15
wait at the door till my husband be gone.

    [*Exit Clincher Senior*]

(*To Tom Errand*) And get you in there till I call you.

    Puts Tom Errand into the next room. Enter Standard

O, sir! are you come? I wonder sir, how you have the confidence
to approach me after so base a trick.

STANDARD O madam, all your artifices won't prevail.   20

LADY LUREWELL Nay sir, your artifices won't avail. I thought, sir,
that I gave you caution enough against troubling me with Sir
Harry Wildair's company when I sent his letters back by you. Yet
you forsooth must tell him where I lodged, and expose me again
to his impertinent courtship.   25

STANDARD I expose you to his courtship!

LADY LUREWELL I'll lay my life you'll deny it now. Come, come,
sir, a pitiful lie is as scandalous to a red coat as an oath to a black.
Did not Sir Harry himself tell me, that he found out by you where
I lodged?   30

STANDARD You're all lies. First, your heart is false, your eyes are
double; one look belies another.° And then your tongue does
contradict them all. Madam, I see a little devil just now hammer-
ing out a lie in your pericranium.

LADY LUREWELL (*aside*) As I hope for mercy he's in the right   35
on't.—Hold, sir, you have got the playhouse cant upon your
tongue, and think that wit may privilege your railing. But I
must tell you, sir, that what is satire upon the stage, is ill manners
here.

STANDARD What is feigned upon the stage, is here in reality. Real   40
falsehood. Yes, yes, madam—I exposed you to the courtship of
your fool Clincher too? I hope your female wiles will impose that
upon me also.

LADY LUREWELL Clincher! Nay, now, you're stark mad. I know no
such person.   45

STANDARD O woman in perfection!° not know him! 'Slife, madam,
can my eyes, my piercing jealous eyes be so deluded? Nay, madam,
my nose could not mistake him; for I smelt the fop by his pulvilio
from the balcony down to the street.

LADY LUREWELL [*aside*] The balcony! Ha, ha, ha, the balcony! I'll   50
be hanged but he has mistaken Sir Harry Wildair's footman with
a new French livery, for a beau.

STANDARD 'Sdeath, madam, what is there in me that looks like a
cully? Did I not see him?

LADY LUREWELL No, no, you could not see him—you're dreaming,   55
Colonel. Will you believe your eyes, now, that I have rubbed them
open? [*Calling*] Here, you friend.

Enter Tom Errand in Clincher Senior's clothes

STANDARD This is illusion all; my eyes conspire against themselves.
'Tis legerdemain.

LADY LUREWELL Legerdemain! Is that all your acknowledgment for   60
your rude behaviour? O, what a curse it is to love as I do! But don't
presume too far, sir, on my affection. For such ungenerous usage will
soon return my tired heart. (*To Tom Errand*) Be gone sir to your
impertinent master, and tell him I shall never be at leisure to receive
any of his troublesome visits. Send to me to know when I should be at   65
home! Begone sir. I am sure he has made me an unfortunate woman.

Weeps

[*Exit Tom Errand*]

STANDARD Nay, then there is no certainty in nature; and truth is
only falsehood well disguised.

LADY LUREWELL Sir, had not I owned my fond foolish passion, I
should not have been subject to such unjust suspicions; but 'tis an   70
ungrateful return. (*Weeping*)

STANDARD [*aside*] Now where are all my firm resolves? I will believe
her just. My passion raised my jealousy; then why mayn't love be
blind in finding faults as in excusing them?—I hope, madam, you'll
pardon me, since jealousy that magnified my suspicion is as much   75
the effect of love as my easiness in being satisfied.

LADY LUREWELL Easiness in being satisfied! You men have got an
insolent way of extorting pardon, by persisting in your faults. No,
no, sir, cherish your suspicions, and feed upon your jealousy. 'Tis
fit meat for your squeamish stomach.   80
With me all women should this rule pursue:
Who thinks us false should never find us true.

*Exit [Lady Lurewell] in a rage. Enter Clincher Senior in [Tom
Errand's] clothes*

CLINCHER SENIOR (*aside*) Well, intriguing is the prettiest pleasantest
thing for a man of my parts. How shall we laugh at the husband when
he is gone! How sillily he looks! He's in labour of horns° already. To   85
make a colonel a cuckold! 'Twill be rare news for the aldermen.

STANDARD [*aside*] All this Sir Harry has occasioned; but he's brave,
and will afford me just revenge. [*Mistaking Clincher Senior for Tom*

Errand] O! this is the porter I sent the challenge by—Well, sir, have you found him? 90

CLINCHER SENIOR [*aside*] What the Devil does he mean now?

STANDARD Have you given Sir Harry the note, fellow?

CLINCHER SENIOR The note! What note?

STANDARD The letter, blockhead, which I sent by you to Sir Harry Wildair—have you seen him? 95

CLINCHER SENIOR [*aside*] O Lord, what shall I say now?—Seen him! Yes sir.—No sir.—I have sir.—I have not sir.

STANDARD The fellow's mad. Answer me directly sirrah, or I'll break your head.

CLINCHER SENIOR I know Sir Harry very well, sir; but as to the note 100 sir, I can't remember a word on't. Truth is, I have a very bad memory.

STANDARD O sir, I'll quicken your memory!
        Strikes him

CLINCHER SENIOR Zauns, sir, hold—I did give him the note.

STANDARD And what answer? 105

CLINCHER SENIOR I mean, sir, I did not give him the note.

STANDARD What, d'ye banter rascal?
        Strikes him again

CLINCHER SENIOR Hold sir, hold—he did send an answer.

STANDARD What was't, villain?

CLINCHER SENIOR Why truly sir, I have forgot it. I told you that I 110 had a very treacherous memory.

STANDARD I'll engage you shall remember me this month, rascal!
        Beats him off and exit [Standard]. Enter Lady Lurewell and Parly

LADY LUREWELL Fort bon,° fort bon, fort bon. This is better than I expected; but fortune still helps the industrious.
        Enter Clincher Senior

CLINCHER SENIOR Ah! The Devil take all intriguing, say I, and him 115 who first invented canes. That cursed colonel has got such a knack of beating his men, that he has left the mark of a collar of bandoleers° about my shoulders.

LADY LUREWELL O my poor gentleman! And was it beaten?

CLINCHER SENIOR Yes, I have been beaten. But where's my clothes, 120 my clothes?

LADY LUREWELL What, you won't leave me so soon, my dear, will ye?

CLINCHER SENIOR Will ye? If ever I peep into a colonel's tent again, may I be forced to run the gauntlet. But my clothes, madam.

LADY LUREWELL I sent the porter downstairs with them. Did not   125
you meet him?

CLINCHER SENIOR Meet him! No, not I.

PARLY No? He went out of the back door, and is run clear away I'm
afraid.

CLINCHER SENIOR Gone, say you? And with my clothes—my fine   130
Jubilee clothes? O the rogue, the thief! I'll have him hanged for
murder. But how shall I get home in this pickle?

PARLY I'm afraid, sir, the colonel will be back presently; for he dines
at home.

CLINCHER SENIOR O, then I must sneak off! Was ever man so   135
managed!°—to have his coat well thrashed, and lose his coat too?
          Exit [Clincher Senior]

LADY LUREWELL Thus the noble poet spoke truth.
Nothing suits worse with vice than want of sense:
Fools are still wicked at their own expense.°

PARLY Methinks madam, the injuries you have suffered by men   140
must be very great, to raise such heavy resentments against the
whole sex.

LADY LUREWELL The greatest injury that woman could sustain.
They robbed me of that jewel, which preserved, exalts our sex
almost to angels, but, destroyed, debases us below the worst of   145
brutes, mankind.°

PARLY But I think, madam, your anger should be only confined to
the author of your wrongs.

LADY LUREWELL The author! Alas, I know him not, which makes
my wrongs the greater.   150

PARLY Not know him! 'Tis odd madam, that a man should rob you
of that same jewel you mentioned, and you not know him.

LADY LUREWELL Leave trifling; 'tis a subject that always sours my
temper; but since by thy faithful service I have some reason to
confide in your secrecy, hear the strange relation. Some twelve,   155
twelve years ago I lived at my father's house in Oxfordshire, blest
with innocence, the ornamental, but weak guard of blooming
beauty. I was then just fifteen, an age oft fatal to the female sex;
our youth is tempting, our innocence credulous, romances moving,
love powerful, and men are—villains. Then it happened that three   160
young gentlemen from the university coming into the country, and
being benighted, and strangers, called at my father's. He was very
glad of their company, and offered them the entertainment of his
house.

PARLY Which they accepted, no doubt. O! these strolling collegians   165
    are never abroad, but upon some mischief.

LADY LUREWELL They had some private frolic or design in their
    heads, as appeared by their not naming one another, which my father
    perceiving, out of civility, made no inquiry into their affairs. Two of
    them had a heavy, pedantic, university air, a sort of disagreeable   170
    scholastic boorishness in their behaviour°—but the third!

PARLY Ay! the third, madam, the third of all things, they say, is very
    critical.

LADY LUREWELL He was—but in short, nature cut him out for my
    undoing; he seemed to be about eighteen.   175

PARLY A fit match for your fifteen as could be.

LADY LUREWELL He had a genteel sweetness in his face, a graceful
    comeliness in his person, and his tongue was fit to soothe soft
    innocence to ruin. His very looks were witty, and his expressive
    eyes spoke softer prettier things than words could frame.   180

PARLY There will be mischief by and by; I never heard a woman talk
    so much of eyes, but there were tears presently after.

LADY LUREWELL His discourse was directed to my father, but his
    looks to me. After supper I went to my chamber, and read
    Cassandra,° then went to bed, and dreamt of him all night, rose in   185
    the morning, and made verses; so fell desperately in love. My
    father was so pleased with his conversation, that he begged their
    company next day; they consented, and next night, Parly—

PARLY Ay, next night, madam—next night (I'm afraid) was a night
    indeed.   190

LADY LUREWELL He bribed my maid with his gold out of her
    honesty, and me with his rhetoric out of my honour: she admitted
    him to my chamber, and there he vowed, and swore, and wept,
    and sighed—and conquered.
    Weeps

PARLY Alack-a-day, poor fifteen!   195
    Weeps

LADY LUREWELL He swore that he would come down from Oxford
    in a fortnight, and marry me.

PARLY (*aside*) The old bait! the old bait; I was cheated just so
    myself.—But had not you the wit to know his name all this while?

LADY LUREWELL Alas! what wit had innocence like mine? He told   200
    me that he was under an obligation to his companions of conceal-
    ing himself then, but that he would write to me in two days, and
    let me know his name and quality. After all the binding oaths of

constancy, joining hands, exchanging hearts, I gave him a ring with
this motto, 'Love and Honour'—then we parted; but I never saw   205
the dear deceiver more.

PARLY No, nor never will, I warrant you.

LADY LUREWELL I need not tell my griefs, which my father's death
made a fair pretence for; he left me sole heiress and executrix to
three thousand pounds a year.° At last my love for this single   210
dissembler turned to a hatred of the whole sex, and resolving to
divert my melancholy, and make my large fortune subservient to
my pleasure and revenge, I went to travel, where in most Courts of
Europe I have done some execution.° Here I will play my last scene;
then retire to my country house, live solitary, and die a penitent. 215

PARLY But don't you still love this dear dissembler?

LADY LUREWELL Most certainly. 'Tis love of him that keeps my
anger warm, representing the baseness of mankind full in view; and
makes my resentments work. We shall have that old impotent
lecher Smuggler here tonight. I have a plot to swinge him and his   220
precise nephew Vizard.

PARLY I think, madam, you manage° everybody that comes in your way.

LADY LUREWELL No, Parly, those men, whose pretensions I found
just and honourable, I fairly dismissed by letting them know my
firm resolutions never to marry. But those villains that would   225
attempt my honour, I've seldom failed to manage.

PARLY What d'ye think of the colonel, madam? I suppose his designs
are honourable.

LADY LUREWELL That man's a riddle. There's something of honour
in his temper that pleases. I'm sure he loves me too, because he's   230
soon jealous, and soon satisfied. But he's a man still. When I once
tried his pulse about marriage, his blood ran as low as a coward's.
He swore indeed that he loved me, but could not marry me
forsooth, because he was engaged elsewhere. So poor a pretence
made me disdain his passion, which otherwise might have been un-   235
easy to me. But, hang him, I have teased him enough. Besides,
Parly, I begin to be tired of my revenge. But this 'Buss and Guinea'
I must maul once more. I'll hansel° his woman's clothes for him.
Go, get me pen and ink; I must write to Vizard too.

> [*Exit Parly*]
> Fortune this once assist me as before—   240
> Two such machines can never work in vain,
> As thy propitious wheel, and my projecting brain.°
> [*Exit*]

4.[1]

Scene, Covent Garden

Sir Harry and Standard meeting

STANDARD I thought, Sir Harry, to have met you ere this in a more convenient place; but since my wrongs were without ceremony, my revenge shall be so too. Draw, sir.

SIR HARRY Draw, sir! What shall I draw?

STANDARD Come, come, sir, I like your facetious humour well enough. It shows courage and unconcern. I know you brave; and therefore use you thus. Draw your sword.

SIR HARRY Nay, to oblige you, I will draw. But the Devil take me if I fight. Perhaps, Colonel, this is the prettiest blade you have seen.

STANDARD I doubt not but the arm is good; and therefore think both worth my resentment. Come, sir.

SIR HARRY But, prithee Colonel, dost think that I am such a madman as to send my soul to the Devil, and my body to the worms upon every fool's errand?

STANDARD I hope you're no coward, sir.

SIR HARRY Coward, sir! I have eight thousand pounds a year, sir.

STANDARD You fought in Flanders to my knowledge.

SIR HARRY Ay, for the same reason that I wore a red coat—because 'twas fashionable.

STANDARD Sir, you fought a French count in Paris.

SIR HARRY True, sir; he was a beau, like myself. Now you're a soldier, Colonel, and fighting's your trade; and I think it downright madness to contend with any man in his profession.

STANDARD Come, sir, no more dallying. I shall take very unseemly methods if you don't show yourself a gentleman.

SIR HARRY A gentleman! Why there again now. A gentleman! I tell you once more, Colonel, that I am a baronet, and have eight thousand pounds a year. I can dance, sing, ride, fence, understand the languages.° Now, I can't conceive how running you through the body should contribute one jot more to my gentility. But pray, Colonel, I had forgot to ask you. What's the quarrel?

STANDARD A woman, sir.

SIR HARRY Then I put up my sword. Take her.

STANDARD Sir, my honour's concerned.

47

SIR HARRY Nay, if your honour be concerned with a woman, get it
out of her hands as soon as you can. An honourable lover is the
greatest slave in nature; some will say, the greatest fool. Come,
come, Colonel, this is something about the Lady Lurewell, I
warrant; I can give you satisfaction in that affair.   40

STANDARD Do so then immediately.

SIR HARRY Put up your sword first. You know I dare fight. But I had
much rather make you a friend than an enemy. I can assure you this
lady will prove too hard for one of your temper. You have too much
honour, too much in conscience, to be a favourite with the ladies.   45

STANDARD I am assured, sir, she never gave you any encouragement.

SIR HARRY A man can never hear reason with a sword in his hand.
Sheathe your weapon; and then if I don't satisfy you, sheathe it in
my body.

STANDARD Give me but demonstration of her granting you any   50
favour, and 'tis enough.

SIR HARRY Will you take my word?

STANDARD Pardon me, sir, I cannot.

SIR HARRY Will you believe your own eyes?

STANDARD 'Tis ten to one whether I shall or no. They have deceived   55
me already.

SIR HARRY That's hard. But some means I shall devise for your
satisfaction.° [Noise of disturbance off] We must fly this place; else
that cluster of mob will overwhelm us.

> Exeunt [Sir Harry and Standard]. Enter mob, Tom Errand's
> wife hurrying in Clincher Senior in Errand's clothes

WIFE O, the villain, the rogue, he has murdered my husband. Ah,   60
my poor Timothy!° (Crying)

CLINCHER SENIOR Demn your Timothy. Your husband has murdered me, woman. For he has carried away my fine Jubilee clothes.

WIFE Ah, you cut-throat, have you not got his clothes upon your back
there? Neighbours, don't you know poor Timothy's coat and apron?   65

MOB Ay, ay, 'tis the same.

FIRST MOB What shall we do with him, neighbours?

SECOND MOB We'll pull him in pieces.

FIRST MOB No, no; then we may be hanged for murder; but we'll
drown him.   70

CLINCHER SENIOR Ah, good people, pray don't drown me; for I
never learned to swim in all my life. Ah, this plaguy intriguing!

MOB Away with him, away with him to the Thames.

CLINCHER SENIOR O, if I had but my swimming-girdle now.

Enter constable°

CONSTABLE Hold, neighbours, I command the peace.   75

WIFE O, Mr Constable, here's a rogue that has murdered my
husband, and robbed him of his clothes.

CONSTABLE Murder and robbery! then he must be a gentleman.
Hands off there—he must not be abused.° Give an account of
yourself. Are you a gentleman?   80

CLINCHER SENIOR No, sir, I am a beau.

CONSTABLE Then you have killed nobody, I'm persuaded. How
came you by these clothes, sir?

CLINCHER SENIOR You must know, sir, that walking along, sir, I
don't know how, sir; I can't tell where, sir; and—so the porter and   85
I changed clothes, sir.

CONSTABLE Very well, the man speaks reason, and like a gentleman.

WIFE But pray Mr Constable, ask him how he changed clothes with
him.

CONSTABLE Silence, woman, and don't disturb the court.—Well, sir,   90
how did you change clothes?

CLINCHER SENIOR Why, sir, he pulled off my coat, and I drew off
his; so I put on his coat, and he puts on mine.

CONSTABLE Why neighbours, I don't find that he's guilty. Search
him; and if he carries no arms about him, we'll let him go.   95

They search his pockets, and pull out his pistols

CLINCHER SENIOR O Gemini!° my Jubilee pistols.

CONSTABLE What, a case of pistols! Then the case is plain. Speak,
what are you, sir? whence come you, and whither go you?

CLINCHER SENIOR Sir, I came from Russell Street, and am going to
the Jubilee.   100

WIFE You shall go to the gallows, you rogue.

CONSTABLE Away with him, away with him to Newgate° straight.

CLINCHER SENIOR I shall go to the Jubilee now indeed.°

*Exeunt [Clincher Senior, wife, constable and mob]. Enter Sir
Harry and Standard*

SIR HARRY In short, Colonel, 'tis all nonsense. Fight for a woman!
Hard by is the lady's house; if you please, we'll wait on her   105
together. You shall draw your sword, I'll draw my snush-box. You
shall produce your wounds received in war; I'll relate mine by
Cupid's dart. You shall look big; I'll ogle. You shall swear; I'll sigh.
You shall *sa, sa*, and I'll *coupée*; and if she flies not to my arms,
like a hawk to its perch, my dancing-master deserves to be   110
damned!°

STANDARD With the generality of women, I grant you, these arts
may prevail.

SIR HARRY Generality of women! Why there again you're out.
They're all alike, sir. I never heard of any one that was particular,   115
but one.

STANDARD Who was she, pray?

SIR HARRY Penelope,° I think she's called; and that's a poetical story
too. When will you find a poet in our age make a woman so chaste?

STANDARD Well, Sir Harry, your facetious humour can disguise   120
falsehood, and make calumny pass for satire. But you have
promised me ocular demonstration that she favours you: make that
good, and I shall then maintain faith and female to be as
inconsistent as truth and falsehood.

SIR HARRY Nay, by what you have told me, I am satisfied that she   125
imposes on us all. And Vizard too seems what I still suspected him;
but his honesty once mistrusted spoils his knavery.° But will you
be convinced if our plot succeeds?

STANDARD I rely on your word and honour, Sir Harry; which, if I
doubted, my distrust would cancel the obligation of their security.°   130

SIR HARRY Then meet me half an hour hence at the Rummer. You
must oblige me by taking a hearty glass with me toward the fitting
me out for a certain project° which this night I undertake.

STANDARD I guess by the preparation, that woman's the design.

SIR HARRY Yes, faith. I am taken dangerously ill with two foolish   135
maladies, modesty and love; the first I'll cure with burgundy, and
my love by a night's lodging with the damsel. A sure remedy.
Probatum est.°

STANDARD I'll certainly meet you, sir.

> *Exeunt [Sir Harry and Standard] severally. Enter Clincher
> Junior and Dicky*

CLINCHER JUNIOR Ah! Dicky, this London is a sad place, a sad   140
vicious place. I wish that I were in the country again. And this
brother of mine! I'm sorry he's so great a rake. I had rather see
him dead than see him thus.

DICKY Ay, sir, he'll spend his whole estate at this same Jubilee. Who,
d'ye think lives at this same Jubilee?   145

CLINCHER JUNIOR Who pray?

DICKY The Pope.°

CLINCHER JUNIOR The Devil he does! My brother go to the place
where the Pope dwells—he's bewitched sure!

> *Enter Tom Errand in Clincher Senior's clothes*

DICKY Indeed I believe he is, for he's strangely altered.   150

CLINCHER JUNIOR Altered! why he looks like a Jesuit already.°

TOM ERRAND (*aside*) This lace will sell. What a blockhead was the fellow to trust me with his coat! If I can get cross the Garden,° down to the waterside, I'm pretty secure.°

CLINCHER JUNIOR Brother!—Alaw! O Gemini? are you my brother?   155

DICKY I seize you in the King's name, sir.

TOM ERRAND O Lord, should this prove some parliament man° now!

CLINCHER JUNIOR Speak you rogue, what are you?

TOM ERRAND A poor porter, sir, and going of an errand.   160

DICKY What errand? speak you rogue.

TOM ERRAND A fool's errand, I'm afraid.

CLINCHER JUNIOR Who sent you?

TOM ERRAND A beau, sir.

DICKY No, no, the rogue has murdered your brother, and stripped   165
him of his clothes.

CLINCHER JUNIOR Murdered my brother! O crimini!° O my poor Jubilee brother! Stay, by Jupiter Ammon, I'm heir though. Speak, sirrah,° have you killed him? Confess that you have killed him, and I'll give you half-a-crown.   170

TOM ERRAND Who I, sir? Alack-a-day, sir, I never killed any man, but a carrier's horse once.

CLINCHER JUNIOR Then you shall certainly be hanged, but confess that you killed him, and we'll let you go.

TOM ERRAND [*aside*] Telling the truth hangs a man, but confessing a   175
lie can do no harm—besides, if the worst comes to the worst, I can but deny it again.—Well, sir, since I must tell you, I did kill him.

CLINCHER JUNIOR Here's your money, sir; but are you sure you killed him dead?

TOM ERRAND Sir, I'll swear it before any judge in England.   180

DICKY But are you sure that he's dead in law?

TOM ERRAND Dead in law! I can't tell whether he be dead in law. But he's as dead as a door-nail; for I gave him seven knocks on the head with a hammer.

DICKY Then you have the estate by the statute. Any man that's   185
knocked o'th' head is dead in law.

CLINCHER JUNIOR But are you sure he was *compos mentis*° when he was killed?

TOM ERRAND I suppose he was, sir, for he told me nothing to the contrary afterwards.   190

CLINCHER JUNIOR Hey! Then I go to the Jubilee.—Strip, sir, strip!
   By Jupiter Ammon, strip!
DICKY Ah! don't swear, sir.
       [*Clincher Junior*] *puts on his brother's clothes*
CLINCHER JUNIOR Swear, sir! Zoons, han't I got the estate? sir?
   Come, sir, now I'm in mourning for my brother.   195
TOM ERRAND I hope you'll let me go now, sir.
CLINCHER JUNIOR Yes, yes, sir, but you must first do me the
   favour, to swear positively before a magistrate, that you killed him
   dead, that I may enter upon the estate without any trouble. By
   Jupiter Ammon all my religion's gone, since I put on these fine   200
   clothes. Hey, call me a coach somebody.
TOM ERRAND Ay, master, let me go, and I'll call one immediately.
CLINCHER JUNIOR No, no, Dicky, carry this spark before a justice,
   and when he has made oath, you may discharge him.
       Exeunt Dicky and Tom Errand
   And I'll go see Angelica. Now that I'm an elder brother, I'll court, 205
   and swear, and rant, and rake, and go to the Jubilee with the best of
   them.
       Exit

4.[2]

Scene, Lady Lurewell's house

Enter Lady Lurewell and Parly

LADY LUREWELL Are you sure that Vizard had my letter?
PARLY Yes, yes, madam, one of your ladyship's footmen gave it to
   him in the Park, and he told the bearer, with all transports of joy,
   that he would be punctual to a minute.
LADY LUREWELL Thus most villains, sometime or other, are punc-   5
   tual to their ruin; and hypocrisy, by imposing on the world, at last
   deceives itself. Are all things prepared for his reception?
PARLY Exactly to your ladyship's order—the alderman too, is just
   come, dressed and cooked up for iniquity.
LADY LUREWELL Then he has got woman's clothes on?   10
PARLY Yes, madam, and has passed upon the family° for your nurse.
LADY LUREWELL Convey him into that closet,° and put out the
   candles, and tell him, I'll wait on him presently.
       As Parly goes to put out the candle[s], somebody knocks

This must be some clown° without manners, or a gentleman above
ceremony. Who's there?   15
SIR HARRY (*sings*)° [*off-stage*]
>   *Thus Damon knock'd at Celia's door,*
>   *He sighed, and begged, and wept, and swore,*
>   *The sign was so—*
(*Knocks*)
>   *She answer'd, 'No,*
>   *No, no, no.'*   20
(*Knocks thrice*)
>   *Again he sighed, again he prayed,*
>   *'No, Damon, no, I am afraid;*
>   *Consider Damon. I'm a maid,*
>   *Consider.'*
>   *'No,'*°   25
>   *'I'm a maid.'*
>   *'No . . .' &c.*
>   *At last his sighs and tears made way,*
>   *She rose, and softly turned the key,*°
>   *'Come in,' said she, 'but do not stay.*   30
>   *I may conclude*
>   *You will be rude,*
>   *But, if you are, you may'*
>   *Exit Parly. Enter Sir Harry*

LADY LUREWELL 'Tis too early for serenading, Sir Harry.

SIR HARRY Wheresoever love is, there music is proper—there's an   35
harmonious consent in their natures, and when rightly joined, they
make up the chorus of earthly happiness.

LADY LUREWELL But, Sir Harry, what tempest drives you here at
this hour?

SIR HARRY No tempest, madam, but as fair weather as ever enticed   40
a citizen's wife to cuckold her husband in fresh air. Love, madam.
(*Taking her by the hand*)

LADY LUREWELL As pure and white as angel's soft desires . . .
>   —Is't not so?

SIR HARRY   Fierce as when ripe consenting beauty fires.°   45

LADY LUREWELL (*aside*) O villain! What privilege has man to our
destruction, that thus they hunt our ruin?
>   *Sir Harry drops a ring; she takes it up*
If this be a love-token, your mistresses'° favours hang very loose
about you sir.

SIR HARRY I can't justly, madam, pay your trouble of taking it up   50
by anything but desiring you to wear it.

LADY LUREWELL You gentlemen have the cunningest ways of
playing the fool, and are so industrious in your profuseness.°
Speak seriously, am I beholding to chance or design for this ring?

SIR HARRY To design upon my honour—(*aside*) and I hope my   55
design will succeed.°

LADY LUREWELL [*singing*]
  And what shall I give you for such a fine thing?

SIR HARRY [*singing*]
  You'll give me another, you'll give me another fine thing.   60

LADY LUREWELL Shall I be free° with you, Sir Harry?

SIR HARRY With all my heart, madam, so I may be free with you.

LADY LUREWELL Then plainly, sir, I shall beg the favour to see you
some other time, for at this very minute I have two lovers in the
house.   65

SIR HARRY Then to be as plain. I must be gone this minute, for I
must see another mistress within these two hours.

LADY LUREWELL Frank and free.

SIR HARRY As you with me. Madam, your most humble servant.
  Exit [*Sir Harry*]

LADY LUREWELL Nothing can disturb his humour. Now for my   70
merchant and Vizard.
  Exit [*Lady Lurewell*], *and takes the candles with her. Enter
  Parly, leading in Smuggler, dressed in woman's clothes.*

PARLY This way, Mr Alderman.

SMUGGLER Well, Mrs Parly, I'm obliged to you for this trouble, here
are a couple of shillings° for you. Times are hard, very hard
indeed, but next time I'll steal a pair of silk stockings from my   75
wife, and bring them to you. What are you fumbling about my
pockets for?°

PARLY Only settling the pleats of your gown, here, sir; get into this
closet, and my lady will wait on you presently.
  Puts him into the closet,° runs out, and returns with Vizard

VIZARD Where wouldst thou lead me, my dear auspicious little pilot?   80

PARLY You're almost in port, sir—my lady's in the closet, and will
come out to you immediately.

VIZARD Let me thank thee as I ought.
  Kisses her

PARLY [*aside*] Pshaw! who has hired me best?—a couple of shillings,
and a couple of kisses.   85

Exit [*Parly*]

VIZARD Propitious darkness guides the lover's steps, and night that shadows outward sense, lights up our inward joy. Night! the great awful ruler of mankind, which, like the Persian monarch, hides its royalty to raise the veneration of the world.° Under thy easy reign dissemblers may speak truth, all slavish forms and ceremonies laid aside, and generous villainy may act without constraint.   90

SMUGGLER (*peeping out of the closet*) Bless me! what voice is this?

VIZARD Our hungry appetites, like the wild beasts of prey, now scour abroad, to gorge their craving maws; the pleasure of hypocrisy, like a chained lion, once broke loose, wildly indulges its new freedom, ranging through all unbounded joys.   95

SMUGGLER My nephew's voice! and certainly possessed with an evil spirit, he talks as profanely, as an actor possessed with a poet.°

VIZARD Ha! I hear a voice.—Madam, my life, my happiness, where are you, madam?   100

SMUGGLER [*aside*] 'Madam!' He takes me for a woman too; I'll try him.—Where have you left your sanctity, Mr Vizard?

VIZARD Talk no more of that ungrateful subject; I left it where it has only business, with daylight—'tis needless to wear a mask in the dark.   105

SMUGGLER [*aside*] O the rogue, the rogue! [*Aloud*] The world takes you for a very sober virtuous gentleman.

VIZARD Ay, madam, that adds security to all my pleasures. With me a cully-squire may squander his estate, and ne'er be thought a spendthrift; with me a holy Elder may zealously be drunk, and toast his tuneful nose° in sack, to make it hold forth clearer. But what is most my praise, the formal rigid she that rails at vice and men, with me secures her loosest pleasures, and her strictest honour—she who with scornful mien, and virtuous pride, disdains the name of whore, with me can wanton, and laugh at the deluded world.   110   115

SMUGGLER [*aside*] How have I been deceived! [*Aloud*] Then you are very great among the ladies.

VIZARD Yes, madam, they know that like a mole in the earth, I dig deep but invisible, not like those fluttering noisy sinners, whose pleasure is the proclamation of their faults, those empty flashes who no sooner kindle, but they must blaze to alarm the world. But come, madam, you delay our pleasures.   120

SMUGGLER [*aside*] He surely takes me for the Lady Lurewell—she has made him an appointment too; but I'll be revenged of both.   125

Well, sir, what are these you are so intimate with?

VIZARD Come, come, madam, you know very well—those who stand
so high, that the vulgar envy even their crimes, whose figure adds
privilege to their sin, and makes it pass unquestioned; fair,
high, pampered females, whose speaking eyes, and piercing voice,   130
would warm the statue of a Stoic, and animate his cold marble
with the soul of an Epicure,° all ravishing, lovely, soft, and kind,
like you.

SMUGGLER [aside] I am very lovely and soft indeed. You shall find
me much harder than you imagine, friend. [Aloud] Well, sir, but   135
I suppose your dissimulation has some other motive besides
pleasure.

VIZARD Yes, madam, the honestest motive in the world—interest.°
You must know, madam, that I have an old uncle, Alderman
Smuggler—you have seen him, I suppose?   140

SMUGGLER Yes, yes, I have some small acquaintance with him.

VIZARD 'Tis the most knavish, precise, covetous old rogue, that ever
died of a gout.°

SMUGGLER [aside] Ah! the young son of a whore. [Aloud] Well, sir,
and what of him?   145

VIZARD Hell hungers not more for wretched souls, than he for ill-got
pelf—and yet (what's wonderful) he that would stick at no
profitable villainy himself, loves holiness in another—he prays all
Sunday for the sins of the week past, he spends all dinner-time in
too tedious graces, and what he designs a blessing to the meat,   150
proves a curse to his family; he's the most—

SMUGGLER Well, well, sir, I know him very well.

VIZARD Then, madam, he has a swingeing estate, which I design to
purchase° as a saint, and spend like a gentleman. He got it by
cheating, and should lose it by deceit. By the pretence of my zeal   155
and sobriety, I'll cozen the old miser one of these days out of a
settlement and deed of conveyance—°

SMUGGLER (aside) It shall be a deed to convey you to the gallows
then, you young dog.

VIZARD And no sooner he's dead, but I'll rattle over his grave with   160
a coach-and-six, to inform his covetous ghost how genteelly I
spend his money.

SMUGGLER (aside) I'll prevent you, boy, for I'll have my money
buried with me.

VIZARD Bless me, madam, here's a light coming this way—I must fly   165
immediately. When shall I see you, madam?

SMUGGLER Sooner than you expect, my dear.

VIZARD Pardon me, dear madam, I would not be seen for the world. I would sooner forfeit my life, nay, my pleasure, than my reputation.

Exit [Vizard]

SMUGGLER Reputation! Reputation! that poor word suffers a great 170
deal. Well! thou art the most accomplished hypocrite that ever made a grave plodding face over a dish of coffee and a pipe of tobacco; he owes me for seven years' maintenance, and shall pay me by seven years' imprisonment; and when I die, I'll leave him the fee-simple of a rope and a shilling. [*Noises off*] Who are these? 175
I begin to be afraid of some mischief. I wish that I were safe within the City Liberties.° I'll hide myself.

Stands close.° Enter butler, with other servants and lights

BUTLER I say there are two spoons wanting, and I'll search the whole house. Two spoons will be no small gap in my quarter's wages.

SERVANT When did you miss them, James? 180

BUTLER Miss them. Why, I miss them now; in short they must be among you, and if you don't return them, I'll go to the cunning-man° tomorrow morning; my spoons I want, and my spoons I will have.

SERVANT Come, come, search about. 185

[They] search and discover Smuggler

Ah! who's this?

BUTLER Hark'ee, good woman, what makes you hide yourself? What are you ashamed of?

SMUGGLER Ashamed of! O Lord, sir, I'm an honest old woman that never was ashamed of anything. 190

BUTLER What are you, a midwife° then? Speak, did not you see a couple of stray spoons in your travels?

SMUGGLER Stray spoons!

BUTLER Ay, ay, stray spoons; in short you stole them, and I'll shake your old limbs to pieces, if you don't deliver them presently. 195

SMUGGLER [*aside*] Bless me! a reverend Elder of seventy years old accused for petty larceny!—Why, search me, good people, search me, and if you find any spoons about me, you shall burn me for a witch.

BUTLER Ay, ay, we will search you mistress. 200

They search and pull the spoons out of his pockets

SMUGGLER O, the Devil, the Devil!

BUTLER Where, where is he? Lord bless us, she is a witch in good earnest, maybe.

SMUGGLER O, it was some devil, some Covent Garden, or St James's
devil° that put them in my pocket.   205

BUTLER Ay, ay, you shall be hanged for a thief, burned for a witch,
and then carted for a bawd. Speak, what are you?

Enter Lady Lurewell

SMUGGLER I'm the Lady Lurewell's nurse.

LADY LUREWELL What noise is this?

BUTLER Here is an old succubus, madam, that has stole two silver   210
spoons, and says, she's your nurse.

LADY LUREWELL My nurse! O the impudent old jade, I never saw
the withered creature before.

SMUGGLER [*aside*] Then I'm finely caught. [*To Lady Lurewell*] O
madam! Madam don't you know me? Don't you remember 'Buss   215
and guinea'?

LADY LUREWELL Was ever such impudence? I know thee! why
thou'rt as brazen as a bawd in the side-box. Take her before a
justice, and then to Newgate, away.

SMUGGLER [*aside to Lady Lurewell*] O! consider, madam, that I'm an   220
alderman.

LADY LUREWELL [*aside to Smuggler*] Consider, sir, that you're a
compound of covetousness, hypocrisy, and knavery, and must be
punished accordingly. You must be in petticoats, gouty monster,
must ye! You must 'Buss and guinea' too, you must tempt a lady's   225
honour, old satyr—away with him!°

[*Butler and servants*] *hurry him off*

Still may our sex thus frauds of men oppose,
Still may our arts delude these tempting foes.
May honour rule, and never fall betrayed,
But vice be caught in nets for virtue laid.   230

5.[1]

Scene, Lady Darling's house

Lady Darling and Angelica

LADY DARLING Daughter, since you have to deal with a man of so peculiar a temper, you must not think the general arts of love can secure him; you may therefore allow such a courtier some encouragement extraordinary, without reproach to your modesty.°

ANGELICA I am sensible, madam, that a formal nicety makes our   5
modesty sit awkward, and appears rather a chain to enslave than bracelet to adorn us; it should show, when unmolested, easy and innocent as a dove, but strong and vigorous as a falcon, when assaulted.

LADY DARLING I'm afraid, daughter, you mistake Sir Harry's gaiety   10
for dishonour.

ANGELICA Though modesty, madam, may wink, it must not sleep, when powerful enemies are abroad. I must confess, that of all men's, I would not see Sir Harry Wildair's faults; nay, I could wrest most suspicious words a thousand ways, to make them look   15
like honour—but, madam, in spite of love I must hate him, and curse those practices which taint our nobility, and rob all virtuous women of the bravest men.

LADY DARLING You must certainly be mistaken, Angelica, for I'm satisfied Sir Harry's designs are only to court, and marry you.   20

ANGELICA His pretence, perhaps, was such, but women now, like enemies, are attacked; whether by treachery, or fairly conquered, the glory of triumph is the same. Pray, madam, by what means were you made acquainted with his designs?

LADY DARLING Means, child! Why my cousin Vizard, who, I'm sure   25
is your sincere friend, sent him. He brought me this letter from my cousin.

Gives the letter which she opens

ANGELICA (*aside*) Ha! Vizard! then I'm abused in earnest. Would Sir Harry, by his instigation, fix a base affront upon me? No, I can't suspect him of so ungenteel a crime—this letter shall trace the   30
truth.—My suspicions, madam, are much cleared, and I hope to satisfy your ladyship in my management, when next I see Sir Harry.

Enter servant

SERVANT Madam, here's a gentleman below calls himself Wildair.

LADY DARLING Conduct him up.   35

     [Exit servant]

Daughter, I won't doubt your discretion.

     Exit Lady Darling. Enter Sir Harry

SIR HARRY O the delights of love and burgundy! Madam, I have
toasted your ladyship fifteen bumpers successively, and swallowed
cupids like loaches,° to every glass.

ANGELICA And what then, sir?   40

SIR HARRY Why then, madam, the wine has got into my head, and
the cupids into my heart; and unless by quenching quick my flame
you kindly ease the smart, I'm a lost man, madam.

ANGELICA Drunkenness, Sir Harry, is the worst pretence a gentleman can make for rudeness. For the excuse is as scandalous as the   45
fault. Therefore pray consider who you are so free with, sir; a
woman of condition, that can call half a dozen footmen upon
occasion.

SIR HARRY Nay, madam, if you have a mind to toss me in a blanket,
half a dozen chambermaids would do better service. Come, come,   50
madam, though the wine makes me lisp, yet has it taught me to
speak plainer. By all the dust of my ancient progenitors, I must
this night quarter my coat-of-arms with yours.°

ANGELICA *[calling to servants off]* Nay, then who waits there?

     Enter footmen

Take hold of that madman, and bind him.   55

SIR HARRY Nay, then 'Burgundy's' the word, and slaughter will
ensue.° Hold—do you know, scoundrels, that I have been drinking
victorious burgundy?

     Draws [his sword]

FOOTMEN We know you're drunk, sir.

SIR HARRY Then how have you the impudence, rascals, to assault a   60
gentleman with a couple of flasks of courage in his head?

FOOTMEN Sir, we must do as our young mistress commands us.

SIR HARRY Nay, then, have among ye, dogs.

     Throws money among them; they scramble and take it up. He
     pelting° them out, shuts the door, and returns

Rascals, poltroons—I have charmed the dragon,° and now the
fruit's my own.   65

ANGELICA O, the mercenary wretches! This was a plot to betray me.

SIR HARRY I have put the whole army to flight. And now take the
general prisoner. (*Laying hold on her*)

ANGELICA I conjure° you, sir, by the sacred name of honour, by your
    dead father's name, and the fair reputation of your mother's   70
    chastity, that you offer not the least offence. Already you have
    wronged me past redress.
SIR HARRY Thou art the most unaccountable creature.
ANGELICA What madness, Sir Harry, what wild dream of loose
    desire could prompt you to attempt this baseness? View me well.   75
    The brightness of my mind, methinks, should lighten outwards,
    and let you see your mistake in my behaviour. I think it shines
    with so much innocence in my face, that it should dazzle all your
    vicious thoughts. Think not I am defenceless 'cause alone. Your
    very self is guard against yourself. I'm sure, there's something   80
    generous° in your soul. My words shall search it out, and eyes shall
    fire it for my own defence.[1]
SIR HARRY [aside] Ha! Her voice bears a commanding accent! Every
    syllable is pointed. By Heavens I love her. I feel her piercing words
    turn the wild current of my blood, and thrill through all my veins.   85
ANGELICA View me well. Consider me with a sober thought, free from
    those fumes of wine that cast a mist before your sight; and you shall
    find that every glance from my reproaching eye is armed with sharp
    resentment, and with repelling rays that look dishonour dead.
SIR HARRY I cannot view you, madam. For when you speak, all the   90
    faculties of my charmed soul crowd to my attentive ears—desert
    my eyes, which gaze insensibly. Whatever charm inspires your
    looks, whether of innocence or vice, 'tis lovely, past expression.

---

[1] *From this point this scene was altered in all editions after the first as follows:*

SIR HARRY (*mimicking*) [*aside*] Tall ti dum, tall ti didi, didum.° A
    million to one now, but this girl is just come flush from reading
    The Rival Queens.° Egad I'll at her in her own cant. [*Quoting aloud*]   85
    'O my Statira! O my angry dear! Turn thy eyes on me'.° Behold
    thy beau in buskins.°
ANGELICA Behold me, sir, view me with a sober thought, free from
    those fumes of wine that throw a mist before your sight, and you
    shall find that every glance from my reproaching eyes is armed   90
    with sharp resentment, and with a virtuous pride that looks
    dishonour dead.
SIR HARRY [*aside*] This is the first whore in heroics that I have met
    with.—Look ye madam, as to that slender particular of your virtue,

ANGELICA If my beauty has power to raise a flame, be sure it is a
virtuous one; if otherwise, 'tis owing to the foulness of your own   95
thought, which throwing this mean affront upon my honour, has
alarmed° my soul, and fires it with a brave disdain.

SIR HARRY Where can the difference lie 'twixt such hypocrisy and
truth? Madam, whate'er my unruly passion did at first suggest, I
now must own you've turned my love to veneration, and my   100
unmannerly demands to a most humble prayer. Your surprising
conduct has quenched the gross material flame, but raised a subtle
piercing fire, which flies like lambent lightning through my blood,
disdaining common fuel, preys upon the nobler part, my soul.°

ANGELICA [aside] Grant, Heavens, his words be true!—Then, as you   105
hope that passion should be happy, tell me without reserve, what
motives have engaged you thus to affront my virtue?

SIR HARRY [aside] Affront her virtue! Ah, something I fear.—Your
question, madam, is a riddle, and cannot be resolved; but the most
proper answer the old gentlewoman can make, who passes for your   110
mother.

ANGELICA Passes for my mother! O indignation! Were I a man, you
durst not use me thus. But the mean poor abuse you cast on me,

we shan't quarrel about it—you may be as virtuous as any woman   95
in England if you please; you may say your prayers all the
time—but pray, madam, be pleased to consider what is this same
virtue that you make such a mighty noise about. Can your virtue
bespeak you a front row in the boxes? No, for the players can't live
upon virtue. Can your virtue keep you a coach-and-six? No,   100
no—your virtuous women walk a-foot. Can your virtue hire you a
pew in a church?° Why the very sexton will tell you, no. Can your
virtue stake for you at piquet? No. Then what business has a
woman with virtue?° Come, come, madam, I offered you fifty
guineas—there's a hundred. [Offering them] The Devil! Virtuous   105
still! Why 'tis a hundred, five score, a hundred guineas.

ANGELICA O indignation! Were I a man, you durst not use me thus;
but the mean, poor abuse you throw on me, reflects upon
yourself—our sex still strikes an awe upon the brave, and only
cowards dare affront a woman.   110

SIR HARRY Affront! 'Sdeath, madam, a hundred guineas will set you
up at basset; a hundred guineas will furnish out your lodgings with
china; a hundred guineas will give you an air of quality; a hundred

reflects upon yourself. Our sex still strikes an awe upon the brave, and only cowards dare affront a woman.   115

SIR HARRY Then, madam, I have a fair claim to courage; for, by all hopes of happiness. I ne'er was awed so much, nor ever felt the power of fear before. But since I can't dissolve this knot, I'll cut it at a stroke.° Vizard, who, I fear, is a villain, told me you were a prostitute; that he had known you, and sent a letter, intimating my   120 designs to the old gentlewoman, who, I supposed, had licensed my proceedings by leaving us so oft in private.

ANGELICA That Vizard is a villain, damned beyond the curses of an injured woman, is most true. But that his letter signified any dishonourable proceedings, is as false.   125

SIR HARRY I appeal to that for pardon or condemnation. He read it to me; and the contents were as I have declared, only with this addition; that I would scruple no price° for the enjoyment of my pleasure.

ANGELICA No price! What have I suffered? To be made a prostitute for sale! 'Tis an unequalled curse upon our sex, that woman's   130

guineas will buy you a rich escritoir for your billets-doux, or a fine Common Prayer Book° for your virtue. A hundred guineas will   115 buy a hundred fine things, and fine things are for fine ladies; and fine ladies are for fine gentlemen; and fine gentlemen are—egad, this burgundy makes a man speak like an angel. Come, come, madam, take it, and put it to what use you please.

ANGELICA I'll use it, as I would the base unworthy giver, thus.   120
            Throws down the purse and stamps upon it

SIR HARRY I have no mind to meddle in state affairs; but these women will make me a parliament man, 'spite of my teeth, on purpose to bring in a bill against their extortion.° She tramples underfoot that deity which all the world adores. O the blooming pride of beautiful eighteen! Pshaw, I'll talk to her no longer—I'll   125 make my markets° with the old gentlewoman, she knows business better.
            Goes to the door [and speaks to servant off-stage]
Here you friend, pray desire the old lady to walk in. [*To Angelica*] Hark'ee, by Gad, madam, I'll tell your 'mother'.
            Enter Lady Darling

LADY DARLING Well, Sir Harry, and d'ye like my daughter, pray?   130

SIR HARRY Like her, madam! Hark'ee, will you take it?° Why faith madam!—take the money, I say, or egad, all's out.

virtue should so much depend on lying fame and scandalous
tongues of men. Read that: then judge how far I'm injured, and
you deceived.

    Hands him a letter

SIR HARRY (*reads*) 'Out of my earnest inclination to serve your
ladyship, and my cousin Angelica, I have sent Sir Harry Wildair   135
to court my cousin.'—The villain read to me a clear different
thing.—'He's a gentleman of great parts and fortune,'—damn his
compliment—'and would make your daughter very happy in a
husband.'—O Lord, O Lord, what have I been doing!—'I hope
your ladyship will entertain him as becomes his birth and fortune,   140
and the friend of, madam, Your ladyship's most devoted and
humble servant, Vizard.'

ANGELICA Now, sir, I hope you need no instigation to redress my
wrongs, since honour points the way.

SIR HARRY Redress your wrongs! Instruct me, madam; for all your   145
injuries tenfold recoiled on me. I have abused innocence, murdered
honour, stabbed it in the nicest part—a fair lady's fame. Instruct

---

ANGELICA All shall out; sir, you're a scandal to the name of gentleman.

SIR HARRY With all my heart, madam.—In short, madam, your
'daughter' has used me somewhat too familiarly, though I have   135
treated her like a woman of quality.

LADY DARLING How sir?

SIR HARRY Why, madam, I have offered her a hundred guineas.

LADY DARLING A hundred guineas! upon what score?

SIR HARRY Upon what score! Lord, Lord, how these old women love   140
to hear bawdy! Why faith madam, I have ne'er *double entendie*°
ready at present, but I'll sing you a song. [*Singing*]

    Behold the goldfinches, tall al de rall,
    And a man of my inches, tall al de rall;
    You shall take 'em, believe me, tall al de rall,   145
    If you will give me your—tall al de rall.

A modish minuet° madam, that's all.

LADY DARLING Sir, I don't understand you.

SIR HARRY Ay, she will have it in plain terms. Then, madam, in
downright English, I offered your daughter a hundred guineas,   150
to—

ANGELICA Hold sir, stop your abusive tongue, too loose for modest
ears to bear. Madam, I did before suspect that his designs were

me, madam. For my reason's fled, and hides its guilty face, as
conscious of its master's shame.

ANGELICA Think, sir, that my blood, for many generations, has run   150
in the purest channel of unsullied honour. Consider what a tender
flower is woman's reputation, which the least air of foul detraction
blasts. Call then to mind your rude and scandalous behaviour.
Remember the base price you offered: then think that Vizard, villain
Vizard, caused all this, yet lives. That's all. Farewell! (*Going*)   155

SIR HARRY Stay, madam; he's too base an offering for such purity.
But justice has inspired me with a nobler thought.

[*Kneels*]

I throw a purer victim at your feet, my honourable love and
fortune. If chastest, purest passion, with a large and fair estate, can
make amends, they're yours this moment. The matrimonial tie   160
shall bind us friends this hour. Nay, madam, no reply, unless you
smile. Let but a pleasing look forerun my sentence—then raise me
up to joy.

ANGELICA Rise, sir, (*smiling*) I'm pleased to find my sentiments of
you, which were always generous, so generously answered. And   165
since I have met a man above the common level of your sex, I think

---

base, now they're too plain; this knight, this mighty man of wit
and humours, is made a tool to a knave: Vizard has sent him on°   155
a bully's errand, to affront a woman; but I scorn the abuse, and
him that offered it.

LADY DARLING How, sir, come to affront us! D'ye know who we
are, sir?

SIR HARRY Know who ye are? Why, your 'daughter' there is Mr   160
Vizard's 'cousin', I suppose; and for you, madam—(*aside*) now to
call her procuress *à la mode France*—[*aloud*] *j'estime votre occupation*° . . .

LADY DARLING Pray sir, speak English.

SIR HARRY [*aside*] Then to define her office, *à la mode Londres!*°—I   165
suppose your ladyship to be one of those civil, obliging, discreet,
old 'gentlewomen', who keep their visiting days for the entertainment of their presenting friends° whom they treat with imperial
tea,° a private room, and a pack of cards. Now I suppose you do
understand me.   170

LADY DARLING This is beyond sufferance. But say, thou abusive
man, what injury have you e'er received from me or mine, thus to

myself disengaged from the formality of mine, and shall therefore venture to inform you, that with joy I receive your honourable love.

SIR HARRY Beauty without art! Virtue without pride! And love without ceremony! The day breaks glorious to my o'erclouded   170 thought, and darts its smiling beams into my soul. My love is heightened by a glad devotion; and virtue rarefies the bliss to feast the purer mind.°

---

engage you in this scandalous aspersion?

ANGELICA Yes, sir, what cause, what motives could induce you thus to debase yourself below your rank?   175

SIR HARRY Hey-day! Now dear Roxana, and you my fair Statira, be not so very heroic in your styles; Vizard's letter may resolve you, and answer all the impertinent questions you have made me.

BOTH WOMEN We appeal to that.

SIR HARRY And I'll stand to't—he read it to me, and the contents   180 were pretty plain, I thought.

ANGELICA Here sir, peruse it, and see how much we are injured, and you deceived.

SIR HARRY (opening the letter) But hold, madam, (to Lady Darling) before I read, I'll make some condition. Mr Vizard says here, that   185 I won't scruple 30 or 40 pieces. Now, madam, if you have clapped in another cipher to the account, and made it three or four hundred, by Gad, I will not stand to't.°

ANGELICA Now can't I tell whether disdain or anger be the most just resentment for this injury.   190

LADY DARLING The letter, sir, shall answer you.

SIR HARRY Well then! (Reads) 'Out of my earnest inclination to serve your ladyship, and my cousin Angelica,'—ay, ay, the very words, I can say it by heart—'I have sent Sir Harry Wildair to court my cousin.' What the Devil's this? '. . . sent Sir Harry Wildair to court   195 my cousin.' He read to me a quite different thing. 'He's a gentleman of great parts and fortune,'—he's a son of a whore and a rascal—'and would make your daughter very happy (whistles) in a husband.'
    Looks foolish and hums a song
O poor Sir Harry, What have thy angry stars designed?

ANGELICA Now sir, I hope you need no instigation to redress our   200 wrongs, since even the injury points the way.

LADY DARLING Think sir, that our blood for many generations, has run in the purest channel of unsullied honour.

ANGELICA You must promise me, Sir Harry, to have a care of
burgundy henceforth.   175

SIR HARRY Fear not sweet innocence: your presence, like a guardian
angel, shall fright away all vice.

> In your sweet eyes and words there is a charm
> To settle madness, or a fiend disarm
> Of all his spite, his torments and his cares,   180
> And make him change his curses into prayers.
>
> *Exeunt*

SIR HARRY Ay, madam.

> *Bows to her*

ANGELICA Consider, what a tender blossom is female reputation,   205
which the least air of foul detraction blasts.

SIR HARRY Yes, madam.

> *Bows to t'other*

LADY DARLING Call then to mind your rude and scandalous behaviour.

SIR HARRY Right, madam.

> *Bows again*

ANGELICA Remember the base price you offered me.   210

> *Exit [Angelica]*

SIR HARRY Very true, madam. [*Aside*] Was ever man so catechized!

LADY DARLING Then think that Vizard, villain Vizard, caused all
this, yet lives; that's all, farewell! (*Going*)

SIR HARRY Stay, madam—one word.

> *He goes to Lady Darling*

Is there no other way to redress your wrongs, but by fighting?   215

LADY DARLING Only one, sir; which, if you can think of, you do.
You know the business I entertained you for.

SIR HARRY I understand you, madam.

> *Exit Lady Darling*

Here am I brought to a very pretty dilemma; I must commit
murder, or commit matrimony—which is best, now? A licence from   220
Doctor's Commons, or a sentence from the Old Bailey?° If I kill
my man, the law hangs me; if I marry my woman, I shall hang
myself. But damn it, cowards dare fight—I'll marry, that's the most
daring action of the two; so my dear cousin Angelica, have at you.

> *Exit*

5.[2]

Scene, Newgate

Clincher Senior alone

CLINCHER SENIOR How severe and melancholy are Newgate reflections! Last week my father died. Yesterday I turned beau. Today I am laid by the heels, and tomorrow shall be hung by the neck. I was agreeing with a bookseller about printing an account of my journey through France to Italy; but now the history of my travels through Holborn to Tyburn,—[*mimicking a ballad-seller*] ' "The Last and Dying Speech of Beau Clincher, That Was Going to the Jubilee." Come, a halfpenny apiece.'° A sad sound, a sad sound, faith. 'Tis one way to have a man's death make a great noise in the world.

Enter Smuggler and gaoler

SMUGGLER [*to gaoler*] Well, friend, I have told you who I am. So send these letters into Thames Street, as directed—they are to gentlemen that will bail me.

Exit gaoler

Eh! this Newgate is a very populous place. Here's robbery and repentance in every corner. Well, friend, what are you, a cut-throat or a bum-bailiff?

CLINCHER SENIOR What are you, mistress, a bawd or a witch? Hark'ee, if you are a witch, d'ye see, I'll give you a hundred pounds to mount me on a broom-staff, and whip me away to the Jubilee.

SMUGGLER [*recognising him*] The Jubilee! O, you young rakehell, what brought you here?

CLINCHER SENIOR Ah, you old rogue, what brought you here, if you go to that?

SMUGGLER I knew, sir, what your powdering, your prinking, your dancing, and your frisking would come to.

CLINCHER SENIOR And I knew what your cozening, your extortion, and your smuggling would come to.

SMUGGLER Ay, sir, you must break your indentures, and run to the Devil in a full-bottom wig,° must you?

CLINCHER SENIOR Ay sir, and you must put off your gravity, and run to the Devil in petticoats. You design to swing in masquerade,° master, d'ye?

SMUGGLER Ay, you must go to plays too, sirrah. Lord, Lord. What business has a 'prentice at a playhouse, unless it be to hear his

master made a cuckold, and his mistress a whore? 'Tis ten to one 35
now, but some malicious poet has my character upon the stage
within this month. 'Tis a hard matter now, that an honest sober
man can't sin in private for this plaguy stage. I gave an honest
gentleman five guineas myself towards writing a book against it.
And it has done no good, we see. 40

CLINCHER SENIOR Well, well, master, take courage; our comfort is,
we have lived together, and shall die together, only with this
difference, that I have lived like a fool, and shall die like a knave,
and you have lived like a knave, and shall die like a fool.

SMUGGLER No, sirrah! I have sent a messenger for my clothes, and 45
shall get out immediately, and shall be upon your jury by and by.
Go to prayers, you rogue, go to prayers.
Exit Smuggler

CLINCHER SENIOR Prayers! 'Tis a hard taking,° when a man must
say grace to the gallows.° Ah, this cursed intriguing! Had I swung
handsomely in a silken garter now, I had died in my duty; but to 50
hang in hemp, like the vulgar, 'tis very ungenteel.°
Enter Tom Errand
A reprieve, a reprieve, thou dear, dear—damned rogue, where have
you been? Thou art the most welcome—son of a whore, where's
my clothes?

TOM ERRAND Sir, I see where mine are. Come, sir, strip, sir, strip. 55

CLINCHER SENIOR What sir, will you abuse a gentleman?

TOM ERRAND A gentleman! ha, ha, ha, d'ye know where you are, sir?
We're all gentlemen here. I stand up for liberty and property.
Newgate's a commonwealth.° No courtier has business among us.
Come, sir. 60

CLINCHER SENIOR Well, but stay, stay till I send for my own
clothes. I shall get out presently.

TOM ERRAND No, no, sir, I'll ha' you into the dungeon, and uncase
you.

CLINCHER SENIOR Sir, you can't master me; for I'm twenty thou- 65
sand strong.°
Exeunt struggling

5.[3]

The scene changes to Lady Darling's house
Enter Sir Harry with letters, servants following

SIR HARRY Here, fly all round and bear these as directed—you to
Westminster—you to St James's—and you into the City. Tell all
my friends a bridegroom's joy invites their presence. Look all of
ye like bridegrooms also. All appear with hospitable looks, and bear
a welcome in your faces. Tell 'em I'm married. If any ask to whom,   5
make no reply; but tell 'em that I'm married, that joy shall crown
the day, and love the night. Begone, fly.
    [*Exeunt servants.*] *Enter Standard*
A thousand welcomes, friend. My pleasure's now complete, since I
can share it with my friend. Brisk joy shall bound from me to you,
then back again—and, like the sun, grow warmer by reflection.°   10
STANDARD You're always pleasant, Sir Harry; but this transcends
yourself. Whence proceeds it?
SIR HARRY Canst thou not guess? My friend, whence flows all
earthly joy? What is the life of man, and soul of pleasure? Woman.
What fires the heart with transport, and the soul with raptures?   15
Lovely woman. What is the master stroke and smile of the
creation, but charming, virtuous woman? When nature, in the
general composition,° first brought woman forth, like a flushed
poet, ravished with his fancy, with ecstasy she° blessed the fair
production. Methinks, my friend, you relish not my joy. What is   20
the cause?
STANDARD Canst thou not guess? What is the bane of man, and
scourge of life, but woman? What is the heathenish idol man sets
up, and is damned for worshipping? Treacherous woman. What
are those whose eyes, like basilisks, shine beautiful for sure   25
destruction, whose smiles are dangerous as the grin of fiends but
false, deluding woman? Woman, whose composition inverts
humanity; their body's heavenly, but their souls are clay.
SIR HARRY Come, come, Colonel, this is too much. I know your
wrongs received from Lurewell may excuse your resentments   30
against her. But 'tis unpardonable to charge the failings of a single
woman upon the whole sex. I have found one, whose virtues—
STANDARD So have I, Sir Harry; I have found one whose pride's above
yielding to a prince. And if lying, dissembling, perjury and falsehood
be no breaches in woman's honour, she's as innocent as infancy.   35

SIR HARRY Well, Colonel, I find your opinion grows stronger by opposition—I shall now therefore waive the argument, and only beg you for this day to make a show of complaisance at least. Here comes my charming bride.

Enter Lady Darling and Angelica

STANDARD (*saluting Angelica*) I wish you, madam, all the joys of love and fortune.   40

Enter Clincher Junior

CLINCHER JUNIOR Gentlemen and ladies, I'm just upon the spur, and have only a minute to take my leave.

SIR HARRY Whither are you bound, sir?

CLINCHER JUNIOR Bound, sir! I'm going to the Jubilee, sir.   45

LADY DARLING Bless me, cousin! how came you by these clothes?

CLINCHER JUNIOR Clothes! ha, ha, ha, the rarest jest! ha, ha, ha, I shall burst, by Jupiter Ammon, I shall burst.

LADY DARLING What's the matter, cousin?

CLINCHER JUNIOR The matter! Ha, ha, ha. Why an honest porter,   50
ha, ha, ha, has knocked out my brother's brains, ha, ha, ha.

SIR HARRY A very good jest, i'faith, ha, ha, ha.

CLINCHER JUNIOR Ay sir, but the best jest of all is, he knocked out his brains with a hammer, and so he is as dead as a door-nail, ha, ha, ha.   55

LADY DARLING And do you laugh, wretch?

CLINCHER JUNIOR Laugh! ha, ha, ha—let me see e'er a younger brother in England that won't laugh at such a jest.

ANGELICA You appeared a very sober pious gentleman some hours ago.   60

CLINCHER JUNIOR Pshaw, I was a fool then. But now, madam, I'm a wit. I can rake now. As for your part, madam, you might have had me once. But now, madam, if you should chance fall to eating chalk, or gnawing the sheets,° 'tis none of my fault. Now, madam, I have got an estate, and I must go to the Jubilee.   65

Enter Clincher Senior in a blanket

CLINCHER SENIOR Must you so, rogue, must ye? You will go to the Jubilee, will you?

CLINCHER JUNIOR A ghost, a ghost! Send for the dean and chapter° presently.

CLINCHER SENIOR A ghost! no, no, sirrah, I'm an elder brother—   70
rogue.

CLINCHER JUNIOR I don't care a farthing for that; I'm sure you're dead in law.

CLINCHER SENIOR Why so, sirrah, why so?

CLINCHER JUNIOR Because, sir, I can get a fellow to swear he   75
knocked out your brains.

SIR HARRY An odd way of swearing a man out of his life.

CLINCHER JUNIOR Smell him, gentlemen, he has a deadly scent
about him.

CLINCHER SENIOR Truly the apprehensions of death may have made   80
me savour a little. O Lord—the colonel! The apprehension of him
may make me savour worse, I'm afraid.

CLINCHER JUNIOR In short, sir, were you ghost, or brother, or devil,
I will go to the Jubilee, by Jupiter Ammon.

STANDARD Go to the Jubilee! go to the bear-garden.° The travel of   85
such fools as you doubly injure our country—you expose our
native follies, which ridicules us among strangers, and return
fraught only with their vices which you vend here for fashionable
gallantry. A travelling fool is as dangerous as a home-bred villain.
Get ye to your native plough and cart, converse with animals like   90
yourselves, sheep and oxen—men are creatures you don't understand.

SIR HARRY Let 'em alone, Colonel, their folly will be now diverting.
Come Gentlemen, we'll dispute this point some other time; I hear
some fiddles tuning; let's hear how they can entertain us. Be   95
pleased to sit.

> [*Enter Musicians.*] *Here singing and dancing, after which a*
> *servant [enters and] whispers [to] Sir Harry*

SIR HARRY (*to Lady Darling*) Madam, shall I beg you to entertain
the company in the next room for a moment?

LADY DARLING With all my heart. Come, gentlemen.

> *Exeunt all but Sir Harry*

SIR HARRY A lady to enquire for me! Who can this be?   100

> *Enter Lady Lurewell*

O, madam, this favour is beyond my expectation, to come unin-
vited to dance at my wedding. What d'ye gaze at, madam?

LADY LUREWELL A monster—if thou art married, thou'rt the most
perjured wretch that e'er avouched deceit.

SIR HARRY Hey-day! Why, madam, I'm sure I never swore to marry   105
you—I made indeed a slight promise, upon condition of your
granting me a small favour, but you would not consent, you know.

LADY LUREWELL [*aside*] How he upbraids me with my shame—can
you deny your binding vows when this appears a witness 'gainst
your falsehood.   110

Shows a ring

Methinks the motto of this sacred pledge should flash confusion in your guilty face. Read, read here the binding words of 'Love and Honour', words not unknown to your perfidious eyes—though utter strangers to your treacherous heart.

SIR HARRY The woman's stark staring mad—that's certain.   115

LADY LUREWELL Was it maliciously designed to let me find my misery when past redress, to let me know you, only to know you false? Had not cursed chance showed me the surprising motto, I had been happy. The first knowledge I had of you was fatal to me, and this second worse.   120

SIR HARRY What the Devil's all this! Madam, I'm not at leisure for raillery at present—I have weighty affairs upon my hands; the business of pleasure, madam, any other time—(*Going*)

LADY LUREWELL Stay, I conjure you stay.

SIR HARRY Faith, I can't—my bride expects me; but hark'ee, when   125
the honeymoon is over, about a month or two hence, I may do you a small favour.

Exit [Sir Harry]

LADY LUREWELL Grant me some wild expressions, Heavens, or I shall burst. Woman's weakness, man's falsehood, my own shame, and love's disdain, at once swell up my breast—words, words, or   130
I shall burst! (*Going*)

Enter Standard

STANDARD Stay, madam, you need not shun my sight; for if you are perfect woman, you have confidence to outface a crime, and bear the charge of guilt without a blush.

LADY LUREWELL The charge of guilt! What—making a fool of you?   135
I've done't, and glory in the act: the height of female justice were to make you all hang or drown—dissembling to the prejudice of men is virtue; and every look, or sigh, or smile, or tear that can deceive is meritorious.

STANDARD Very pretty principles truly—if there be truth in woman,   140
'tis now in thee. Come, madam, you know that you're discovered, and being sensible you can't escape, you would now turn to bay. That ring, madam, proclaims you guilty.

LADY LUREWELL O monster, villain, perfidious villain! Has he told you?   145

STANDARD I'll tell it you, and loudly too.

LADY LUREWELL O name it not—yes, speak it out—'tis so just punishment for putting faith in man, that I will bear it all; and let credulous maids that trust their honour to the tongues of men, thus hear their shame proclaimed. Speak now, what his busy scandal, and your improving malice both dare utter. 150

STANDARD Your falsehood can't be reached by malice, nor by satire; your actions are the justest libel on your fame. Your words, your looks, your tears, I did believe in spite of common fame. Nay, 'gainst my own eyes, I still maintained your truth. I imagined 155 Wildair's boasting of your favours to be the pure result of his own vanity; at last he urged your taking presents of him, as a convincing proof of which you yesterday from him received that ring—which ring, that I might be sure he gave it, I lent him for that purpose.

LADY LUREWELL Ha! you lent him for that purpose! 160

STANDARD Yes, yes, madam, I lent him for that purpose—no denying it. I know it well, for I have worn it long, and desire you now, madam, to restore it to the just owner.

LADY LUREWELL The just owner—think, sir, think but of what importance 'tis to own it, if you have love and honour in your soul. 165 'Tis then most justly yours—if not, you are a robber, and have stolen it basely.

STANDARD Ha—your words, like meeting flints, have struck a light to show me something strange—but tell me instantly, is not your real name Manly?° 170

LADY LUREWELL Answer me first—did not you receive this ring about twelve years ago?

STANDARD I did.

LADY LUREWELL And were not you about that time entertained two nights at the house of Sir Oliver Manly in Oxfordshire? 175

STANDARD I was, I was.

Runs to her, and embraces her

The blest remembrance fires my soul with transport: I know the rest—you are the charming she, and I the happy man.

LADY LUREWELL How has blind Fortune stumbled on the right! But where have you wandered since?—'twas cruel to forsake me. 180

STANDARD The particulars of my fortune were too tedious now; but to discharge myself from the stain of dishonour, I must tell you, that immediately upon my return to the university, my elder brother and I quarrelled; my father, to prevent further mischief, posts me away to travel. I writ to you from London, but fear the 185 letter came not to your hands.

LADY LUREWELL I never had the least account of you, by letter or otherwise.

STANDARD Three years I lived abroad, and at my return, found you
were gone out of the kingdom, though none could tell me whither;   190
missing you thus, I went to Flanders, served my King till the peace
commenced, then fortunately going on board at Amsterdam, one
ship transported us both to England. At the first sight I loved,
though ignorant of the hidden cause. You may remember, madam,
that talking once of marriage, I told you I was engaged; to your   195
dear self I meant.

LADY LUREWELL Then men are still most generous and brave—and
to reward your truth, an estate of three-thousand pounds a year
waits your acceptance; and if I can satisfy you in my past conduct,
and the reasons that engaged me to deceive all men, I shall expect   200
the honourable performance of your promise, and that you would
stay with me in England.

STANDARD Stay—not fame nor glory e'er shall part us more. My
honour can be nowhere more concerned than here.

  Enter Sir Harry, Angelica, [and] both Clinchers

O, Sir Harry, Fortune has acted miracles—the story's strange and   205
tedious, but all amounts to this: that woman's mind is charming as
her person, and I am made a convert too to beauty.

SIR HARRY I wanted only this to make my pleasure perfect.

  Enter Smuggler

SMUGGLER So, gentlemen and ladies, is my gracious nephew Vizard
among ye?   210

SIR HARRY Sir, he dares not show his face among such honourable
company, for your gracious nephew is a—

SMUGGLER What, sir? Have a care what you say—

SIR HARRY A villain, sir.

SMUGGLER With all my heart—I'll pardon you the beating me for   215
that very word. And pray, Sir Harry, when you see him next, tell
him this news from me, that I have disinherited him, that I will
leave him as poor as a disbanded quartermaster. And this is the
positive and stiff resolution of three score and ten; an age that
sticks as obstinately to its purpose, as to the old fashion of its cloak.   220

SIR HARRY (*to Angelica*) You see, madam, how industriously Fortune
has punished his offence to you.

ANGELICA I can scarcely, sir, reckon it an offence, considering the
happy consequences of it.

SMUGGLER O, Sir Harry, he's as hypocritical—   225

LADY LUREWELL As yourself, Mr Alderman—how fares my good
old nurse, pray, sir?

SMUGGLER O, madam, I shall be even with you before I part with your writings and money that I have in my hands.

STANDARD A word with you, Mr Alderman—do you know this pocket-book? 230

SMUGGLER (*aside*) O Lord, it contains an account of all my secret practices in trading.—How came you by it, sir?

STANDARD Sir Harry here dusted it out of your pocket, at this lady's house, yesterday. It contains an account of some secret practices in 235 your merchandizing; among the rest, the counterpart of an agreement with a correspondent at Bordeaux, about transporting French wine in Spanish casks. First return this lady all her writings, then I shall consider whether I shall lay your proceedings before the parliament or not, whose justice will never suffer your smuggling 240 to go unpunished.

SMUGGLER O my poor ship and cargo.

CLINCHER SENIOR Hark'ee, master, you had as good come along with me to the Jubilee, now.

ANGELICA Come, Mr Alderman, for once let a woman advise. Would 245 you be thought° an honest man, banish covetousness, that worst gout of age; avarice is a poor pilfering quality of the soul, and will as certainly cheat, as a thief would steal. Would you be thought a reformer of the times, be less severe in your censures, less rigid in your precepts, and more strict in your example. 250

SIR HARRY Right, madam, virtue flows freer from imitation, than compulsion, of which, Colonel, your conversion and mine are just examples.

> In vain are musty morals taught in schools,
> By rigid teachers, and as rigid rules; 255
> Where virtue with a frowning aspect stands,
> And frights the pupil from its rough commands.
> But woman—
> Charming woman can true converts make;
> We love the precepts for the teacher's sake. 260
> Virtue in them appears so bright, so gay,
> We hear with transport, and with pride obey.

Epilogue

spoken by Mr Wilks

Now all depart, each his respective way,
To spend an evening's chat upon the play;
Some to Hippolito's, one homeward goes,°
And one with loving she retires to th' Rose.°
The amorous pair in all things frank and free,   5
Perhaps may save the play, in number three.°
The tearing spark, if Phillis aught gainsays,°
Breaks th'drawer's head, kicks her, and murders Bays.°
To coffee some retreat to save their pockets,
Others more generous damn the play at Locket's;°   10
But there, I hope, the author's fears are vain—
Malice ne'er spoke in generous champagne.
That poet merits an ignoble death,
Who fears to fall over a brave Monteith.°
The privilege of wine we only ask: 15
You'll taste again, before you damn the flask.
Our author fears not you; but those he may
Who, in cold blood, murder a man in tea:°
Those men of spleen, who fond the world should know it,
Sit down, and for their two-pence damn a poet.   20
Their criticism's good, that we can say for't;
They understand a play—too well to pay for't.
From box to stage, from stage to box they run—
First steal the play, then damn it when they've done.°
But now to know what fate may us betide,   25
Among our friends in Cornhill and Cheapside:°
But those I think have but one rule for plays;
They'll say they're good, if so the world says.°
If it should please them, and their spouses know it,
They straight inquire what kind of man's the poet.   30
But from side-box we dread a fearful doom;
All the good-natured beaux are gone to Rome.
The ladies' censure I'd almost forgot—°
Then for a line or two t'engage their vote.
But that way's old, below our author's aim—   35
No less than his whole play is compliment to them.

For their sakes then the play can't miss succeeding—
Though critics may want wit, they have good breeding.
They won't, I'm sure, forfeit the ladies' graces,
By showing their ill-nature to their faces.   40
Our business with good manners may be done;
Flatter us here, and damn us when you're gone.°

THE TWIN RIVALS

A Comedy

Sic vos non vobis°

DRAMATIS PERSONAE

The play was first staged at the Theatre Royal, Drury Lane, on 14 December 1702, with the following cast:

[MEN]

Elder Wouldbe [Hermes]	*Mr Wilks*
Younger Wouldbe [Benjamin]	*Mr Cibber*
Richmore	*Mr Husband*
Trueman	*Mr Mills*
Subtleman	*Mr Pinkethman*
Balderdash° and Alderman	*Mr Johnson*
Clearaccount, *a Steward*	*Mr Fairbank*
Fairbank, *a Goldsmith*	*Mr Minns*
Teague°	*Mr Bowen*

[WOMEN]

Constance	*Mrs Rogers*
Aurelia°	*Mrs Hook*
Mandrake°	*Mr Bullock*
Steward's wife	*Mrs Moor*

Constable, Watch, etc.

SCENE

London

THE DEDICATION
To Henry Bret° Esq.

The Commons of England have a right of petitioning, and since by your place in the Senate you are obliged to hear and redress the subject,° I presume upon the privilege of the people to give you the following trouble.

As prologues introduce plays on the stage, so dedications usher   5
them into the great theatre of the world;° and as we choose some staunch actor to address the audience, so we pitch upon some gentleman of undisputed ingenuity to recommend us to the reader. Books, like metals, require to be stamped with some valuable effigies before they become popular and current.°   10

To escape the critics I resolved to take sanctuary with one of the best, one who differs from the fraternity in this, that his good nature is ever predominant, can discover an author's smallest fault, and pardon the greatest.

Your generous approbation, sir, has done this play service, but has   15
injured the author; for it has made him insufferably vain, and he thinks himself authorised to stand up for the merit of his performance, when so great a master of wit has declared in its favour.

The Muses are the most coquettish of their sex, fond of being admired, and always putting on their best airs to the finest gentlemen.   20
But alas, sir! their addresses are stale, and their fine things but repetition; for there is nothing new in wit, but what is found in your own conversation.

Could I write by the help of study, as you talk without it, I would venture to say something in the usual strain of dedication; but as you   25
have too much wit to suffer it, and I too little to undertake it, I hope the world will excuse my deficiency, and you will pardon the presumption of,

Sir,

Your most obliged,   30
and most humble servant,
George Farquhar.

December 23
1702

81

THE PREFACE

The success and countenance that debauchery has met with in plays, was the most severe and reasonable charge against their authors in Mr Collier's *Short View*:° and indeed this gentleman had done the drama considerable service, had he arraigned the stage only to punish its misdemeanours, and not to take away its life; but there is an advantage to be made sometimes of the advice of an enemy, and the only way to disappoint his designs, is to improve upon his invective, and to make the stage flourish by virtue of that satire by which he thought to suppress it.

I have therefore in this piece endeavoured to show that an English comedy may answer the strictness of poetical justice;° but indeed, the greater share of the English audience—I mean that part which is no further read than in plays of their own language—have imbibed other principles, and stand up as vigorously for the old poetic licence, as they do for the liberty of the subject.° They take all innovations for grievances; and, let a project be never so well laid for their advantage, yet the undertaker is very likely to suffer by't. A play without a beau, cully, cuckold, or coquette is as poor an entertainment to some palates, as their Sunday's dinner would be without beef and pudding. And this I take to be one reason that the galleries were so thin during the run of this play. I thought indeed to have soothed the splenetic zeal of the City, by making a gentleman a knave, and punishing their great grievance—a whoremaster; but a certain virtuoso of that fraternity has told me since, that the citizens were never more disappointed in any entertainment—'For,' said he, 'however pious we may appear to be at home, yet we never go to that end of the Town,° but with an intention to be lewd.'

There was an odium cast upon this play before it appeared, by some persons who thought it their interest to have it suppressed. The ladies were frighted from seeing it by formidable stories of a midwife,° and were told no doubt, that they must expect no less than a labour upon the stage; but I hope the examining into that aspersion will be enough to wipe it off, since the character of the midwife is only so far touched as is necessary for carrying on the plot, she being principally deciphered in her procuring capacity; and I dare not affront the ladies so far, as to imagine they could be offended at the exposing of a bawd.

82

Some critics complain, that the design is defective for want of Clelia's appearance in the scene; but I had rather they should find this fault than I forfeit my regard to the fair, by showing a lady of figure under a misfortune; for which reason I made her only nominal,° and chose to expose the person that injured her; and if the ladies don't agree that I have done her justice in the end, I'm very sorry for't.

Some people are apt to say, that the character of Richmore points at a particular person, though I must confess I see nothing but what is very general in his character, except his marrying his own mistress; which, by the way, he never did, for he was no sooner off the stage, but he changed his mind,° and the poor lady is still *in statu quo*;° but upon the whole matter, 'tis application only makes the ass, and characters in plays are like Long Lane clothes, not hung out for the use of any particular people, but to be bought by only those° they happen to fit.°

The most material objection against this play, is the importance of the subject, which necessarily leads into sentiments too grave for diversion, and supposes vices too great for comedy to punish. 'Tis said, I must own, that the business of comedy is chiefly to ridicule folly; and that the punishment of vice falls rather into the province of tragedy; but if there be a middle sort of wickedness, too high for the sock, and too low for the buskin,° is there any reason that it should go unpunished? What are more obnoxious to human society than the villainies exposed in this play, the frauds, plots and contrivances upon the fortunes of men and the virtue of women? But the persons are too mean for the heroic—then what must we do with them? Why, they must of necessity drop into comedy. For it is unreasonable to imagine that the lawgivers in poetry would tie themselves up from executing that justice which is the foundation of their constitution; or to say that exposing vice is the business of the drama, and yet make rules to screen it from persecution.

Some have asked the question, why the Elder Wouldbe, in the fourth act, should counterfeit madness in his confinement—don't mistake, there was no such thing in his head; and the judicious could easily perceive that it was only a start° of humour put on to divert his melancholy; and when gaiety is strained to cover misfortune, it may very naturally be overdone, and rise to a semblance of madness, sufficient to impose on the constable, and perhaps on some of the audience; who taking everything at sight, impute that as a fault, which I am bold to stand up for, as one of the most masterly strokes of the whole piece.

This I think sufficient to obviate what objections I have heard made; but there was no great occasion for making this defence, having had the opinion of some of the greatest persons in England, both for quality and parts, that the play has merit enough to hide more faults than have been found; and I think their approbation sufficient to excuse some pride that may be incident to the author upon this performance.

I must own myself obliged to Mr Longueville° for some lines in the part of Teague, and something of the lawyer; but above all, for his hint of the twins, upon which I formed my plot. But having paid him all due satisfaction and acknowledgment, I must do myself the justice to believe, that few of our modern writers have been less beholden to foreign assistance° in their plays, than I have been in the following scenes.

Prologue

by Mr Motteux° and spoken by Mr Wilks°

An alarm sounded
With drums and trumpets in this warring age,°
A martial prologue should alarm the stage.
New plays, ere acted, a full audience near,
Seem towns invested, when a siege they fear.°
Prologues are like a 'forlorn hope' sent out°   5
Before the play, to skirmish, and to scout.
Our dreadful foes the critics, when they spy
They cock, they charge, they fire—then back they fly.
The siege is laid: there, gallant chiefs abound;
Here, foes intrenched; there, glittering troops around,   10
And the loud batteries roar—from yonder rising ground.
In the first act, brisk sallies (miss or hit)
With volleys of small-shot, or snip-snap wit°
Attack, and gall the trenches of the pit.
The next, the fire continues, but at length°   15
Grows less, and slackens like a bridegroom's strength.
The third, feints, mines, and countermines abound—
Your critic-engineers safe underground
Blow up our works, and all our art confound.°
The fourth brings on most action, and 'tis sharp—   20
Fresh foes crowd on, at your remissness carp,
And desperate, though unskilled, insult our counterscarp.°
Then comes the last—the general storm is near,
The poet-governor now quakes for fear,°
Runs wildly up and down, forgets to huff,   25
And would give all h'as plundered—to get off.
So *Don* and *Monsieur*, bluff before the siege,°
Were quickly tamed—at Venlo, and at Liège.°
'Twas '*Viva Spagnia!*' '*Vive France!*' before;°
Now, '*Quartier! Monsieur!*' '*Quartier! Ah! Senor!*'°   30
But what your resolution can withstand?
You master all, and awe the sea and land.
In war your valour makes the strong submit;
Your judgment humbles all attempts in wit.
What play, what fort, what beauty can endure   35

All fierce assaults, and always be secure!
Then grant 'em generous terms who *dare* to write,°
Since now—that seems as desperate as to fight.
If we must yield, yet ere the day be fixed,
Let us hold out the third—and, if we may, the sixth.°   40

1.1

[Scene.] Lodgings

The curtain drawn up, discovers Young Wouldbe a-dressing, and his Valet [Jack] buckling his shoes

YOUNG WOULDBE Here is such a plague every morning with buckling shoes, gartering, combing, and powdering—pshaw! Cease thy impertinence, I'll dress no more today.

[Exit Jack]

Were I an honest brute,° that rises from his litter, shakes himself, and so is dressed, I could bear it!   5

Enter Richmore

RICHMORE No further yet, Wouldbe? 'tis almost one.

YOUNG WOULDBE Then blame the clockmakers, they made it so; the sun has neither fore-nor afternoon. Prithee, what have we to do with time? Can't we let it alone as nature made it? Can't a man eat when he's hungry, go to bed when he's sleepy, rise when he wakes, dress   10 when he pleases, without the confinement of hours to enslave him?

RICHMORE Pardon me, sir, I understand your stoicism°—you have lost your money last night.

YOUNG WOULDBE No, no, Fortune took care of me there—I had none to lose.   15

RICHMORE 'Tis that gives you the spleen.

YOUNG WOULDBE Yes, I have got the spleen; and something else.° Hark'ee—*(whispers)*

RICHMORE How!

YOUNG WOULDBE Positively. The lady's kind reception was the   20 most severe usage I ever met with. Shan't I break her windows,° Richmore?

RICHMORE A mighty revenge truly. Let me tell you, friend, that breaking the windows of such houses are° no more than writing over a vintner's door as they do in Holland, *Vin te koop*.° 'Tis no   25 more than a bush° to a tavern, a decoy to trade,° and to draw in customers; but upon the whole matter, I think, a gentleman should put up an affront° got in such little company; for the pleasure, the pain, and the resentment are all alike scandalous.

YOUNG WOULDBE Have you forgot, Richmore, how I found you one   30 morning with the *Flying Post*° in your hand, hunting for physical advertisements?°

RICHMORE That was in the days of Dad, my friend, in the days of
dirty linen, pit-masks,° hedge-taverns,° and beefsteaks; but now I
fly at nobler game; the Ring,° the Court, Pawlet's° and the   35
Park.° I despise all women that I apprehend any danger from, less
than the having my throat cut; and should scruple to converse even
with a lady of fortune, unless her virtue were loud enough to give
me pride in exposing it. Here's a letter I received this morning;
you may read it.   40

    Gives a letter

YOUNG WOULDBE (*reads*) 'If there be solemnity in protestation,
justice in heaven, or fidelity on earth, I may still depend on the
faith of my Richmore. Though I may conceal my love, I no longer
can hide the effects on't from the world. Be careful of my honour,
remember your vows, and fly to the relief of the disconsolate   45
Clelia.' The fair, the courted, blooming Clelia!

RICHMORE The credulous, troublesome, foolish Clelia. Did you ever
read such a fulsome harangue? 'Lard, sir, I am near my time, and
want your assistance.' Does the silly creature imagine that any man
would come near her in those circumstances, unless it were Doctor   50
Chamberlain?° You may keep the letter.

YOUNG WOULDBE But why would you trust it with me?—you know
I can't keep a secret that has any scandal in't.

RICHMORE For that reason I communicate.° I know thou art a
perfect *Gazette*,° and will spread the news all over the Town. For   55
you must understand, that I am now besieging another; and I
would have the fame of my conquests upon the wing, that the town
may surrender the sooner.

YOUNG WOULDBE But if the report of your cruelty goes along with
that of your valour, you'll find no garrison of any strength will   60
open their gates to you.

RICHMORE No, no, women are cowards, and terror prevails upon
them more than clemency. My best pretence to my success with
the fair, is my using 'em ill. 'Tis turning their own guns upon 'em,
and I have always found it the most successful battery to assail one   65
reputation by sacrificing another.

YOUNG WOULDBE I could love thee for thy mischief, did I not envy
thee for thy success in't.

RICHMORE You never attempt a woman of figure.

YOUNG WOULDBE How can I? This confounded hump of mine is   70
such a burden at my back, that it presses me down here in the dirt
and diseases of Covent Garden,° the low suburbs of pleasure.

Curst fortune! I am a younger brother, and yet cruelly deprived of my birthright of a handsome person; seven thousand a year in a direct line would have straightened my back to some purpose. But I look, in my present circumstances, like a branch of another kind, grafted only upon the stock, which makes me grow so crooked.°

RICHMORE Come, come, 'tis no misfortune, your father is so as well as you.

YOUNG WOULDBE Then why should not I be a lord as well as he? Had I the same title to the deformity I could bear it.

RICHMORE But how does my lord bear the absence of your twin-brother?

YOUNG WOULDBE My twin-brother! Ay, 'twas his crowding me that spoiled my shape, and his coming half-an-hour before me that ruined my fortune. My father expelled me his house some two years ago, because I would have persuaded him that my twin-brother was a bastard. He gave me my portion, which was about fifteen hundred pound, and I have spent two thousand of it already. As for my brother, he don't care a farthing for me.

RICHMORE Why so, pray?

YOUNG WOULDBE A very odd reason—because I hate him.

RICHMORE How should he know that?

YOUNG WOULDBE Because he thinks it reasonable it should be so.°

RICHMORE But did your actions ever express any malice to him?

YOUNG WOULDBE Yes. I would fain have kept him company, but being aware of my kindness, he went abroad. He has travelled these five years, and I am told, is a grave sober fellow, and in danger of living a great while. All my hope is, that when he gets into his honour and estate, the nobility will soon kill him by drinking him up to his dignity.° But come, Frank, I have but two eyesores in the world, a brother before me, and a hump behind me, and thou art still laying 'em in my way. Let us assume an argument of less severity—canst thou lend me a brace of hundred pounds?

RICHMORE What would you do with 'em?

YOUNG WOULDBE Do with 'em! There's a question indeed. Do you think I would eat 'em?

RICHMORE Yes, o' my troth, would you, and drink 'em together. Look'ee, Mr Wouldbe, whilst you kept well with your father, I could have ventured to have lent you five guineas. But as the case stands, I can assure you, I have lately paid off my sisters' fortunes,° and—

YOUNG WOULDBE Sir, this put-off looks like an affront; and you
   know I don't use to take such things.   115

RICHMORE Sir, your demand is rather an affront, when you know I
   don't use to give such things.

YOUNG WOULDBE Sir, I'll pawn my honour.

RICHMORE That's mortgaged already for more than it is worth; you
   had better pawn your sword there, 'twill bring you forty shillings.   120

YOUNG WOULDBE 'Sdeath, sir.
        Takes his sword off the table

RICHMORE Hold, Mr Wouldbe. Suppose I put an end to your
   misfortunes all at once?

YOUNG WOULDBE How, sir?

RICHMORE Why, go to a magistrate, and swear you would have   125
   robbed me of two hundred pounds. Look'ee, sir, you have been
   often told that your extravagance would some time or other be the
   ruin of you; and it will go a great way in your indictment, to have
   turned the pad upon° your friend.

YOUNG WOULDBE This usage is the height of ingratitude from you,   130
   in whose company I have spent my fortune.

RICHMORE I'm therefore a witness, that it was very ill spent. Why
   would you keep company, be at equal expenses with me that have
   fifty times your estate? What was gallantry in me, was prodigality
   in you; mine was my health, because I could pay for't; yours a   135
   disease, because you could not.

YOUNG WOULDBE And is this all I must expect from our friendship?

RICHMORE Friendship! Sir, there can be no such thing without an
   equality.°

YOUNG WOULDBE That is, there can be no such thing when there   140
   is occasion for't.

RICHMORE Right sir—our friendship was over a bottle only, and
   whilst you can pay your club of friendship,° I'm that way your
   humble servant, but when once you come borrowing, I'm this
   way—your humble servant.   145
        Exit [Richmore]

YOUNG WOULDBE Rich, big, proud, arrogant villain! I have been
   twice his second,° thrice sick of the same love, and thrice cured by
   the same physic, and now he drops me for a trifle. That an honest
   fellow in his cups should be such a rogue when he's sober—the
   narrow-hearted rascal has been drinking coffee this morning.   150
   [*Looking at a coin*] Well! thou dear solitary half-crown, adieu!
   Here, Jack!

Enter Jack

Take this; pay for a bottle of wine, and bid Balderdash bring it himself.

Exit [Jack]

How melancholy are my poor breeches, not one chink! Thou art a   155
villainous hand, for thou hast picked my pocket. This vintner now
has all the marks of an honest fellow, a broad face, a copious look,°
a strutting belly, and a jolly mien. I have brought him above three
pound a night for these two years successively. The rogue has
money I'm sure, if he will but lend it.   160

Enter Balderdash with a bottle and glass[es], [Jack attending]

O, Mr Balderdash, good morrow.

BALDERDASH Noble Mr Wouldbe, I'm your most humble servant. I
have brought you a whetting-glass, the best old hock in Europe; I
know 'tis your drink in a morning.

YOUNG WOULDBE I'll pledge you,° Mr Balderdash.   165

BALDERDASH Your health sir—(*drinks*).

YOUNG WOULDBE Pray Mr Balderdash, tell me one thing—but first
sit down—now tell me plainly what you think of me.

BALDERDASH Think of you, sir! I think that you are the honestest,
noblest gentleman, that ever drank a glass of wine; and the best   170
customer that ever came into my house.

YOUNG WOULDBE And you really think as you speak?

BALDERDASH May this wine be my poison, sir, if I don't speak from
the bottom of° my heart.

YOUNG WOULDBE And how much money do you think I have spent   175
in your house?

BALDERDASH Why truly, sir, by a moderate computation, I do
believe that I have handled of your money, the best part of five
hundred pounds within these two years.

YOUNG WOULDBE Very well! And do you think that you lie under   180
any obligation for the trade I have promoted to your advantage?

BALDERDASH Yes, sir; and if I can serve you in any respect, pray
command me to the utmost of my ability.

YOUNG WOULDBE Well! Thanks to my stars, there is still some
honesty in wine. Mr Balderdash, I embrace you and your kindness.   185
I am at present a little low in cash, and must beg you to lend me
a hundred pieces.

BALDERDASH Why truly Mr Wouldbe, I was afraid it would come
to this—I have had it in my head several times to caution you upon
your expenses, but you were so very genteel in my house, and your   190

liberality became you so very well, that I was unwilling to say anything that might check your disposition; but truly, sir, I can forbear no longer to tell you, that you have been a little too extravagant.

YOUNG WOULDBE But since you reaped the benefit of my extra-   195
vagance, you will I hope consider my necessity.

BALDERDASH Consider your necessity! I do with all my heart, and must tell you moreover, that I will be no longer accessory to it. I desire you, sir, to frequent my house no more.

YOUNG WOULDBE How, sir!   200

BALDERDASH I say, sir, that I have an honour for° my good lord your father, and will not suffer his son to run into any unconveni-ence; sir, I shall order my drawers not to serve you with a drop of wine. Would you have me connive at a gentleman's destruction?

YOUNG WOULDBE But methinks, sir, that a person of your nice   205
conscience should have cautioned me before.

BALDERDASH Alas! Sir, it was none of my business. Would you have me be saucy to a gentleman that was my best customer? Lackaday, sir, had you money to hold it out still, I had been hanged rather than be rude to you. But truly, sir, when a man is ruined, 'tis but   210
the duty of a Christian to tell him of it.

YOUNG WOULDBE Will you lend me the money, sir?

BALDERDASH Will you pay me this bill, sir?
    [*Presents his account*]

YOUNG WOULDBE Lend me the hundred pound, and I will pay the bill.   215

BALDERDASH Pay me the bill, and I will not lend the hundred pound, sir. But pray consider with yourself—now sir, would not you think me an arrant coxcomb, to trust a person with money that has always been so extravagant under my eye, whose profuseness I have seen, I have felt, I have handled? Have not I known you,   220
sir, throw away ten pound of a night upon a covey of pit-partridges,° and a setting-dog? Sir, you have made my house an ill house; my very chairs will bear you no longer. In short, sir, I desire you to frequent the Crown no more, sir.

YOUNG WOULDBE Thou sophisticated tun of iniquity;° have I   225
fattened your carcass, and swelled your bags with my vital blood? Have I made you my companion to be thus saucy to me? But now I will keep you at your due distance.
    Kicks him

JACK [*to Balderdash*] Welcome sir!

92

YOUNG WOULDBE Well said Jack.   230
    Kicks him again
JACK [*to Balderdash*] Very welcome sir! I hope we shall have your
company another time. Welcome sir!
    [*Balderdash is*] *kicked off*
YOUNG WOULDBE Pray wait on him down stairs, and give him a
welcome at the door too.
    Exit Jack
This is the punishment of Hell; the very devil that tempted me to   235
the sin, now upbraids me with the crime. I have villainously
murdered my fortune; and now its ghost, in the lank shape of
Poverty, haunts me. Is there no charm to conjure down° the fiend?
    Enter Jack
JACK O sir, here's sad news!
YOUNG WOULDBE Then keep it to thyself—I have enough of that   240
already.
JACK Sir, you will hear it too soon.
YOUNG WOULDBE What! Is Broad° below?
JACK No, no, sir; better twenty such as he were hanged. Sir, your
father's dead.   245
YOUNG WOULDBE My father. Good night, my lord. Has he left me
anything?
JACK I heard nothing of that, sir.
YOUNG WOULDBE Then I believe you heard all there was of it. Let
me see—my father dead! And my elder brother abroad! If necessity   250
be the mother of invention, she was never more pregnant than with
me.
    Pauses
Here, sirrah, run to Mrs Mandrake, and bid her come hither
presently.
    Exit Jack
That woman was my mother's midwife when I was born, and has   255
been my bawd these ten years. I have had her endeavours to
corrupt my brother's mistress; and now her assistance will be
necessary to cheat him of his estate; for she's famous for understanding the right side of a woman, and the wrong side of the law.
    Exit

1.[2]

Scene changes to Mandrake's house

Mandrake and maid

MANDRAKE Who is there?

MAID Madam.

MANDRAKE Has any message been left for me today?

MAID Yes, madam. Here has been one from my Lady Stillborn, that
desired you not to be out of the way, for she expected to cry out   5
every minute.

MANDRAKE How! every minute! Let me see.

Takes out her pocket-book

Stillborn—ay—she reckons with her husband from the first of
April;° and with Sir James, from the first of March. Ay, she's
always a month before her time. (*Knocking at the door*) Go see   10
who's at the door.

MAID Yes, madam.

Exit maid

MANDRAKE Well! Certainly there is not a woman in the world
so willing to oblige mankind° as myself; and really I have been so
ever since the age of twelve, as I can remember—I have deliv-   15
ered as many women of great bellies, and helped as many to
'em as any person in England; but my watching and cares
have broken me quite—I am not the same woman I was forty
years ago.

Enter Richmore

O, Mr Richmore! You're a sad man, a barbarous man, so you are.   20
What will become of poor Clelia, Mr Richmore? The poor creature
is so big with her misfortunes, that they are not to be borne.

Weeps

RICHMORE You, Mrs Mandrake, are the fittest person in the world,
to ease her of 'em.

MANDRAKE And won't you marry her, Mr Richmore?   25

RICHMORE My conscience won't allow it; for I have sworn since, to
marry another.

MANDRAKE And will you break your vows to Clelia?

RICHMORE Why not, when she has broke hers to me?

MANDRAKE How's that, sir?   30

RICHMORE Why, she swore a hundred times never to grant me the
favour, and yet you know she broke her word.

MANDRAKE But she loved Mr Richmore, and that was the reason she
forgot her oath.

RICHMORE And I love Mr Richmore, and that is the reason I forgot   35
mine. Why should she be angry that I follow her own example, by
doing the very same thing from the very same motive?

MANDRAKE Well, well! Take my word, you'll never thrive—I wonder how you can have the face to come near me, that am the
witness of your horrid oaths and imprecations! Are not you afraid   40
that the guilty chamber above-stairs should fall down upon your
head?° Yes, yes, I was accessory, I was so; but if ever you involve
my honour in such a villainy the second time—Ah, poor Clelia! I
loved her as I did my own daughter. You seducing man—
　　Weeps

RICHMORE Hey-ho, my Aurelia!   45

MANDRAKE Hey-ho, she's very pretty.

RICHMORE Dost thou know her, my dear Mandrake?

MANDRAKE Hey-ho, she's very pretty. Ah, you're a sad° man. Poor
Clelia was handsome, but indeed, breeding, puking, and longing,
has broken her much. 'Tis a hard case, Mr Richmore, for a young   50
lady to see a thousand things, and long for a thousand things, and
yet not dare to own that she longs for one. She had liked to have
miscarried t'other day for the pith of a loin of veal. Ah, you
barbarous man.

RICHMORE But my Aurelia! Confirm me that you know her, and I'll   55
adore thee.

MANDRAKE You would fling five hundred guineas at my head, that
you knew as much of her as I do. Why, sir, I brought her into the
world; I have had her sprawling in my lap. Ah! She was as plump
as a puffin, sir.   60

RICHMORE I think she has no great portion to value herself upon;
her reputation only will keep up the market. We must first make
that cheap, by crying it down, and then she'll part with it at an
easy rate.°

MANDRAKE But you won't provide for poor Clelia?   65

RICHMORE Provide! Why, han't I taught her a trade? Let her set up
when she will—I'll engage her customers enough, because I can
answer for the goodness of the ware.

MANDRAKE Nay, but you ought to set her up with credit, and take
a shop; that is, get her a husband. Have you no pretty gentleman   70
your relation now that wants a young virtuous lady with a
handsome fortune? No young Templer° that has spent his estate

in the study of the law, and starves by the practice? No spruce officer that wants a handsome wife to make court for him among the major-generals? Have you none of these, sir?   75

RICHMORE Pho, pho, madam—you have tired me upon that subject. Do you think a lady that gave me so much trouble before possession shall ever give me any after it? No, no, had she been more obliging to me when I was in her power, I should be more civil to her, now she's in mine. My assiduity beforehand was an   80 overprice; had she made a merit of the matter, she should have yielded sooner.°

MANDRAKE Nay, nay, sir. Though you have no regard to her honour, yet you shall protect mine. How d'ee think I have secured my reputation so long among the people of best figure, but by keeping   85 all mouths stopped? Sir, I'll have no clamours at me—Heavens help me, I have clamours enough at my door early and late in my t'other capacity. In short, sir, a husband for Clelia; or I banish you my presence for ever.

RICHMORE [aside] Thou art a necessary devil, and I can't want thee.   90

MANDRAKE Look'ee, sir; 'tis your own advantage; 'tis only making over your estate into the hands of a trustee; and though you don't absolutely command the premises, yet you may exact enough out of 'em for necessaries, when you will.°

RICHMORE Patience a little, madam—I have a young nephew that is   95 captain of horse. He mortgaged the last morsel of his estate to me, to make up his equipage for the last campaign. Perhaps you know him: he's a brisk fellow, much about Court, Captain Trueman.

MANDRAKE Trueman! Adsmylife, he's one of my babies. I can tell you the very minute he was born—precisely at three o'clock next   100 St George's day, Trueman will be two and twenty, a stripling, the prettiest good-natured child, and your nephew! He must be the man, and shall be the man; I have a kindness for him.

RICHMORE But we must have a care; the fellow wants neither sense nor courage.   105

MANDRAKE Phu, phu, never fear her part—she shan't want instructions, and then for her lying-in a little abruptly, 'tis my business to reconcile matters there—a fright or a fall excuses that. Lard sir, I do these things every day.

RICHMORE 'Tis pity then to put you out of your road; and Clelia   110 shall have a husband.

MANDRAKE Spoke like a man of honour. And now I'll serve you again. This Aurelia, you say—

RICHMORE O she distracts me!° Her beauty, family, and virtue make   115
her a noble pleasure.

MANDRAKE And you have a mind for that reason to get her a
husband?

RICHMORE Yes, faith. I have another young relation at Cambridge—
he's just going into orders; and I think such a fine woman, with
fifteen hundred pound, is a better presentation than any living in   120
my gift;° and why should he like the cure the worse that an
incumbent was there before?°

MANDRAKE Thou art a pretty fellow—at the same moment you
would persuade me that you love a woman to madness, are you
contriving how to part with her?   125

RICHMORE If I loved her not to madness, I should not run into these
contradictions. Here (*offering her money*), my dear 'mother',°
Aurelia's the word.

MANDRAKE Pardon me, sir. (*Refusing the money*) Did you ever know
me mercenary? No, no, sir; virtue is its own reward.   130

RICHMORE Nay, but madam, I owe you for the teeth-powder you
sent me.

MANDRAKE O, that's another matter, sir.
Takes the money
I hope you liked it sir.

RICHMORE Extremely madam—(*aside*) but it was somewhat dear   135
of° twenty guineas.
Enter servant

SERVANT Madam, here is Mr Wouldbe's footman below with a
message from his master.

MANDRAKE I come to him presently.
Exit servant
Do you know that Wouldbe loves Aurelia's cousin and companion,   140
Mrs Constance with the great fortune, and that I solicit for him?

RICHMORE Why, she's engaged to his elder brother. Besides, young
Wouldbe has no money to prosecute an affair of such consequence—you can have no hopes of success there, I'm sure.

MANDRAKE Truly, I have no great hopes; but an industrious body   145
you know, would do anything rather than be idle. The aunt is very
near her time, and I have access to the family when I please.

RICHMORE Now I think on't; prithee get the letter from Wouldbe
that I gave him just now; it would be proper to our designs upon
Trueman, that it should not be exposed.   150

MANDRAKE And you showed Clelia's letter to Wouldbe?

RICHMORE Yes.

MANDRAKE Eh, you barbarous man. Who the Devil would oblige
   you? What pleasure can you take in exposing the poor creature?
   Dear little child, 'tis pity; indeed it is.   155

RICHMORE Madam, the messenger waits below; so I'll take my leave.

   Exit [Richmore]

MANDRAKE Ah, you're a sad man!

   Exit

2.[1]

Scene, the Park°

Constance and Aurelia

AURELIA Prithee cousin Constance, be cheerful. Let the dead lord
sleep in peace, and look up to the living. Take pen, ink, and paper,
and write immediately to your lover, that he is now a baron of
England, and that you long to be a baroness.

CONSTANCE Nay, Aurelia, there is some regard due to the memory   5
of the father, for the respect I bear the son; besides, I don't know
how, I could wish my young lord were at home in this juncture.
This brother of his—some mischief will happen—I had a very ugly
dream last night. In short, I am eaten up with the spleen, my dear.

AURELIA Come, come; walk about and divert it—the air will do you   10
good; think of other people's affairs a little. When did you see
Clelia?

CONSTANCE I'm glad you mentioned her. Don't you observe her
gaiety to be much more forced than formerly?—her humour don't
sit so easily upon her.   15

AURELIA No, nor her stays neither, I can assure you.

CONSTANCE Did you observe how she devoured the pomegranates
yesterday?

AURELIA She talks of visiting a relation in Leicestershire.

CONSTANCE She fainted away in the country dance t'other night.   20

AURELIA Richmore shunned her in the Walk last week.

CONSTANCE And his footman laughed.

AURELIA She takes laudanum to make her sleep a' nights.

CONSTANCE Ah, poor Clelia! What will she do cousin?

AURELIA Do! Why nothing till the nine months be up.   25

CONSTANCE That's cruel, Aurelia. How can you make merry with
her misfortunes? I am positive she was no easy conquest; some
singular villainy has been practised upon her.

AURELIA Yes, yes, the fellow would be practising upon me too, I
thank him.   30

CONSTANCE Have a care, cousin, he has a promising person.

AURELIA Nay, for that matter, his promising person may as soon be
broke as his promising vows. Nature indeed has made him a giant,
and he wars with heaven like the giants of old.°

CONSTANCE Then why will you admit his visits?   35

AURELIA I never did, but all the servants are more his than our own. He has a golden key to every door in the house; besides, he makes my uncle believe that his intentions are honourable; and indeed he has said nothing yet to disprove it. But cousin, do you see who comes yonder, sliding along the Mall?   40

CONSTANCE Captain Trueman, I protest. The campaign has improved him—he makes a very clean well-furnished° figure.

AURELIA Youthful, easy, and good-natured—I could wish he would know us.

CONSTANCE Are you sure he's well-bred?   45

AURELIA I tell you he's good-natured, and I take good manners to be nothing but a natural desire to be easy and agreeable to whatever conversation we fall into; and a porter with this is mannerly in his way; and a duke without it has but the breeding of a dancing-master.   50

CONSTANCE I like him for his affection to my young lord.

AURELIA And I like him for his affection to my young person.

CONSTANCE How, how, cousin? You never told me that.

AURELIA How should I? He never told it me, but I have discovered it by a great many signs and tokens, that are better security for his   55
heart than ten thousand vows and promises.

CONSTANCE He's Richmore's nephew.

AURELIA Ah! Would he were his heir too. He's a pretty fellow. But then he's a soldier, and must share his time with his mistress, Honour, in Flanders. No, no, I'm resolved against a man that   60
disappears all the summer, like a woodcock.°

> *As these last words are spoken, Trueman enters behind them, as passing over the stage*

TRUEMAN That's for me, whoever spoke it.

> *The Ladies turn about. [Trueman is] surprised*

Aurelia!

CONSTANCE What, Captain, you're afraid of everything but the enemy.   65

TRUEMAN I have reason, ladies, to be most apprehensive where there is most danger. The enemy is satisfied with a leg or an arm, but here I'm in hazard of losing my heart.

AURELIA None in the world, sir—nobody here designs to attack it.

TRUEMAN But suppose it be assaulted, and taken already, madam.   70

AURELIA Then we'll return it without ransom.

TRUEMAN But suppose, madam, the prisoner choose to stay where it is.

AURELIA That were to turn deserter, and you know Captain, what
such deserve.   75

TRUEMAN The punishment it undergoes this moment—shot to
death.

CONSTANCE Nay, then, 'tis time for me to put in.° Pray, sir, have
you heard the news of my Lord Wouldbe's death?

TRUEMAN (to Constance) People mind not the death of others,   80
madam, that are expiring themselves. (To Aurelia) Do you consider
madam, the penalty of wounding a man in the Park?°

AURELIA Hey-day! Why Captain, d'ee intend to make a Vigo business of it, and break the boom at once?° Sir, if you only rally, pray
let my cousin have her share; or if you would be particular, pray   85
be more respectful—not so much upon the declaration, I beseech
you, sir.°

TRUEMAN I have been, fair creature, a perfect coward in my passion;
I have had hard strugglings with my fear before I durst engage,
and now perhaps behave but too desperately.   90

AURELIA Sir, I am very sorry you have said so much; for I must
punish you for't, though it be contrary to my inclination. [To
Constance] Come, cousin, will you walk?

CONSTANCE [saluting Trueman] Servant, sir.
        Exeunt ladies

TRUEMAN Charming creature! 'I must punish you for't, though it be   95
contrary to my inclination.' Hope and despair in a breath. But I'll
think the best.
        Exit

2.[2]

Scene changes to Young Wouldbe's lodgings

Young Wouldbe and Mandrake meeting

YOUNG WOULDBE Thou life and soul of secret dealings, welcome.

MANDRAKE My dear child, bless thee. Who would have imagined
that I brought this great rogue into the world? He makes me an
old woman I protest. But adso, my child, I forgot; I'm sorry for
the loss of your father, sorry at my heart, poor man.   5
        Weeps
Mr Wouldbe, have you got a drop of brandy in your closet? I an't
very well today.

YOUNG WOULDBE That you shan't want. But please to sit, my dear
'mother'. [*Calling*] Here, Jack, the brandy bottle. Now madam.
I have occasion to use you in dressing up a handsome cheat for   10
me.

MANDRAKE I defy any chambermaid in England to do it better—I
have dressed up a hundred and fifty cheats in my time.

    Enter Jack with the brandy bottle [*and a glass*]

Here, boy, this glass is too big—carry it away, I'll take a sup out
of the bottle.   15

    [*Exit Jack with glass*]

YOUNG WOULDBE Right madam—and my business being very
urgent—in three words, 'tis this.

MANDRAKE Hold, sir, till I take advice of my counsel.

    Drinks

There is nothing more comfortable to a poor creature, and fitter
to revive wasting spirits, than a little plain brandy. I an't for your   20
hot spirits, your *rosa solis*, your ratifias, your orange waters, and
the like. A moderate glass of cool Nantes is the thing.

YOUNG WOULDBE But to our business, madam—my father is dead,
and I have a mind to inherit his estate.

MANDRAKE You put the case very well.   25

YOUNG WOULDBE One of two things I must choose—either to be a
lord or a beggar.

MANDRAKE Be a lord to choose°—though I have known some that
have chosen both.

YOUNG WOULDBE I have a brother that I love very well; but since   30
one of us must want, I had rather he should starve than I.

MANDRAKE Upon my conscience, dear heart, you're in the right on't.

YOUNG WOULDBE Now your advice upon these heads.

MANDRAKE They be matters of weight, and I must consider.

    Drinks

Is there a will in the case?   35

YOUNG WOULDBE There is; which excludes me from every foot of
the estate.

MANDRAKE That's bad. Where's your brother?

YOUNG WOULDBE He's now in Germany, in his way to England,
and is expected very soon.   40

MANDRAKE How soon?

YOUNG WOULDBE In a month or less.

MANDRAKE O ho! A month is a great while; our business must be
done in an hour or two. We must—(*drinks*)—suppose your brother

to be dead; nay, he shall be actually dead—and my lord, my 45
humble service t'ee.

YOUNG WOULDBE O Madam, I'm your ladyship's most devoted.
Make your words good, and I'll—

MANDRAKE Say no more, sir; you shall have it, you shall have it.

YOUNG WOULDBE Ay, but how, dear Mrs Mandrake? 50

MANDRAKE 'Mrs Mandrake!' Is that all? Why not 'Mother', 'Aunt',
'Grandmother'? Sir, I have done more for you this moment, than
all the relations you have in the world.

YOUNG WOULDBE Let me hear it.

MANDRAKE By the strength of this potent inspiration,° I have made 55
you a peer of England, with seven thousand pound a year. My
lord, I wish you joy.
    Drinks

YOUNG WOULDBE [*aside*] The woman's mad, I believe.

MANDRAKE Quick, quick, my lord! Counterfeit a letter presently
from Germany, that your brother is killed in a duel. Let it be 60
directed to your father, and fall into the hands of the steward when
you are by. What sort of fellow is the steward?

YOUNG WOULDBE Why, a timorous half-honest man, that a little
persuasions will make a whole knave. He wants courage to be
thoroughly just, or entirely a villain—but good backing will make 65
him either.

MANDRAKE And he shan't want that! I tell you the letter must
come into his hands when you are by; upon this you take
immediate possession, and so you have the best part of the law of
your side. 70

YOUNG WOULDBE But suppose my brother comes in the mean time?

MANDRAKE This must be done this very moment. Let him come
when you're in possession, I'll warrant we'll find a way to keep
him out.

YOUNG WOULDBE But, how, my dear contriver? 75

MANDRAKE By your father's will, man, your father's will. That is,
one that your father might have made, and which we will make for
him. I'll send you a nephew of my own, a lawyer, that shall do the
business. Go, get into possession, possession, I say; let us have but
the estate to back the suit, and you'll find the law too strong for 80
justice, I warrant you.

YOUNG WOULDBE My oracle! How shall we revel in delight when
this great prediction is accomplished. But one thing yet remains—
my brother's mistress, the charming Constance: let her be mine—

MANDRAKE Pho, pho, she's yours a' course;° she's contracted to you;   85
for she's engaged to marry no man but my Lord Wouldbe's son
and heir. Now you being the person, she's recoverable by law.

YOUNG WOULDBE Marry her! No, no, she's contracted to him—
'twere injustice to rob a brother of his wife—an easier favour will
satisfy me.   90

MANDRAKE Why, truly, as you say, that favour is so easy, that I
wonder they make such a bustle about it. But get you gone and
mind your affairs, I must about mine. Oh—I had forgot—where's
that foolish letter you had this morning from Richmore?

YOUNG WOULDBE I have posted it up in the Chocolate House.   95

MANDRAKE (shrieks) Yaw, I shall fall into fits; hold me—

YOUNG WOULDBE No, no, I did but jest. Here it is—but be assured
madam, I wanted only time to have exposed it.

MANDRAKE Ah! You barbarous man, why so?

YOUNG WOULDBE Because, when knaves of our sex, and fools of   100
yours meet, they make the best jest in the world.

MANDRAKE Sir—the world has a better share in the jest when we are
the knaves and you the fools. But lookee, sir, if ever you open your
mouth about this trick°—I'll discover all your tricks; therefore
silence and safety on both sides.   105

YOUNG WOULDBE Madam, you need not doubt my silence at
present; because my own affairs will employ me sufficiently; so
there's your letter.

> *Gives the letter*

And now to write my own.

> *Exit [Young Wouldbe]*

MANDRAKE Adieu, my lord. Let me see.   110

> *Opens the letter and reads*

'If there be solemnity in protestations'—that's foolish, very foolish.
Why should she expect solemnity in protestations? um, um, um.
'I may still depend on the faith of my Richmore'—Ah poor Clelia!
um, um, um. 'I can no longer hide the effects on't from the world.'
The effects on't! How modestly is that expressed! Well, 'tis a   115
pretty letter, and I'll keep it.

> *Puts the letter in her pocket, and exit[s]*

2.[3]

Scene, Lord Wouldbe's house

Enter Clearaccount, and his wife

WIFE You are to blame, you are much to blame, husband, in being so scrupulous.

CLEARACCOUNT 'Tis true. This foolish conscience of mine has been the greatest bar to my fortune.

WIFE And will ever be so. Tell me but one that thrives, and I'll 5
show you a hundred that starve by it. Do you think 'tis four
score pound a year makes my Lord Gouty's steward's wife
live at the rate of four hundred? Upon my word, my dear,
I'm as good a gentlewoman as she, and I expect to be maintained accordingly. 'Tis conscience I warrant, that buys 10
her the point-heads, and diamond necklace? Was it conscience
that bought her the fine house in Jermyn Street?° Is it conscience that enables the steward to buy when the lord is forced
to sell?

CLEARACCOUNT But what would you have me do? 15

WIFE Do! Now's your time. That small morsel of an estate your lord
bought lately, a thing not worth mentioning; take it towards your
daughter Molly's portion. What's two hundred a year?—'twill
never be missed.

CLEARACCOUNT 'Tis but a small matter, I must confess; and as a 20
reward for my past faithful service, I think it but reasonable I
should cheat a little now.

WIFE Reasonable! All the reason that can be—if the ungrateful world
won't reward an honest man, why let an honest man reward
himself. There's five hundred pound you received but two days 25
ago—lay them aside. You may easily sink it in the charge of the
funeral. Do, my dear, now—kiss me, and do it.

CLEARACCOUNT Well, you have such a winning way with you! But,
my dear, I'm so much afraid of my young lord's coming home;
he's a cunning close man they say, and will examine my accounts 30
very narrowly.

WIFE Ay, my dear, would you had the younger brother to deal
with—you might manage him as you pleased. I see him coming.
Let us weep, let us weep.

> *They pull out their handkerchiefs, and seem to mourn. Enter*
> *Young Wouldbe*

CLEARACCOUNT Ah, sir; we have all lost a father, a friend, and a   35
supporter.

YOUNG WOULDBE Ay, Mr Steward, we must submit to fate, as he
has done. And it is no small addition to my grief, honest Mr
Clearaccount, that it is not in my power to supply my father's
place to you and yours—your sincerity and justice to the dead   40
merits the greatest regard from those that survive him. Had I but
my brother's ability,° or he my inclinations—I'll assure you, Mrs
Clearaccount, you should not have such cause to mourn.

WIFE Ah, good noble sir!

CLEARACCOUNT Your brother, sir, I hear, is a very severe man.   45

YOUNG WOULDBE He is what the world calls a prudent man, Mr
Steward. I have often heard him very severe upon men of your
business; and has declared, that for form's sake indeed he would
keep a steward, but that he would inspect into all his accounts
himself.   50

WIFE Ay, Mr Wouldbe, you have more sense than to do these things.
You have more honour than to trouble your head with your own
affairs—would to Heavens we were to serve you.

YOUNG WOULDBE Would I could serve you, madam—without
injustice to my brother.   55

Enter a servant

SERVANT A letter for my Lord Wouldbe.

CLEARACCOUNT It comes too late, alas! for his perusal—let me see it.

Opens and reads

'Frankfort, October 10, new style.'° Frankfort! where's Frankfort,
sir?

YOUNG WOULDBE In Germany. The letter must be from my   60
brother—I suppose he's a-coming home.

CLEARACCOUNT 'Tis none of his hand. Let me see.

Reads [apart]

'My Lord, I am troubled at this unhappy occasion of sending to
your lordship; your brave son, and my dear friend, was yesterday
unfortunately killed in a duel by a German count—' I shall love a   65
German Count as long as I live. [*To Young Wouldbe*] My lord, my
lord, now I may call you so, since your elder brother's—dead.

YOUNG WOULDBE and WIFE How?

CLEARACCOUNT Read there.

Gives the letter; Young Wouldbe peruses it

YOUNG WOULDBE O, my fate! A father and a brother in one day!   70
Heavens! 'Tis too much. Where is the fatal messenger?

SERVANT A gentleman, sir, who said he came post on purpose. He was afraid the contents of the letter would unqualify my lord for company; so he would take another time to wait on him.

[*Exit servant*]

YOUNG WOULDBE Nay, then 'tis true; and there is truth in dreams. 75
Last night I dreamt—

WIFE Nay, my lord, I dreamt too; I dreamt I saw your brother dressed in a long minister's gown—Lord bless us!—with a book in his hand, walking before a dead body to the grave.

YOUNG WOULDBE Well, Mr Clearaccount, get mourning ready. 80

CLEARACCOUNT Will your lordship have the old coach covered, or a new one made?

YOUNG WOULDBE A new one—the old coach with the grey horses, I give to Mrs Clearaccount here; 'tis not fit she should walk the streets. 85

WIFE (*aside*) Heavens bless the German count, I say.—But, my lord—

YOUNG WOULDBE No reply, madam, you shall have it—and receive it but as the earnest of my favours. Mr Clearaccount, I double your salary, and all the servants' wages, to moderate their grief for our 90
great losses. Pray, sir, take order about these affairs.

CLEARACCOUNT I shall, my lord.

Exeunt Clearaccount and Wife

YOUNG WOULDBE So! I have got possession of the castle, and if I had but a little law to fortify me now, I believe we might hold it out a great while. O! here comes my attorney. 95

Enter Subtleman

Mr Subtleman, your servant.

SUBTLEMAN My lord, I wish you joy; my aunt Mandrake has sent me to receive your commands.

YOUNG WOULDBE Has she told you anything of the affair?

SUBTLEMAN Not a word, my lord. 100

YOUNG WOULDBE Why then—come nearer—can you make a man right heir to an estate during the life of an elder brother?

SUBTLEMAN I thought you had been the eldest.

YOUNG WOULDBE That we are not yet agreed upon; for you must know, there is an impertinent fellow that takes a fancy to dispute 105
the seniority with me. For, look'ee, sir, my mother has unluckily sowed discord in the family by bringing forth twins. My brother, 'tis true, was first-born, but, I believe from the bottom of my heart, I was the first-begotten.

SUBTLEMAN I understand—you are come to an estate and dignity,   110
that by justice indeed is your own, but by law it falls to your
brother.

YOUNG WOULDBE I had rather, Mr Subtleman, it were his by justice
and mine by law, for I would have the strongest title, if possible.

SUBTLEMAN I am very sorry there should happen any breach   115
between brethren—so I think it would be but a christian and
charitable act to take away all further disputes, by making you true
heir to the estate by the last will of your father. Look'ee, I'll divide
stakes—you shall yield the eldership and honour to him, and he
shall quit his estate to you.   120

YOUNG WOULDBE Why, as you say, I don't much care if I do grant
him the eldest—half-an-hour is but a trifle. But how shall we do
about this will? Who shall we get to prove it?

SUBTLEMAN Never trouble yourself for that—I expect a cargo of
witnesses and *usquebaugh*° by the first fair wind.   125

YOUNG WOULDBE But we can't stay for them, it must be done
immediately.

SUBTLEMAN Well, well. We'll find somebody I warrant you, to make
oath of his last words.

YOUNG WOULDBE That's impossible. For my father died of an   130
apoplexy, and did not speak at all.

SUBTLEMAN That's nothing, sir. He's not the first dead man that I
have made to speak.

YOUNG WOULDBE You're a great master of speech, I don't question,
sir, and I can assure you there will be ten guineas for every word   135
you extort from him in my favour.

SUBTLEMAN O sir; that's enough to make your great-grandfather
speak.

YOUNG WOULDBE Come then, I'll carry you to my steward. He shall
give you the names of the manors, and the true titles and   140
denominations of the estate, and then you shall go to work.
    Exeunt

2.[4]

Scene changes to the Park

Richmore and Trueman meeting

RICHMORE O brave coz! You're very happy with the fair, I find. Pray which of those two ladies you encountered just now has your adoration?

TRUEMAN She that commands by forbidding it. And since I had courage to declare to herself, I dare now own it to the world; 5
Aurelia, sir, is my angel.

RICHMORE Ha! (*A long pause*) Sir, I find you're of everybody's religion; but methinks you make a bold flight at first. Do you think your captain's pay will stake against so high a gamester?°

TRUEMAN What do you mean? 10

RICHMORE Mean, bless me, sir, mean! You're a man of mighty honour, we all know, but I'll tell you a secret—the thing is public already.

TRUEMAN I should be proud that all mankind were acquainted with it; I should despise the passion that could make me either ashamed or afraid to own it. 15

RICHMORE Ha, ha, ha, prithee dear Captain, no more of these rodomontados. You may as soon put a standing army upon us.°
I'll tell you another secret—five hundred pound is the least penny.

TRUEMAN Nay, to my knowledge, she has fifteen hundred.

RICHMORE Nay, to my knowledge, she took five. 20

TRUEMAN Took five! How? Where?

RICHMORE In her lap, in her lap, Captain. Where should it be?

TRUEMAN I'm amazed!

RICHMORE So am I—that she could be so unreasonable. Fifteen hundred pound! 'Sdeath! Had she that price from you? 25

TRUEMAN 'Sdeath, I meant her portion.

RICHMORE Why, what have you to do with her portion?

TRUEMAN I loved her up to marriage, by this light.

RICHMORE Marriage! Ha, ha, ha, I love the gypsy for her cunning.
A young, easy, amorous, credulous fellow of two and twenty, was 30
just the game she wanted; I find she presently singled you out from the herd.

TRUEMAN You distract me.

RICHMORE A soldier too, that must follow the wars abroad, and leave her to engagements at home. 35

TRUEMAN Death and furies; I'll be revenged.

RICHMORE Why? What can you do? You'll challenge her, will you?

TRUEMAN Her reputation was spotless when I went over.

RICHMORE So was the reputation of Marshal Boufflers;° but d'ee think, that while you were beating the French abroad, that we were idle at home? No, no, we have had our sieges, our capitulations,° and surrendries and all that—we have cut ourselves out good winter-quarters as well as you.   40

TRUEMAN And are you billeted there?

RICHMORE Look'ee Trueman. You ought to be very trusty to a secret, that has saved you from destruction. In plain terms, I have buried five hundred pounds in that little spot, and I should think it very hard, if you took it over my head.   45

TRUEMAN Not by a lease for life, I can assure you, but I shall—

RICHMORE What! You han't five hundred pounds to give?° Look'ee, since you can make no sport, spoil none. In a year or two, she dwindles to a perfect basset-bank°—everybody may play at it that pleases, and then you may put in for a piece or two.   50

TRUEMAN Dear sir, I could worship you for this.

RICHMORE Not for this, nephew; for I did not intend it, but I came to seek you upon another affair—were not you in the presence° last night?   55

TRUEMAN I was.

RICHMORE Did not you talk to Clelia, my Lady Taper's niece?

TRUEMAN A fine woman.   60

RICHMORE Well! I met her upon the stairs, and handing her to her coach, she asked me, if you were not my nephew, and said two or three warm things that persuade me she likes you. Her relations have interest at Court, and she has money in her pocket.

TRUEMAN But—this devil Aurelia still sticks with me.   65

RICHMORE What then? The way to love in one place with success, is to marry in another with convenience. Clelia has four thousand pound. This applied to your reigning ambition, whether love or advancement, will go a great way. And for her virtue and conduct, be assured, that nobody can give a better account of it than myself.   70

TRUEMAN I am willing to believe from this late accident, that you consult my honour and interest in what you propose, and therefore I am satisfied to be governed.

RICHMORE I see the very lady in the walk—we'll about it.

TRUEMAN I wait on you.   75

    Exeunt

2.[5]

Scene changes to Lord Wouldbe's house

Young Wouldbe, Subtleman and Clearaccount

YOUNG WOULDBE Well, Mr Subtleman, you are sure the will is firm and good in law?

SUBTLEMAN I warrant you, my lord. And for the last words to prove it, here they are. Look'ee Mr Clearaccount, 'Yes'—that is an answer to the question that was put to him, you know, by those   5
about him when he was a-dying. 'Yes' or 'No' he must have said; so we have chosen 'Yes'. 'Yes, I have made my will, as it may be found in the custody of Mr Clearaccount my steward; and I desire it may stand as my last will and testament.' Did you ever hear a dying man's words more to the purpose? An apoplexy! I tell you,   10
my lord had intervals° to the last.

CLEARACCOUNT Ay, but how shall these words be proved?

SUBTLEMAN My lord shall speak 'em now.

YOUNG WOULDBE Shall he, 'faith?

SUBTLEMAN Ay, now—if the corpse ben't buried. Look'ee, sir;   15
these words must be put into his mouth, and drawn out again before us all; and if they won't be his last words then—I'll be perjured.

YOUNG WOULDBE What! Violate the dead! It must not be, Mr Subtleman.   20

SUBTLEMAN With all my heart, sir! But I think you had better violate the dead of a tooth or so, than violate the living of seven thousand pound a year.

YOUNG WOULDBE But is there no other way?

SUBTLEMAN No, sir. Why? D'ee think Mr Clearaccount here will   25
hazard soul and body to swear they are his last words, unless they be made his last words? For my part, sir, I'll swear to nothing but what I see with my eyes come out of a man's mouth.

YOUNG WOULDBE But it looks so unnatural.

SUBTLEMAN What! To open a man's mouth, and put in a bit of   30
paper—this is all.

YOUNG WOULDBE But the body is cold, and his teeth can't be got asunder.

SUBTLEMAN But what occasion has your father for teeth now? I tell you what—I knew a gentleman, three days buried, taken out of his   35
grave, and his dead hand set to his last will—unless somebody

made him sign another afterwards—and I know the estate to be
held by that tenure to this day; and a firm tenure it is; for a dead
hand holds fastest;° and let me tell you, dead teeth will fasten as
hard.   40

YOUNG WOULDBE Well, well; use your pleasure—you understand
the law best.

    Exeunt Subtleman and Clearaccount

What a mighty confusion is brought into families by sudden
deaths! Men should do well to settle their affairs in time—had my
father done this before he was taken ill, what a trouble had he   45
saved us! But he was taken suddenly, poor man.

    Enter Subtleman

SUBTLEMAN Your father still bears you the old grudge, I find. It was
with much struggling he consented; I never knew a man so loth to
speak in my life.

YOUNG WOULDBE He was always a man of few words.   50

SUBTLEMAN Now I may safely bear witness, myself, as the scrivener
there present—I love to do things with a clear conscience.

    Subscribes°

YOUNG WOULDBE But the law requires three witnesses.

SUBTLEMAN O! I shall pick up a couple more, that perhaps
may take my word for't. But is not Mr Clearaccount in your   55
interest?

YOUNG WOULDBE I hope so.

SUBTLEMAN Then he shall be one. A witness in the family goes a
great way; besides these foreign evidences are risen confoundedly
since the wars.° I hope if mine escape the privateers, to make a   60
hundred pound an ear of every head of 'em.° But the steward is
an honest man, and shall save you the charges.

    Exit [Subtleman]

YOUNG WOULDBE (*alone*) The pride of birth, the heats of appetite,
and fears of want, are strong temptations to injustice. But why
injustice? The world has broke all civilities with me; and left me   65
in the eldest state of nature, wild, where force, or cunning first
created right. I cannot say I ever knew a father.° 'Tis true, I
was begotten in his lifetime, but I was posthumous born, and
lived not till he died. My hours indeed I numbered, but ne'er
enjoyed 'em, till this moment. My brother! What is brother?   70
We are all so; and the first two were enemies.° He stands before
me in the road of life to rob me of my pleasures. My senses,
formed by nature for delight, are all alarmed. My sight, my

hearing, taste, and touch, call loudly on me for their objects, and they shall be satisfied.

     Exit

75

3.[1]

Scene, a levée [in Lord Wouldbe's house]

Young Wouldbe dressing, and several gentlemen whispering [to] him by turns, [Clearaccount and Frisure, the Valet, in attendance]

YOUNG WOULDBE [*aside*] Surely the greatest ornament of quality is a clean and a numerous levée. Such a crowd of attendance for the cheap reward of words and promises distinguishes the nobility from those that pay wages to their servants.

    A gentleman whispers

Sir, I shall speak to the Commissioners,° and use all my interest I   5
can assure you, sir.

    Another whispers

Sir, I shall meet some of your Board° this evening; let me see you tomorrow.

    A third whispers

Sir, I'll consider of it. (*Aside*) That fellow's breath stinks of
tobacco. [*Aloud*] O, Mr Comic, your servant.   10

COMIC My lord, I wish you joy; I have something to show your lordship.

YOUNG WOULDBE What is it, pray, sir?

COMIC I have an elegy upon the dead lord, and a panegyric upon the living one. *In utrumque paratus,*° my lord.   15

YOUNG WOULDBE Ha, ha, very pretty, Mr Comic—but pray, Mr Comic, why don't you write plays? It would give one an opportunity of serving you.

COMIC My lord, I have writ one.

YOUNG WOULDBE Was it ever acted?   20

COMIC No, my lord, but it has been a-rehearsing these three years and a half.°

YOUNG WOULDBE A long time. There must be a great deal of business in it surely.

COMIC No, my lord, none at all. I have another play just finished,   25
but that I want a plot for't.°

YOUNG WOULDBE A plot! You should read the Italian, and Spanish plays,° Mr Comic. I like your verses here mightily. Here, Mr Clearaccount.

COMIC (*aside*) Now for five guineas at least.   30

YOUNG WOULDBE Here, give Mr Comic, give him—give him the
Spanish play that lies in the closet window. [*To an officer*] Captain,
can I do you any service?

CAPTAIN Pray, my lord, use your interest with the general for that
vacant commission;° I hope, my lord, the blood I have already lost   35
may entitle me to spill the remainder in my country's cause.

YOUNG WOULDBE All the reason in the world—Captain, you may
depend upon me for all the service I can.

GENTLEMAN I hope your lordship won't forget to speak to the
general about that vacant commission, although I have never made   40
a campaign; yet my lord, my interest in the country can raise me
men; which I think should prefer me to that gentleman whose
bloody disposition frightens the poor people from listing.

YOUNG WOULDBE All the reason in the world, sir; you may depend
upon me for all the service in my power. [*To the captain*] Captain,   45
I'll do your business for you. (*To the gentleman*) Sir, I'll speak to
the general; I shall see him at the House.°
    Enter [an alderman]
O, Mr Alderman—your servant. Gentlemen all, I beg your pardon.
    Exeunt [all but alderman and Frisure]
Mr Alderman, have you any service to command me?

ALDERMAN Your lordship's humble servant—I have a favour to beg.   50
You must know, I have a graceless son, a fellow that drinks and
swears eternally, keeps a whore in every corner of the town. In
short, he's fit for no kind of thing but a soldier—I am so tired of
him, that I intend to throw him into the army, let the fellow be
ruined, if he will.   55

YOUNG WOULDBE I commend your paternal care, sir—can I do you
any service in this affair?

ALDERMAN Yes, my lord. There is a vacant company in Colonel
Whatdeecalum's regiment, and if your lordship would but speak
to the general.   60

YOUNG WOULDBE Has your son ever served?

ALDERMAN Served! Yes, my lord; he's an ensign in the trainbands.°

YOUNG WOULDBE Has he ever signalised his courage?

ALDERMAN Often, often, my lord; but one day particularly, you   65
must know, his captain was so busy shipping off a cargo of cheeses,
that he left my son to command in his place. Would you believe
it my lord? He charged up Cheapside in the front of the buff-coats
with such bravery and courage, that I could not forbear wishing in

the loyalty of my heart, for ten thousand such officers upon the   70
Rhine.° Ah! my lord, we must employ such fellows as him, or we
shall never humble the French king. Now, my lord, if you could
find a convenient time to hint these things to the general.

YOUNG WOULDBE All the reason in the world, Mr Alderman—I'll
do you all the service I can.   75

ALDERMAN You may tell him, he's a man of courage, fit for the
service; and then he loves hardship—he sleeps every other night
in the Round House.°

YOUNG WOULDBE I'll do you all the service I can.

ALDERMAN Then, my lord, he salutes with his pike so very hand-   80
somely, it went to his mistress's heart t'other day. Then he beats
a drum like an angel.

YOUNG WOULDBE (*not taking the least notice of the alderman all this
while, but dressing himself in the glass*) Sir, I'll do you all the service
I can.   85

ALDERMAN But, my lord, the hurry of your lordship's affairs may
put my business out of your head; therefore, my lord, I'll presume
to leave you some memorandum.

YOUNG WOULDBE (*not minding him*) I'll do you all the service I can.

ALDERMAN Pray, my lord, (*pulling him by the sleeve*) give me leave   90
for a memorandum; my glove,° I suppose, will do. Here, my lord,
pray remember me—
    [*Alderman*] *lays his glove upon the table, and exit*[*s*]

YOUNG WOULDBE I'll do you all the service I can. What, is he gone?
'Tis the most rude familiar fellow. Faugh, what a greasy gauntlet
is here.   95
    A purse drops out of the glove
O! no, no, the glove is a clean well-made glove, and the owner of
it—the most respectful person I have seen this morning: he knows
what distance (*chinking the purse*) is due to a man of quality—but
what must I do for this? (*To his valet*) Frisure, do you remember
what the alderman said to me?   100

FRISURE No, my lord, I thought your lordship had.

YOUNG WOULDBE This blockhead thinks a man of quality can mind
what people say—when they do something, 'tis another case; here,
call him back.
    Exit Frisure
He talked something of the general, and his son, and trainbands, I   105
know not what stuff.
    Enter alderman and Frisure

O, Mr Alderman, I have put your memorandum in my pocket.

ALDERMAN O, my lord, you do me too much honour.

YOUNG WOULDBE But Mr Alderman, the business you were talking of; it shall be done, but if you gave a short note of it to my secretary, it would not be amiss. But Mr Alderman, han't you the fellow to this glove? It fits me mighty well (*putting on the glove*)—it looks so like a challenge° to give a man an odd glove, and I would have nothing that looks like emnity between you and I,° Mr Alderman.

ALDERMAN Truly my lord, I intended the other glove for a memorandum to the colonel, but since your lordship has a mind to't—(*gives the glove*)

YOUNG WOULDBE Here Frisure, lead this gentleman to my secretary, and bid him take a note of his business.

ALDERMAN But, my lord, *don't* 'do me all the service you can' now.

YOUNG WOULDBE Well! I *won't* 'do you all the service I can'.

    [*Exeunt Frisure and*] ALDERMAN

These citizens have a strange capacity of soliciting sometimes.°

    Enter Clearaccount

CLEARACCOUNT My lord, here are your tailor, your vintner, your bookseller, and half a dozen more with their bills at the door, and they desire their money.

YOUNG WOULDBE Tell 'em, Mr Clearaccount, that when I was a private gentleman, I had nothing else to do but to run in debt, and now that I have got into a higher rank, I'm so very busy I can't pay it. As for that clamorous rogue of a tailor speak him fair, till he has made up my liveries°—then about a year and a half hence, be at leisure to put him off, for a year and a half longer.

CLEARACCOUNT My lord, there's a gentleman below calls himself Mr Basset—he says your lordship owes him fifty guineas that he won of you at cards.

YOUNG WOULDBE Look'ee sir, the gentleman's money is a debt of honour,° and must be paid immediately.

CLEARACCOUNT Your father thought otherwise, my lord—he always took care to have the poor tradesmen satisfied, whose only subsistence lay in the use of their money, and was used to say, that nothing was honourable but what was honest.

YOUNG WOULDBE My father might say what he pleased—he was a noble man of very singular humours—but in my notion, there are not two things in nature more different than honour and honesty: now your honesty is a little mechanic quality, well enough among citizens, people that do nothing but pitiful mean actions according to law, but your honour flies a much higher pitch, and will do anything that's free and spontaneous, but scorns to level itself to what is only just.

CLEARACCOUNT But I think it a little hard to have these poor people   150
starve for want of their money, and yet pay this sharping rascal fifty guineas.

YOUNG WOULDBE Sharping rascal! What a barbarism that is! Why, he wears as good wigs, as fine linen, and keeps as good company as any at White's;° and between him and I sir, this sharping   155
rascal, as you are pleased to call him, shall make more interest among the nobility with his cards and counters, than a soldier shall with his sword and pistol. Pray let him have fifty guineas immediately.
    Exeunt

3.[2]

Scene, the street [before Lord Wouldbe's house]

Elder Wouldbe, writing in a pocket-book in a riding habit

ELDER WOULDBE 'Monday the . . . 1702.° I arrived safe in London and so concluding my travels.' (*Putting up his book*)
Now welcome country, father, friends,
My brother too (if brothers can be friends),
But above all, my charming fair, my Constance.   5
Through all the mazes of my wandering steps,
Through all the various climes that I have run,°
Her love has been the loadstone of my course,
Her eyes the stars that pointed me the way.
Had not her charms my heart entire possessed,   10
Who knows what Circe's artful voice and look°
Might have ensnared my travelling youth,
And fixed me to enchantment?
        Enter Teague with a portmantle. He throws it down and sits on it
Here comes my fellow traveller. What makes you sit upon the portmantle, Teague? You'll rumple the things.   15

TEAGUE Be me shoul, maishter, I did carry the portmantle till it tired me; and now the portmantle shall carry me till I tire him.°

ELDER WOULDBE And how d'ye like London, Teague, after our
   travels?

TEAGUE Fet,° dear joy,° 'tis the bravest plaase I have sheen in my   20
   peregrinations, exshepting my nown brave shitty of Carrickfergus.°
   [*Sniffing*] Uf, uf, dere ish a very fragrant shmell hereabouts.
   Maishter, shall I run to that paishtry-cook's for shix pennyworths
   of boiled beef?

ELDER WOULDBE Though this fellow travelled the world over he   25
   would never lose his brogue nor his stomach. Why, you cormorant,° so hungry and so early!

TEAGUE Early! Deel tauk° me, maishter, 'tish a great deal more than
   almost twelve a'clock.°

ELDER WOULDBE Thou art never happy unless thy guts be stuffed   30
   up to thy eyes.

TEAGUE O maishter, dere ish a dam way of distance, and the deel a
   bit between.
       Enter Young Wouldbe in a chair, with four or five footmen
       before him, and passes over the stage

ELDER WOULDBE Hey-day—who comes here? with one, two, three,
   four, five footmen! Some young fellow just tasting the sweet vanity   35
   of fortune. Run, Teague, inquire who that is.

TEAGUE Yes, maishter.
       Runs to one of the footmen
   Sir will you give my humble shervish to your maishter and tell him
   to send me word fat naam° ish upon him.

FOOTMAN You would know 'fat naam ish upon him?'   40

TEAGUE Yesh, fet would I.

FOOTMAN Why, what are you, sir?

TEAGUE Be me shoul I am a shentleman bred and born,° and dere
   ish my maishter.

FOOTMAN Then your master would know it?°   45

TEAGUE Arrah, you fool, ish it not the saam ting?

FOOTMAN Then tell your master 'tis the young Lord Wouldbe just
   come to his estate by the death of his father and elder brother.
       Exit footman

ELDER WOULDBE What do I hear?

TEAGUE You hear that you are dead, maishter; fere vil° you please to   50
   be buried?

ELDER WOULDBE But art thou sure it was my brother?

TEAGUE Be me shoul it was him nown self; I know'd him fery well,
   after his man told me.

ELDER WOULDBE The business requires that I be convinced with my   55
own eyes; I'll follow him and know the bottom on't. Stay here till
I return.

TEAGUE Dear maishter, have a care upon yourself. Now they know
you are dead, by my shoul they may kill you.

ELDER WOULDBE Don't fear; none of his servants know me, and I'll   60
take care to keep my face from his sight. It concerns me to conceal
myself, till I know the engines of this contrivance. Be sure you stay
till I come to you; and let nobody know whom you belong to.
      Exit [Elder Wouldbe]

TEAGUE O, O, *hone,*° poor Teague is left all alone.
      Sits on the portmantle. Enter Subtleman and Clearaccount

SUBTLEMAN And you won't swear to the Will?   65

CLEARACCOUNT My conscience tells me I dare not do't with safety.

SUBTLEMAN But if we make it lawful, what should you fear? We now
think nothing against conscience, till the cause be thrown out of
court.

CLEARACCOUNT In you, sir, 'tis no sin, because 'tis the principle of   70
your profession; but in me, sir, 'tis downright perjury indeed. You
can't want witnesses enough, since money won't be wanting—and
you must lose no time; for I heard just now, that the true Lord
Wouldbe was seen in Town, or his ghost.

SUBTLEMAN It was his ghost, to be sure; for a nobleman without an   75
estate is but the shadow of a lord. Well; take no care.° Leave me
to myself; I'm near the Friars,° and ten to one, shall pick up an
evidence.

CLEARACCOUNT Speed you well, sir.
      Exit [Clearaccount]

SUBTLEMAN [*seeing Teague*] There's a fellow that has hunger and the   80
gallows pictured in his face, and looks like my countryman.°—
How now, honest friend, what have you got under you there?

TEAGUE Noting, dear joy.

SUBTLEMAN Nothing? Is it not a portmantle?

TEAGUE That is nothing to you.   85

SUBTLEMAN The fellow's a wit.

TEAGUE Fet am I. My grandfader was an Irish poet.° He did write
a great book of verses concerning the vars between St Patrick and
the wolf-dogs.

SUBTLEMAN Then thou art poor, I'm afraid.   90

TEAGUE Be me shoul, my fole generation ish so. I have nothing but
thish poor portmantle, and dat itshelf ish not my own.

120

SUBTLEMAN Why, who does it belong to?

TEAGUE To my maishter, dear joy.

SUBTLEMAN Then you have a master?   95

TEAGUE Fet have I, but he's dead.

SUBTLEMAN Right! And how do you intend to live?

TEAGUE By eating, dear joy, fen I can get it, and by sleeping fen I
can get none—'tish the fashion of Ireland.

SUBTLEMAN What was your master's name, pray?   100

TEAGUE (aside) I will tell a lee now; but it shall be a true one.—Mac-
fadin, dear joy, was his naam. He vent over vith King Jamish into
France.° (Aside) He was my master once. Deere ish de true lee,
noo.

SUBTLEMAN What employment had he?   105

TEAGUE Je ne sais pas.°

SUBTLEMAN What! you can speak French?

TEAGUE Oui, monsieur.° I did travel France, and Spain, and Italy.
Dear joy, I did kish the Pope's toe, and dat will excuse me all
the sins of my life; and fen I am dead, St Patrick will excuse the   110
rest.°

SUBTLEMAN (aside) A rare fellow for my purpose.—Thou look'st like
an honest fellow; and if you'll go with me to the next tavern, I'll
give thee a dinner, and a glass of wine.

TEAGUE Be me shoul, 'tis dat I wanted, dear joy; come along, I will 115
follow you.

        [Teague] runs out before Subtleman with the portmantle on his
        back. Exit Subtleman. Enter Elder Wouldbe

ELDER WOULDBE My father dead! my birthright lost! How have my
drowsy stars slept o'er my fortune? Ha! [Looking about] my servant
gone! The simple, poor, ungrateful wretch has left me. I took him
up from poverty and want; and now he leaves me just as I found   120
him. My clothes and money too!—but why should I repine? Let
man but view the dangers he has passed, and few will fear what
hazards are to come. That Providence that has secured my life
from robbers, shipwreck, and from sickness, is still the same; still
kind whilst I am just.° My death, I find, is firmly believed; but   125
how it gained so universal credit, I fain would learn. Who comes
here?—honest Mr Fairbank! my father's goldsmith,° a man of
substance and integrity. The alteration of five years' absence, with
the report of my death, may shade me from his knowledge, till I
inquire some news.   130

        Enter Fairbank

Sir, your humble servant.

FAIRBANK (*shunning him*) Sir, I don't know you.

ELDER WOULDBE I intend you no harm, sir; but seeing you come
from my Lord Wouldbe's house, I would ask you a question or
two. Pray what distemper did my lord die of?   135

FAIRBANK I am told it was an apoplexy.

ELDER WOULDBE And pray sir, what does the world say? Is his
death lamented?

FAIRBANK Lamented! my eyes that question should resolve.° Friend,
thou knewest him not; else thy own heart had answered thee.   140

ELDER WOULDBE [*aside*] His grief, methinks, chides my defect of
filial duty.—But I hope, sir, his loss is partly recompensed in the
merits of his successor.

FAIRBANK It might have been; but his eldest son, heir to his virtue
and his honour, was lately and unfortunately killed in Germany.   145

ELDER WOULDBE How unfortunately, sir?

FAIRBANK Unfortunately for him and us. I do remember him. He
was the mildest, humblest, sweetest youth.

ELDER WOULDBE (*aside*) Happy indeed, had been my part in life, if
I had left this human stage, whilst this so spotless and so fair   150
applause had crowned my going off. [*Aloud*] Well, sir.

FAIRBANK But those that saw him in his travels, told such wonders
of his improvement, that the report recalled his father's years; and
with the joy to hear his Hermes praised, he oft would break the
chains of gout and age; and leaping up with strength of greenest   155
youth, cry, 'My Hermes is myself. Methinks I live my sprightly
days again, and I am young in him.'

ELDER WOULDBE (*aside*) Spite of all modesty, a man must own a
pleasure in the hearing of his praise.

FAIRBANK You're thoughtful, sir. Had you any relation to the family   160
we talk of?

ELDER WOULDBE None, sir, beyond my private concern in the
public loss. But pray, sir, what character does the present lord
bear?

FAIRBANK Your pardon, sir. As for the dead, their memories are left   165
unguarded, and tongues may touch them freely; but for the living,
they have provided for the safety of their names by a strong
enclosure of the law. There is a thing called *scandalum magnatum*,°
sir.

ELDER WOULDBE I commend your caution, sir; but be assured I   170
intend not to entrap you. I am a poor gentleman; and having heard

much of the charity of the old Lord Wouldbe, I had a mind to
apply to his son; and therefore enquired his character.

FAIRBANK Alas, sir, things are changed. That house was once
what poverty might go a pilgrimage to seek, and have its pains   175
rewarded. The noble lord, the truly noble lord, held his estate,
his honour, and his house, as if they were only lent upon the
interest of doing good to others. He kept a porter, not to exclude,
but serve the poor. No creditor was seen to guard his going out,
or watch his coming in. No craving eyes, but looks of smiling   180
gratitude. But now, that family, which like a garden fairly kept,
invited every stranger to its fruit and shade, is now run o'er
with weeds. Nothing but wine and revelling within, a crowd of
noisy creditors without, a train of servants insolently proud.
Would you believe it, sir, as I offered to go in just now, the   185
rude porter pushed me back with his staff. I am at this present
(thanks to Providence and my industry) worth twenty thousand
pounds. I pay the fifth part of this to maintain the liberty of the
nation;° and yet this slave, the impudent Swiss slave,° offered to
strike me.   190

ELDER WOULDBE 'Twas hard, sir, very hard. And if they used a man
of your substance so roughly, how will they manage me, that am
not worth a groat?

FAIRBANK I would not willingly defraud your hopes of what may
happen. If you can drink and swear, perhaps—   195

ELDER WOULDBE I shall not pay that price for his lordship's bounty
would it extend to half he's worth. Sir, I give you thanks for your
caution, and shall steer another course.

FAIRBANK Sir, you look like an honest, modest gentleman. Come
home with me; I am as able to give you a dinner as my lord; and   200
you shall be very welcome to eat at my table every day, till you are
better provided.

ELDER WOULDBE (aside) Good man. [Aloud] Sir, I must beg you to
excuse me today. But I shall find a time to accept of your favours,
or at least to thank you for 'em.   205

FAIRBANK Sir, you shall be very welcome whenever you please.
    Exit [Fairbank]

ELDER WOULDBE Gramercy, citizen! Surely if Justice were an
herald,° she would give this tradesman a nobler coat of arms than
my brother. But I delay. I long to vindicate the honour of my
station, and to displace this bold usurper. But one concern   210
methinks is nearer still, my Constance! Should she upon the

rumour of my death, have fixed her heart elsewhere—then I were
dead indeed. But if she still proves true—brother, sit fast.

> I'll shake your strength, all obstacles remove,
> Sustained by Justice and inspired by Love.   215

Exit

3.[3]

Scene, an apartment

Constance, Aurelia

CONSTANCE For Heaven's° sake, cousin, cease your impertinent consolation. It but makes me angry, and raises two passions in me instead
of one. You see I commit no extravagance—my grief is silent enough.
My tears make no noise to disturb anybody. I desire no companion
in my sorrows. Leave me to myself, and you comfort me.   5

AURELIA But, cousin, have you no regard to your reputation? This
immoderate concern for a young fellow—what will the world say?
You lament him like a husband.

CONSTANCE No, you mistake. I have no rule nor method for my
grief; no pomp of black and darkened rooms; no formal month for   10
visits on my bed.° I am content with the slight mourning of a
broken heart; and all my form is tears.

Weeps. Enter Mandrake

MANDRAKE Madam Aurelia, madam, don't disturb her. Everything
must have its vent. 'Tis a hard case to be crossed in one's first love.
(*To Constance*) But you should consider, madam, that we are all   15
born to die, some young, some old.

CONSTANCE Better we all died young, than be plagued with age, as
I am. I find other folks' years are as troublesome to us as our own.

MANDRAKE You have reason, you have cause to mourn. He was the
handsomest man, and the sweetest babe—that I know; though I   20
must confess too, that Ben had much the finer complexion when
he was born. But then Hermes—O yes, Hermes had the shape—
that he had! But of all the infants that I ever beheld with my eyes,
I think Ben had the finest ear, waxwork, perfect waxwork;° and
then he did so sputter at the breast. His nurse° was a hale,   25
well-complexioned sprightly jade as ever I saw; but her milk was
a little too stale; though at the same time 'twas as blue and clear
as a cambric.

AURELIA Do you intend all this, madam, for a consolation to my cousin? 30

MANDRAKE No, no, madam, that's to come. I tell you, fair lady, you have only lost the man; the estate and title are still your own; and this very moment I would salute you Lady Wouldbe, if you pleased.

CONSTANCE Dear madam, your proposal is very tempting; let me 35 but consider till tomorrow, and I'll give you an answer.

MANDRAKE I knew it, I knew it; I said when you were born you would be a lady; I knew it. Tomorrow you say. My lord shall know it immediately.

Exit [Mandrake]

AURELIA What d'ye intend to do, cousin? 40

CONSTANCE To go into the country this moment, to be free from the impertinence of condolence, the persecution of that monster of a man, and that devil of a woman. O Aurelia, I long to be alone. I am become so fond of grief, that I would fly where I might enjoy it all, and have no interruption in my darling sorrow. 45

Enter Elder Wouldbe unperceived

ELDER WOULDBE In tears! perhaps for me! I'll try.

Drops a picture,° and goes back to the entrance, and listens

AURELIA If there be aught in grief delightful, don't grudge me a share.

CONSTANCE No, my dear Aurelia, I'll engross it all. I loved him so, methinks I should be jealous if any mourned his death besides 50 myself. What's here.

Takes up the picture

Ha! see cousin—the very face and features of the man! Sure some officious° angel has brought me this for a companion in my solitude. Now I'm fitted out for sorrow. With this I'll sigh, with this converse, gaze on his image till I grow blind with weeping. 55

AURELIA I'm amazed! how came it here?

CONSTANCE Whether by miracle or human chance, 'tis all alike; I have it here. Nor shall it ever separate from my breast. It is the only thing could give me joy—because it will increase my grief. 60

ELDER WOULDBE [*coming forward*] Most glorious woman! Now I am fond of life.

AURELIA Ha! what's this? Your business, pray sir?

ELDER WOULDBE With this lady.

Goes to Constance, takes her hand and kneels

Here let me worship that perfection, whose virtue might attract the   65
listening angels, and make 'em smile to see such purity, so like
themselves in human shape.

CONSTANCE Hermes?

ELDER WOULDBE Your living Hermes, who shall die yours too.

CONSTANCE Now passion, powerful passion, would bear me like a   70
whirlwind to his arms. But my sex has bounds.° 'Tis wondrous,
sir.

ELDER WOULDBE Most wondrous are the works of fate for man, and
most closely laid is the serpentine line that guides him into
happiness—that hidden power which did permit those arts to cheat   75
me of my birthright, had this surprise of happiness in store, well
knowing that grief is the best preparative for joy.

CONSTANCE I never found the true sweets of love, till this romantic
turn: dead, and alive! my stars are poetical. For Heaven's sake, sir,
unriddle your fortune.   80

ELDER WOULDBE That my dear brother must do; for he made the
enigma.

AURELIA Methinks I stand here like a fool all this while. Would I
had somebody or other to say a fine thing or two to me.

ELDER WOULDBE Madam, I beg ten thousand pardons. I have my   85
excuse in my hand.

AURELIA My lord, I wish you joy.

ELDER WOULDBE Pray madam, don't trouble me with a title till I
am better equipped for it. My peerage would look a little shabby
in these robes.   90

CONSTANCE You have a good excuse, my lord. You can wear better
when you please.

ELDER WOULDBE I have a better excuse, madam. These are the best
I have.

CONSTANCE How, my lord?   95

ELDER WOULDBE Very true, madam; I am at present, I believe, the
poorest peer in England. Heark'ee, Aurelia, prithee lend me a
piece° or two.

AURELIA Ha, ha, ha; poor peer indeed! he wants a guinea.

CONSTANCE I'm glad on't with all my heart!   100

ELDER WOULDBE Why so, madam?

CONSTANCE Because I can furnish you with five thousand.

ELDER WOULDBE Generous woman!

    Enter Trueman

Ha, my friend too!

TRUEMAN I'm glad to find you here, my lord. Here's a current report 105
about Town that you were killed. I was afraid it might reach this
family; so I came to disprove the story by your letter to me by last
post.

AURELIA [*aside to Constance*] I'm glad he's come; now it will be my
turn, cousin. 110

TRUEMAN Now, my lord, I wish you joy; and I expect the same from
you.

ELDER WOULDBE With all my heart; but upon what score?

TRUEMAN The old score, marriage.

ELDER WOULDBE To whom? 115

TRUEMAN To a neighbour lady here. (*Looking at Aurelia*)

AURELIA (*aside*) Impudence! [*Aloud*] The lady mayn't be so near as
you imagine, sir.

TRUEMAN The lady mayn't be so near as you imagine, madam.
*Constance and Elder Wouldbe entertain one another in dumb-
show*

AURELIA Don't mistake me, sir. I did not care if the lady were in 120
Mexico.

TRUEMAN Nor I neither, madam.

AURELIA You're very short, sir.

TRUEMAN The shortest pleasures are the sweetest, you know.

AURELIA Sir, you appear very different to me, from what you were 125
lately.

TRUEMAN Madam, you appear very indifferent to me, to what you
were lately.

AURELIA Strange!

TRUEMAN Miraculous! 130

AURELIA I could never have believed it.

TRUEMAN Nor I, as I hope to be saved.

AURELIA Ill manners!

TRUEMAN Worse.

AURELIA How have I deserved it, sir? 135

TRUEMAN How have I deserved it, madam?

AURELIA What?

TRUEMAN You.

AURELIA Riddles!

TRUEMAN Women!—My lord, you'll hear of me at White's. Fare- 140
well!
[*Trueman*] *runs off*

ELDER WOULDBE What, Trueman gone!

AURELIA Yes.

> *Walks about in disorder*

CONSTANCE Bless me! what's the matter, cousin?

AURELIA Nothing.   145

CONSTANCE Why are you uneasy?

AURELIA Nothing.

CONSTANCE What ails you then?

AURELIA Nothing. I don't love the fellow—yet to be affronted—I
can't bear it.   150

> [*Aurelia*] *bursts out a-crying, and runs off*

CONSTANCE Your friend, my lord, has affronted Aurelia.

ELDER WOULDBE Impossible! His regard to me were sufficient
security for his good behaviour here, though it were in his nature
to be rude elsewhere. She has certainly used him ill.

CONSTANCE Too well rather.   155

ELDER WOULDBE Too well? Have a care madam; that with some
men is the greatest provocation to a slight.

CONSTANCE Don't mistake, my lord—her usage never went further
than mine to you; and I should take it very ill to be abused for it.

ELDER WOULDBE I'll follow him, and know the cause of it.   160

CONSTANCE No, my lord, I'll follow her, and know it. Besides, your
own affairs with your brother require you at present.

> *Exeunt*

4.[1]

Scene, Lord Wouldbe's house

Young Wouldbe and Subtleman

YOUNG WOULDBE Returned! Who saw him? Who spoke with him? He can't be returned.

SUBTLEMAN My lord, he's below at the gate parleying with the porter, who has private orders from me to admit nobody till you send him word, that we may have the more time to settle our affairs. 5

YOUNG WOULDBE 'Tis a hard case, Mr Subtleman, that a man can't enjoy his right without all this trouble.

SUBTLEMAN Ay, my lord, you see the benefit of law now, what an advantage it is to the public for securing of property. Had you not 10 the law o' your side, who knows what devices might be practised to defraud you of your right. But I have secured all. The will is in true form; and you have two witnesses already to swear to the last words of your father.

YOUNG WOULDBE Then you have got another? 15

SUBTLEMAN Yes, yes, a right one, and I shall pick up another time enough before the term; and I have planted three or four constables in the next room, to take care of your brother if he should be boisterous.

YOUNG WOULDBE Then you think we are secure. 20

SUBTLEMAN Ay, ay; let him come now when he pleases. I'll go down and give orders for his admittance.

[Exit Subtleman]

YOUNG WOULDBE Unkind brother! to disturb me thus, just in the swing and stretch of my full fortune! Where is the tie of blood and nature, when brothers will do this? Had he but stayed till 25 Constance had been mine, his presence or his absence had been then indifferent.

Enter Mandrake

MANDRAKE Well, my lord, (*pants as out of breath*) you'll ne'er be satisfied till you have broken my poor heart. I have had such ado yonder about you with Madam Constance. But she's your own. 30

YOUNG WOULDBE How! my own? Ah, my dear helpmate, I'm afraid we are routed in that quarter: my brother's come home.

MANDRAKE Your brother come home! then I'll go travel. (*Going*)

YOUNG WOULDBE Hold, hold, madam, we are all secure: we have
provided for his reception; your nephew Subtleman has stopped   35
up all passages to the estate.

MANDRAKE Ay, Subtleman is a pretty, thriving, ingenious boy.
Little do you think who is the father of him. I'll tell you: Mr
Moabite the rich Jew in Lombard Street.°

YOUNG WOULDBE Moabite the Jew?   40

MANDRAKE You shall hear, my lord. One evening as I was very grave
in my own house, reading the—*Weekly Preparation*°—ay, it was
the *Weekly Preparation*, I do remember particularly well—what
hears me I,° but pat, pat, pat very softly at the door? 'Come in,'
cries I, and presently enters Mr Moabite, followed by a snug chair,   45
the windows close drawn,° and in it a fine young virgin just upon
the point of being delivered. We were all in a great hurly-burly for
a while, to be sure; but our production was a fine boy. I had fifty
guineas for my trouble; the lady was wrapped up very warm,
placed in her chair, and reconveyed to the place she came from.   50
Who she was, or what she was, I could never learn, though my
maid said that the chair went through the Park—but the child was
left with me. The father would have made a Jew on't° presently,
but I swore, if he committed such a barbarity on the infant, that I
would discover all—so I had him brought up a good Christian,°   55
and bound 'prentice to an attorney.

YOUNG WOULDBE Very well!

MANDRAKE Ah, my lord, there's many a pretty fellow in London
that knows as little of their true father and mother as he does; I
have had several such jobs in my time—there was one Scotch   60
nobleman that brought me four in half a year.

YOUNG WOULDBE Four! and how were they all provided for?

MANDRAKE Very handsomely indeed; they were two sons and two
daughters—the eldest son rides in the first troop of Guards, and
the t'other is a very pretty fellow, and his father's *valet de*   65
chambre.°

YOUNG WOULDBE And what is become of the daughters, pray?

MANDRAKE Why one of 'em is a manteau-maker,° and the youngest
has got into the playhouse. Ay, ay, my lord, let Subtleman alone,
I'll warrant he'll manage your brother—adsmylife here's somebody   70
coming. I would not be seen.

YOUNG WOULDBE 'Tis my brother, and he'll meet you upon the
stairs—adso, get into this closet° till he be gone.

Shuts her into the closet. Enter Elder Wouldbe and Subtleman

My brother! dearest brother, welcome!
>   *Runs and embraces him*

ELDER WOULDBE I can't dissemble, sir, else I would return your   75
false embrace.

YOUNG WOULDBE False embrace! still suspicious of me! I thought
that five years' absence might have cooled the unmanly heats of
our childish days: that I am overjoyed at your return, let this
testify—this moment I resign all right and title to your honour,   80
and salute you lord.

ELDER WOULDBE I want not your permission to enjoy my right; here
I am lord and master without your resignation; and the first use I
make of my authority is to discard that rude bull-faced fellow at
the door. Where is my steward?   85
>   *Enter Clearaccount*

Mr Clearaccount, let that pampered sentinel below this minute be
discharged. Brother, I wonder you could feed such a swarm of lazy
idle drones about you, and leave the poor industrious bees that fed
you from their hives, to starve for want. Steward, look to't, if I
have not discharges for every farthing of my father's debts upon   90
my toilet tomorrow morning, you shall follow the tipstaff° I can
assure you.

YOUNG WOULDBE Hold, hold, my lord, you usurp too large a
power, methinks, o'er my family.

ELDER WOULDBE Your family!   95

YOUNG WOULDBE Yes, my family—you have no title to lord it here.
Mr Clearaccount, you know your master.

ELDER WOULDBE How! a combination against me! Brother, take
heed how you deal with one that, cautious of your falsehood,
comes prepared to meet your arts, and can retort your cunning to   100
your infamy.° Your black unnatural designs against my life before
I went abroad my charity can pardon; but my prudence must
remember to guard me from your malice for the future.

YOUNG WOULDBE Our father's weak and fond surmise! which he
upon his death-bed owned; and to recompense me for that   105
injurious unnatural suspicion, he left me sole heir to his estate.
Now, my lord, my house and servants are—at your service.

ELDER WOULDBE Villainy beyond example! have I not letters from
my father, of scarce a fortnight's date, where he repeats his fears
for my return, lest it should again expose me to your hatred?   110

SUBTLEMAN Well, well, these are no proofs, no proofs, my lord; they
won't pass in court against positive evidence—here is your father's

will, *signatum et sigillatum*,° besides his last words to confirm it, to
which I can take my positive oath in any court of Westminster.

ELDER WOULDBE What are you, sir?   115

SUBTLEMAN Of Clifford's Inn,° my lord—I belong to the law.

ELDER WOULDBE Thou art the worm and maggot of the law, bred
in the bruised and rotten parts, and now art nourished on the same
corruption that produced thee.° The English law as planted first,
was like the English oak, shooting its spreading arms around to   120
shelter all that dwelt beneath its shade—but now whole swarms of
caterpillars, like you, hang in such clusters upon every branch, that
the once thriving tree now sheds infectious vermin on our heads.

YOUNG WOULDBE My lord, I have some company above—if your
lordship will drink a glass of wine, we shall be proud of the   125
honour; if not, I shall attend you at any court of judicature
whenever you please to summon me. (*Going*)

ELDER WOULDBE Hold, sir—(*aside*) perhaps my father's dying
weakness was imposed on, and he has left him heir; if so, his will
shall freely be obeyed.—Brother, you say you have a will.   130

SUBTLEMAN Here it is. (*Showing a parchment*)

ELDER WOULDBE Let me see it.

SUBTLEMAN There's no precedent for that, my lord.

ELDER WOULDBE Upon my honour I'll restore it.

YOUNG WOULDBE Upon my honour but you shan't.   135
   Takes it from Subtleman and puts it in his pocket

ELDER WOULDBE This over-caution, brother, is suspicious.

YOUNG WOULDBE Seven thousand pound a year is worth looking after.

ELDER WOULDBE Therefore you can't take it ill that I am a little
inquisitive about it. Have you witnesses to prove my father's dying
words?   140

YOUNG WOULDBE A couple, in the house.

ELDER WOULDBE Who are they?

SUBTLEMAN Witnesses, my lord. 'Tis unwarrantable to enquire into
the merits of the cause out of court—my client shall answer no
more questions.   145

ELDER WOULDBE Perhaps, sir, upon a satisfactory account of his
title, I intend to leave your client to the quiet enjoyment of his
right, without troubling any court with the business. I therefore
desire to know what kind of persons are these witnesses.

SUBTLEMAN (*aside*) Oho, he's a-coming about—I told your lordship   150
already, that I am one—another is in the house, one of my lord's
footmen.

132

ELDER WOULDBE Where is this footman?

YOUNG WOULDBE Forthcoming.

ELDER WOULDBE Produce him.   155

SUBTLEMAN That I shall presently. (*To Young Wouldbe*) The day's
our own, sir. [*To Elder Wouldbe*] But you shall engage first to ask
him no cross questions.°
> *Exit Subtleman*

ELDER WOULDBE I am not skilled in such. But pray brother, did my
father quite forget me, left me nothing?   160

YOUNG WOULDBE Truly, my lord, nothing—he spake but little, left
no legacies.

ELDER WOULDBE 'Tis strange! he was extremely just, and loved me
too—but perhaps—
> *Enter Subtleman with Teague*

SUBTLEMAN My lord, here's another evidence.   165

ELDER WOULDBE Teague!

YOUNG WOULDBE My brother's servant!°
> *They all four stare upon one another*

SUBTLEMAN His servant!

TEAGUE Maishter! see here, maishter, I did get all dish (*chinks money*)
for being an evidensh, dear joy, an be me shoul I will give the half   170
of it to you, if you will give me your permission to maake swear°
against you.

ELDER WOULDBE My wonder is divided between the villainy of the
fact, and the amazement of the discovery. Teague! my very
servant! sure I dream.   175

TEAGUE Fet, dere is no dreaming in the cashe—I'm sure the croon
pieceish are awake, for I have been taaking° with dem dish half hour.

YOUNG WOULDBE [*to Subtleman*] Ignorant, unlucky° man, thou hast
ruined me; why had not I a sight of him before?

SUBTLEMAN I thought the fellow had been too ignorant to be a knave.   180

TEAGUE Be me shoul, you lee, dear joy—I can be a knave as well as
you, fen I think it conveniency.

ELDER WOULDBE Now brother! Speechless! Your oracle too silenced!
Is all your boasted fortune sunk to the guilty blushing for a crime?
But I scorn to insult—let disappointment be your punishment. But   185
for your lawyer there—Teague, lay hold of him.

SUBTLEMAN Let none dare to attach me without a legal warrant.

TEAGUE Attach! no dear joy, I cannot attach you—but I can catch
you by the troat, after the fashion of Ireland.
> *Takes Subtleman by the throat*

SUBTLEMAN An assault! An assault!   190

TEAGUE No, no, 'tish nothing but choking, nothing but choking.

ELDER WOULDBE Hold him fast Teague. (*To Young Wouldbe*) Now
  sir, because I was your brother you would have betrayed me; and
  because I am your brother, I forgive it—dispose yourself as you
  think fit; I'll order Mr Clearaccount to give you a thousand   195
  pounds. Go take it, and pay me by your absence.

YOUNG WOULDBE I scorn your beggarly benevolence. Had my
  designs succeeded, I would not have allowed you the weight of a
  wafer, and therefore will accept none. As for that lawyer, he
  deserves to be pilloried, not for his cunning in deceiving you, but 200
  for his ignorance in betraying me. The villain has defrauded me of
  seven thousand pounds a year. Farewell. (*Going*)
      *Enter Mandrake out of the closet, runs to Young Wouldbe and
      kneels*

MANDRAKE My lord! my dear Lord Wouldbe, I beg you ten
  thousand pardons.

YOUNG WOULDBE What offence hast thou done to me?   205

MANDRAKE An offence the most injurious. I have hitherto concealed
  a secret in my breast to the offence of justice, and the defrauding
  your lordship of your true right and title. You Benjamin Wouldbe
  with the crooked back, art the eldest-born, and true heir to the
  estate and dignity.   210

ALL How!

TEAGUE Arah, how?

MANDRAKE None, my lord, can tell better than I, who brought you
  both into the world. My deceased lord, upon the sight of your
  deformity, engaged me by a considerable reward, to say you were   215
  the last born, that the beautiful twin, likely to be the greater
  ornament to the family, might succeed him in his honour. This
  secret my conscience has long struggled with. Upon the news that
  you were left heir to the estate, I thought justice was satisfied, and
  I was resolved to keep it a secret still; but by strange chance   220
  overhearing what passed just now, my poor conscience was racked,
  and I was forced to declare the truth.

YOUNG WOULDBE By all my forward hopes I could have sworn it.
  I found the spirit of eldership in my blood. My pulses beat, and
  swelled for seniority. (*Foppishly*) Mr Hermes Wouldbe—I'm your 225
  most humble servant.

ELDER WOULDBE Hermes is my name, my christian name; of which
  I am prouder than of all titles that honour gives, or flattery

bestows. But thou, vain bubble, puffed up with the empty breath
of that more empty woman; to let thee see how I despise thy pride,   230
I'll call thee 'Lord', dress thee up in titles like a King at Arms;°
you shall be blazoned round like any church in Holland; thy
pageantry shall exceed the Lord Mayor's; and yet this Hermes,
plain Hermes, shall despise thee.

SUBTLEMAN Well, well, this is nothing to the purpose. Mistress, will   235
you make an affidavit of what you have said, before a Master in
Chancery?°

MANDRAKE That I can, though I were to die the next minute after
it.

TEAGUE Den, dear joy, you would be dam the nex minute after dat.   240

ELDER WOULDBE All this is trifling; I must purge my house of this
nest of villainy at once. Here Teague.
        Whispers to Teague
Go, make haste!

TEAGUE Dat I can.
        As he runs out Young Wouldbe stops him

YOUNG WOULDBE Where are you going, sir?   245

TEAGUE Only for a pot of ale, dear joy, for you and my maishter to
drink friends.

YOUNG WOULDBE You lie, sirrah.
        Pushes him back

TEAGUE Fet, I do so.

ELDER WOULDBE What! Violence to my servant! Nay, then I'll force   250
him a passage.
        Draws

SUBTLEMAN [*to the constables off-stage*] An assault, an assault upon
the body of a peer—within there!
        *Enter three or four constables, one of 'em with a black patch on
        his eye. They disarm Elder Wouldbe, and secure Teague*

ELDER WOULDBE This plot was laid for my reception. Unhand me,
Constable!   255

YOUNG WOULDBE Have a care, Mr Constable; the man is mad; he's
possessed with an odd frenzy, that he's my brother, and my elder
too. So because I would not very willingly resign my house and
estate, he attempted to murder me.

SUBTLEMAN [*pointing to Teague*] Gentlemen, take care of that fellow: 260
he made an assault upon my body, *vi et armis.*°

TEAGUE Arah, fat is dat 'wy at armish'?

SUBTLEMAN No matter, sirrah; I shall have you hanged.

TEAGUE Hanged! dat is nothing, dear joy; we are used to't.

ELDER WOULDBE Unhand me, villains, or by all—   265

TEAGUE Have a caar, dear maishter; don't swear. We shall be had in
the Croon Offish.° (*Looking about on them that hold him*) You know
dere ish sharpers about us.

YOUNG WOULDBE Mr Constable, you know your directions. Away
with 'em.   270

ELDER WOULDBE Hold—

CONSTABLE No, no; force him away.

> *They all hurry off. Young Wouldbe and Mandrake remain*

YOUNG WOULDBE Now, my dear prophetess, my sibyl.° By all my
dear desires and ambitions, I do believe you have spoken the truth.
I am the elder.   275

MANDRAKE No, no, sir, the Devil a word on't is true. I would not
wrong my conscience neither. For, faith and troth, as I am an
honest woman, you were born above three-quarters-of-an-hour
after him; but I don't much care if I do swear that you are the
eldest. What a blessing it was, that I was in the closet at that pinch. 280
Had I not come out that moment, you would have sneaked off;
your brother had been in possession, and then we had lost all; but
now you are established. Possession gets you money, that gets you
law, and law, you know. Down on your knees, sirrah, and ask me
blessing.   285

YOUNG WOULDBE No, my dear 'mother', I'll give thee a blessing, a
rent-charge° of five hundred pound a year, upon what part of the
estate you will, during your life.

MANDRAKE Thank you, my lord. That five hundred a year will
afford me a leisurely life, and a handsome retirement in the   290
country, where I mean to repent me of my sins, and die a good
Christian. For Heaven knows, I am old, and ought to bethink me
of another life. Have you none of the cordial left that we had in
the morning?

YOUNG WOULDBE Yes, yes, we'll go to the fountain-head.   295

> *Exeunt*

4.[2]

Scene, the street

Enter Teague

TEAGUE Deel tauke me but dish ish a most shweet business indeed; maishters play the fool, and shervants must shuffer for it. I am prishoner in the constable's house, be me shoul, and shent abrode to fetch some bail for my maishter; but foo shall bail° poor Teague agra?   5

Enter Constance

O, dere ish my maishter's old love. Indeed, I fear dish bishness will spoil his fortune.

CONSTANCE Who's here? Teague!

He turns from her

TEAGUE [*aside*] Deel tauke her, I did tought she could not know me agen.°   10

Constance goes about to look him in the face. He turns from her

Dish ish not shivil, be me shoul, to know a shentleman fither he will or no.

CONSTANCE Why this, Teague? What's the matter? are you ashamed of me or yourself, Teague?

TEAGUE Of bote, be me shoul.   15

CONSTANCE How does your master, sir?

TEAGUE Very well, dear joy, and in prishon.

CONSTANCE In prison! how, where?

TEAGUE Why, in the little Bashtile° yonder at the end of the street.

CONSTANCE Show me the way immediately.   20

TEAGUE Fet, I can show you the hoose yonder. Shee yonder; be me shoul, I she his faace yonder, peeping troo the iron glash window.°

CONSTANCE I'll see him though a dungeon were his confinement.

[Constance] runs out

TEAGUE Ah—auld kindnesh, be me shoul, cannot be forgotten. Now if my maishter had but grash° enough to get her wit child, her   25 word would go for two;° and she would bail him and I bote.

Exit

4.[3]

Scene, a room miserably furnished, Elder Wouldbe sitting and writing

ELDER WOULDBE
   The Tower confines the great,°
    The sponging-house the poor.
   Thus there are degrees of state
    That ev'n the wretched must endure.

   Virgil, though cherish'd in courts,   5
    Relates but a splenetic tale;°
   Cervantes revels and sports,
    Although he writ in a goal.°
Then hang reflections.
  Starts up
Tell the Lieutenant of the Tower° that I would speak with him. 10
  Enter constable

CONSTABLE Ay, ay the man is mad. Lieutenant o'th' Tower! Ha, ha, ha; would you could make your words good, master.

ELDER WOULDBE Why, am not I a prisoner there? I know it by the stately apartments. What is that, pray, that hangs streaming down upon the wall yonder? 15

CONSTABLE Yonder? 'Tis cobweb, sir.

ELDER WOULDBE 'Tis false, sir; 'tis as fine tapestry as any in Europe.

CONSTABLE The Devil it is.

ELDER WOULDBE Then your damask° bed, here; the flowers are so bold,° I took 'em for embroidery; and then the headwork! *Point de* 20 *Venise*,° I protest.

CONSTABLE As good Kidderminster° as any in England, I must confess; and though the sheets be a little soiled, yet I can assure you, sir, that many an honest gentleman has lain in them.

ELDER WOULDBE Pray sir, what did those two Indian pieces° cost 25 that are fixed up in the corner of the room?

CONSTABLE Indian pieces? What the Devil, sir, they are my old jack boots, my militia boots.

ELDER WOULDBE I took 'em for two china jars, upon my word. But heark'ee, friend, art thou content that these things should be as 30 they are?

CONSTABLE Content! ay, sir.

ELDER WOULDBE Why then should I complain?
>   *One calls within*

[SERVANT *off-stage*] Mr Constable, here's a woman will force her way
>   upon us. We can't stop her.   35

CONSTABLE Knock her down then, knock her down; let no woman
>   come up, the man's mad enough already.
>   *Enter Constance*

CONSTANCE Who dares oppose me?
>   *Throws him a handful of money*

CONSTABLE Not I truly madam.
>   *Gathers up the money*

ELDER WOULDBE My Constance! my guardian angel here! Then   40
>   naught can hurt me.

CONSTABLE Heark'ee, sir, you may suppose the bed to be a damask
>   bed for half-an-hour if you please.

CONSTANCE No, no, sir, your prisoner must along with me.

CONSTABLE Ay? Faith the woman's madder than the man.   45
>   *Enter Trueman and Teague*

ELDER WOULDBE Ha! Trueman too! I'm proud to think that many
>   a prince has not so many true friends in his palace, as I have here
>   in my prison. Two such—

TEAGUE Tree, be me shoul.°

TRUEMAN My lord, just as I heard of your confinement, I was going   50
>   to make myself a prisoner. Behold the fetters. I had just bought
>   the wedding ring.

CONSTANCE I hope they are golden fetters,° Captain!

TRUEMAN They weigh four thousand pound, madam, besides the
>   purse,° which is worth a million. My lord, this very evening was   55
>   I to be married; but the news of your misfortune has stopped me.
>   I would not gather roses in a wet hour.

ELDER WOULDBE Come, the weather shall be clear; the thoughts of
>   your good fortune will make me easy, more than my own can do,
>   if purchased by your disappointment.   60

TRUEMAN Do you think, my lord, that I can go to the bed of pleasure
>   whilst you lie in a hovel? Here, where is this constable—how dare
>   you do this, insolent rascal?

CONSTABLE Insolent rascal! do you know who you speak to, sir?

TRUEMAN Yes, sirrah, don't I call you by your proper name? How   65
>   dare you confine a peer of the realm?°

CONSTABLE Peer of the realm? you may give good words though,° I
>   hope.

ELDER WOULDBE Ay, ay, Mr Constable is in the right—he did but
his duty; I suppose he had twenty guineas for his pains.   70

CONSTABLE No, I had but ten.

[*Constance talks quietly to the constable*]

ELDER WOULDBE Heark'ee Trueman, this fellow must be soothed—
he'll be of use to us; I must employ you too in this affair with my
brother.

TRUEMAN Say no more, my lord, I'll cut his throat—'tis but flying   75
the kingdom.

ELDER WOULDBE No, no, 'twill be more revenge to worst him at his
own weapons. Could I but force him out of his garrison, that I
might get into possession, his claim would vanish immediately.
Does my brother know you?   80

TRUEMAN Very little, if at all.

ELDER WOULDBE Heark'ee—(*whispers*)

TRUEMAN It shall be done. Look'ee Constable, you're drawn into a
wrong cause, and it may prove your destruction if you don't
change sides immediately—we desire no favour but the use of your   85
coat, wig, and staff,° for half-an-hour.

CONSTABLE Why truly sir, I understand now, by this gentlewoman
that I know to be our neighbour, that he is a lord, and I heartily
beg his worship's pardon, and if I can do your honour any service,
your grace° may command me.   90

ELDER WOULDBE I'll reward you, but we must have the black patch
for the eye too.

TEAGUE I can give your lordship wan—here fet, 'tis a plaishter for a
shore finger, and I have worn it but twice.

CONSTANCE But pray, Captain, what was your quarrel at Aurelia   95
today?

TRUEMAN With your permission, madam, we'll mind my lord's
business at present; when that's done, we'll mind the lady's. My
lord, I shall make an excellent constable—I never had the honour
of a civil employment before; we'll equip ourselves in another   100
place. [*To constable*] Here you Prince of Darkness, have you ne'er
a better room in your house? These iron grates° frighten the lady.

CONSTABLE I have a handsome neat parlour below, sir.

TRUEMAN Come along then, you must conduct us—we don't intend
to be out of your sight—(*aside*) that you mayn't be out of ours.   105

Exeunt

4.[4]

Scene changes to an apartment

Enter Aurelia in a passion, Richmore following

AURELIA Follow me not—age and deformity with quiet were prefer-
able to this vexatious persecution; for Heaven's sake, Mr Richmore,
what have I ever shown to vindicate this presumption of yours?

RICHMORE You show it now madam—your face, your wit, your
shape, are all temptations to undergo even the rigour of your   5
disdain, for the bewitching pleasure of your company.

AURELIA Then be assured, sir, you shall reap no other benefit by my
company, and if you think it a pleasure to be constantly slighted,
ridiculed, and affronted, you shall have admittance to such entertainment whenever you will.   10

RICHMORE I take you at your word, madam—I am armed with
submission against all the attacks of your severity, and your
ladyship shall find that my resignation can bear much longer than
your rigour can inflict.

AURELIA That is in plain terms, your sufficiency° will presume much 15
longer than my honour can resist. Sir, you might have spared the
unmannerly declaration to my face, having already taken care to
let me know your opinion of my virtue, by your impudent
settlement, proposed by Mrs Mandrake.

RICHMORE By those fair eyes I'll double the proposal; this soft, this 20
white, this powerful hand (*takes her hand*) shall write its own
conditions.

AURELIA Then it shall write this—(*strikes him*) and if you like the
terms you shall have more another time.

    Exit [Aurelia]

RICHMORE Death and madness! a blow! Twenty thousand pound   25
sterling for one night's revenge upon her dear proud disdainful
person! Am I rich as many a sovereign prince, wallow in wealth,
yet can't command my pleasure? Woman! If there be power in
gold, I yet shall triumph o'er thy pride.

    Enter Mandrake

MANDRAKE O my troth, and so you shall, if I can help it.   30

RICHMORE Madam, madam, here, here, here's money, gold, silver,
take, take, all, all—my rings too; all shall be yours—make me but
happy in this presumptuous beauty, I'll make thee rich as avarice
can crave; if not, I'll murder thee, and myself too.

MANDRAKE Your bounty is too large, too large indeed sir.   35

RICHMORE Too large! no, 'tis beggary without her. Lordships,
    manors, acres, rents, tithes, and trees, all, all shall fly for my dear
    sweet revenge.

MANDRAKE Say no more, this night I'll put you in a way.

RICHMORE This night!   40

MANDRAKE The lady's aunt is very near her time—she goes abroad
    this evening a-visiting; in the meantime I send to your mistress,
    that her aunt is fallen in labour at my house. She comes in a hurry,
    and then—

RICHMORE Shall I be there to meet her?   45

MANDRAKE Perhaps.

RICHMORE In a private room?

MANDRAKE Mum.

RICHMORE No creature to disturb us?

MANDRAKE Mum, I say, but you must give me your word not to   50
    ravish her; nay, I can tell you, she won't be ravished.

RICHMORE Ravish! let me see, I'm worth five thousand pound a year,
    twenty thousand guineas in my pocket, and may not I force a toy
    that's scarce worth fifteen hundred pound? I'll do't.

> Her beauty sets my heart on fire, beside   55
> The injurious blow has set on fire my pride:
> The bare fruition were not worth my pain,
> The joy will be to humble her disdain;
> Beyond enjoyment will the transport last
> In triumph when the ecstasy is past.   60

Exeunt

5.[1]

Scene, Lord Wouldbe's house
Young Wouldbe alone

YOUNG WOULDBE Show me that proud stoic° that can bear success
and champagne—philosophy can support us in hard fortune, but
who can have patience in prosperity? The learned may talk what
they will of human bodies, but I am sure there is not one atom in
mine, but what is truly epicurean.° My brother is secured, I   5
guarded with my friends, my lewd and honest midnight friends.
[*Calling*] Holla, who waits there?
    Enter servant

SERVANT My lord?

YOUNG WOULDBE A fresh battalion of bottles to reinforce the
cistern—are the ladies come?   10

SERVANT Half-an-hour ago, my lord—they're below in the bathing
chamber.

YOUNG WOULDBE Where did you light on 'em?

SERVANT One in the passage at the old playhouse,° my lord—I found
another very melancholy paring her nails by Rosamond's Pond°—   15
and a couple I got at the Chequer ale-house in Holborn;° the two
last came to Town yesterday in a west-country waggon.

YOUNG WOULDBE Very well, order Baconface to hasten supper—
and d'y' hear?—and bid the Swiss admit no stranger without
acquainting me.   20
    Exit servant
Now Fortune I defy thee—this night's my own at least.
    Enter servant

SERVANT My lord, here's the constable below with the black eye, and
he wants to speak with your lordship in all haste.

YOUNG WOULDBE Ha! the constable! should Fortune jilt me now?
Bid him come up—I fear some cursed chance to thwart me.   25
    Enter Trueman in the constable's clothes

TRUEMAN Ah, my lord, here is sad news—your brother is—

YOUNG WOULDBE Got away, made his escape, I warrant you.

TRUEMAN Worse, worse, my lord.

YOUNG WOULDBE Worse, worse! What can be worse?

TRUEMAN I dare not speak it.   30

YOUNG WOULDBE Death and hell fellow, don't distract me!

TRUEMAN He's dead.

YOUNG WOULDBE Dead!

TRUEMAN Positively.

YOUNG WOULDBE *Coup de grace, ciel gramerci.*°   35

TRUEMAN (*aside*) Villain, I understand you.

YOUNG WOULDBE But how, how, Mr Constable? Speak it aloud—
kill me with the relation.

TRUEMAN I don't know how—the poor gentleman was very melancholy upon his confinement, and so he desired me to send for a   40
gentlewoman that lives hard by here—mayhap your worship may
know her.

YOUNG WOULDBE At the gilt balcony in the square.

TRUEMAN The very same, a smart woman truly. I went for her
myself, but she was 'otherwise engaged'—not she truly: she would 45
not come. Would you believe it, my lord?—at hearing of this the
poor man was like to drop down dead.

YOUNG WOULDBE Then he was but likely to drop dead.

TRUEMAN Would it were no more. Then I left him, and coming
about two hours after, I found him hanged in his sword-belt.   50

YOUNG WOULDBE Hanged!

TRUEMAN Dangling.

YOUNG WOULDBE *Le coup d'éclat!*° done like the noblest Roman of
'em all!° But are you sure he's past all recovery? Did you send for
no surgeon to bleed him?   55

TRUEMAN No, my lord, I forgot that—but I'll send immediately.

YOUNG WOULDBE No, no, Mr Constable, 'tis too late now, too
late—and the lady would not come, you say?

TRUEMAN Not a step would she stir.

YOUNG WOULDBE Inhuman, barbarous. [*Aside*] Dear, delicious   60
woman thou now art mine.—Where is the body, Mr Constable? I
must see it.

TRUEMAN By all means, my lord—it lies in my parlour. There's a
power of company come in, and among the rest one . . . one . . . one
. . . Trueman I think they call him, a devilish hot fellow—he had   65
like to have pulled the house down about our ears, and swears—I
told him he should pay for his swearing—he gave me a slap in the
face, said he was in the army, and had a commission for't.

YOUNG WOULDBE Captain Trueman!—a blustering kind of rakehelly officer.   70

TRUEMAN Ay, my lord, one of those scoundrels that we pay wages
to for being knocked o'th' head for us.

YOUNG WOULDBE Ay, ay, one of those fools that have only brains
to be knocked out.

TRUEMAN (*aside*) Son of a whore. [*Aloud.*] He's a plaguy impudent   75
fellow, my lord; he swore that you were the greatest villain upon
the earth.

YOUNG WOULDBE Ay, ay; but he durst not say that to my face, Mr
Constable.

TRUEMAN No, no, hang him, he said it behind your back, to be sure;   80
and he swore, moreover—have a care, my lord—he swore that he
would cut your throat whenever he met you.

YOUNG WOULDBE Will you swear that you heard him say so?

TRUEMAN Heard him! ay, as plainly as you hear me. He spoke the
very words that I speak to your lordship.   85

YOUNG WOULDBE Well, well, I'll manage him. But now I think on't,
I won't go see the body. It will but increase my grief. Mr Constable,
do you send for the coroner: they must find him *non compos*.° He
was mad before, you know. Here's something for your trouble.
         Gives money

TRUEMAN Thank your honour. But pray, my lord, have a care of that   90
Trueman; he swears that he'll cut your throat; and he will do't,
my lord, he will do't.

YOUNG WOULDBE Never fear, never fear.

TRUEMAN But he swore it, my lord, and he will certainly do't. Pray
have a care.   95
         Exit [*Trueman*]

YOUNG WOULDBE Well, well—so—the Devil's in't if I ben't the
eldest now. What a pack of civil relations have I had here! My
father takes a fit of the apoplexy, makes a face, and goes off one
way; my brother takes a fit of the spleen, makes a face, and goes
off t'other way. Well, I must own he has found the way to mollify   100
me, and I do love him now with all my heart—since he was so
very civil to justle into the world before me, I think he did very
civilly to justle out of it before me. But now my joys! [*Calling*]
Without there—hollo—take off the inquistion of the gate; the heir
may now enter unsuspected.   105
The wolf is dead, the shepherds may go play;
Ease follows care; so rolls the world away.
'Tis a question whether adversity or prosperity makes the most poets.
         Enter servant

SERVANT My lord, a footman brought this letter, and waits for an
answer.   110

YOUNG WOULDBE Nothing from the Elysian fields,° I hope. (*Opening the letter*) What do I see—'Constance'? Spells and magic in every letter of the name. Now for the sweet contents. 'My Lord, I'm pleased to hear of your happy change of fortune, and shall be glad to see your lordship this evening to wish you joy. Constance.'   115
Now the Devil's in this Mandrake; she told me this afternoon that the wind was chopping about; and has it got into the warm corner already? [*To servant*] Here, my coach-and-six to the door. I'll visit my sultana in state. As for the seraglio below stairs, you, my bashaws, may possess 'em.°   120

    Exeunt

5.[2]

    Scene, the street [*before Mandrake's house*]

    Teague with a lantern. Trueman in the constable's habit following

TRUEMAN Blockhead, thou hast led us out of the way; we have certainly passed the constable's house.

TEAGUE Be me shoul, dear joy, I am never oot of my ways; for poor Teague has been a vanderer ever since he vas borned.

TRUEMAN Hold up the lantern. What sign° is that? The St Alban's   5
Tavern!° Why, you blundering fool, you have led me directly to St James's Square, when you should have gone towards Soho.°

    Shrieking within

Hark! What noise is that over the way? A woman's cry!

TEAGUE Fet is it—shome daumsel in distress I believe, that has no mind to be relieved.   10

TRUEMAN I'll use the privilege of my office to know what the matter is.

TEAGUE Hold, hold, maishter Captain; be me fet, dat ish not the way home.

[AURELIA] (*within*) Help, help, murder, help.

TRUEMAN Ha! here must be mischief. Within there, open the door   15
in the King's name,° or I'll force it open. Here, Teague, break down the door.

    Teague takes the staff, thumps at the door

TEAGUE Deel tauke him, I have knock so long as I am able. Arah, maishter, get a great long ladder to get in the window of the firsht room, and sho open the door, and let in yourshelf.   20

[AURELIA] (*within*) Help, help, help.

TRUEMAN Knock harder; let's raise the mob.

TEAGUE O maishter, I have tink just now of a brave invention to
maake dem come out; and be St Patrick, dat very bushiness did
maake my nown shelf and my fader run like de Devil out of mine   25
nown hoose in my nown countrey. Be me shoul, set the hoose
a-fire.

        Enter the mob

MOB What's the matter, Master Constable?

TRUEMAN Gentlemen, I command your assistance in the King's
name, to break into the house. There is murder cried within.   30

MOB Ay, ay, break open the door.

        Mandrake [appears] at the balcony°

MANDRAKE What noise is that below?

TEAGUE Arah, vat noise ish dat above?

MANDRAKE Only a poor gentlewoman in labour; 'twill be over
presently. Here, Mr Constable, there's something for you to drink.   35

        Throws down a purse. Teague takes it up

TEAGUE (*going*) Come maishter, we have no more to shay, be me
shoul. Arah, if you vill play de constable right now, fet you vill
come away.

TRUEMAN No, no, there must be villainy by this bribe. Who lives in
this house?   40

MOB A midwife, a midwife—'tis none of our business. Let us be
gone.

        Aurelia [appears] at the window

AURELIA Gentlemen, dear gentlemen, help; a rape, a rape, villainy.

TRUEMAN Ha! That voice I know. Give me the staff; I'll make a
breach, I warrant you.   45

        Breaks open the door, and all go in

5.[3]

        Scene changes to the inside of the house

        Enter Trueman and mob°

TRUEMAN Gentlemen, search all about the house; let not a soul
escape.

        *Enter Aurelia, running, with her hair about her ears, and out of
        breath*

AURELIA Dear Mr Constable—had you—stayed—but a moment longer, I had been ruined.

TRUEMAN [*aside*] Aurelia! [*Aloud*]—Are you safe madam?   5

AURELIA Yes, yes, I am safe—I think—but with enough ado. He's a devilish strong fellow.

TRUEMAN Where is the villain that attempted it?

AURELIA Pshaw—never mind the villain—look out the woman of the house, the devil, the monster, that decoyed me hither.   10

Enter Teague, haling in Mandrake by the hair

TEAGUE Be me shoul I have taken my shaare of the plunder. Let me shee fat I have gotten.

Takes her to the light

Ububboo, a witch, a witch; the very saame witch dat would swaar my maishter was de youngest.

TRUEMAN [*aside*] How! Mandrake! This was the luckiest disguise.   15
[*To Mandrake*] Come, my dear Proserpine,° I'll take care of you.

MANDRAKE Pray, sir, let me speak with you.

TRUEMAN No, no, I'll talk with you before a magistrate. A cart, Bridewell°—you understand me. Teague, let her be your prisoner—I'll wait on this lady.   20

AURELIA Mr Constable, I'll reward you.

TEAGUE It ish convenient noo by the law of armsh, that I search my prishoner, for fear she may have some pocket-pishtols. Dere ish a joak for you.°

Searches her pockets

MANDRAKE Ah! don't use an old woman so barbarously.   25

TEAGUE Dear joy, den fy vere you an old woman? Dat is your falt, not mine, joy! Uboo, here ish nothing but scribble scrabble papers, I tink.

Pulls out a handful of letters

TRUEMAN Let me see 'em; they may be of use.

Looks over the letters

'For Mr Richmore.' Ay! does he traffic hereabouts?   30

AURELIA That is the villain that would have abused me.

TRUEMAN Ha! then he has abused you. Villain indeed! Was his name Richmore, mistress? a lusty handsome man?

AURELIA Ay, ay, the very same; a lusty ugly fellow.

TRUEMAN Let me see—(*opens a letter*) whose scrawl is this? (*Aside*)   35
Death and confusion to my sight; Clelia! my bride! His whore. I've passed a precipice unseen, which to look back upon, shivers me with terror. This night, this very moment, had not my friend been

in confinement, had not I worn this dress, had not Aurelia been in
danger, had not Teague found this letter, had the least minutest   40
circumstance been omitted, what a monster° had I been? [*Aloud*]
Mistress, is this same Richmore in the house still think'ee?

AURELIA 'Tis very probable he may.

TRUEMAN Very well. Teague, take these ladies over to the tavern and
stay there till I come to you. (*To Aurelia*) Madam, fear no   45
injury—your friends are near you.

AURELIA What does he mean!

TEAGUE Come, dear joy, I vill give you a pot of wine, out of your
own briberies here.

> *Teague hales out Mandrake.* [*Exeunt*] *Aurelia and mob. True-*
> *man remains. Enter Richmore*

RICHMORE [*aside*] Since my money won't prevail on this cross   50
fellow, I'll try what my authority can do. [*Aloud*] What's the
meaning of this riot, Constable? I have the commission of the
peace,° and can command you. Go about your business, and leave
your prisoners with me.

TRUEMAN No sir, the prisoners shall go about their business, and I'll 55
be left with you. Look'ee, master, we don't use to make up these
matters before company.° So you and I must be in private a little.
You say sir, that you are a justice of peace.

RICHMORE Yes sir, I have my commission in my pocket.

TRUEMAN I believe it. Now sir, one good turn deserves another. And   60
if you will promise to do me a kindness, why you shall have as
good as you bring.

RICHMORE What is it?

TRUEMAN You must know sir, there is a neighbour's daughter that
I had a woundy kindness for. She had a very good repute all over   65
the parish, and might have married very handsomely (that I must
say). But I don't know how—we came together after a very kindly
natural manner, and I swore (that I must say) I did swear
confoundedly, that I would marry her. But I don't know how—I
never cared for marrying of her since.   70

RICHMORE How so?

TRUEMAN Why, because I did my business without it: that was the
best way, I thought. The truth is, she has some foolish reasons to
say she's with child, and threatens mainly to have me taken up
with a warrant, and brought before a justice of peace.° Now sir,   75
I intend to come before you, and I hope your worship will bring
me off.°

RICHMORE Look'ee sir, if the woman prove with child, and you
swore to marry her, you must do't.

TRUEMAN Ay master; but I am for liberty and property. I vote for   80
parliament-men. I pay taxes, and truly I don't think matrimony
consistent with the liberty of the subject.°

RICHMORE But in this case, sir, both law and justice will oblige you.

TRUEMAN Why if it be the law of the land—I found a letter here. I
think it is for your worship.   85

RICHMORE Ay sir; how came you by it?

TRUEMAN By a very strange accident truly. [*Looking at the letter*]
'Clelia'—she says here you swore to marry her. Eh! Now sir, I
suppose that what is law for a petty-constable may be law for a
justice of peace.   90

RICHMORE [*aside*] This is the oddest fellow—

TRUEMAN Here was the t'other lady that cried out so. I warrant now,
if I were brought before you for ravishing a woman—the gallows
would ravish me for't.

RICHMORE But I did not ravish her.   95

TRUEMAN (*aside*) That I'm glad to hear. I wanted to be sure of that.

RICHMORE [*aside*] I don't like this fellow.—Come sir, give me my
letter, and go about your business; I have no more to say to you.

TRUEMAN But I have something to say to you. (*Coming up to him*)

RICHMORE What!   100

TRUEMAN Dog!
        Strikes him

RICHMORE Ha! struck by a peasant!
        Draws [this sword]
Slave, thy death is certain.
        Runs at Trueman

TRUEMAN O brave Don John,° rape and murder in one night!
        Disarms him

RICHMORE Rascal, return my sword, and acquit your prisoners; else   105
will I prosecute thee to beggary. I'll give some pettifogger a
thousand pound to starve thee and thy family according to law.

TRUEMAN I'll lay you a thousand pound you won't.
        (*Discovering himself*)

RICHMORE Ghosts and apparitions! Trueman!

TRUEMAN Words are needless to upbraid you: my very looks are   110
sufficient, and if you have the least sense of shame, this sword
would be less painful in your heart, than my appearance is in
your eye.

RICHMORE Truth, by Heavens.

TRUEMAN Think on the contents of this. (*Showing the letter*) Think 115
next on me; reflect upon your villainy to Aurelia; then view thyself.

RICHMORE Trueman, canst thou forgive me?

TRUEMAN Forgive thee! (*A long pause*) Do one thing, and I will.

RICHMORE Anything. I'll beg thy pardon.

TRUEMAN The blow excuses that. 120

RICHMORE I'll give thee half my estate.

TRUEMAN Mercenary.

RICHMORE I'll make thee my sole heir.

TRUEMAN I despise it.

RICHMORE What shall I do? 125

TRUEMAN You shall—marry Clelia.

RICHMORE How! That's too hard.

TRUEMAN Too hard! why was it then imposed on me? If you marry
her yourself, I shall believe you intended me no injury; so your
behaviour will be justified, my resentment appeased, and the lady's 130
honour repaired.

RICHMORE 'Tis infamous.

TRUEMAN No, by Heavens, 'tis justice, and what is just is honourable; if promises from man to man have force, why not from man
to woman? Their very weakness is the charter of their power, and 135
they should not be injured, because they can't return it.

RICHMORE Return my sword.

TRUEMAN In my hand 'tis the sword of justice, and I should not part
with it.

RICHMORE Then sheathe it here [*pointing to his own body*]—I'll die 140
before I consent so basely.

TRUEMAN Consider, sir, the sword is worn for a distinguishing mark
of honour—promise me one, and receive t'other.

RICHMORE I'll promise nothing, till I have that in my power.

TRUEMAN Take it. 145
Throws him his sword

RICHMORE I scorn to be compelled even to justice, and now that I
may resist, I yield. Trueman, I have injured thee, and Clelia I have
severely wronged.

TRUEMAN Wronged indeed sir, and to aggravate the crime, the fair
afflicted loves you. Marked you with what confusion she received 150
me? She wept, the injured innocence wept, and with a strange
reluctance gave consent; her moving softness pierced my heart,
though I mistook the cause.

RICHMORE Your youthful virtue warms my breast, and melts it into
    tenderness.   155
TRUEMAN Indulge it sir—justice is noble in any form; think of the
    joys and raptures will possess her, when she finds you instead of
    me; you the dear dissembler, the man she loves, the man she gave
    for lost, to find him true, returned, and in her arms.
RICHMORE No new possession can give equal joy—it shall be done;   160
    the priest that waits for you shall tie the knot this moment—in the
    morning I'll expect you'll give me joy.
        Exit [*Richmore*]°
TRUEMAN So, is not this better now than cutting of throats? I have
    got my revenge, and the lady will have hers without bloodshed.
        Exit

5.[4]

Scene changes to an apartment

Constance and Servant

SERVANT He's just a-coming up, madam.
        [*Exit servant*]
CONSTANCE My civility to this man will be as great a constraint
    upon me as rudeness would be to his brother; but I must bear it a
    little, because our designs require it.
        Enter Young Wouldbe
    [*Aside*] His appearance shocks me. [*Aloud*] My lord, I wish you joy.   5
YOUNG WOULDBE Madam, 'tis only in your power to give it, and
    would you honour me with a title to be really proud of, it should
    be that of your humblest servant.
CONSTANCE I never admitted anybody to the title of an humble
    servant, that I did not intend should command me°—if your   10
    lordship will bear with the slavery, you shall begin when you please,
    provided you take upon you the authority when I have a mind.
YOUNG WOULDBE Our sex, madam, make much better lovers than
    husbands, and I think it highly unreasonable, that you should put
    yourself in my power when you can so absolutely keep me in   15
    yours.
CONSTANCE No, my lord, we never truly command till we have
    given our promise to obey; and we are never in more danger of
    being made slaves, than when we have 'em at our feet.

YOUNG WOULDBE True, madam, the greatest empires are in most   20
danger of falling, but it is better to be absolute there, than to act
by a prerogative that's confined.

CONSTANCE Well, well, my lord, I like the constitution we live
under; I'm for a limited power or none at all.

YOUNG WOULDBE You have so much the heart of the subject,   25
madam, that you may rule as you please; but you have weak
pretences to a limited sway, where your eyes have already played
the tyrant. I think one privilege of the people is to kiss their
sovereign's hand. (*Taking her hand*)

CONSTANCE Not till they have taken the oaths, my lord; and he that   30
refuses them in the form the law prescribes, is, I think, no better
than a rebel.°

YOUNG WOULDBE By shrines and altars, (*kneeling*) by all that you
think just, and I hold good, by this (*taking her hand*) the fairest,
and the dearest vow—(*kissing her hand*)   35

CONSTANCE Fie my lord. (*Seemingly yielding*)

YOUNG WOULDBE Your eyes are mine, they bring me tidings from
your heart, that this night I shall be happy.

CONSTANCE Would not you despise a conquest so easily gained?

YOUNG WOULDBE Yours will be the conquest, and I shall despise all   40
the world but you.

CONSTANCE But will you promise to make no attempts upon my honour?

YOUNG WOULDBE (*aside*) That's foolish. [*Aloud*] Not angels sent on
messages to earth, shall visit with more innocence.°

CONSTANCE (*aside*) Ay, ay, to be sure. [*Aloud*] My lord, I'll send one   45
to conduct you.
        Exit [*Constance*]

YOUNG WOULDBE Ha, ha, ha—no attempts upon her honour! When
I can find the place where it lies, I'll tell her more of my mind.
Now do I feel ten thousand cupids tickling me all over with the
points of their arrows. Where's my deformity now? I have read   50
somewhere these lines:°
Though Nature cast me in a rugged mould,
Since Fate has changed the bullion into gold.°
Cupid returns, breaks all his shafts of lead,
And tips each arrow with a golden head;   55
Feathered with title, the gay lordly dart
Flies proudly on, whilst every virgin's heart
Swells with ambition to receive the smart.
        Enter Elder Wouldbe behind him

ELDER WOULDBE

> Thus to adorn dramatic story,
> Stage-hero struts in borrowed glory, 60
> Proud and august as ever man saw,
> And ends his empire in a stanza.°

Slaps him on the shoulder

YOUNG WOULDBE Ha! my brother!

ELDER WOULDBE No, perfidious man; all kindred and relation I disown; the poor attempts upon my fortune I could pardon, but 65 thy base designs upon my love I never can forgive: my honour, birthright, riches, all I could more freely spare, than the least thought of thy prevailing here.

YOUNG WOULDBE How! my hopes deceived! Cursed be the fair delusions of her sex; whilst only man opposed my cunning, I stood 70 secure, but soon as woman interposed, luck changed hands, and the Devil was immediately on her side. Well, sir, much good may do you with your mistress, and may you love, and live, and starve together. (*Going*)

ELDER WOULDBE Hold sir, I was lately your prisoner, now you are 75 mine; when the ejectment is executed, you shall be at liberty.

YOUNG WOULDBE Ejectment!

ELDER WOULDBE Yes, sir—by this time, I hope, my friends have purged my father's house of that debauched and riotous swarm that you had hived together. 80

YOUNG WOULDBE Confusion, sir, let me pass, I am the elder, and will be obeyed.

Draws [his sword]

ELDER WOULDBE Darest thou dispute the eldership so nobly?

YOUNG WOULDBE I dare, and will, to the last drop of my inveterate blood. 85

They fight. Enter Trueman [in his own clothes] and Teague. Trueman strikes down their swords

TRUEMAN Hold, hold, my lord, I have brought those shall soon decide the controversy.

YOUNG WOULDBE If I mistake not, that is the villain that decoyed me abroad.

Runs at Trueman. Teague catches his arm behind, and takes away his sword

TEAGUE Ay, be me shoul, thish ish the besht guard upon the rules 90 of fighting, to catch a man behind his back.

TRUEMAN My lord, a word.

Whispers [to] Elder Wouldbe
Now, gentlemen, please to hear this venerable lady.
Goes to the door and brings in Mandrake
ELDER WOULDBE Mandrake in custody!°
TEAGUE In my custody, fet.   95
TRUEMAN Now, madam, you know what punishment is destined for
the injury offered to Aurelia, if you don't immediately confess the
truth.
MANDRAKE Then I must own—Heaven forgive me (*weeping*)—I
must own that Hermes, as he was still esteemed,° so he is the   100
first-born.
TEAGUE A very honesht woman, be me shoul.
YOUNG WOULDBE That confession is extorted by fear, and therefore
of no force.
TRUEMAN Ay sir, but here is your letter to her, with the ink scarce 105
dry, where you repeat your offer of five hundred pound a year to
swear in your behalf.
TEAGUE Dat was Teague's finding out, and I believe St Patrick put
it in my toughts to pick her pockets.
Enter Constance and Aurelia
CONSTANCE I hope, Mr Wouldbe, you will make no attempts upon 110
my person.
YOUNG WOULDBE Damn your person!
ELDER WOULDBE (*to Aurelia*) But pray madam where have you been
all this evening?
AURELIA Very busy I can assure you sir; here's an honest constable 115
that I could find in my heart to marry, had the greasy rogue but
one drop of genteel blood in his veins. What's become of him?
(*Looking about*)
CONSTANCE Bless me cousin, marry a constable!
AURELIA Why truly, madam, if that constable had not come in a very 120
critical minute, by this time I had been glad to marry anybody.
TRUEMAN I take you at your word, madam, you shall marry him this
moment; and if you don't say that I have genteel blood in my veins
by tomorrow morning—
AURELIA And was it you sir?   125
TRUEMAN Look'ee, madam, don't be ashamed; I found you a little
in the *déshabillé*,° that's the truth on't, but you made a brave
defence.
AURELIA I am obliged to you, and though you were a little whimsical
today, this late adventure has taught me how dangerous it is to   130

155

provoke a gentleman by ill usage; therefore if my lord and this lady will show us a good example, I think we must follow our leaders, Captain.

TRUEMAN As boldly as when honour calls.

CONSTANCE My lord, there was taken among your brother's jovial crew, his friend Subtleman, whom we have taken care to secure. 135

ELDER WOULDBE For him, the pillory. (*To Mandrake*) For you, madam—

TEAGUE Be me shoul, she shall be married to maishter Fuller.°

ELDER WOULDBE For you, brother— 140

YOUNG WOULDBE Poverty and contempt—
      To which I yield as to a milder fate
      Than obligations from the man I hate.
    Exit [Young Wouldbe]

ELDER WOULDBE Then take thy wish—and now I hope all parties have received their due rewards and punishments. 145

TEAGUE But what will you do for poor Teague, maishter?

ELDER WOULDBE What shall I do for thee?

TEAGUE Arah, maak me a justice of peash, dear joy.

ELDER WOULDBE Justice of peace! thou art not qualified, man.

TEAGUE Yesh,° fet am I—I can take the oats, and write my mark—I 150 can be an honesht man myshelf, and keep a great rogue for my clark.°

ELDER WOULDBE Well, well, you shall be taken care of, and now, Captain, we set out for happiness.
      Let none despair, whate'er their fortunes be; 155
      Fortune must yield, would men but act like me.°
      Choose a brave friend as partner of your breast,
      Be active when your right is in contest;
      Be true to love, and Fate will do the rest.

Epilogue

spoken by Mrs Hook

Our poet opened with a loud warlike blast,
But now weak woman is his safest cast
To bring him off with quarter at the last.°
Not that he's vain to think that I can say,
Or he can write, fine things to help the play.   5
The various scenes have drained his strength and art;
And I, you know, had a hard struggling part.°
But then he brought me off with life and limb;
Ah! would that I could do as much for him.
Stay, let me think—your favours to excite,   10
I still must act the part I played tonight.
For whatsoe'er may be your sly pretence,
You like those best, that make the best defence.°
But this is needless—'tis in vain to crave it:
If you have damned the play, no power can save it.   15
Not all the wits of Athens and of Rome,°
Not Shakespeare, Jonson, could revoke its doom;
Nay, what is more—if once your anger rouses—
Not all the courted beauties of both houses.
He would have ended here—but I thought meet°   20
To tell him there was left one safe retreat,
Protection sacred, at the ladies' feet.
To that he answered in submissive strain,
He paid all homage to this female reign,°
And therefore turned his satire—'gainst the men.   25
From your great Queen, this sovereign right ye draw,
To keep the wits, as she the world, in awe;
To her bright sceptre, your bright eyes they bow—
Such awful splendour sits on every brow,
All scandal on the sex were treason now.   30
The play can tell with what poetic care
He laboured to redress the injured fair,
And if you won't protect, the men will damn him there.
Then save the Muse, that flies to ye for aid;
Perhaps my poor request may some persuade   35
Because it is the first I ever made.

THE RECRUITING
OFFICER

A Comedy

—*Captique dolis, donisque coacti.*°
(Virgil, *Aeneid*, Book 2)

DRAMATIS PERSONAE

The play was first staged at the Theatre Royal, Drury Lane, on 8 April 1706, with the following cast:

[MEN]

Mr Balance	} three justices	Mr Keen
Mr Scale		Mr Phillips
Mr Scruple°		Mr Kent
Mr Worthy, *a gentleman of Shropshire,*		Mr Williams
Captain Plume	} two recruiting officers	Mr Wilks
Captain Brazen°		Mr Cibber
Kite, *sergeant to Plume*		Mr Estcourt
Bullock, *a country clown*		Mr Bullock
Costar Pearmain°	} two recruits	Mr Norris
Thomas Appletree		Mr Fairbank

[WOMEN]

Melinda, *a lady of fortune*	Mrs Rogers
Silvia, *daughter to Balance, in love with Plume*	Mrs Oldfield
Lucy, *Melinda's maid*	Mrs Sapsford
Rose, *a country wench*	Mrs Mountford

Constable, recruits, mob, servants, and attendants

SCENE

Shrewsbury

To All Friends Round the Wrekin°

My Lords and Gentlemen,
Instead of the mercenary expectations that attend addresses of this
nature, I humbly beg, that this may be received as an acknowledgment
for the favours you have already conferred;° I have transgressed the
rules of dedication in offering you anything in that style, without first   5
asking your leave. But the entertainment I found in Shropshire
commands me to be grateful, and that's all I intend.

'Twas my good fortune to be ordered some time ago into the place
which is made the scene of this comedy; I was a perfect stranger to
everything in Salop,° but its character of loyalty, the number of its   10
inhabitants, the alacrity of the gentlemen in recruiting the army,° with
their generous and hospitable reception of strangers.

This character I found so amply verified in every particular, that
you made recruiting, which is the greatest fatigue upon earth to
others, to be the greatest pleasure in the world to me.   15

The kingdom cannot show better bodies of men, better inclinations
for the service, more generosity, more good understanding, nor more
politeness than is to be found at the foot of the Wrekin.

Some little turns of humour that I met with almost within the shade
of that famous hill, gave the rise to this comedy,° and people were   20
apprehensive, that, by the example of some others, I would make the
Town merry at the expense of the country gentlemen. But they forgot
that I was to write a comedy, not a libel; and that whilst I held to
nature, no person of any character in your country could suffer by
being exposed. I have drawn the justice and the clown in their *puris*   25
naturabilis°—the one an apprehensive,° sturdy, brave blockhead, and
the other a worthy, honest, generous gentleman, hearty in his
country's cause, and of as good an understanding as I could give him,
which I must confess is far short of his own.°

I humbly beg leave to interline a word or two of the adventures of   30
The Recruiting Officer upon the stage. Mr Rich,° who commands the
company for which those recruits were raised, has desired me to
acquit him before the world of a charge which he thinks lies heavy
upon him for acting this play on Mr Durfey's third night.°

Be it known unto all men by these presents, that it was my act and   35
deed,° or rather Mr Durfey's; for he would play his third night
against the first of mine. He brought down a huge flight of frightful

birds upon me, when, Heaven knows, I had not a feathered fowl in
my play, except one single Kite. But I presently made Plume a bird,
because of his name, and Brazen another, because of the feather in his
hat; and with these three I engaged his whole empire, which I think
was as great a wonder as any in the sun.°

But to answer his complaints more gravely, the season was far
advanced; the officers that made the greatest figures in my play were
all commanded to their posts abroad,° and waited only for a wind,
which might possibly turn in less time than a day. And I know none
of Mr Durfey's birds that had posts abroad but his woodcocks, and
their season is over;° so that he might put off a day with less prejudice
than the Recruiting Officer could, who has this further to say for
himself, that he was posted° before the other spoke, and could not
with credit recede from his station.

These and some other rubs this comedy met with before it
appeared. But on the other hand, it had powerful helps to set it
forward. The Duke of Ormonde° encouraged the author, and the Earl
of Orrery° approved the play. My recruits were reviewed by my
general and my colonel, and could not fail to pass muster;° and still
to add to my success, they were raised among my Friends round the
Wrekin.

This health has the advantage over our other celebrated toasts,
never to grow worse for the wearing.° 'Tis a lasting beauty, old
without age, and common without scandal. That you may live long
to set it cheerfully round, and to enjoy the abundant pleasures of your
fair and plentiful country, is the hearty wish of,

> My lords and gentlemen,
>   Your most obliged,
>   and most obedient servant,
>   Geo. Farquhar.

The Prologue

In ancient times, when Helen's fatal charms
Roused the contending universe to arms,°
The Grecian council happily deputes
The sly Ulysses forth—to raise recruits.
The artful captain found, without delay,   5
Where great Achilles, a deserter, lay.
Him Fate had warned to shun the Trojan blows;
Him Greece required—against their Trojan foes.
All the recruiting arts were needful here
To raise this great, this tim'rous volunteer.   10
Ulysses well could talk: he stirs, he warms°
The warlike youth—he listens to the charms
Of plunder, fine laced coats, and glittering arms.°
Ulysses caught the young aspiring boy,
And listed him who wrought the fate of Troy.   15
Thus by recruiting was bold Hector slain.°
Recruiting thus fair Helen did regain.
If for one Helen such prodigious things
Were acted, that they even listed kings;
If for one Helen's artful vicious charms,   20
Half the transported world was found in arms;
What for so many Helens may we dare,
Whose minds, as well as faces, are so fair?
If, by one Helen's eyes, old Greece could find
Its Homer fired to write—ev'n Homer blind—   25
The Britons sure beyond compare may write,
That view so many Helens every night.

1.1

Scene, the market place

Drum beats the 'Grenadier March'.° Enter Sergeant Kite, followed by the mob

KITE (*making a speech*) If any gentlemen-soldiers.° or others, have a mind to serve her Majesty,° and pull down the French king; if any 'prentices have severe masters, any children have undutiful parents; if any servants have too little wages, or any husband too much wife, let them repair to the noble Sergeant Kite, at the sign of the Raven,° in this good town of Shrewsbury, and they shall receive present relief and entertainment.° 5

Gentlemen, I don't beat my drums here to ensnare or inveigle any man; for you must know, gentlemen, that I am a man of honour. Besides, I don't beat up for common soldiers; no, I list only grenadiers°—grenadiers, gentlemen. Pray gentlemen observe this cap.° [*Pointing to his own regimental cap*] This is the cap of honour—it dubs a man a gentleman in the drawing of a trigger; and he that has the good fortune to be born six foot high, was born to be a great man. (*To one of the mob*) Sir, will you give me leave to try this cap upon your head? 10

to be a great man. (*To one of the mob*) Sir, will you give me leave to try this cap upon your head? 15

[MAN]° Is there no harm in't? Won't the cap list me?

KITE No, no, no more than I can. Come, let me see how it becomes you.

[MAN] Are you sure there be no conjuration° in it, no gunpowder plot° upon me? 20

KITE No, no, friend; don't fear, man.

[MAN] My mind misgives me plaguily. Let me see it. (*Going to put it on*) It smells woundily of sweat and brimstone; pray, Sergeant, what writing is this upon the face of it? 25

KITE 'The Crown, or the Bed of Honour.'°

[MAN] Pray now, what may be that same 'Bed of Honour'?

KITE O, a mighty large bed, bigger by half than the great bed of Ware°—ten thousand people may lie in't together, and never feel one another. 30

[MAN] My wife and I would do well to lie in't, for we don't care for feeling one another. But do folk sleep sound in this same 'Bed of Honour'?

KITE Sound! Ay, so sound that they never wake.

[MAN] Wauns! I wish again that my wife lay there.   35

KITE Say you so? Then, I find, brother—

[MAN] Brother! hold there, friend—I'm no kindred to you that I
know of, as yet. Look ye Sergeant, no coaxing, no wheedling d'ye
see; if I have a mind to list, why so. If not, why 'tis not so.
Therefore take your cap and your brothership back again, for I an't   40
disposed at this present writing.° No coaxing, no brothering me,
faith.

KITE I coax! I wheedle! I'm above it! Sir, I have served twenty
campaigns. But, sir, you talk well, and I must own that you are a
man, every inch of you—a pretty young sprightly fellow; I love a   45
fellow with a spirit, but I scorn to coax—'tis base; though I must
say, that never in my life have I seen a better built man. How firm
and strong he treads, he steps like a castle! But I scorn to wheedle
any man. Come, honest lad, will you take share of a pot?

[MAN] Nay, for that matter, I'll spend my penny with the best he   50
that wears a head, that is, begging your pardon sir, and in a fair
way.

KITE Give me your hand then; and now gentlemen, I have no more
to say but this. Here's a purse of gold, and there is a tub of
humming ale at my quarters; 'tis the Queen's money, and the   55
Queen's drink. She's a generous queen, and loves her subjects. I
hope, gentlemen, you won't refuse the Queen's health.

ALL MOB No, no, no.

KITE Huzza then, huzza for the Queen, and the honour of Shropshire.   60

ALL MOB Huzza.

KITE Beat drum
        Exeunt [Kite and mob], drum beating the 'Grenadier March'.
        Enter° Plume in a riding habit

PLUME By the 'Grenadier March' that should be my drum, and by
that shout it should beat with success. Let me see.
        Looks on his watch
Four o'clock—at ten yesterday morning I left London. A hundred   65
and twenty miles in thirty hours is pretty smart riding, but nothing
to the fatigue of recruiting.
        Enter Kite

KITE Welcome to Shrewsbury, noble Captain—from the banks of the
Danube to the Severn side, noble Captain, you are welcome.

PLUME A very elegant reception indeed, Mr Kite—I find you are   70
fairly entered into your recruiting strain. Pray what success?

KITE   I have been here but a week, and I have recruited five.

PLUME   Five! Pray, what are they?

KITE   I have listed the strong man of Kent,° the king of the gypsies,°
a Scotch pedlar, a scoundrel attorney, and a Welsh parson.°   75

PLUME   An attorney! Wert thou mad? List a lawyer! Discharge him,
discharge him this minute.

KITE   Why sir?

PLUME   Because I will have nobody in my company that can write; a
fellow that can write, can draw petitions. I say, this minute   80
discharge him.

KITE   And what shall I do with the parson?

PLUME   Can he write?

KITE   Umh. He plays rarely upon the fiddle.

PLUME   Keep him by all means. But how stands the country affected?   85
Were the people pleased with the news of my coming to town?

KITE   Sir, the mob are so pleased with your honour, and the justices
and better sort of people are so delighted with me, that we shall
soon do our business. But, sir, you have got a recruit here that you
little think of.   90

PLUME   Who?

KITE   One that you beat up for last time you were in the country; you
remember your old friend Molly at the Castle.°

PLUME   She's not with child, I hope.

KITE   No, no, sir; she was brought to bed yesterday.   95

PLUME   Kite, you must father the child.

KITE   Humph. And so° her friends will oblige me to marry the
mother.

PLUME   If they° should, we'll take her with us; she can wash you
know, and make a bed upon occasion.   100

KITE   Ay, or unmake it upon occasion—but your honour knows that
I'm married already.

PLUME   To how many?

KITE   I can't tell readily. I have set them down here upon the back of
the muster-roll.   105
      Draws out the muster-roll
Let me see. '*Imprimis*, Mrs Sheely Snikereyes'°—she sells potatoes
upon Ormonde Key in Dublin—'Peggy Guzzle'—the brandy
woman at the Horseguard° at Whitehall—'Dolly Waggon'—the
carrier's daughter in Hull—'Mademoiselle Van-Bottomflat'—at
the Buss.° Then—'Jenny Oakum'°—the ship-carpenter's widow,   110
at Portsmouth; but I don't reckon upon her, for she was married

at the same time to two lieutenants of Marines, and a man-of-war's boatswain.

PLUME A full company—you have named five. Come, make 'em half a dozen, Kite. Is the child a boy or a girl?   115

KITE A chopping boy.

PLUME Then set the mother down in your list, and the boy in mine; enter him a grenadier by the name of Francis Kite, absent upon furlough. I'll allow you a man's pay for his subsistence,° and now go comfort the wench in the straw.   120

KITE I shall, sir.

PLUME But hold, have you made any use of your German doctor's habit° since you arrived?

KITE Yes, yes, sir; and my fame's all about the country, for the most famous° fortune-teller that ever told a lie; I was obliged to let my   125 landlord into the secret for the convenience of keeping it so; but he's an honest fellow, and will be trusty° to any roguery that is confided° to him. This device, sir, will get you men, and me money, which I think is all we want at present. But yonder comes your friend, Mr Worthy. Has your honour any further commands?   130

PLUME None at present.

    Exit Kite

'Tis indeed the picture of Worthy, but the life's departed.

    Enter Worthy

What! Arms across, Worthy! Methinks you should hold 'em open when a friend's so near. The man has got the vapours in his ears,° I believe. I must expel this melancholy spirit.   135

Spleen, thou worst of fiends below,

Fly, I conjure thee by this magic blow.

    Slaps Worthy on the shoulder.

WORTHY Plume! My dear Captain, welcome, safe and sound returned!

PLUME I 'scaped safe from Germany, and sound I hope from   140 London—you see I have lost neither leg, arm, nor nose.° Then for my inside, 'tis neither troubled with sympathies nor antipathies,° and I have an excellent stomach for roast beef.

WORTHY Thou art a happy fellow—once I was so.

PLUME What ails thee, man? No inundations nor earthquakes in   145 Wales, I hope? Has your father rose from the dead, and reassumed his estate?

WORTHY No.

PLUME Then you are married surely.

WORTHY No.   150

PLUME Then you are mad, or turning Quaker.°

WORTHY Come, I must out with it. Your once gay roving friend is
   dwindled into an obsequious, thoughtful, romantic, constant coxcomb.

PLUME And pray, what is all this for?   155

WORTHY For a woman.

PLUME Shake hands brother, if you° go to that. Behold me as
   obsequious, as thoughtful, and as constant a coxcomb as your
   worship.

WORTHY For whom?   160

PLUME For a regiment. But for a woman, 'sdeath, I have been
   constant to fifteen at a time, but never melancholy for one; and can
   the love of one bring you into this pickle?° Pray, who is this
   miraculous° Helen?

WORTHY A Helen indeed, not to be won under a ten years' siege, as   165
   great a beauty, and as great a jilt.

PLUME A jilt! Pho—is she as great a whore?

WORTHY No, no.

PLUME 'Tis ten thousand pities. But who is she? Do I know her?

WORTHY Very well.   170

PLUME Impossible. I know no woman that will hold out a ten years'
   siege.

WORTHY What think you of Melinda?

PLUME Melinda! Why she began to capitulate this time twelve-
   month, and offered to surrender upon honourable terms;° and I   175
   advised you to propose a settlement of five hundred pound a year
   to her, before I went last abroad.

WORTHY I did, and she hearkened to't, desiring only one week to
   consider; when, beyond her hopes, the town was relieved, and I
   forced to turn my siege into a blockade.°   180

PLUME Explain, explain.

WORTHY My Lady Richly her aunt in Flintshire dies, and leaves her
   at this critical time twenty thousand pound.

PLUME O the Devil, what a delicate woman was there spoiled. But by
   the rules of war now, Worthy, your blockade was foolish. After such   185
   a convoy of provisions was entered the place, you could have no
   thought of reducing it by famine. You should have redoubled your
   attacks, taken the town by storm, or have died upon the breach.°

WORTHY I did make one general assault, and pushed it with all my
   forces; but I was so vigorously repulsed, that despairing of ever   190

gaining her for a mistress, I have altered my conduct, given my
addresses the obsequious and distant turn, and court her now for
a wife.

PLUME So, as you grew obsequious, she grew haughty, and because
you approached her as a goddess, she used you like a dog.   195

WORTHY Exactly.

PLUME 'Tis the way of 'em all. Come Worthy, your obsequious and
distant airs will never bring you together; you must not think to
surmount her pride by your humility. Would you bring her° to
better thoughts of you, she must be reduced to a meaner opinion   200
of herself. Let me see. The very first thing that I would do, should
be to lie with her chambermaid, and hire three or four wenches in
the neighbourhood to report that I had got them with child.
Suppose we lampooned all the pretty women in town, and left her
out? Or what if we made a ball, and forgot to invite her, with one 205
or two of the ugliest?

WORTHY These would be mortifications, I must confess. But we live
in such a precise, dull place, that we can have no balls, no
lampoons, no—

PLUME What! No bastards! and so many recruiting officers in town; 210
I thought 'twas a maxim among them to leave as many recruits in
the country as they carried out.

WORTHY Nobody doubts your good-will, noble Captain, in serving
your country with your best blood.° Witness our friend Molly at
the Castle. There have been tears in town about that business,   215
Captain.

PLUME I hope Sylvia has not heard of't?

WORTHY O sir, have you thought of her? I began to fancy you had
forgot poor Silvia.

PLUME Your affairs had put my own quite out of my head. 'Tis true, 220
Silvia and I had once agreed to go to bed together, could we have
adjusted preliminaries; but she would have the wedding before
consummation, and I was for consummation before the wedding.
We could not agree—she was a pert, obstinate fool, and would lose
her maidenhead her own way, so she may keep it for Plume.   225

WORTHY But do you intend to marry upon no other conditions?

PLUME Your pardon, sir, I'll marry upon no conditions at all—if I
should, I'm resolved never to bind myself to a woman for my
whole life, till I know whether I shall like her company for half an
hour. Suppose I married a woman that wanted a leg? Such a thing 230
might be, unless I examined the goods beforehand; if people would

but try one another's constitutions before they engaged, it would
prevent all these elopements, divorces, and the Devil knows what.

WORTHY Nay, for that matter, the town did not stick to say, that—

PLUME [*interrupting him*] I hate country towns for that reason. If   235
your town has a dishonourable thought of Silvia, it deserves to be
burnt to the ground. I love Silvia—I admire her frank, generous
disposition; there's something in that girl more than woman—her
sex is but a foil to her. The ingratitude, dissimulation, envy, pride,
avarice, and vanity of her sister females, do but set off their   240
contraries in her. In short, were I once a general, I would marry
her.

WORTHY Faith you have reason; for were you but a corporal, she
would marry you. But my Melinda coquettes it with every fellow
she sees. I lay fifty pound she makes love to you.°   245

PLUME I'll lay fifty pound that I return it, if she does. Lookye,
Worthy, I'll win her, and give her to you afterwards.

WORTHY If you win her, you shall wear her, faith; I would not give
a fig for° the conquest, without the credit of the victory.

        Enter Kite

KITE Captain, Captain, a word in your ear.   250

PLUME You may speak out, here are none but friends.

KITE You know, sir, that you sent me to comfort the good woman in
the straw, Mrs Molly—my wife, Mr Worthy.

WORTHY Oho, very well—I wish you joy, Mr Kite.

KITE Your worship very well may, for I have got both a wife and a   255
child in half an hour—but as I was a-saying, you sent me to
comfort Mrs Molly—my wife, I mean. But what d'ye think sir?
She was better comforted before I came.

PLUME As how?

KITE Why, sir, a footman in a blue livery had brought her ten guineas   260
to buy her baby clothes.

PLUME Who, in the name of wonder, could send them?

KITE Nay, sir, I must whisper that.

        Whispers [*to*] *Plume*
Mrs Silvia.

PLUME Silvia! Generous creature.   265

WORTHY Silvia! Impossible.

KITE Here be the guineas, sir; I took the gold as part of my wife's
portion. Nay further, sir, she sent word that the child should be
taken all imaginable care of, and that she intended to stand
godmother. The same footman, as I was coming to you with this   270

news, called after me, and told me that his lady would speak with
me. I went; and upon hearing that you were come to town, she
gave me half a guinea for the news, and ordered me to tell you,
that Justice Balance her father, who is just come out of the
country, would be glad to see you.   275

PLUME There's a girl for you, Worthy. Is there anything of woman
in this? No, 'tis noble and generous, manly friendship—show me
another woman that would lose an inch of her prerogative that
way,° without tears, fits, and reproaches. The common jealousy of
her sex, which is nothing but their avarice of pleasure, she   280
despises; and can part with the lover, though she dies for the man.
Come Worthy. Where's the best wine? For there I'll quarter.

WORTHY Horton° has a fresh pipe of choice Barcelona,° which I
would not let him pierce before, because I reserved the maidenhead of it for your welcome to town.   285

PLUME Let's away then. Mr Kite, wait on the lady° with my humble
service, and tell her that I shall only refresh a little, and wait on
her.

WORTHY Hold, Kite. Have you seen the other recruiting captain?

KITE No, sir.   290

PLUME Another—who is he?

WORTHY My rival in the first place, and the most unaccountable
fellow. But I'll tell you more as we go.
         Exeunt

1.2

Scene, an apartment [in Melinda's house]
Melinda and Silvia meeting

MELINDA Welcome to town, cousin Silvia.
         [*They*] *salute°*
I envied you your retreat in the country; for Shrewsbury, methinks, and all your heads of shires,° are the most irregular places
for living; here we have smoke, noise, scandal, affectation, and
pretension; in short, everything to give the spleen, and nothing to 5
divert it. Then the air is intolerable.°

SILVIA O! Madam, I have heard the town commended for its air.

MELINDA But you don't consider, Silvia, how long I have lived in it;
for I can assure you, that to a lady the least nice in her constitution,

no air can be good above half a year; change of air I take to be the   10
most agreeable of any variety in life.

SILVIA As you say, cousin Melinda, there are several sorts of airs, airs
in conversation, airs in behaviour, airs in dress; then we have our
quality airs, our sickly airs, our reserved airs, and sometimes our
impudent airs.°   15

MELINDA Pshaw—I talk only of the air we breathe, or more properly
of that we taste. Have not you, Silvia, found a vast difference in
the taste of airs?

SILVIA Pray cousin, are not vapours a sort of air? Taste air! You may
as well tell me I might feed upon air; but prithee, my dear   20
Melinda, don't put on such airs to me—your education and mine
were just the same, and I remember the time when we never
troubled our heads about air, but when the sharp air from the
Welsh mountains made our noses drop° in a cold morning at the
boarding-school.   25

MELINDA Our education, cousin, was the same, but our tempera-
ments had nothing alike; you have the constitution of a horse—

SILVIA So far as to be troubled with neither spleen, colic, nor
vapours. I need no salts° for my stomach, no hartshorn for my
head, nor wash for my complexion; I can gallop all the morning   30
after the hunting horn, and all the evening after a fiddle. In short,
I can do everything with my father but drink and shoot flying;°
and I'm sure I can do everything my mother could, were I put to
the trial.

MELINDA You are in a fair way of being put to't; for I'm told, your   35
captain is come to town.

SILVIA Ay, Melinda, he is come, and I'll take care he shan't go
without a companion.

MELINDA You're certainly mad, cousin.

SILVIA 'And there's a pleasure sure in being mad.   40
              Which none but madmen know.'°

MELINDA Thou poor romantic Quixote,° hast thou the vanity to
imagine that a young sprightly officer that rambles over half the
globe in half a year, can confine his thoughts to the little daughter
of a country justice, in an obscure corner° of the world?   45

SILVIA Pshaw! What care I for his thoughts? I should not like a man
with confined thoughts—it shows a narrowness of soul. Constancy
is but a dull, sleepy quality at best; they will hardly admit it among
the manly virtues, nor do I think it deserves a place with bravery,
knowledge, policy, justice, and some other qualities that are proper   50

to that noble sex. In short, Melinda, I think a petticoat a mighty simple thing, and I'm heartily tired of my sex.

MELINDA That is, you are tired of an appendix to our sex,° that you can't so handsomely get rid of in petticoats as if you were in breeches. O' my conscience, Silvia, hadst thou been a man, thou hadst been the greatest rake in Christendom.

SILVIA I should endeavour to know the world, which a man can never do thoroughly without half a hundred friendships, and as many amours. But now I think on't, how stands your affair with Mr Worthy?

MELINDA He's my aversion.

SILVIA Vapours.

MELINDA What do you say, madam?

SILVIA I say, that you should not use that honest fellow so inhumanly—he's a gentleman of parts and fortune, and beside that, he's my Plume's friend; and by all that's sacred, if you don't use him better, I shall expect satisfaction.°

MELINDA Satisfaction! You begin to fancy yourself in breeches in good earnest. But to be plain with you, I like Worthy the worse for being so intimate with your captain; for I take him to be a loose, idle, unmannerly coxcomb.

SILVIA O! Madam, you never saw him, perhaps, since you were mistress of twenty thousand pound; you only knew him when you were capitulating with Worthy for a settlement, which perhaps might encourage him to be a little loose and unmannerly with you.

MELINDA What do you mean, madam?

SILVIA My meaning needs no interpretation, madam.

MELINDA Better it had, madam—for methinks you're too plain.

SILVIA If you mean the plainness of my person, I think your ladyship as plain as me to the full.

MELINDA Were I assured of that, I should be glad to take up with a rakehelly officer as you do.

SILVIA Again! Look'ee, madam—you're in your own house.

MELINDA And if you had kept in yours, I should have excused you.

SILVIA Don't be troubled, madam—I shan't desire to have my visit returned.

MELINDA The sooner therefore you make an end of this, the better.

SILVIA I'm easily advised° to follow my inclinations. So madam. Your humble servant.
        Exit [Silvia]

MELINDA Saucy thing!
>   *Enter Lucy*

LUCY What's the matter, madam!

MELINDA Did you not see the proud nothing, how she swells upon the arrival of her fellow?

LUCY Her fellow has not been long enough arrived to occasion any   95
great swelling, madam—I don't believe she has seen him yet.

MELINDA Nor shan't if I can help it; let me see—I have it. Bring me pen and ink. Hold, I'll go write in my closet.

LUCY An answer to this letter, I hope, madam.
>   *Presents a letter*

MELINDA Who sent it?   100

LUCY Your captain, madam.

MELINDA He's a fool, and I'm tired of him; send it back unopened.

LUCY The messenger's gone, madam.

MELINDA Then how shall I send an answer? Call him back immediately, while I go write.   105
>   *Exeunt [Melinda and Lucy] severally*

2.1

Scene, an apartment [in Justice Balance's house]

Enter Justice Balance and Plume

BALANCE Look'ee, Captain, give us but blood for our money, and you shan't want men; I remember, that for some years of the last war, we had no blood nor wounds but in the officers' mouths, nothing for our millions but newspapers not worth a-reading—our armies did nothing but play at 'prison bars',° and 'hide-and-seek' with the enemy; but now ye have brought us colours, and standards,° and prisoners. Odsmylife, Captain, get us but another Marshal of France,° and I'll go myself for a soldier.   5

PLUME Pray, Mr Balance, how does your fair daughter?

BALANCE Ah! Captain, what is my daughter to° a Marshal of France? We're upon a nobler subject—I want to have a particular description of the battle of Hockstadt.°   10

PLUME The battle, sir, was a very pretty battle as one should desire to see, but we were all so intent upon victory, that we never minded the battle; all that I know of the matter is, our general° commanded us to beat the French, and we did so, and if he pleases to say the word, we'll do't again. But pray, sir, how does Mrs Silvia?   15

BALANCE Still upon Silvia! For shame, Captain—you're engaged already, wedded to the war—war is° your mistress, and it is below a soldier to think of any other.   20

PLUME As a mistress, I confess, but as a friend, Mr Balance.

BALANCE Come, come, Captain, never mince the matter—would not you debauch my daughter if you could?

PLUME How sir! I hope she is not to be debauched.   25

BALANCE Faith but she is, sir, and any woman in England of her age and complexion, by a man of your youth and vigour. Look'ee, Captain, once I was young, and once an officer as you are; and I can guess at your thoughts now by what mine were then, and I remember very well, that I would have given one of my legs to have deluded the daughter of an old plain country gentleman, as like me as I then was like you.   30

PLUME But, sir, was that country gentleman your friend and benefactor?

BALANCE Not much of that.   35

175

PLUME There the comparison breaks; the favours, sir, that—

BALANCE Pho! I hate speeches; if I have done you any service, Captain, 'twas to please myself, for I love thee; and if I could part with my girl, you should have her as soon as any young fellow I know; but I hope you have more honour than to quit the service, and she more prudence than to follow the camp. But she's at her own disposal°—she has fifteen hundred pound in her pocket, and so, (*calls*) Silvia, Silvia! 40

> *Enter Silvia*

SILVIA There are some letters, sir, come by post from London—I left them upon the table in your closet. 45

BALANCE And here is a gentleman from Germany. (*Presents Plume to her*) Captain, you'll excuse me, I'll go read my letters and wait on you.

> *Exit Balance*

SILVIA Sir, you're welcome to England.[1]

PLUME Blessings in heaven we should receive in a prostrate posture—let me receive my welcome thus. 50

> *Kneels and kisses her hand*

SILVIA Pray rise, sir—I'll give you fair quarter.°

PLUME All quarter I despise—the height of conquest is to die at your feet. (*Kissing her hand again*)

SILVIA Well, well, you shall die° at my feet, or where you will; but first let me desire you to make your will°—perhaps you'll leave me something.° 55

---

[1] *Between lines 48 and 56 the second edition reads*:

PLUME You are indebted to me° a welcome, madam, since the hopes of receiving it from this fair hand was the principal cause of my seeing England. 50

SILVIA I have often heard, that soldiers were sincere°—shall I venture to believe public report?

PLUME You may, when 'tis backed by private insurance;° for I swear, madam, by the honour of my profession, that whatever dangers I went upon, it was with the hope of making myself more worthy of your esteem, and if ever I had thoughts of preserving my life, 'twas for the pleasure of dying at your feet. 55

SILVIA Well, well, you shall die at my feet, or where you will; but you know, sir, there is a certain will and testament to be made beforehand. 60

PLUME My will, madam, is made already, and there it is, (*gives her a parchment*) and if you please to open that parchment, which was drawn the evening before the battle of Blenheim,° you will find whom I left my heir.   60
    Silvia opens the will and reads

SILVIA 'Mrs Silvia Balance.' Well, Captain, this is a handsome and substantial compliment, but I can assure you I am much better pleased with the bare knowledge of your intention, than I should have been in the possession of your legacy; but methinks, sir, you should have left something to your little boy at the Castle.   65

PLUME (*aside*) That's home. [*Aloud*] My little boy!—Lack-a-day, madam, that alone may convince you 'twas none of mine; why the girl, madam, is my sergeant's wife, and so the poor creature gave out that I was father, in hopes that my friends might support her in case of necessity—that was all, madam. My boy! no, no.   70
    Enter servant

SERVANT Madam, my master has received some ill news from London, and desires to speak with you immediately, and he begs the captain's pardon, that he can't wait on him as he promised.

PLUME Ill news! Heavens avert it. Nothing could touch me nearer than to see that generous worthy gentleman afflicted; I'll leave you   75
to comfort him, and be assured that if my life and fortune can be any way serviceable to the father of my Silvia, she shall freely command both.

SILVIA The necessity must be very pressing, that would engage me to do either.°   80
    Exeunt Plume, Silvia and servant severally.

2.[2]

    Scene changes to another apartment
    Enter Balance and Silvia

SILVIA Whilst there is life there is hope, sir; perhaps my brother may recover.

BALANCE We have but little reason to expect it. Doctor Kilman acquaints me here, that before this comes to my hands, he fears I shall have no son. Poor Owen!° But the decree is just—I was   5
pleased with the death of my father, because he left me an estate, and now I'm punished with the loss of an heir to inherit mine. I

must now look upon you as the only hopes of my family, and I
expect that the augmentation of your fortune will give you fresh
thoughts and new prospects.   10

SILVIA My desire of being punctual in my obedience, requires that
you would be plain in your commands, sir.

BALANCE The death of your brother makes you sole heiress to my
estate, which three or four years hence will amount to twelve
hundred pound *per annum*;° this fortune gives you a fair claim to   15
quality and a title°—you must set a just value upon yourself, and
in plain terms think no more of Captain Plume.

SILVIA You have often commended the gentleman, sir.

BALANCE And I do so still, he's a very pretty fellow; but though I
liked him well enough for a bare son-in-law, I don't approve of   20
him for an heir to my estate and family. Fifteen hundred pound,
indeed, I might trust in his hands, and it might do the young
fellow a kindness, but odsmylife, twelve hundred pound a year
would ruin him, quite turn his brain. A captain of foot worth
twelve hundred pound a year!° 'Tis a prodigy in nature. Besides   25
this, I have five or six thousand pounds in woods upon my estate.°
O! That would make him stark mad, for you must know that all
captains have a mighty aversion to timber—they can't endure to
see trees standing. Then I should have some rogue of a builder by
the help of his damned magic art transform my noble oaks and   30
elms into cornices, portals, sashes, birds, beasts, gods and devils,
to adorn some maggotty, new-fashioned bauble upon the Thames;°
and then you should have a dog of a gardener bring a *habeas
corpus*° for my *terra firma*,° remove it to Chelsea or Twickenham,
and clap it into grass-plots and gravel-walks.   35

    Enter a servant

SERVANT Sir, here's one below with a letter for your worship, but he
will deliver it into no hands but your own.

BALANCE Come, show me the messenger.

    Exit [Balance] with servant

SILVIA Make the dispute between love and duty, and I am Prince
Prettyman° exactly. If my brother dies, 'Ah! poor brother'; if he   40
lives, 'Ah! poor sister'. 'Tis bad both ways; I'll try again—follow
my own inclinations and break my father's heart, or obey his
commands and break my own—worse and worse. Suppose I take
it° thus: a moderate fortune, a pretty fellow and a pad—or a fine
estate, a coach-and-six, and an ass.° That will never do neither.   45

    Enter Balance and servant

BALANCE (*to servant*) Put four horses into the coach.
        [*Exit servant*]
    Silvia.
SILVIA Sir.
BALANCE How old were you when your mother died?
SILVIA So young that I don't remember I ever had one; and you have   50
    been so careful, so indulgent to me since, that indeed I never
    wanted one.
BALANCE Have I ever denied you anything you asked of me?
SILVIA Never, that I remember.
BALANCE Then Silvia, I must beg that once in your life you would   55
    grant me a favour.
SILVIA Why should you question it, sir?
BALANCE I don't, but I would rather counsel than command—I
    don't propose this with the authority of a parent, but as the advice
    of your friend, that you would take the coach this moment and go   60
    into the country.
SILVIA Does this advice proceed from the contents of the letter you
    received just now?
BALANCE No matter—I shall be with you in three or four days, and
    then give you my reasons. But before you go, I expect you will   65
    make me one solemn promise.
SILVIA Propose the thing, sir.
BALANCE That you will never dispose of yourself to any man,
    without my consent.
SILVIA I promise.   70
BALANCE Very well, and to be even with you, I promise, that I will
    never dispose of you without your own consent. And so Silvia, the
    coach is ready—farewell.
        Leads her to the door and returns. [*Exit Silvia*]
    Now she's gone, I'll examine the contents of this letter a little
    nearer. (*Reads*) 'Sir—my intimacy with Mr Worthy has drawn a   75
    secret from him, that he had from his friend Captain Plume, and
    my friendship and relation to your family oblige me to give you
    timely notice of it; the captain has dishonourable designs upon my
    cousin Silvia. Evils of this nature are more easily prevented than
    amended, and that you would immediately send my cousin into the   80
    country is the advice of, sir, your humble servant, Melinda.' Why
    the Devil's in the young fellows of this age—they're ten times
    worse than they were in my time. Had he made my daughter a
    whore, and foreswore it like a gentleman, I could have almost

pardoned it; but to tell tales beforehand is monstrous! Hang it, I   85
can fetch down a woodcock or snipe, and why not a hat and
feather?° I have a case of good pistols, and have a good mind to
try.

    Enter Worthy

Worthy, your servant.

WORTHY I'm sorry, sir, to be the messenger of ill news.   90

BALANCE I apprehend it, sir; you have heard that my son Owen is
past recovery.

WORTHY My advices° say he's dead, sir.

BALANCE He's happy, and I am satisfied; the strokes of Heaven I can
bear, but injuries from men, Mr Worthy, are not so easily   95
supported.

WORTHY I hope, sir, you are under no apprehension of wrong from
anybody?

BALANCE You know I ought to be.

WORTHY You wrong my honour, sir, in believing I could know   100
anything to your prejudice without resenting it as much as you
should.

BALANCE This letter, sir, which I tear in pieces to conceal the person
that sent it, informs me that Plume has a design upon Silvia, and
that you are privy to't.   105

    Tears the letter

WORTHY Nay, then sir, I must do myself justice, and endeavour to
find out the author.

    Takes up a piece of the letter

Sir, I know the hand, and if you refuse to discover the contents,
Melinda shall tell me. (*Going*)

BALANCE Hold, sir—the contents I have told you already, only with   110
this circumstance, that her intimacy with Mr Worthy had drawn
the secret from him.

WORTHY Her intimacy with me! Dear sir, let me pick up the
pieces of this letter—'twill give me such a hank upon° her pride,
to have her own an intimacy under her hand; 'twas the luckiest   115
accident. (*Gathering up the letter*) The aspersion, sir, was nothing but malice, the effect of a little quarrel between her and Mrs
Silvia.

BALANCE Are you sure of that, sir?

WORTHY Her maid gave me the history of part of the battle just now,   120
as she overheard it.

BALANCE 'Tis probable—I am satisfied.°

WORTHY But I hope, sir, your daughter has suffered nothing upon
the account?

BALANCE No, no. Poor girl, she is so afflicted with the news of her   125
brother's death, that to avoid company she begged leave to be gone
into the country.

WORTHY And is she gone?

BALANCE I could not refuse her, she was so pressing—the coach
went from the door the minute before you came.   130

WORTHY So pressing to be gone, sir. I find her fortune will give her
the same airs with° Melinda, and then Plume and I may laugh at
one another.

BALANCE Like enough. Women are as subject to pride as we are, and
why mayn't great women as well as great men forget their old   135
aquaintance? But come, where's this young fellow? I love him so
well, it would break the heart of me to think him a rascal. (*Aside*)
I'm glad my daughter's fairly gone off though. (*Aloud*) Where does
the Captain quarter?

WORTHY At Horton's—I'm to meet him there two hours hence, and   140
we should be glad of your company.

BALANCE Your pardon, dear Worthy—I must allow a day or two to
the death of my son; the decorum of mourning is what we owe the
world, because they pay it to us. Afterwards° I'm yours over a
bottle, or how you will.   145

WORTHY Sir, I'm your humble servant.
     Exeunt [*Balance and Plume*] *severally.*

2.[3]

Scene, the street

Enter Kite, with one of the mob [*Costar and Pearmain*] *in each
hand, drunk*

KITE (*sings*)

> Our prentice Tom may now refuse
> To wipe his scoundrel master's shoes;
> For now he's free to sing and play,
> Over the hills and far away.   5
> —*Over the hills, &c.*

The Mob sing the Chorus

> *We all shall lead more happy lives,*
> *By getting rid of brats and wives,*
> *That scold and brawl both night and day;*
> *Over the hills and far away.*
> *—Over the hills, &c.°*   10

Hey boys. Thus we soldiers live; drink, sing, dance, play; we live,
as one should say . . . We live—'tis impossible to tell how we
live. We're all princes. Why—why, you're a king. You're an
emperor, and I'm a prince. Now, an't we—

COSTAR° No, Sergeant—I'll be no emperor.   15

KITE No!

COSTAR No, I'll be a justice of peace.

KITE A justice of peace, man!

COSTAR Ay, wauns will I, for since this Pressing Act they are greater
than any emperor under the sun.°   20

KITE Done—you're a justice of peace, and [*to Thomas*] you're a king,
and I'm a duke, and a rum duke,° an't I?

THOMAS° No, but I'll be no king.

KITE What then?

THOMAS I'll be a queen.   25

KITE A queen!

THOMAS Ay, Queen of England. That's greater than any king of 'em all.

KITE Bravely said! Faith: huzza for the Queen.

> *All huzza*

But heark'ee, you Mr Justice, and you Mr Queen, did you ever
see the Queen's picture?   30

[COSTAR and THOMAS] No, no.

KITE I wonder at that—I have two of 'em set in gold, and as like her
Majesty, God bless the mark.

> *He takes two broad pieces° out of his pocket*

See here, they're set in gold.

> *Gives one to each*

COSTAR (*looking earnestly upon the piece*) The wonderful works of   35
Nature!

THOMAS What's this written about?° Here's a posy, I believe.

> [*Tries to read the inscription*]

'Ca-ro-lus.'° What's that, Sergeant?

KITE O '*Carolus*.' Why '*Carolus*' is Latin for 'Queen Anne', that's all.

[THOMAS] 'Tis a fine thing to be a scollard,° Sergeant—will you part with   40 this? I'll buy it on you, if it come within the compass of a crawn.°

KITE A crown! Never talk of buying. 'Tis the same thing among friends, you know—I present them to you both: you shall give me as good a thing. Put them up,° and remember your old friend, when I'm—(singing) 'over the hills and far away.'   45

    They sing and put up the money. Enter Plume singing

PLUME   *Over the hills and o'er the main,*
        To Flanders, Portugal, or Spain;
        The Queen commands, and we'll obey,
        Over the hills and far away.°

Come on my men of mirth, away with it°—I'll make one among   50
ye. Who are these hearty lads?

KITE Off with your hats, ouns, off with your hats; this is the captain, the captain.

[COSTAR] We have seen captains afore now, mun.

[THOMAS] Ay, and lieutenant-captains° too; flesh, I'se keep on my   55
nab.°

[COSTAR] And I'se scarcely doff mine for any captain in England— my vether's a freeholder.°

PLUME Who are these jolly lads, Sergeant?

KITE A couple of honest brave fellows, that are willing to serve the   60
Queen; I have entertained them just now as volunteers under your honour's command.

PLUME And good entertainment they shall have—volunteers are the men I want, those are the men fit to make soldiers, captains, generals.   65

[COSTAR] Wauns, Tummas, what's this? Are you listed?

[THOMAS] Flesh, not I—are you, Costar?

[COSTAR] Wauns, not I!

KITE What, not listed! Ha, ha, ha, a very good jest, faith.

[COSTAR] Come, Tummas, we'll go whome.   70

[THOMAS] Ay, ay, come.

KITE Home! For shame, gentlemen, behave yourselves better before your captain. Dear Tummas, honest Costar—

[THOMAS] No, no, we'll be gone. (*Going*)

KITE Nay, then I command you to stay—I place you both sentinels in   75
this place for two hours to watch the motion of St Mary's clock you, and you the motion of St Chad's,° and he that dare stir from his post till he be relieved, shall have my sword in his guts the next minute.

PLUME What's the matter, Sergeant? I'm afraid you're too rough with these gentlemen.   80

KITE I'm too mild, sir—they disobey command, sir, and one of them
should be shot for an example to the other.

[COSTAR] Shot! Tummas.

PLUME Come, gentlemen, what is the matter?

[COSTAR] We don't know—the noble sergeant is pleased to be in a   85
passion, sir, but—

KITE They disobey command, they deny their being listed.

THOMAS Nay, Sergeant, we don't downright deny it neither—that
we dare not do for fear of being shot; but we humbly conceive in
a civil way, and begging your worship's pardon, that we may go   90
home.

PLUME That's easily known—have either of you received any of the
Queen's money?

[COSTAR] Not a brass farthing, sir.

KITE Sir, they have each of them received three and twenty shillings   95
and sixpence, and 'tis now in their pockets.

[COSTAR] Wauns! If I have a penny in my pocket but a bent
sixpence, I'll be content to be listed, and shot into the bargain!

THOMAS And I, look'e here, sir.

COSTAR Ay, here's my stock too [taking out coin]—nothing but the   100
Queen's picture, that the sergeant gave me just now.

KITE See there, a broad piece, three and twenty shillings and
sixpence—the t'other has the fellow on't.

PLUME The case is plain, gentlemen—the goods are found upon you;
those pieces of gold are worth three and twenty and sixpence each.   105

[COSTAR] So it seems that 'Carolus' is 'three and twenty shillings and
sixpence' in Latin.

[THOMAS] 'Tis the same thing in the Greek, for we are listed.

[COSTAR] Flesh, but we an't, Tummas. I desire to be carried before
the Mayar,° Captain.   110

       While they talk, [Plume] and [Kite] whisper

PLUME 'Twill never do, Kite; your damned tricks will ruin me at
last—I won't lose the fellows though, if I can help it. [Aloud] Well,
gentlemen, there must be some trick in this—my sergeant offers
here to take his oath that you're fairly listed.

[THOMAS]° Why, Captain, we know that you soldiers have more   115
liberty of conscience° than other folks, but for me or neighbour
Costar here to take such an oath, 'twould be downright perjuration.

PLUME [to Kite] Look'ee, you rascal, you villain, if I find that you
have imposed upon these two honest fellows, I'll trample you to
death, you dog! Come, how was't.   120

[THOMAS] Nay, then, we will speak—your sergeant, as you say, is a
   rogue, begging your worship's pardon. And—
[COSTAR] Nay, Tummas, let me speak—you know I can read. And
   so, sir, he gave us those two pieces of money for pictures of the
   Queen, by way of a present.   125
PLUME How! By way of a present! The son of a whore! I'll teach him
   to abuse honest fellows like you. Scoundrel, rogue, villain . . .
   etc.°
      Beats [Kite] off the stage and follows him out
[COSTAR and THOMAS] O brave noble Captain—huzza, a brave
   captain, faith!   130
[COSTAR] Now Tummas, 'Carolus' is Latin for a beating. This is the
   bravest captain I ever saw—wauns, I have a month's mind° to go
   with him.
      Enter Plume
PLUME A dog! To abuse two such pretty° fellows as you. Look'ee,
   gentlemen, I love a pretty fellow—I come among you here as an   135
   officer to list soldiers, not as a kidnapper, to steal slaves.°
[COSTAR] Mind that, Tummas.
PLUME I desire no man to go with me, but as I went myself. I went
   a volunteer, as you or you may go—for a little time carried a
   musket,° and now I command a company.   140
[THOMAS] Mind that, Costar—a sweet gentleman.
PLUME 'Tis true, gentlemen, I might take an advantage of you—the
   Queen's money was in your pockets, my sergeant was ready to take
   his oath that you were listed; but I scorn to do a base thing—you
   are both of you at your liberty.   145
[COSTAR] Thank you, noble Captain. Ecod, I cannot find in my heart
   to leave him, he talks so finely.
[THOMAS] Ay, Costar, would he alway hold in this mind.
PLUME Come, my lads, one thing more I'll tell you—you're both
   young tight fellows, and the army is the place to make you men   150
   for ever. Every man has his lot, and you have yours. What think
   you now of a purse full of French gold out of a monsieur's pocket,
   after you have dashed out his brains with the butt of your firelock,
   eh?
[COSTAR] Wauns, I'll have it, Captain—give me a shilling, I'll follow   155
   you to the end of the world.
[THOMAS] Nay, dear Costar, duna°—be advised.
PLUME Here, my hero, here are two guineas for thee, as earnest of
   what I'll do further for thee.

[THOMAS] Duna take it, duna, dear Costar.   160
  Cries and pulls back his arm

[COSTAR] I wull, I wull—wauns, my mind gives me that I shall be a
captain myself; I take your money, sir, and now I'm a gentleman.

PLUME Give me thy hand. And now you and I will travel the world
o'er, and command° wherever we tread. (*Aside*) Bring your friend
with you if you can.   165

[COSTAR] Well, Tummas, must we part?

[THOMAS] No, Costar, I cannot leave thee. Come, Captain, (*crying*)
I'll e'en go along too; and if you have two honester, simpler lads
in your company than we twa been—I'll say no more.

PLUME Here, my lad.   170
  Gives him money
Now your name?

[THOMAS] Tummas Appletree.

PLUME And yours?

COSTAR Costar Pearmain.°

PLUME Born where?   175

THOMAS Both in Herefordshire.°

PLUME Very well; courage, my lads—now we will sing 'Over the hills
and far away.'
  [*Sings*]
    Courage, boys, 'tis one to ten
    But we return all gentlemen, &c.
  Exeunt   180

3.1

Scene, the market place
Plume and Worthy

WORTHY I can't forbear admiring the equality of our two fortunes.
  We loved two ladies; they met us half way, and just as we were
  upon the point of leaping into their arms, fortune drops into their
  laps, pride possesses their hearts, a maggot fills their heads,
  madness takes 'em by the tails, they snort, kick up their heels, and   5
  away they run.

PLUME And leave us here to mourn upon the shore—a couple of
  poor melancholy monsters.° What shall we do?

WORTHY I have a trick for mine; the letter you know, and the
  fortune-teller.   10

PLUME And I have a trick for mine.

WORTHY What is't?

PLUME I'll never think of her again.

WORTHY No!

PLUME No; I think myself above administering to the pride of   15
  any woman, were she worth twelve thousand a year, and I
  han't the vanity to believe I shall ever gain a lady worth twelve
  hundred. The generous good-natured Silvia in her smock° I
  admire, but the haughty scornful Silvia, with her fortune, I
  despise.   20

> [*Plume sings*]
>   *Come, fair one, be kind*
>   *You never shall find*
>   *A fellow so fit for a lover.*
>   *The world shall view*
>   *My passion for you,*
>   *But never your passion discover.*   25
>
>
>   *I still will complain*
>   *Of your frowns and disdain,*
>   *Though I revel through all your charms.*
>   *The world shall declare,*   30
>   *That I die with despair,*
>   *When I only die in your arms.*

> *I still will adore,*
> *And love more and more,*
> *But, by Jove, if you chance to prove cruel,*   35
> *I'll get me a miss*
> *That freely will kiss,*
> *Though I afterwards drink water-gruel.*°

What! Sneak out o' town, and not so much as a word, a line, a
compliment! 'Sdeath, how far off does she live? I'd go and break   40
her windows.°

WORTHY Ha, ha, ha; ay, and the window-bars too to come at her.
Come, come, friend, no more of your rough military airs.
        Enter Kite

KITE Captain, sir, look yonder, she's a-coming this way—'tis the
prettiest, cleanest little tit—   45

PLUME Now, Worthy, to show you how much I'm in love: here she
comes, and what is that great country fellow with her?

KITE I can't tell, sir.
        Enter Rose and her brother Bullock, Rose with a basket on her
        arm, crying chickens°

ROSE Buy chickens, young and tender. Young and tender chickens.

PLUME Here, you chickens—   50

ROSE Who calls?

PLUME Come hither, pretty maid.

ROSE Will you please to buy, sir?

WORTHY Yes, child, we'll both buy.

PLUME Nay, Worthy, that's not fair—market for yourself. Come, my   55
child, I'll buy all you have.

ROSE Then all I have is at your sarvice.°
        Curtsies

WORTHY Then I must shift for myself, I find.
        Exit [Worthy]

PLUME Let me see—young and tender, you say?
        Chucks her under the chin

ROSE As ever you tasted in your life, sir.   60
        Curtsies

PLUME Come, I must examine your basket to the bottom, my dear.

ROSE Nay, for that matter, put in your hand, feel, sir;° I warrant my
ware as good as any in the market.

PLUME And I'll buy it all, child, were it ten times more.

ROSE Sir, I can furnish you.   65

PLUME Come then; we won't quarrel about the price—they're fine
birds. Pray what's your name, pretty creature.

ROSE Rose, sir. My father is a farmer within three short mile o'th'
town; we keep this market;° I sell chickens, eggs, and butter, and
my brother Bullock there sells corn.   70

BULLOCK Come, sister, hast ye, we shall be liate a-whome.°
    All this while Bullock whistles about the stage

PLUME [*aside*] Kite!
    He tips the wink upon Kite, who returns it
Pretty Mrs Rose! you have—let me see—how many?

ROSE A dozen, sir. And they are richly worth a crawn.

BULLOCK Come, Ruose, Ruose, I sold fifty stracke o'° barely today   75
in half this time; but you will higgle and higgle for a penny more
than the commodity° is worth.

ROSE What's that to you, oaf? I can make as much out of a groat, as
you can out of fourpence,° I'm sure. The gentleman bids fair, and
when I meet with a chapman, I know how to make the best on   80
him. [*To Plume, while Kite draws Bullock aside and talks with him*]
And so, sir, I say, for a crawn piece the bargain is yours.

PLUME Here's a guinea, my dear.

ROSE I con't change your money, sir.

PLUME Indeed, indeed but you can. My lodging is hard by—you   85
shall bring home the chickens,° and we'll make change there.°
    Goes off: she follows him

KITE So, sir, as I was telling you, I have seen one of these hussars eat up
a ravelin for his breakfast, and afterwards pick his teeth with a palisado.

BULLOCK Ay, you soldiers see very strange things. But pray sir, what
is a ravelin?   90

KITE Why 'tis like a modern minced-pie, but the crust is confounded
hard, and the plums are somewhat hard of digestion!

BULLOCK Then your palisado, pray what may he be?—Come, Ruose,
pray ha' done.

KITE Your palisado is a pretty sort of bodkin, about the thickness of   95
my leg.

BULLOCK (*aside*) That's a fib, I believe. Eh, where's Ruose?—Ruose!
Ruose! 'sflesh, where's Ruose gone?

KITE She's gone with the captain.

BULLOCK The captain! Wauns, there's no pressing of women, sure.   100

KITE But there is, sir.

BULLOCK If the captain should press Ruose, I should be ruined. Which
way went she? O! The Devil take your rablins and palisaders.

Exit [Bullock]

KITE You shall be better acquainted with them, honest Bullock, or I
shall miss of my aim.   105

Enter Worthy

WORTHY Why, thou'rt the most useful fellow in nature to your
captain, admirable in your way, I find.

KITE Yes, sir, I understand my business, I will say it. You must
know, sir, I was born a gypsy,° and bred among that crew till I
was ten year old; there I learned canting and lying. I was bought   110
from my mother Cleopatra by a certain nobleman for three
pistoles, who liking my beauty made me his page; there I learned
impudence and pimping. I was turned off for wearing my lord's
linen, and drinking my lady's brandy,° and then turned bailliff's
follower;° there I learned bullying and swearing. I at last got into 115
the army, and there I learned whoring and drinking. So that if your
worship pleases to cast up the whole sum, *viz.* canting, lying,
impudence, pimping, bullying, swearing, whoring, drinking, and a
halberd, you will find the sum total will amount to a recruiting
sergeant.   120

WORTHY And pray, what induced you to turn soldier?

KITE Hunger and ambition. The fears of starving and hopes of a
truncheon,° led me along to a gentleman with a fair tongue and
fair periwig, who loaded me with promises; but egad 'twas the
lightest load that I ever felt in my life. He promised to advance   125
me, and indeed he did so—to a garret in the Savoy.° I asked him
why he put me in prison—he called me lying dog, and said I was
in garrison, and indeed 'tis a garrison that may hold out till
doomsday before I should desire to take it again.° But here comes
Justice Balance.   130

Enter Balance and Bullock

BALANCE Here, you Sergeant, where's your captain? Here's a poor
foolish fellow comes clamouring to me with a complaint, that your
captain has pressed his sister—do you know anything of this
matter, Worthy?

WORTHY Ha, ha, ha, I know his sister is gone with Plume to his   135
lodgings to sell him some chickens.

BALANCE Is that all? The fellow's a fool.

BULLOCK I know that, an't° please you; but if your worship
pleases to grant me a warrant to bring her before you for fear o'th'
worst.   140

BALANCE Thou art a mad fellow—thy sister's safe° enough.

KITE (*aside*) I hope so too.

WORTHY Hast thou no more sense, fellow, than to believe that the captain can list women?

BULLOCK I know not whether they list them, or what they do with them, but I'm sure they carry as many women as men with them out of the country.

BALANCE But how came you not to go along with your sister?

BULLOCK Luord, sir, I thought no more of her going than I do of the day I shall die; but this gentleman, here, not suspecting any hurt neither, I believe—you thought no harm, friend, did ye?

KITE Lackaday, sir, not I. (*Aside*) Only that I believe I shall marry her tomorrow.

BALANCE [*aside*] I begin to smell powder.° [*To Bullock*] Well, friend, but what did that gentleman with you?

BULLOCK Why, sir, he entertained me with a fine story of a great fight between the Hungarians, I think it was, and the Irish;° and so, sir, while we were in the heat of the battle, the captain carried off the baggage.°

BALANCE Sergeant, go along with this fellow to your captain, give him my humble service, and I° desire him to discharge the wench, though he has listed her.

BULLOCK Ay. And if he ben't free for that, he shall have another man in her place.

KITE [*to Bullock*] Come, honest friend. (*Aside*) You shall go to my quarters instead of the captain's.

    Exeunt Kite and Bullock

BALANCE We must get this mad captain his complement of men, and send him a-packing, else he'll overrun the country.

WORTHY You see, sir, how little he values your daughter's disdain.

BALANCE I like him the better—I was much° such another fellow at his age; I never set my heart upon any woman so much as to make me uneasy at the disappointment—but what was very surprising both to myself and friends, I changed o'th' sudden from the most fickle lover to be the most constant husband in the world. But how goes your affair with Melinda?

WORTHY Very slowly—Cupid had° formerly wings, but I think in this age he goes upon crutches, or I fancy Venus has been dallying with her cripple Vulcan° when my amour commenced, which has made it go on so lamely; my mistress has got a captain too, but such a captain! As I live yonder he comes.

BALANCE Who? That bluff fellow in the sash. I don't know him.

WORTHY But I engage he knows you, and everybody at first sight; his impudence were a prodigy, were not his ignorance proportionable; he has the most universal acquaintance of any man living, for he won't be alone, and nobody will keep him company twice; then he's a Caesar among the women—*veni, vidi, vici*,° that's all. If he has but talked with the maid, he swears he has lain with the mistress: but the most surprising part of his character is his memory, which is the most prodigious, and the most trifling in the world.

BALANCE I have met with such men, and I take this good-for-nothing memory to proceed from a certain contexture of the brain, which is purely adapted to impertinencies, and there they lodge secure, the owner having no thoughts of his own to disturb them. I have known a man as perfect as a chronologer as to the day and year of most unimportant° transactions, but be altogether ignorant of the causes, springs, or consequences of any one thing of moment. I have known another acquire so much by travel, as to tell you the names of most places in Europe, with their distances of miles, leagues or hours,° as punctually as a postboy; but for anything else, as ignorant as the horse that carries the mail.

WORTHY This is your man, sir, add but the traveller's privilege of lying, and even that he abuses; this is the picture, behold the life!
    Enter Brazen°

BRAZEN Mr Worthy, I'm your servant, and so forth. Hark'ee, my dear.

WORTHY Whispering, sir, before company is not manners, and when nobody's by, 'tis foolish.

BRAZEN Company! *Mort de ma vie*.° I beg the gentleman's pardon—who is he?

WORTHY Ask him.

BRAZEN So I will. [*To Balance*] My dear, I'm your servant, and so forth—your name, my dear?

BALANCE Very laconic, sir.

BRAZEN Laconic, a very good name, truly; I have known several of the Laconics abroad—poor Jack Laconic! He was killed at the battle of Landen.° I remember that he had a blue ribbon in his hat that very day, and after he fell, we found a piece of neat's tongue in his pocket.

BALANCE Pray, sir, did the French attack us, or we them, at Landen?

BRAZEN The French attack us! Oons, sir, are you a Jacobite?°

BALANCE Why that question?

BRAZEN Because none but a Jacobite could think that the French
durst attack us. No, sir, we attacked them on the—I have reason
to remember the time, for I had two and twenty horses killed
under me that day.°   225

WORTHY Then, sir, you rid mighty hard.

BALANCE Or perhaps, sir, like my countryman,° you rid upon half a
dozen horses at once.

BRAZEN What d'e mean, gentlemen? I tell you they were killed; all
torn to pieces by cannon-shot, except six that I staked to death   230
upon the enemy's *chevaux de frise*.°

BALANCE Noble Captain, may I crave your name?

BRAZEN Brazen, at your service.

BALANCE O, Brazen! A very good name, I have known several of the
Brazens abroad.   235

WORTHY Do you know Captain Plume, sir?

BRAZEN Is he anything related to Frank Plume in Northampton-
shire? Honest Frank! Many, many a dry bottle have we cracked
hand to fist;° you must have known his brother Charles that was
concerned in the India Company°—he married the daughter of old   240
Tonguepad° the Master in Chancery,° a very pretty woman, only
squinted a little. She died in childbed of her first child, but the
child survived—'twas a daughter, but whether 'twas called Margaret or Margery, upon my soul, I can't remember. But, gentlemen
(*looking on his watch*) I must meet a lady, a twenty thousand   245
pounder° presently, upon the walk by the water. Worthy, your
servant. Laconic, yours.
          Exit [Brazen]

BALANCE If you can have so mean an opinion of Melinda, as to be
jealous of this fellow, I think she ought to give you cause to be so.

WORTHY I don't think she encourages him so much for gaining   250
herself a lover, as to set me up a rival; were there any credit to be
given to his words, I should believe Melinda had made him this
assignation. I must go see—sir, you'll pardon me.

BALANCE Ay, ay, sir, you're a man of business.
          [*Exit Worthy*]
But what have we got here?   255
          Enter Rose singing what she pleases°

ROSE And I shall be a lady, a captain's lady; and ride single upon a
white horse with a star,° upon a velvet side-saddle, and I shall go
to London and see the tombs and the lions, and the Queen.° Sir,
an't please your worship, I have often seen your worship ride

through our grounds a-hunting, begging your worship's pardon.   260
Pray what may this lace be worth a yard? (*Showing some lace*)

BALANCE Right Mechlin,° by this light! Where did you get this lace,
child?

ROSE No matter for that, sir, I come honestly by't.

BALANCE I question it much.   265

ROSE And see here, sir, a fine turkey-shell° snuff-box, and fine
manageree,° see here.

> *She takes snuff affectedly*

The captain learned me° how to take it with an air.

BALANCE Oho, the captain! Now the murder's out. And so the
captain taught you to take it with an air?   270

ROSE Yes, and give it with an air, too. Will your worship please to
taste my snuff?

> *Offers the box affectedly*

BALANCE You're a very apt scholar, pretty maid, and pray what did
you give the captain for these fine things?

ROSE He's to have my brother for a soldier, and two or three   275
sweethearts that I have in the country—they shall all go with the
captain. O he's the finest man, and the humblest withal°—would
you believe it, sir? He carried me up with him to his own chamber
with as much familiarity° as if I had been the best lady in the land.

BALANCE O he's a mighty familiar gentleman as can be.   280

ROSE But I must beg your worship's pardon—I must go seek out my
brother Bullock.

> *Runs off singing*

BALANCE If all officers took the same method of recruiting with this
gentleman,° they might come in time to be fathers as well as
captains of their companies.°   285

> *Enter Plume singing [with Rose]*

PLUME   *But it is not so*
             With those that go
             Through frost and snow
             Most apropos,
             My maid with the milking-pail.°   290

> *Takes hold on Rose*

[*Aside*] How, the Justice! Then I'm arraigned, condemned, and
executed.

BALANCE O, my noble captain.

ROSE And my noble captain too, sir.

PLUME 'Sdeath, child, are you mad? Mr Balance, I am so full of   295

business about my recruits, that I han't a moment's time to—I
have just now three or four people to—

BALANCE Nay, Captain, I must speak to you.

ROSE And so must I too, Captain.

PLUME Any other time, sir; I cannot for my life, sir—

BALANCE Pray, sir—

PLUME Twenty thousand things—I would but—now, sir, pray—
Devil take me—I cannot—I must—
          Breaks away [and exit]

BALANCE Nay, I'll follow you.
          Exit [Balance]

ROSE And I too.
          Exit

3.2

Scene, the walk, by the Severn side

Enter Melinda and her maid Lucy

MELINDA And pray, was it a ring, or buckle, or pendants, or knots;
or in what shape was the almighty gold transformed that has bribed
you so much in his favour?

LUCY Indeed, madam, the last bribe I had was from the captain, and
that was only a small piece of Flanders edging for pinners.°

MELINDA Ay, Flanders lace is as constant a present from officers to
their women as something else is from their women to them. They
every year bring over a cargo of lace to cheat the Queen of her
duty,° and her subjects of their honesty.

LUCY They only barter one sort of prohibited goods for another,
madam.

MELINDA Has any of them been bartering with you, Mrs Pert, that
you talk so like a trader?

LUCY Madam, you talk as peevishly to me as if it were my fault—the
crime is none of mine though I pretend to excuse it; though he
should not see you this week, can I help it? But as I was saying,
madam, his friend Captain Plume has so taken him up these two
days—

MELINDA Psha! would his friend, the captain, were tied on his back.°
I warrant he has never been sober since that confounded captain

came to town. The Devil take all officers, I say—they do the nation more harm by debauching us at home, than they do good by defending us abroad. No sooner a captain comes to town, but all the young fellows flock about him, and we can't keep a man to ourselves.   25

LUCY One would imagine, madam, by your concern for Worthy's absence, that you should use him better when he's with you.

MELINDA Who told you, pray, that I was concerned for his absence? I'm only vexed that I've had nothing said to me these two days. One may like the love, and despise the lover, I hope; as one may   30 love the treason, and hate the traitor. O, here comes another captain, and a rogue that has the confidence to make love to me; but indeed I don't wonder at that, when he has the assurance to fancy himself a fine gentleman.

LUCY (aside) If he should speak o'th' assignation, I should be ruined.   35
    Enter Brazen

BRAZEN (aside) True to the touch,° faith. I'll draw up all my compliments into one grand platoon, and fire upon her at once.
    [Aloud] Thou peerless Princess of Salopian plains,
            Envied by nymphs, and worshipped by the swains,
            Behold how humbly does the Severn glide,   40
            To greet thee, Princess of the Severn side.°
    Madam, I'm your humble servant, and all that, madam. A fine river this same Severn—do you love fishing, madam?

MELINDA 'Tis a pretty, melancholy amusement° for lovers.

BRAZEN I'll go buy hooks and lines presently; for you must know,   45 madam, that I have served in Flanders against the French, in Hungary against the Turks, and in Tangier against the Moors,° and I was never so much in love before; and split me, madam, in all the campaigns I ever made I have not seen so fine a woman as your ladyship.   50

MELINDA And from all the men I ever saw I never had so fine a compliment; but you soldiers are the best bred men—that we must allow.

BRAZEN Some of us, madam, but there are brutes among us too, very sad brutes; for my own part, I have always had the good luck to   55 prove agreeable. I have had very considerable offers, madam—I might have married a German princess worth fifty thousand crowns a year, but her stove disgusted me;° the daughter of a Turkish bashaw fell in love with me too when I was prisoner among the infidels—she offered to rob her father of his treasure,   60

and make her escape with me,° but I don't know how, my time
was not come. Hanging and marriage, you know, go by destiny;
Fate has reserved me for a Shropshire lady with twenty thousand
pound. Do you know any such person, madam?

MELINDA [*aside*] Extravagant coxcomb! [*Aloud*] To be sure a great   65
many ladies of that fortune would be proud of the name of Mrs
Brazen.

BRAZEN Nay, for that matter, madam, there are women of very good
quality of the name of Brazen.
      Enter Worthy

MELINDA [*aside*] O! are you there, gentleman? [*Aloud to Brazen*]   70
Come, Captain, we'll walk this way—give me your hand.

BRAZEN My hand, heart's blood and guts are at your service. Mr
Worthy—your servant, my dear.
      Exit [Brazen,] leading Melinda, [Lucy following]

WORTHY Death and fire! This is not to be borne!
      Enter Plume

PLUME No more it is, faith.   75

WORTHY What?

PLUME The March beer at the Raven;° I have been doubly serving
the Queen—raising men, and raising the excise.° Recruiting and
elections are good friends to the excise.

WORTHY You an't drunk?   80

PLUME No, no, whimsical only; I could be mighty foolish, and fancy
myself mighty witty; reason still keeps its throne, but it nods a
little, that's all.

WORTHY Then you're just fit for a frolic?

PLUME As fit as close pinners for a punk in the pit.°   85

WORTHY There's your play then—recover me that vessel from that
Tangerine.°

PLUME She's well rigged, but how is she manned?

WORTHY By Captain Brazen that I told you of today; the frigate° is
called the Melinda, a first-rate, I can assure you; she sheered off   90
with him just now on purpose to affront me, but according to your
advice I would take no notice, because I would seem to be above
a concern for her behaviour; but have a care of a quarrel.

PLUME No, no, I never quarrel with anything in my cups but with
an oyster-wench or a cookmaid, and if they ben't civil, I knock 'em   95
down. But heark'ee my friend, I will make love, and I must make
love—I tell 'ee what. I'll make love like a platoon.

WORTHY A platoon! how's that?

PLUME I'll kneel, stoop and stand, faith; most ladies are gained by
platooning.°   100

WORTHY Here they come; I must leave you.
        Exit [Worthy]

PLUME So. Now I must° look as sober and demure as a whore at a
christening.
        Enter Brazen and Melinda

BRAZEN Who's that, madam?

MELINDA A brother officer of yours, I suppose.   105

BRAZEN Ay! (*To Plume*) My dear!

PLUME My dear!
        They run and embrace

BRAZEN My dear boy, how is't? Your name, my dear? If I be not
mistaken, I have seen your face.

PLUME I never see yours in my life, my dear. [*Looking towards*   110
Melinda] But there's a face well known as the sun's, that shines on
all, and is by all adored.

BRAZEN Have you any pretensions, sir?

PLUME Pretensions!

BRAZEN That is, sir, have you ever served abroad?   115

PLUME I have served at home, sir; for ages served this cruel fair. And
that will serve the turn, sir.

MELINDA (*aside*) So! Between the fool and the rake, I shall bring a
fine spot of work upon my hands. I see Worthy yonder—I could
be content to be friends with him would he come this way.   120

BRAZEN Will you fight for the lady, sir?

PLUME No, sir, but I'll have her notwithstanding.
        Thou peerless Princess of Salopian plains,
        Envied by nymphs, and worshipped by the swains.

BRAZEN Oons, sir, not fight for her!   125

PLUME Prithee be quiet—I shall be out.°
            Behold how humbly does the Severn glide
            To greet thee, Princess of the Severn side!

BRAZEN Don't mind him, madam—if he were not so well dressed I
should take him for a poet; but I'll show the difference presently.   130
Come, madam, we'll place you between us, and now the longest
sword carries her.
        Draws; Melinda shrieks
        Enter Worthy

MELINDA O! Mr Worthy, save me from these madmen.
        Runs off with Worthy

PLUME Ha, ha, ha, why don't you follow, sir, and fight the bold
ravisher? 135

BRAZEN No, sir, you're my man.

PLUME I don't like the wages, and I won't be 'your man'.°

BRAZEN Then you're not worth my sword.

PLUME No! Pray what did it cost?

BRAZEN It cost my enemies thousands of lives,° sir. 140

PLUME Then they had a dear bargain.

Enter Silvia dressed in man's apparel

SILVIA Save ye, save ye, gentlemen.

BRAZEN My dear, I'm yours.

PLUME Do you know the gentleman?

BRAZEN No, but I will presently. [*To Silvia*] Your name, my dear. 145

SILVIA Wilful, Jack Wilful, at your service.

BRAZEN What! The Kentish Wilfuls, or those of Staffordshire?

SILVIA Both sir, both; I'm related to all the Wilfuls in Europe, and
I'm head of the family at present.

PLUME Do you live in the country,° sir? 150

SILVIA Yes, sir, I live where I should;° I have neither home, house,
nor habitation beyond this spot of ground.

BRAZEN What are you, sir?

SILVIA A rake.

PLUME In the army I presume. 155

SILVIA No, but I intend to list immediately. Look'ee, gentlemen, he
that bids me fairest shall have° me.

BRAZEN Sir, I'll prefer you—I'll make you a corporal this minute.

PLUME A corporal! I'll make you my companion—you shall eat with me.

BRAZEN You shall drink with me. 160

PLUME You shall lie with me,° you young rogue.

Kisses her°

BRAZEN You shall receive your pay, and do no duty.

SILVIA Then you must make me a field officer.°

PLUME Pho, pho, I'll do more than all this—I'll make you a corporal,
and give you a brevet for sergeant. 165

BRAZEN Can you read and write, sir?

SILVIA Yes.

BRAZEN Then your business is done—I'll make you chaplain to the
regiment.

SILVIA Your promises are so equal, that I'm at a loss to choose— 170
there is one Plume that I hear much commended in town; pray
which of you is Captain Plume?

PLUME I'm Captain Plume.

BRAZEN No, no, I am Captain Plume.

SILVIA Hey-day!   175

PLUME [to Brazen] Captain Plume, I'm your servant, my dear.

BRAZEN Captain Brazen, I'm yours. The fellow dare not fight.

        Enter Kite. Goes to whisper [to] Plume

KITE Sir, if you please—

PLUME No, no, there's your captain. [To Brazen] Captain
        Plume, your sergeant here° has got so drunk he mistakes me for   180
        you.

BRAZEN He's an incorrigible sot. [To Silvia] Here, my Hector of
        Holborn,° forty shillings for you.

PLUME I forbid the banns.° [To Silvia] Look'ee, friend, you shall list
        with Captain Brazen.   185

SILVIA I will see Captain Brazen hanged first—I will list with
        Captain Plume. I'm a freeborn Englishman, and will be a slave my
        own way. (To Brazen) Look'ee, sir, will you stand by me?

BRAZEN I warrant you, my lad.

SILVIA (to Plume) Then I will tell you, Captain Brazen, that you are   190
        an ignorant, pretending, impudent coxcomb.

BRAZEN Ay, ay, a sad dog.

SILVIA A very sad dog. [To Brazen] Give me the money, noble
        Captain Plume.

PLUME Hold, hold°—then you won't list with Captain Brazen?   195

SILVIA I won't.

BRAZEN [to Silvia] Never mind him, child—I'll end the dispute
        presently. [To Plume] Heark'ee, my dear.

        *Takes Plume to one side of the stage, and entertains him in dumb
        show*

KITE [to Silvia] Sir, he in the plain coat is Captain Plume—I'm his
        sergeant, and will take my oath on't.   200

SILVIA What!—are you Sergeant Kite?

KITE At your service.

SILVIA Then I would not take your oath for a farthing.

KITE A very understanding youth of his age! Pray sir, let me look
        you full in the face.   205

SILVIA Well, sir, what have you to say to my face?

KITE The very image and superscription° of my brother—two bullets
        of the same caliber were never so like; sure it must be Charles,
        Charles—

SILVIA What d'ye mean by 'Charles'?   210

KITE The voice too, only a little variation in C fa ut flat.° My dear
    brother, for I must call you so, if you should have the fortune to
    enter into the most noble society of the sword, I bespeak you for
    a comrade.

SILVIA No, sir, I'll be your captain's comrade if anybody's.   215

KITE Ambition! There again, 'tis a noble passion for a soldier; by that
    I gained this glorious halberd. Ambition! I see a commission in his
    face already—pray, noble Captain, give me leave to salute you.
            Offers to kiss her

SILVIA What! Men kiss one another!

KITE We officers do, 'tis our way; we live together like man and wife,   220
    always either kissing or fighting. [*Looking towards Brazen and
    Plume*] But I see a storm a-coming.

SILVIA Now, Sergeant, I shall see who is your captain by your
    knocking down the t'other.

KITE My captain scorns assistance, sir.   225

BRAZEN How dare you contend for anything, and not dare to draw
    your sword? But you're a young fellow, and have not been much
    abroad—I excuse that; but prithee resign the man, prithee do—
    you're a very honest fellow.

PLUME You lie, and you're a son of a whore.   230
            Draws and makes up to Brazen

BRAZEN (*retiring*) Hold! hold—did not you refuse to fight for the
    lady?

PLUME I always do, but for a man I'll fight knee deep, so you lie
    again.
            *Plume and Brazen fight a traverse or two about the stage; Silvia
            draws and is held by Kite, who sounds 'To arms' with his
            mouth,° takes Silvia in his arms, and carries her off the stage*

BRAZEN Hold. Where's the man?   235

PLUME Gone.

BRAZEN Then what do we fight for?
            Puts up
    Now let's embrace, my dear.

PLUME With all my heart, my dear.
            Puts up
    [*Aside*] I suppose Kite has listed him by this time.   240
            They embrace

BRAZEN You're a brave fellow—I always fight with a man before I
    make him my friend; and if once I find he will fight, I never
    quarrel with him afterwards. And now I'll tell you a secret, my

dear friend—that lady that we frighted out o'the walk just now I
found in bed this morning, so beautiful, so inviting. I presently   245
locked the door . . . But I'm a man of honour. But I believe I shall
marry her nevertheless; her twenty thousand pound you know will
be a pretty convenience. I had an assignation with her here, but
your coming spoiled my sport, curse ye, my dear. But don't do so
again.   250

PLUME No, no, my dear, men are my business at present.
    Exeunt

4.[1]

Scene of the walk continues

Rose and Bullock, meeting

ROSE Where have you been, you great booby?—you're always out o'th' way in the time of preferment.

BULLOCK Preferment! Who should prefer me?

ROSE I would prefer you—who should prefer a man but a woman? Come throw away that great club,° hold up your head, cock your hat, and look big.   5

BULLOCK Ah! Ruose, Ruose, I fear somebody will look big sooner than folk think of; this genteel breeding never comes into the country without a train of followers.° Here has been Cartwheel your sweetheart—what will become o' him?   10

ROSE Look'ee, I'm a great woman, and will provide for my relations. I told the captain how finely he could play upon the tabor and pipe, so he has set him down for a drum-major.

BULLOCK Nay, sister, why did not you keep that place for me? You know I always loved to be a-drumming, if it were but on a table,   15
or on a quart pot.

Enter Silvia

SILVIA [*aside*] Had I but a commission° in my pocket, I fancy my breeches would become me as well as any ranting fellow of 'em all; for I take a bold step, a rakish toss, a smart cock,° and an impudent air to be the principal ingredients in the composition of a captain.   20
What's here—Rose, my nurse's daughter! I'll go and practise.— Come child, kiss me at once.

Kisses Rose

And her brother too! Well, honest dungfork, do you know the difference between a horse-cart and a cart-horse, eh?

BULLOCK I presume that your worship is a captain by your clothes   25
and your courage.

SILVIA Suppose I were, would you be contented to list, friend?

ROSE No, no, though your worship be a handsome man, there be others as fine as you; my brother is engaged to Captain Plume.

SILVIA Plume! do you know Captain Plume?   30

ROSE Yes, I do, and he knows me. He took the very ribbons out of his shirt sleeves, and put them into my shoes. See there. I can assure you° that I can do anything with the captain.

BULLOCK That is, in a modest way, sir. Have a care what you say, Ruose—don't shame your parentage.   35

ROSE Nay, for that matter I am not so simple as to say that I can do anything with the captain, but what I may do with anybody else.

SILVIA So!—and pray what do you expect from this captain, child?

ROSE I expect, sir! I expect—but he ordered me to tell nobody. But suppose that he should promise to marry me.   40

SILVIA You should have a care, my dear—men will promise anything beforehand.

ROSE I know that, but he promised to marry me afterwards.

BULLOCK Wauns, Ruose, what have you said?

SILVIA Afterwards! After what?   45

ROSE After I had sold him my chickens—I hope there's no harm in that, though there be an ugly song of chickens and sparagus.°
     Enter Plume

PLUME What! Mr Wilful, so close with my market-woman!

SILVIA (*aside*) I'll try if he loves her. (*Aloud*) Close, Sir! ay, and closer yet, sir. Come, my pretty maid, you and I will withdraw a   50
     little—[*holding her*]

PLUME [*holding her also*] No, no, friend, I han't done with her yet.

SILVIA Nor have I begun with her, so I have as good a right as you have.[1]

PLUME Thou art a bloody,° impudent fellow—let her go, I say.   55

SILVIA Do you let her go.

PLUME *Entendez vous français, mon petit garçon?*

SILVIA *Oui.*

PLUME *Si voulez-vous donc vous enroller dans ma companie, la demoiselle sera à vous.*   60

SILVIA *Avez-vous couché avec elle?*

---

[1] *Between lines 55 and 67 the second edition reads:*

PLUME Thou art a bloody, impudent fellow.

SILVIA Sir, I would qualify myself for the service.   55

PLUME Hast thou really a mind to the service?

SILVIA Yes, sir. So let her go.

ROSE Pray, gentlemen, don't be so violent.

PLUME Come, leave it to the girl's own choice. Will you belong to me or to that gentleman?   60

ROSE Let me consider—you're both very handsome.

PLUME *Non.*

SILVIA *Assurement?*

PLUME *Ma foi.*

SILVIA *C'est assez. Je serai votre soldat.* 65

PLUME *La prenez donc.*° I'll change a woman for a man at any time.

ROSE But I hope Captain, you won't part with me.
  Cries
  I have heard before indeed that you captains use to sell° your men.

BULLOCK (*crying*) Pray, Captain, don't send Ruose to the West
  Indies.° 70

PLUME Ha, ha, ha, West Indies! No, no, my honest lad, give me thy
  hand—nor you, nor she shall move a step farther than I do. This
  gentleman is one of us, and will be kind to you, Mrs Rose.

ROSE [*to Silvia*] But will you be so kind to me, sir, as the captain would?

SILVIA I can't be altogether so kind to you—my circumstances are not 75
  so good as the captain's—but I'll take care of you, upon my word.

PLUME Ay, ay, we'll all take care of her—she shall live like a princess,
  and her brother here shall be—[*To Bullock*] What would you be?

BULLOCK Ah! sir, if you had not promised the place of drum-major.

PLUME Ay, that is promised—but what think ye of barrack-master? 80
  You're a person of understanding, and barrack-master you shall be.

PLUME [*aside*] Now the natural unconstancy of her sex begins to
  work.

ROSE [*to Silvia*] Pray, sir, what will you give me?

BULLOCK Don't be angry, sir, that my sister should be mercenary, 65
  for she's but young.

SILVIA Give thee, child! I'll set thee above scandal; you shall have a
  coach with six before and six behind;° an equipage to make vice
  fashionable, and put virtue out of countenance.

PLUME Pho, that's easily done; I'll do more for thee, child—I'll buy 70
  you a furbelow scarf, and give you a ticket to see a play.

BULLOCK A play—wauns, Ruose, take the ticket, and let's see the
  show.

SILVIA Look'ee, Captain, if you won't resign, I'll go list with Captain
  Brazen this minute. 75

PLUME Will you list with me if I give up my title?

SILVIA I will.

PLUME Take her—I'll change a woman for a man at any time.

[*To Rose*] But what's become of this same Cartwheel you told me of, my dear?

ROSE We'll go fetch him. [*To Bullock*] Come, brother barrack-master. We shall find you at home, noble Captain? 85
Exeunt Rose and Bullock

PLUME Yes, yes. And now, sir, here are your forty shillings.

SILVIA Captain Plume, I despise your listing money—if I do serve, 'tis purely for love—of that wench, I mean; for you must know, that among my other sallies, I have spent the best part of my fortune in search of a maid, and could never find one hitherto; so 90 you may be assured that I won't sell my freedom under a less purchase than I did my estate, so before I list I must be certified that this girl is a virgin.

PLUME Mr Wilful, I can't tell how you can be certified in that point till you try, but upon my honour she may be a vestal° for aught 95 that I know to the contrary. I gained her heart indeed by some trifling presents and promises, and knowing that the best security for a woman's soul is her body, I would have made myself master of that too, had not the jealousy of my impertinent landlady interposed. 100

SILVIA So you only want an opportunity for accomplishing your designs upon her.

PLUME Not at all—I have already gained my ends, which were only the drawing in one or two of her followers; the women, you know, are the loadstones everywhere—gain the wives, and you're caressed 105 by the husbands; please the mistresses,° and you are valued by their° gallants; secure an interest with the finest women at Court, and you procure the favour of the greatest men. So kiss the prettiest country wenches, and you are sure of listing the lustiest fellows. Some people may call this artifice, but I term it stratagem, 110 since it is so main a part of the service. Besides, the fatigue of recruiting is so intolerable, that unless we could make ourselves some pleasure amidst the pain, no mortal man would be able to bear it.

SILVIA Well, sir, I'm satisfied as to the point in debate. But now let 115 me beg you to lay aside your recruiting airs, put on the man of honour, and tell me plainly what usage I must expect when I'm under your command.

PLUME You must know in the first place then, that I hate to have gentlemen in my company, for they are always troublesome and 120 expensive, sometimes dangerous; and 'tis a constant maxim among us, that those who know the least, obey the best. Notwithstanding all this, I find something so agreeable about you, that engages me to court your company; and I can't tell how it is, but I should be uneasy to see you under the command of anybody else. Your usage will chiefly depend upon your behaviour; only this you must expect, that if you commit a small fault I will excuse it, if a great one, I'll discharge you, for something tells me I shall not be able to punish you.

SILVIA And something tells me, that if you do discharge me 'twill be the greatest punishment you will inflict; for were we this moment to go upon the greatest dangers in your profession, they would be less terrible to me, than to stay behind you. And now your hand [*shakes hands with Plume*]—this lists me—and now you are my captain.

PLUME Your friend.
        Kisses her
    'Sdeath! there's something in this fellow that charms me.

SILVIA One favour I must beg. This affair will make some noise, and I have some friends that would censure my conduct if I threw myself into the circumstances of a private sentinel of my own head;° I must therefore take care to be impressed by the Act of Parliament—you shall leave that to me.

PLUME What you please as to that. Will you lodge at my quarters in the meantime? You shall have part of my bed.

SILVIA O fie, lie with a common soldier! Would not you rather lie with a common woman?

PLUME No, faith, I am not that rake that the world imagines; I have got an air of freedom, which people mistake for lewdness in me, as they mistake formality in others for religion; the world is all a cheat, only I take mine which is undesigned to be more excusable than theirs, which is hypocritical; I hurt nobody but myself, and they abuse all mankind. Will you lie with me?

SILVIA No, no, Captain, you forget Rose; she's to be my bedfellow, you know.

PLUME I had forgot—pray be kind to her.
        Exeunt [*Silvia and Plume*] *severally. Enter Melinda and Lucy*°

MELINDA [*aside*] 'Tis the greatest misfortune in nature for a woman to want a confidante—we are so weak that we can do nothing without assistance, and then a secret racks us worse than the colic; I'm at this minute so sick of a secret, that I'm ready to faint away. [*Aloud*] Help me, Lucy.

LUCY Bless me, madam, what's the matter?

MELINDA Vapours only—I begin to recover. If Silvia were in town, I could heartily forgive her faults for the ease of discovering my own.

LUCY You're thoughtful, madam—am not I worthy to know the cause? 165

MELINDA You're a servant, and a secret would make you saucy.

LUCY Not unless you should find fault without a cause, madam.

MELINDA Cause or not cause, I must not lose the pleasure of chiding when I please; women must discharge their vapours somewhere, 170 and before we get husbands, our servants must expect to bear with 'em.

LUCY Then, madam, you had better raise me to a degree above a servant. You know my family, and that five hundred pound would set me upon the foot of° a gentlewoman, and make me worthy the 175 confidence of any lady in the land; besides, madam, 'twill extremely encourage me in the great design° that I now have in hand.

MELINDA I don't find that your design can be of any great advantage to you. 'Twill please me indeed in the humour I have of being revenged on the fool for his vanity of making love to me, so I don't 180 much care if I do promise you five hundred pound the day of my° marriage.

LUCY That is the way, madam, to make me diligent in the vocation of a confidante, which I think is generally to bring people together.

MELINDA O, Lucy, I can hold my secret no longer. You must know 185 that hearing of the famous fortune-teller in town, I went disguised to satisfy a curiosity which has cost me dear; that fellow is certainly the Devil, or one of his bosom favourites—he has told me the most surprising things of my past life.

LUCY Things past, madam, can hardly be reckoned surprising, 190 because we know them already. Did he tell you anything surprising that was to come?

MELINDA One thing very surprising—he said I should die a maid.

LUCY Die a maid. Come into the world for nothing! Dear madam, if you should believe him, it might come to pass; for the bare thought 195 on't might kill one in four and twenty hours. And did you ask him any questions about me?

MELINDA You! Why, I passed for you.

LUCY So 'tis I that am to die a maid. [Aside] But the Devil was a liar from the beginning—he can't make me die a maid; I have put it 200 out of his power already.

MELINDA I do but jest—I would have passed for you, and called
myself Lucy, but he presently told me my name, my quality,
my fortune, and gave me the whole history of my life; he told
me of a lover I had in this country, and described worthy   205
exactly, but in nothing so well as in his present indifference. I
fled to him for refuge here today. He never so much as encouraged
me in my fright, but coldly told me that he was sorry for the
accident, because it might give the town cause to censure my
conduct; excused his not waiting on me home, made me a careless   210
bow, and walked off. 'Sdeath, I could have stabbed him, or
myself—'twas the same thing. Yonder he comes—I will so slave°
him.

LUCY Don't exasperate him—consider what the fortune-teller told
you; men are scarce; and as times go, it is not impossible for a   215
woman to die a maid.
Enter Worthy

MELINDA No matter.

WORTHY [*aside*] I find she's warmed—I must strike while the iron is
hot. [*Aloud*] You have a great deal of courage, madam, to venture
into the walks where you were so late° frighted.   220

MELINDA And you have a quantity of impudence to appear before
me, that you have so lately affronted.

WORTHY I had no design to affront you, nor appear before you
either, madam; I left you here, because I had business in another
place, and came hither thinking to meet another person.   225

MELINDA Since you find yourself disappointed, I hope you'll withdraw to another part of the walk.

WORTHY The walk is as free for me as you, madam, and° broad
enough for us both.
*They walk one by another, he with his hat cocked, she fretting
and tearing her fan*
Will you please to take snuff, madam?   230
*He offers her his box. She strikes it out of his hand; while he is
gathering it up, enter Brazen*

BRAZEN What? Here before me! My dear.
[*He*] *takes Melinda about the middle.*

MELINDA What means this insolence?
She cuffs him

LUCY (*runs to Brazen*) Are you mad? Don't you see Mr Worthy?

BRAZEN No, no, I'm struck blind—Worthy! Adso, well turned—my
mistress has wit at her fingers' ends.° [*To Melinda*] Madam, I ask   235

your pardon, 'tis our way abroad. Mr Worthy, you're the happy man.

WORTHY I don't envy your happiness very much, if the lady can afford no other sort of favours but what she has bestowed upon you.

MELINDA I'm sorry the favour miscarried, for it was designed for you, Mr Worthy; and be assured, 'tis the last and only favour you must expect at my hands. Captain, I ask your pardon.

    Exit [*Melinda with Lucy*]

BRAZEN I grant it. You see, Mr Worthy, 'twas only a random shot—it might ha' taken off your head as well as mine. Courage, my dear—'tis the fortune of war. But the enemy has thought fit to withdraw, I think.

WORTHY Withdraw! Oons, sir, what d'ye mean by withdraw?

BRAZEN I'll show you.

    Exit [*Brazen*]

WORTHY She's lost, irrecoverably lost, and Plume's advice has ruined me. 'Sdeath, why should I that knew her haughty spirit be ruled by a man that is a stranger to her pride?

    Enter Plume

PLUME Ha, ha, ha, a battle royal; don't frown so, man—she's your own, I tell'ee; I saw the fury of her love in the extremity of her passion: the wildness of her anger is a certain sign that she loves you to madness. That rogue, Kite, began the battle with abundance of conduct,° and will bring you off victorious, my life on't; he plays his part admirably—she's to be with him again presently.

WORTHY But what could be the meaning of Brazen's familiarity with her?

PLUME You are no logician if you pretend to draw consequences from the actions of fools—there's no arguing by the rule of reason upon a science without principles, and such is their conduct; whim, unaccountable whim, hurries them on, like a man drunk with brandy before ten o'clock in the morning. But we lose our sport—Kite has opened above an hour ago; let's away.

    Exeunt

4.[2]

Scene, a chamber: a table with books and globes

Kite disguised in a strange habit, and sitting at the table

KITE (*rising*) By the position of the heavens, gained from my observation upon these celestial globes, I find that Luna was a tidewaiter, Sol a surveyor, Mercury a thief, Venus a whore, Saturn an alderman, Jupiter a rake, and Mars a sergeant of grenadiers.° And this is the system of Kite the conjurer.   5

Enter Plume and Worthy [with servant]

PLUME Well, what success?

KITE I have sent away a shoemaker and a tailor already—one's to be a captain of marines, and the other a major of dragoons.° I am to manage° them at night. Have you seen the lady, Mr Worthy?   10

WORTHY Ay, but it won't do. Have you showed her her name that I tore off from the bottom of the letter.

KITE No, sir, I reserve that for the last stroke.

PLUME What letter?

WORTHY One that I would not let you see, for fear you should break   15
Melinda's windows° in good earnest.

Knocking at the door

KITE Officers to your post.

Exeunt Worthy and Plume

[*To servant*] Tycho,° mind the door.

Servant opens the door, and enter a smith

SMITH Well, master, are you the cunning man?

KITE I am the learned Copernicus.°   20

SMITH Well, Master Coppernose,° I'm but a poor man, and I can't afford above a shilling for my fortune.

KITE Perhaps that is more than 'tis worth.

SMITH Look'ee, Doctor, let me have something that's good for my shilling, or I'll have my money again.   25

KITE If there be faith in the stars, you shall have your shilling fortyfold. Your hand, countryman.

Takes the smith's hand and studies it

You are by trade a smith.

SMITH How the Devil should you know that?

KITE Because the Devil and you are brother-tradesmen—you were   30
born under Forceps.°

SMITH Forceps! What's that?

KITE One of the signs; there's Leo, Sagittarius, Forceps, Furns, Dixmude, Namur, Brussels, Charleroy,° and so forth—twelve of 'em. Let me see—did you ever make any bombs or cannons' bullets?   35

SMITH Not I.

KITE You either have, or will. The stars have decreed that you shall be—I must have more money, sir, your fortune's great.

SMITH Faith, Doctor, I have no more.   40

KITE O, sir, I'll trust you, and take it out of your arrears.

SMITH Arrears! What arrears?

KITE The five hundred pound that's owing to you from the government.

SMITH Owing me!   45

KITE Owing you, sir. Let me see your t'other hand.
    Takes and studies it
  I beg your pardon, it will be owing to you; and the rogue of an agent will demand fifty per cent for a fortnight's advance.°

SMITH I'm in the clouds, Doctor, all this while.

KITE So am I, sir,° among the stars. In two years, three months, and two hours, you will be made Captain of the Forges to the Grand Train of Artillery,° and will have ten shillings a day, and two servants; 'tis the decree of the stars, and of the fixed stars, that are as immovable as your anvil. Strike, sir, while the iron is hot. Fly, sir, begone—   55

SMITH What, what would you have me do, Doctor? I wish the stars would put me in a way for this fine place.

KITE The stars do. Let me see. Ay, about an hour hence walk carelessly into the market-place, and you'll see a tall, slender gentleman cheapening a pen'worth° of apples, with a cane hanging upon his button.° This gentleman will ask you 'What's o'clock?' He's your man, and the maker of your fortune; follow him, follow him. And now go home, and take leave of your wife and children. An hour hence exactly is your time.   60

SMITH A tall slender gentleman you say! With a cane—pray what sort of a head has the cane?   65

KITE An amber head, with a black ribbon.

SMITH But pray, of what employment is the gentleman?

KITE Let me see. He's either a collector of the excise, a plenipotentiary, or a captain of grenadiers°—I can't tell exactly which. But he'll call you 'honest . . .'—your name is—?   70

SMITH Thomas.

KITE Right,° he'll call you 'Honest Tom'.

SMITH But how the Devil should he know my name?

KITE O, there are several sorts of Toms—Tom o' Lincoln,° Tom-   75
tit,° Tom Telltroth,° Tom o' Bedlam,° Tom Fool.°
     Knocking at the door
Begone. An hour hence precisely.

SMITH You say he'll ask me what's o'clock?

KITE Most certainly, and you'll answer—you don't know, and be
sure you look at St Mary's dial, for the sun won't shine, and if it   80
should, you won't be able to tell the figures.

SMITH I will, I will.
     Exit [smith]

PLUME (*behind*) Well done, conjurer—go on and prosper.

KITE As you were.
     Enter a butcher
(*Aside*) What? My old friend Pluck,° the butcher. I offered the   85
surly bull-dog five guineas this morning, and he refused it.

BUTCHER So, Master Conjurer, here's half-a-crown. And now you
must understand—

KITE Hold, friend, I know your business beforehand.

BUTCHER You're devilish cunning then; for I don't well know it   90
myself.

KITE I know more than you, friend. You have a foolish saying, that
such a one knows no more than the man in the moon; I tell you
the man in the moon knows more than all the men under the sun.
Don't the moon see all the world?   95

BUTCHER All the world see the moon, I must confess.

KITE Then she must see all the world, that's certain. Give me your
hand. [*Studying it*] You are by trade either a butcher or a surgeon.

BUTCHER True, I am a butcher.

KITE And a surgeon you will be—the employments differ only in the   100
name. He that can cut up an ox, may dissect a man; and the same
dexterity that cracks a marrow-bone, will cut off a leg or an arm.

BUTCHER What d'ye mean, Doctor, what d'ye mean?

KITE Patience, patience, Mr Surgeon-General—the stars are great
bodies, and move slowly.   105

BUTCHER But what d'ye mean by 'Surgeon-General', Doctor?

KITE Nay, sir, if your worship won't have patience, I must beg the
favour of your worship's absence.

BUTCHER My worship, my worship! But why my worship?

KITE Nay, then I have done.   110
      Sits
BUTCHER Pray, Doctor.
KITE Fire and fury, sir! (*rises in a passion*)—do you think the stars
      will be hurried? Do the stars owe you any money, sir, that you
      dare to dun their lordships at this rate? Sir, I am porter to the stars,
      and I am ordered to let no dun come near their doors.   115
BUTCHER Dear Doctor, I never had any dealings with the stars—
      they don't owe me a penny. But since you are the porter, please
      to accept of this half-crown to drink their healths, and don't be
      angry.
KITE Let me see your hand then, once more. [*Studying it*] Here   120
      has been gold—five guineas, my friend, in this very hand this
      morning.
BUTCHER Nay, then he is the Devil. Pray, Doctor, were you born of
      a woman, or did you come into the world of your own head?
KITE That's a secret. This gold was offered you by a proper   125
      handsome man, called Hawk, or Buzzard, or—
BUTCHER Kite you mean.
KITE Ay, ay, Kite.
BUTCHER As arrant a rogue as ever carried a halberd—the impudent
      rascal would have decoyed me for a soldier.   130
KITE A soldier! a man of your substance for a soldier! Your mother
      has a hundred pound in hard money lying at this minute in the
      hands of a mercer,° not forty yards from this place.
BUTCHER Oons, and so she has, but very few know so much.
KITE I know it, and that rogue, what's his name, Kite, knew it! And 135
      offered you five guineas to list, because he knew your poor mother
      would give the hundred for your discharge.
BUTCHER There's a dog now. 'Flesh, Doctor, I'll give you t'other
      half-crown, and tell me that this same Kite will be hanged.
KITE He's in as much danger as any man in the county of Salop.   140
BUTCHER There's your fee.
      Gives him a coin
      But you have forgot the Surgeon-General all this while.
KITE You put the stars in a passion.
      Looks on his books
      But now they're pacified again. Let me see. Did you never cut off
      a man's leg?   145
BUTCHER No.
KITE Recollect, pray.

BUTCHER I say no.

KITE That's strange, wonderful strange; but nothing is strange to me, such wonderful changes have I seen. The second, or third, ay, the third campaign that you make in Flanders, the leg of a great officer will be shattered by a great shot; you will be there accidentally, and with your cleaver chop off the limb at a blow. In short, the operation will be performed with so much dexterity, that with the° general applause you will be made Surgeon-General of the whole army.

BUTCHER Nay, for the matter of cutting off a limb, I'll do't, I'll do't with any surgeon in Europe, but I have no thoughts of making a campaign.

KITE You have no thoughts! What matter for your thoughts? The stars have decreed it, and you must go.

BUTCHER The stars decree it! Oons, sir, the justices can't press me.

KITE Nay, friend, 'tis none of my business—I ha' done. Only mind this—you'll know more an hour and a half hence—that's all. Farewell. (Going)

BUTCHER Hold, hold, Doctor—Surgeon-General! Pray what is the place worth, pray?

KITE Five hundred pound a year, beside guineas for claps.°

BUTCHER Five hundred pound a year! An hour and half hence you say?

KITE Prithee friend be quiet—don't be so troublesome. Here's such a work to make a booby butcher accept of five hundred pound a year. But if you must hear it—I tell you in short. You'll be standing in your stall an hour and half hence, and a gentleman will come by with a snuff-box in his hand, and the tip of his handkerchief hanging out of his right pocket. He'll ask you the price of a loin of veal, and at the same time stroke your great dog upon the head, and call him Chopper.

BUTCHER Mercy upon us—Chopper is the dog's name.

KITE Look'ee there. What I say is true—things that are to come must come to pass. Get you home, sell off your stock, don't mind the whining and the snivelling of your mother and your sister—women always hinder preferment; make what money you can,° and follow that gentleman. His name begins with a P—mind that. There will be the barber's daughter too, that you promised marriage to—she will be pulling and haling you to pieces.

BUTCHER What! Know Sally too? He's the Devil, and he needs must go that the Devil drives.° (Going) The tip of his handkerchief out of his left pocket?

KITE No, no, his right pocket—if it be the left, 'tis none of the man.

BUTCHER Well, well, I'll mind him.   190

    Exit [butcher]

PLUME (*behind with his pocket-book*) The right pocket, you say?

KITE I hear the rustling of silks.

    Knocking

  Fly, sir—'tis Madam Melinda.

    [*Plume hides again.*] *Enter Melinda and Lucy*

  Tycho, chairs for the ladies.

MELINDA Don't trouble yourself, we shan't stay, Doctor.   195

KITE Your ladyship is to stay much longer than you imagine.

MELINDA For what?

KITE For a husband. (*To Lucy*) For your part, madam, you won't stay for a husband.

LUCY Pray, Doctor, do you converse with the stars, or with the   200
Devil?

KITE With both; when I have the destinies of men in search, I consult the stars, when the affairs of women come under my hands, I advise with my t'other friend.

MELINDA And have you raised the Devil upon my account?   205

KITE Yes, madam, and he's now under the table.

LUCY O! Heavens protect us—dear madam, let us be gone.

KITE If you be afraid of him, why do you come to consult him?

MELINDA [*to Lucy*] Don't fear, fool. Do you think, sir, that because I'm a woman, I'm to be fooled out of my reason, or frighted out   210
of my senses? Come, show me this Devil.

KITE He's a little busy at present, but when he has done he shall wait on you.

MELINDA What is he doing?

KITE Writing your name in his pocket-book.   215

MELINDA Ha, ha, ha, my name! Pray what have you or he to do with my name?

KITE Look'ee, fair lady, the Devil is a very modest person—he seeks nobody unless they seek him first; he's chained up like a mastiff, and cannot stir unless he be let loose. You come to me to have   220
your fortune told—do you think, madam, that I can answer you of my own head? No, madam, the affairs of women are so irregular, that nothing less than the Devil can give any account of 'em. Now to convince you of your incredulity, I'll show you a trial of my skill. Here, you *Cacodemon del fuego*,° exert your power—draw me   225
this lady's name, the word 'Melinda' in the proper letters and

character of her own handwriting. Do it at three motions—one, two, three—'tis done. Now, madam, will you please to send your maid to fetch it.

LUCY I fetch it! The Devil fetch me if I do. 230

MELINDA My name in my own handwriting!—that would be convincing indeed.

KITE Seeing's believing.
> *Goes to the table, lifts up the carpet*
Here, Tre, Tre, poor Tre, give me the bone, sirrah.
> *He puts his hand under the table; Plume steals to the other side of the table and catches him by the hand*
O! O! the Devil, the Devil in good earnest—my hand, my hand, 235
the Devil, my hand!
> *Melinda and Lucy shriek, and run to a corner of the stage. Kite discovers Plume, and gets away his hand*
A plague o' your pincers, he has fixed his nails in my very flesh. O! Madam, you put the demon into such a passion with your scruples, that it has almost cost me my hand.

MELINDA It has cost us our lives almost—but have you got the 240
name?

KITE Got it! Ay, madam, I have got it here—I'm sure the blood comes°—but there's your name upon that square piece of paper—behold.

MELINDA 'Tis wonderful. My very letters to a tittle. 245

LUCY 'Tis like your hand, madam, but not so like your hand neither, and now I look nearer—'tis not like your hand at all.

KITE Here's a chambermaid now that will outlie the Devil.

LUCY Look'ee, madam, they shan't impose upon us; people can't remember their hands no more than they can their faces. Come, 250
madam, let us be certain—write your name upon this paper
> *Takes out paper and folds it*
Then we'll compare the two names.

KITE Anything for your satisfaction, madam—here's pen and ink.
> *Melinda writes, and Lucy holds the paper*

LUCY Let me see it, madam—'tis the same, the very same. (*Aside*) But I'll secure one copy for my own affairs. 255

MELINDA This is demonstration.

KITE 'Tis so, madam.—the word 'demonstration' comes from 'Demon' the father of lies.°

MELINDA Well, Doctor, I'm convinced; and now pray what account can you give me of my future fortune? 260

KITE Before the sun has made one course round this earthly globe, your fortune will be fixed for happiness or misery.

MELINDA What! so near the crisis of my fate!

KITE Let me see—about the hour of ten tomorrow morning you will be saluted by a gentleman who will come to take his leave of you, being designed for travel. His intention of going abroad is sudden, and the occasion a woman. Your fortune and his are like the bullet and the barrel—one runs plump into the t'other. In short, if the gentleman travels he will die abroad; and if he does you will die before he comes home.

MELINDA What sort of man is he?

KITE Madam, he is a fine gentleman, and a lover—that is, a man of very good sense, and a very great fool.

MELINDA How is that possible, Doctor?

KITE Because, madam—because it is so. A woman's reason is the best for a man's being a fool.

MELINDA Ten o'clock you say?

KITE Ten—about the hour of tea-drinking throughout the kingdom.

MELINDA Here. Doctor.
            Gives him money
        Lucy, have you any questions to ask?

LUCY O! Madam, a thousand.

KITE I must beg your patience till another time, for I expect more company this minute; besides, I must discharge the gentleman under the table.

LUCY Pray, sir, discharge us first.

KITE Tycho, wait on the ladies down stairs.
            Exeunt Melinda and Lucy. Enter Plume and Worthy [out of hiding] laughing

KITE Ay, you may well laugh, gentlemen—not all the cannon of the French army could have frighted me so much as that gripe you gave me under the table.

PLUME I think, Mr Doctor, I out-conjured you that bout.

KITE I was surprised, for I should not have taken a captain for a conjurer.

PLUME No more than I should a sergeant for a wit.°

KITE Mr Worthy, you were pleased to wish me joy today—I hope to be able to return the compliment tomorrow.

WORTHY I'll make it the best compliment to you that ever I made in my life,° if you do; but I must be a traveller you say?

KITE No farther than the chops of the Channel,° I presume, sir.

PLUME That we have concerted already.
    Knocking hard
  Hey-day!—you don't profess midwifery, Doctor?   300
KITE Away to your ambuscade.
    Exeunt Plume and Worthy [to their former hiding place]. Enter
    Brazen
BRAZEN Your servant, servant, my dear.
KITE Stand off—I have my familiar° already.
BRAZEN Are you bewitched, my dear?
KITE Yes, my dear, but mine is a peaceable spirit, and hates   305
  gunpowder. Thus I fortify myself.
    Draws a circle round him
  And now, Captain, have a care how you force my lines.°
BRAZEN Lines! What dost talk of lines? You have something like a
  fishing rod there, indeed; but I come to be acquainted with you,
  man. What's your name, my dear?   310
KITE Conundrum.
BRAZEN Conundrum! Rat me, I know a famous doctor in London of
  your name—where were you born?
KITE I was born in Algebra.
BRAZEN Algebra! 'Tis no country in Christendom I'm sure, unless it   315
  be some pitiful place in the Highlands of Scotland.
KITE Right! I told you I was bewitched.
BRAZEN So am I, my dear—I'm going to be married. I've had two
  letters from a lady of fortune that loves me to madness, fits, colic,
  spleen, and vapours. Shall I marry her in four and twenty hours,   320
  ay, or no?
KITE I must have the year and day o'th' month when these letters
  were dated.
BRAZEN Why, you old bitch, did you ever hear of love-letters dated
  with the year and day o'th' month? Do you think billets-doux are 325
  like bank bills?°
KITE They are not so good. But if they bear no date, I must examine
  the contents.
BRAZEN Contents? That you shall, old boy—here they be both.
    [Produces the letters]
KITE Only the last you received, if you please.   330
    Takes [a] letter
  Now sir, if you please to let me consult my books for a minute,
  I'll send this letter enclosed to you with the determination of the
  stars upon it to your lodgings.

BRAZEN With all my heart. I must give him.
>   *Puts his hand in's pocket*

Algebra! I fancy, Doctor, 'tis hard to calculate the place of your   335
nativity. Here.
>   *Gives him money*

And if I succeed, I'll build a watch-tower upon the top of the
highest mountain in Wales for the study of astrology, and the
benefit of Conundrums.
>   *Exit [Brazen]. Enter Plume and Worthy*

WORTHY O! Doctor, that letter's worth a million—let me see it.   340
>   *Takes the letter*

And now I have it, I'm afraid to open it.

PLUME Pho, let me see it! (*Opening the letter*) If she be a jilt—damn
her, she is one—there's her name at the bottom on't.

WORTHY How! Then I will travel in good earnest. [*Looking at the
letter*] By all my hopes, 'tis Lucy's hand!   345

PLUME Lucy's!

WORTHY Certainly—'tis no more like Melinda's character than black
is to white.

PLUME Then 'tis certainly Lucy's contrivance to draw in Brazen for
a husband—but are you sure 'tis not Melinda's hand?   350

WORTHY You shall see—where's the bit of paper I gave you just now
that the Devil writ 'Melinda' upon?

KITE Here, sir.

PLUME 'Tis plain, they're not the same. And is this the malicious
name that was subscribed to the letter which made Mr Balance   355
send his daughter into the country?

WORTHY The very same; the other fragments I showed you just
now—I once intended it for another use, but I think I have turned
it now to better advantage.°

PLUME But 'twas barbarous to conceal this so long, and to continue   360
me so many hours in the pernicious heresy of believing that angelic
creature could change—poor Silvia!

WORTHY Rich Silvia you mean, and poor captain—ha, ha, ha. Come,
come, friend, Melinda is true and shall be mine; Silvia is constant,
and may be yours.   365

PLUME No, she's above my hopes—but for her sake I'll recant my
opinion of her sex.
>   By some the sex is blamed without design,
>   Light harmless censure, such as yours and mine,
>   Sallies of wit, and vapours of our wine.   370

Others the justice of the sex condemn,
And wanting merit to create esteem,
Would hide their own defects by cens'ring them.
But they, secure in their all-conqu'ring charms,
Laugh at the vain efforts of false alarms;°   375
He magnifies their conquests who complains,
For none would struggle were they not in chains.
[*Exeunt*]

5.[1]

Scene,° an antechamber [in Silvia's lodgings] with a periwig, hat and sword upon the table

Enter Silvia in her nightcap

SILVIA I have rested but indifferently, and I believe my bedfellow was as little pleased; poor Rose! Here she comes.

Enter Rose

Good morrow, my dear, how d'ye this morning?

ROSE Just as I was last night, neither better nor worse for you.

SILVIA What's the matter? Did not you like your bedfellow?   5

ROSE I don't know whether I had a bedfellow or not.

SILVIA Did not I lie with you?

ROSE No—I wonder you could have the conscience to ruin a poor girl for nothing.

SILVIA I have saved thee from ruin, child; don't be melancholy—I   10
can give you as many fine things as the captain can.

ROSE But you can't, I'm sure.

Knocking at the door

SILVIA Odso! My acoutrements.

Puts on her periwig, hat and sword

Who's at the door?

[CONSTABLE] (*without*) Open the door, or we'll break it down.   15

SILVIA Patience a little.

Opens the door. Enter constable and mob

CONSTABLE We have 'em, we have 'em—the duck and the mallard both in the decoy.°

SILVIA What means this riot? Stand off.

Draws

The man dies that comes within reach of my point.   20

CONSTABLE That is not the point, master—put up your sword or I shall knock you down; and so I command the Queen's peace.

SILVIA You are some blockhead of a constable.

CONSTABLE I am so, and have a warrant to apprehend the bodies of you and your whore there.   25

ROSE Whore! Never was poor woman so abused.

Enter Bullock unbuttoned

BULLOCK What's matter now? O! Mr Bridewell,° what brings you abroad so early?

CONSTABLE This, sir.
          Lays hold of Bullock
    You're the Queen's prisoner.   30
BULLOCK Wauns, you lie, sir—I'm the Queen's soldier.
CONSTABLE No matter for that, you shall go before Justice Balance.
SILVIA Balance! 'Tis what I wanted. Here, Mr Constable, I resign
    my sword.
ROSE Can't you carry us before the captain, Mr Bridewell.   35
CONSTABLE Captain! han't you got your bellyful of captains yet?
    Come, come, make way there.
          Exeunt

5.[2]

Scene, Justice Balance's house
Balance and Scale

SCALE I say 'tis not to be borne, Mr Balance.
BALANCE Look'ee, Mr Scale, for my own part I shall be very tender
    in what regards the officers of the army; they expose their lives to
    so many dangers for us abroad, that we may give them some grains
    of allowance at home.   5
SCALE Allowance! This poor girl's father is my tenant, and if I
    mistake not, her mother nursed a child for you; shall they debauch
    our daughters to our faces?
BALANCE Consider, Mr Scale, that were it not for the bravery of
    these officers we should have French dragoons among us, that   10
    would leave us neither liberty, property, wife, nor daughter. Come,
    Mr Scale, the gentlemen are vigorous and warm, and may they
    continue so; the same heat that stirs them up to love, spurs them
    on to battle. You never knew a great general in your life that did
    not love a whore. This I only speak in reference to Captain Plume,   15
    for the other spark° I know nothing of.
SCALE Nor can I hear of anybody that does. O! here they come.
          Enter Silvia, Bullock, [and] Rose, prisoners: constable and mob
CONSTABLE May it please your worships, we took them in the very
    act, *re infecta*,° sir. The gentleman indeed behaved himself like a
    gentleman, for he drew his sword and swore, and afterwards laid   20
    it down and said nothing.
BALANCE Give the gentleman his sword again—wait you without.

Exit constable [with mob]

(*To Silvia*) I'm sorry, sir, to know a gentleman upon such terms, that the occasion of our meeting should prevent the satisfaction of an acquaintance.   25

SILVIA Sir, you need make no apology for your warrant, no more than I shall do for my behaviour. My innocence is upon an equal foot with your authority.

SCALE Innocence! Have you not seduced that young maid?

SILVIA No, Mr Goosecap,° she seduced me.   30

BULLOCK So she did I'll swear—for she proposed marriage first.

BALANCE (*to Rose*) What? Then you're married, child?

ROSE Yes, sir, to my sorrow.

BALANCE Who was witness?

BULLOCK That was I—I danced, threw the stocking, and spoke jokes   35
by their bedside,° I'm sure.

BALANCE Who was the minister?

BULLOCK Minister! We are soldiers, and want no ministers—they were married by the Articles of War.

BALANCE Hold thy prating, fool! [*To Silvia*] Your appearance, sir,   40
promises some understanding—pray what does this fellow mean?

SILVIA He means marriage, I think—but that, you know, is so odd a thing, that hardly any two people under the sun agree in the ceremony; some make it a sacrament,° others a convenience, and others make it a jest; but among soldiers 'tis most sacred. Our   45
sword, you know, is our honour; that we lay down—the hero jumps over it first, and the Amazon after—leap rogue, follow whore—the drum beats a ruff, and so to bed; that's all—the ceremony is concise.°

BULLOCK And the prettiest ceremony, so full of pastime and prodig-   50
ality.

BALANCE What! are you a soldier?

BULLOCK Ay, that I am. Will your worship lend me your cane, and I'll show you how I can exercise.°

BALANCE Take it.   55

Strikes him over the head

(*To Silvia*) Pray, sir, what commission may you bear?

SILVIA I'm called 'Captain', sir, by all the coffeemen, drawers, whores, and groom-porters in London, for I wear a red coat, a sword, a hat *bien troussé*,° a martial twist in my cravat,° a fierce knot in my periwig,° a cane upon my button,° piquet in my head,   60
and dice in my pocket.

SCALE Your name, pray, sir?

SILVIA 'Captain Pinch';° I cock my hat with a pinch, I take snuff with a pinch, pay my whores with a pinch. In short, I can do anything at a pinch, but fight and fill my belly.   65

BALANCE And pray, sir, what brought you into Shropshire?

SILVIA A pinch, sir: I knew that you country gentlemen want wit, and you know that we Town gentlemen want money, and so—

BALANCE I understand you, sir. Here, Constable—
          Enter constable
Take this gentleman into custody till further orders.   70

ROSE Pray your worship, don't be uncivil to him, for he did me no hurt—he's the most harmless man in the world, for all he talks so.

SCALE Come, come, child, I'll take care of you.

SILVIA What, gentlemen, rob me of my freedom and my wife at once! 'Tis the first time they ever went together.   75

BALANCE Heark'ee Constable.
          Whispers [to] the constable

CONSTABLE It shall be done, sir. [*To Silvia*] Come along, sir.
          Exeunt constable, Bullock and Silvia

BALANCE Come, Mr Scale, we'll manage the spark presently.
          Exeunt

5.[3]

Scene changes to Melinda's apartment

Melinda and Worthy

MELINDA (*aside*) So far the prediction is right, 'tis ten exactly.—And pray, sir, how long have you been in this travelling humour?

WORTHY 'Tis natural, madam, for us to avoid what disturbs our quiet.

MELINDA Rather the love of change, which is more natural, may be the occasion of it.   5

WORTHY To be sure, madam, there must be charms in variety, else neither you nor I should be so fond of it.

MELINDA You mistake, Mr Worthy—I am not so fond of variety, as to travel for it; nor do I think it prudence in you to run yourself into a certain expense and danger, in hopes of precarious pleasures, 10 which at best never answer expectation, as 'tis evident from the example of most travellers, that long more to return to their own country than they did to go abroad.

WORTHY What pleasures I may receive abroad are indeed uncertain; but this I am sure of—I shall meet with less cruelty among the most barbarous nations, than I have found at home. 15

MELINDA Come, sir, you and I have been jangling a great while—I fancy if we made up our accounts, we should the sooner come to an agreement.

WORTHY Sure, madam, you won't dispute your being in my debt. 20 My fears, sighs, vows, promises, assiduities, anxieties, jealousies, have run on for a whole year, without any payment.

MELINDA A year! O Mr Worthy, what you owe to me is not to be paid under a seven years' servitude.° How did you use me the year before, when taking the advantage of my innocence, and necessity, 25 you would have made me your mistress, that is, your slave. Remember the wicked insinuations, artful baits, deceitful arguments, cunning pretences; then your impudent behaviour, loose expressions, familiar letters, rude visits—remember those, those, Mr Worthy. 30

WORTHY (aside) I do remember, and am sorry I made no better use of 'em.—But you may remember, madam—that—

MELINDA Sir, I'll remember nothing—'tis your interest that I should forget; you have been barbarous to me, I have been cruel to you. Put that and that together, and let one balance the other. Now if 35 you will begin upon a new score,° lay aside your adventuring airs, and behave yourself handsomely till Lent be over.° Here's my hand—I'll use you as a gentleman should be.

WORTHY And if I don't use you as a gentlewoman should be, may this be my poison. (Kissing her hand) 40
        Enter servant

SERVANT Madam, the coach is at the door.
        [Exit servant]

MELINDA I'm going to Mr Balance's country house to see my cousin Silvia—I have done her an injury, and can't be easy till I have asked her pardon.

WORTHY I dare not hope for the honour of waiting on you. 45

MELINDA My coach is full, but if you will be so gallant as to mount your own horses° and follow us, we shall be glad to be overtaken; and if you bring Captain Plume with you, we shan't have the worse reception.

WORTHY I'll endeavour it. 50
        Exit Worthy leading Melinda

5.[4]

Scene, the market-place

Plume and Kite

PLUME A baker, a tailor, a smith, and a butcher—I believe the first colony planted at Virginia° had not more trades in their company than I have in mine.

KITE The butcher, sir, will have his hands full; for we have two sheep-stealers among us. I hear of a fellow too committed just now   5
for stealing of horses.

PLUME We'll dispose of him among the dragoons. Have we never a poulterer among us?

KITE Yes, sir, the king of the gypsies is a very good one—he has an excellent hand at a goose or a turkey.° Here's Captain Brazen. Sir,   10
I must go look after the men.

Exit [Kite]. Enter Brazen, reading a letter [to himself]

BRAZEN Um, um, um, the canonical hour.° Um, um, very well.—My dear Plume! Give me a buss.

PLUME Half a score, if you will, my dear. What hast got in thy hand, child?   15

BRAZEN 'Tis a project for laying out a thousand pound.

PLUME Were it not requisite to project first how to get it in?

BRAZEN You can't imagine, my dear, that I want a thousand pound;° I have spent twenty times as much in the service. Now, my dear, pray advise me; my head runs much upon architecture:° shall I   20
build a privateer or a playhouse?°

PLUME An odd question—a privateer or a playhouse! 'Twill require some consideration. Faith, I'm for a privateer.

BRAZEN I'm not of your opinion, my dear. For in the first place a privateer may be ill built.   25

PLUME And so may a playhouse.

BRAZEN But a privateer may be ill manned.

PLUME And so may a playhouse.

BRAZEN But a privateer may run upon the shallows.

PLUME Not so often as a playhouse.   30

BRAZEN But, you know, a privateer may spring a leak.

PLUME And I know that a playhouse may spring a great many.

BRAZEN But suppose the privateer come home with a rich booty, we should never agree about our shares.

PLUME 'Tis just so in a playhouse. So by my advice, you shall fix   35
upon the privateer.

BRAZEN Agreed. But if this twenty thousand should not be *in
specie*—°

PLUME What twenty thousand?

BRAZEN Heark'ee.   40
Whispers

PLUME Married!

BRAZEN Presently—we're to meet about half a mile out of town at
the water-side. And so forth.
Reads
'For fear I should be known by any of Worthy's friends, you must
give me leave to wear my mask till after the ceremony, which will   45
make me ever yours.' Look'ee there, my dear dog.
Shows the bottom of the letter to Plume

PLUME Melinda! And by this light, her own hand!° Once more, if
you please, my dear—her hand exactly! Just now you say?

BRAZEN This minute I must be gone.

PLUME Have a little patience, and I'll go with you.   50

BRAZEN No, no, I see a gentleman coming this way that may be
inquisitive; 'tis Worthy—do you know him?

PLUME By sight only.

BRAZEN Have a care, the very eyes discover secrets.
Exit [Brazen]. Enter Worthy

WORTHY To boot, and saddle, Captain—you must mount.°   55

PLUME Whip and spur, Worthy, or you won't mount.

WORTHY But I shall. Melinda and I are agreed—she is gone to visit
Silvia; we are to mount and follow, and could we carry a parson
with us, who knows what might be done for us both?

PLUME Don't trouble your head—Melinda has secured a parson   60
already.

WORTHY Already! Do you know more than I?

PLUME Yes, I saw it under her hand: Brazen and she are to meet half
a mile hence at the water-side, there to take boat—I suppose to be
ferried over to the Elysian Fields,° if there be any such thing in   65
matrimony.

WORTHY I parted with Melinda just now; she assured me she hated
Brazen, and that she resolved to discard Lucy for daring to write
letters to him in her name.

PLUME Nay, nay, there's nothing of Lucy in this—I tell ye I saw   70
Melinda's hand as surely as this is mine.

WORTHY But I tell you, she's gone this minute to Justice Balance's
country house.

PLUME But I tell you, she's gone this minute to the water-side.
     Enter a servant

[SERVANT] (*to Worthy*) Sir, Madam Melinda has sent word that you   75
need not trouble yourself to follow her, because her journey to
Justice Balance's is put off, and she's gone to take the air another
way.

WORTHY How! Her journey put off?

PLUME That is, her journey was a put-off to you.   80

WORTHY 'Tis plain, plain. But how, where, when is she to meet
Brazen?

PLUME Just now, I tell you, half a mile hence at the water-side.

WORTHY Up, or down the water?

PLUME That I don't know.   85

WORTHY I'm glad my horses are ready. [*To servant*] Jack, get 'em out.
     [*Exit servant*]

PLUME Shall I go with you?

WORTHY Not an inch—I shall return presently.
     Exit [*Worthy*]

PLUME You'll find me at the hall; the justices are sitting by this time,
and I must attend them.   90
     Exit

5.5

*Scene, a Court of Justice, Balance, Scale, Scruple, upon the
Bench*

Constable, Kite, [a married man, a collier, two women]

Kite and Constable advance to the front of the stage

KITE [*to constable*] Pray, who are those honourable gentlemen upon
the bench?

CONSTABLE He in the middle is Justice Balance, he on the right is
Justice Scale, and he on the left is Justice Scruple, and I am Mr
Constable, four very honest gentlemen.   5

KITE (*saluting° the constable*) O dear Sir, I'm your most obedient
servant. I fancy, sir, that your employment and mine are much the
same, for my business is to keep people in order, and if they
disobey, to knock 'em down; and then we're both staff-officers.°

CONSTABLE Nay, I'm a sergeant myself—of the militia.° Come,   10
brother, you shall see me exercise. Suppose this a musket now.
            He puts his staff on his right shoulder
Now I'm shouldered.

KITE Ay, you're shouldered pretty well for a constable's staff, but for
a musket, you must put it on t'other shoulder, my dear.

CONSTABLE Adso, that's true. Come, now give the word o' com-   15
mand.

KITE Silence.

CONSTABLE Ay, ay, so we will. We will be silent.

KITE Silence, you dog, silence.
            Strikes him over the head with his halberd

CONSTABLE That's the way to silence a man with a witness.° What   20
d'ye mean, friend?

KITE Only to exercise you, sir.

CONSTABLE Your exercise differs so from ours, that we shall ne'er
agree about it; if my own captain had given me such a rap, I had
taken the law of him.   25
            Enter Plume

BALANCE Captain, you're welcome.

PLUME Gentlemen, I thank'ee.

SCRUPLE Come, honest Captain, sit by me.
            Plume ascends, and sits upon the Bench°
Now produce your prisoners. Here, that fellow there [*pointing to
married man*]—set him up. Mr Constable, what have you to say   30
against this man?

CONSTABLE I have nothing to say against him, an't please ye.

BALANCE No! What made you bring him hither?

CONSTABLE I don't know, an't please your worship.

SCRUPLE° Did not the contents of your warrant direct you what sort   35
of men to take up?

CONSTABLE I can't tell, an't please ye—I can't read.

SCRUPLE A very pretty constable truly! I find we have no business
here.

KITE May it please the worshipful Bench, I desire to be heard in this   40
case, as being Counsel for the Queen.°

BALANCE Come, Sergeant, you shall be heard, since nobody else will
speak; we won't come here for nothing.

KITE This man is but one man, the country may spare him, and the
army wants him—besides he's cut out by nature for a grenadier: 45
he's five foot ten inches high,° he shall box, wrestle, or dance the

Cheshire Round° with any man in the county, he gets drunk every
sabbath day, and he beats his wife.

WIFE You lie, sirrah, you lie, an't please your worship; he's the
best-natured, painstaking° man in the parish—witness my five   50
poor children.

SCRUPLE A wife and five children! You Constable, you rogue, how
durst you impress a man that has a wife and five children?°

SCALE Discharge him, discharge him.

BALANCE Hold, gentlemen. Heark'ee, friend, how do you maintain   55
your wife and children?

PLUME They live upon wildfowl and venison, sir—the husband keeps
a gun, and kills all the hares and partridges within five miles round.°

BALANCE A gun! Nay, if he be so good at gunning he shall have
enough on't. He may be of use against the French, for he shoots   60
flying° to be sure.

SCRUPLE But his wife and children, Mr Balance!

WIFE Ay, ay, that's the reason you would send him away. You know
I have a child every year, and you're afraid they should come upon
the parish at last.   65

PLUME Look'ee there, gentlemen, the honest woman has spoke it at
once—the parish had better maintain five children this year than
six or seven the next; that fellow upon his high feeding may get
you two or three beggars at a birth.°

WIFE Look'ee, Mr Captain, the parish shall get nothing by sending   70
him away, for I won't lose my teeming time if there be a man left
in the parish.

BALANCE Send that woman to the house of correction°—and the
man—

KITE I'll take care o'him, if you please.   75
          Takes the man down°

SCALE Here, you Constable, the next. Set up that black-faced
fellow—he has a gunpowder look. What can you say against this
man, Constable?

CONSTABLE Nothing, but that he's a very honest man.

PLUME Pray, gentlemen, let me have one honest man in my company   80
for the novelty's sake.

BALANCE What are you, friend?

[COLLIER] A collier—I work in the coal-pits.

SCRUPLE Look'ee, gentlemen, this fellow has a trade, and the Act of
Parliament here expresses, that we are to impress no man that has   85
any visible means of a livelihood.

KITE May it please your worships, this man has no visible means of
a livelihood, for he works underground.

PLUME Well said Kite. Besides, the army wants miners.

BALANCE Right! and had we an order of government for't, we could   90
raise you in this and the neighbouring county of Stafford five
hundred colliers that would run you underground like moles, and
do more service in a siege° than all the miners in the army.

SCRUPLE Well, friend, what have you to say for yourself?

[COLLIER] I'm married.   95

KITE Lack-a-day, so am I.

[COLLIER] Here's my wife, poor woman.

BALANCE Are you married, good woman?

WOMAN I'm married in conscience.

KITE May it please your worship, she's with child in conscience.   100

SCALE Who married you, mistress?

WOMAN My husband. We agreed that I should call him husband to
avoid passing for a whore, and that he should call me wife to shun
going for a soldier.

SCRUPLE A very pretty couple. Pray, Captain, will you take 'em both?   105

PLUME What say you, Mr Kite—will you take care of the woman?

KITE Yes, sir, she shall go with us to the seaside, and there, if she
has a mind to drown herself, we'll take care that nobody shall
hinder her.

BALANCE Here, Constable, bring in my man.   110

    Exit constable

Now Captain, I'll fit you with a man, such as you ne'er listed in
your life.

    Enter constable and Silvia

O! my friend Pinch—I'm very glad to see you.

SILVIA Well sir, and what then?

SCALE What then! Is that your respect to the Bench?   115

SILVIA Sir, I don't care a farthing for you nor your Bench neither.

SCRUPLE Look'ee, gentlemen, that's enough—he's a very impudent
fellow, and fit for a soldier.

SCALE A notorious rogue, I say, and very fit for a soldier.

CONSTABLE A whoremaster, I say, and therefore fit to go.   120

BALANCE What think you, Captain?

PLUME I think he's a very pretty fellow, and therefore fit to serve.

SILVIA Me for a soldier! Send your own lazy lubberly sons at home,
fellows that hazard their necks every day in pursuit of a fox, yet
dare not peep abroad to look an enemy in the face.   125

CONSTABLE May it please your worships, I have a woman at the door
　　to swear a rape against this rogue.

SILVIA Is it your wife or daughter, booby? I ravished 'em both
　　yesterday.

BALANCE Pray, Captain, read the Articles of War, we'll see him   130
　　listed immediately.

PLUME (*reads*) 'Articles of War against mutiny and desertion—'.°

SILVIA Hold, sir. Once more, gentlemen, have a care what you do, for
　　you shall severely smart for any violence you offer to me, and you,
　　Mr Balance, I speak to you particularly, you shall heartily repent it.   135

PLUME Look'ee, young spark, say but one word more and I'll build
　　a horse for you as high as the ceiling, and make you ride the most
　　tiresome journey that ever you made in your life.°

SILVIA You have made a fine speech, good Captain Huffcap.° But
　　you had better be quiet—I shall find a way to cool your courage.   140

PLUME Pray, gentlemen, don't mind him, he's distracted.

SILVIA 'Tis false. I'm descended of as good a family as any in your
　　county—my father is as good a man as any upon your Bench, and
　　I am heir to twelve hundred pound a year.

BALANCE He's certainly mad. Pray, Captain, read the Articles of War.   145

SILVIA Hold once more. Pray, Mr Balance, to you I speak—suppose
　　I were your child, would you use me at this rate?

BALANCE No faith, were you mine, I would send you to Bedlam,°
　　first, and into the army afterwards.

SILVIA But consider my father, sir—he's as good, as generous, as   150
　　brave, as just a man as ever served his country; I'm his only
　　child—perhaps the loss of me may break his heart.

BALANCE He's a very great fool if it does. Captain, if you don't list
　　him this minute, I'll leave the court.

PLUME Kite, do you distribute the levy-money° to the men whilst I   155
　　read.

KITE Ay, sir. Silence, gentlemen.

　　　　Plume reads the Articles of War

BALANCE Very well; now, Captain, let me beg the favour of you, not
　　to discharge this fellow upon any account whatsoever.—Bring in
　　the rest.   160

CONSTABLE There are no more, an't please your worship.

BALANCE No more! There were five two hours ago.

SILVIA 'Tis true, sir, but this rogue of a constable let the rest escape
　　for a bribe of eleven shillings a man, because he said that the act
　　allows him but ten,° so the odd shilling was clear gains.   165

ALL JUSTICES How!

SILVIA Gentlemen, he offered to let me get away for two guineas, but I had not so much about me. This is truth, and I'm ready to swear it.

KITE And I'll swear it—give me the book, 'tis for the good of the   170
service.

COLLIER May it please your worship, I gave him half-a-crown to say that I was an honest man—and now that your worships have made me a rogue, I hope I shall have my money again.

BALANCE 'Tis my opinion that this constable be put into the   175
captain's hands, and if his friends don't bring four good men for his ransom by tomorrow night, Captain, you shall carry him to Flanders.

SCALE, SCRUPLE Agreed, agreed!

PLUME Mr Kite, take the constable into custody.   180

KITE Ay, ay, sir. (*To the constable*) Will you please to have your office taken from you, or will you handsomely lay down your staff as your betters have done before you?°
    The constable drops his staff

BALANCE Come, gentlemen, there needs no great ceremony in adjourning this court. Captain, you shall dine with me.   185

KITE Come, Mr Militia Sergeant, I shall silence you now, I believe, without your taking the law of me.
    Exeunt all

5.[6]

Scene changes to the fields, Brazen leading in Lucy masked

BRAZEN The boat is just below here.
    Enter Worthy with a case of pistols under his arm, parts Brazen and Lucy

WORTHY Here, sir, take your choice. (*Offering the pistols*)

BRAZEN What! Pistols! are they charged, my dear?

WORTHY With a brace of bullets each.

BRAZEN But I'm a foot-officer,° my dear, and never use pistols—the   5
sword is my way—and I won't be put out of my road to please any man.

WORTHY Nor I neither, so have at you.
    Cocks one pistol

BRAZEN Look'ee, my dear, I do not care for pistols. Pray oblige me
and let us have a bout at sharps—damn't, there's no parrying these   10
bullets.

WORTHY Sir, if you han't your bellyful of these, the swords shall
come in for second course.

BRAZEN Why then, fire and fury! I have eaten smoke from the mouth
of a cannon. Sir, don't think I fear powder, for I live upon't; let   15
me see (takes a pistol), and now, sir, how many paces distant shall
we fire?

WORTHY Fire when you please—I'll reserve my shot till I be sure of
you.°

BRAZEN Come, where's your cloak?   20

WORTHY Cloak! what d'ye mean?

BRAZEN To fight upon—I always fight upon a cloak,° 'tis our way
abroad.

LUCY Come, gentlemen, I'll end the strife.
        Pulls off her mask

WORTHY Lucy! Take her.   25

BRAZEN The Devil take me if I do—Huzza!
        Fires his pistol
D'ye hear, d'ye hear, you plaguy harridan, how those bullets
whistle—suppose they had been lodged in my gizzard now?

LUCY Pray, sir, pardon me.

BRAZEN I can't tell, child, till I know whether my money be safe.   30
(*Searching his pockets*) Yes, yes, I do pardon you, but if I had you
in the Rose Tavern, Covent Garden,° with three or four hearty
rakes, and three or four smart napkins,° I would tell you another
story, my dear.
        Exit [Brazen]

WORTHY And was Melinda privy to this?   35

LUCY No, sir, she wrote her name upon a piece of paper at the
fortune-teller's last night, which I put in my pocket, and so writ
above it to the captain.

WORTHY And how came Melinda's journey put off?

LUCY At the town's end she met Mr Balance's steward, who told her   40
Mrs Silvia was gone from her father's, and nobody could tell
whither.

WORTHY Silvia gone from her father's! This will be news to Plume.
Go home, and tell your lady how near I was being shot for her.
        Exeunt

5.[7]

[Scene,° Justice Balance's house]

Enter Balance with a napkin in his hand as risen from dinner, talking with his steward

STEWARD We did not miss her till the evening, sir, and then searching for her in the chamber that was my young master's, we found her clothes there, but the suit that your son left in the press when he went to London, was gone.

BALANCE The white trimmed with silver?   5

STEWARD The same.

BALANCE You han't told that circumstance to anybody.

STEWARD To none but your worship.

BALANCE And be sure you don't. Go into the dining room, and tell Captain Plume that I beg to speak with him.   10

STEWARD I shall.

    Exit [steward]

BALANCE Was ever man so imposed upon? I had her promise indeed that she should never dispose of herself without my consent. I have consented with a witness, given her away as my act and deed; and this, I warrant, the captain thinks will pass; no, I shall never   15
pardon him the villainy, first of robbing me of my daughter, and then the mean opinion he must have of me to think that I could be so wretchedly imposed upon. Her extravagant passion might encourage her in the attempt, but the contrivance must be his—I'll know the truth presently.   20

    Enter Plume

Pray, Captain, what have you done with your young gentleman soldier?

PLUME He's at my quarters, I suppose, with the rest of my men.

BALANCE Does he keep company with the common soldiers?

PLUME No, he's generally with me.   25

BALANCE He lies with you, I presume?

PLUME No, faith, I offered him part of my bed, but the young rogue fell in love with Rose, and has lain with her, I think, since he came to town.

BALANCE So that between you both Rose has been finely managed.   30

PLUME Upon my honour, sir, she had no harm from me.

BALANCE *[aside]* All's safe, I find! *[Aloud]* Now Captain, you must know that the young fellow's impudence in court was well grounded; he said that I should heartily repent his being listed, and I do from my soul. 35

PLUME Ay! for what reason?

BALANCE Because he is no less than what he said he was, born of as good a family as any in this county, and is heir to twelve hundred pound a year.

PLUME I'm very glad to hear it, for I wanted but a man of that 40 quality to make my company a perfect representative of the whole commons of England.

BALANCE Won't you discharge him?

PLUME Not under a hundred pound sterling.

BALANCE You shall have it, for his father is my intimate friend. 45

PLUME Then you shall have him for nothing.

BALANCE Nay, sir, you shall have your price.

PLUME Not a penny, sir; I value an obligation to you much above a hundred pound.

BALANCE Perhaps, sir, you shan't repent your generosity. Will you 50 please to write his discharge in my pocket-book?
        Gives his book
    In the meantime we'll send for the gentleman. [*Calling off-stage*] Who waits there?
        Enter servant
    Go to the captain's lodgings, and inquire for Mr Wilful—tell him his captain wants him here immediately. 55

SERVANT Sir, the gentleman's below at the door inquiring for the captain.

PLUME Bid him come up. [*To Balance*] Here's the discharge, sir.
    [*Exit servant*]

BALANCE Sir, I thank you. (*Aside*) 'Tis plain he had no hand in't.
        Enter Silvia

SILVIA I think, Captain, you might have used me better, than to leave 60 me yonder among your swearing, drunken crew. And you, Mr Justice, might have been so civil as to have invited me to dinner, for I have eaten with as good a man as your worship.

PLUME Sir, you must charge our want of respect upon our ignorance of your quality, but now you're at liberty—I have discharged 65 you.

SILVIA Discharged me!

BALANCE Yes, sir, and you must once more go home to your father.

SILVIA My father! then I'm discovered. O, sir, (*kneeling*) I expect no pardon.
 70

BALANCE Pardon! No, no, child; your crime shall be your punishment. Here, Captain, I deliver her over to the conjugal power for her chastisement; since she will be a wife, be you a husband, a very husband. When she tells you of her love, upbraid her with her folly; be modishly ungrateful, because she has been unfashionably 75 kind; and use her worse than you would anybody else, because you can't use her so well as she deserves.

PLUME And are you Silvia in good earnest?

SILVIA Earnest! I have gone too far to make it a jest, sir.

PLUME And do you give her to me in good earnest? 80

BALANCE° If you please to take her, sir.

PLUME Why then I have saved my legs and arms, and lost my liberty; secure from wounds I'm prepared for the gout—farewell subsistence, and welcome taxes. Sir, my liberty and hopes of being a general are much dearer to me than your twelve hundred pound 85 a year, but to your love, madam, I resign my freedom, and to your beauty, my ambition; greater in obeying at your feet, than commanding at the head of an army.

    Enter Worthy

WORTHY I'm sorry to hear, Mr Balance, that your daughter is lost.

BALANCE So am not I, sir, since an honest gentleman has found her. 90

    Enter Melinda

MELINDA Pray, Mr Balance, what's become of my cousin Silvia?

BALANCE Your cousin Silvia is talking yonder with your cousin Plume.

MELINDA and WORTHY How!

SILVIA Do you think it strange, cousin, that a woman should change? But I hope you'll excuse a change that has proceeded from 95 constancy; I altered my outside, because I was the same within, and only laid by the woman to make sure of my man—that's my history.

MELINDA Your history is a little romantic, cousin, but since success has crowned your adventures you will have the world o' your side, and I shall be willing to go with the tide, provided you pardon an 100 injury I offered you in the letter to your father.

PLUME That injury, madam, was done to me, and the reparation I expect shall be made to my friend—make Mr Worthy happy, and I shall be satisfied.

MELINDA A good example, sir, will go a great way. When my cousin 105 is pleased to surrender, 'tis probable I shan't hold out much longer.

    Enter Brazen

BRAZEN Gentlemen, I am yours. [*To Melinda*] Madam, I am not yours.

MELINDA I'm glad on't, sir.

BRAZEN So am I. You have got a pretty house here, Mr Laconic.   110

BALANCE 'Tis time to right all mistakes. My name, sir, is Balance.

BRAZEN Balance! Sir, I'm your most obedient. I know your whole generation. Had not you an uncle that was Governor of the Leeward Islands° some years ago?

BALANCE Did you know him?   115

BRAZEN Intimately, sir—he played at billiards to a miracle. You had a brother too, that was captain of a fireship:° poor Dick, he had the most engaging way with him—of making punch—and then his cabin was so neat; but his boy Jack was the most comical bastard—ha, ha, ha—a pickled dog, I shall never forget him.   120

PLUME Well, Captain, are you fixed in your project yet—are you still for the privateer?

BRAZEN No, no, I had enough of a privateer just now—I had like to have been picked up by a cruiser under false colours, and a French picaroon° for aught I know.   125

PLUME But have you got your recruits, my dear?

BRAZEN Not a stick, my dear.

PLUME Probably I shall furnish you.

Enter Rose and Bullock

ROSE Captain, Captain, I have got loose once more, and have persuaded my sweetheart Cartwheel to go with us, but you must   130
promise not to part with me again.

SILVIA I find Mrs Rose has not been pleased with her bedfellow.

ROSE Bedfellow! I don't know whether I had a bedfellow or not.

SILVIA Don't be in a passion, child—I was as little pleased with your company as you could be with mine.   135

BULLOCK Pray, sir, dunna be offended at my sister—she's something underbred, but if you please I'll lie with you in her stead.

PLUME I have promised, madam, to provide for this girl; now will you be pleased to let her wait upon you, or shall I take care of her?

SILVIA She shall be my charge, sir—you may find it business enough   140
to take care of me.

BULLOCK Ay, and of me, Captain, for wauns! if ever you lift your hand against me, I'll desert.

PLUME Captain Brazen shall take care o' that. [*To Brazen*] My dear, instead of the twenty thousand pound you talked of, you shall have   145
the twenty brave recruits that I have raised, at the rate they cost me. My commission I lay down to be taken up by some braver fellow, that has more merit, and less good fortune, whilst I

endeavour by the example of this worthy gentleman to serve my
Queen and country at home.   150

> With some regret I quit the active field,
> Where glory full reward for life does yield;
> But the recruiting trade with all its train
> Of lasting plague, fatigue, and endless pain,°
> I gladly quit, with my fair spouse to stay—   155
> And raise recruits the matrimonial way.

Epilogue

All ladies and gentlemen, that are willing to see the comedy called *The Recruiting Officer*, let them repair tomorrow night by six o' clock to the sign of the Theatre Royal in Drury Lane, and they shall be kindly entertained.°

We scorn the vulgar ways to bid you come— 5
Whole Europe now obeys the call of drum.
The soldier, not the poet, here appears,
And beats up for a corps of volunteers:
He finds that music chiefly does delight ye,
And therefore chooses music to invite ye. 10
Beat the 'Grenadier March'.

[*Music plays*]

Row, row, tow, Gentlemen, this piece of music, called 'An Overture to a Battle',° was composed by a famous Italian master, and was performed with wonderful success, at the great operas of Vigo, Schellenberg, and Blenheim;° it came off with the applause of all 15 Europe, excepting France; the French found it a little too rough for their *delicatesse*.°

Some that have acted on those glorious stages,
Are here to witness to succeeding ages
That no music like the grenadier's engages. 20

Ladies, we must own, that this music of ours is not altogether so soft as Bononcini's, yet we dare affirm that it has laid more people asleep than all the *Camillas* in the world;° and you'll condescend to own, that it keeps one awake, better than any opera that ever was acted. 25

The 'Grenadier March' seems to be a composure excellently adapted to the genius of the English; for no music was ever followed so far by us, nor with so much alacrity; and with all deference to the present subscription,° we must say that the 'Grenadier March' has been subscribed for by the whole Grand Alliance;° and we presume 30 to inform the ladies, that it always has the pre-eminence abroad, and is constantly heard by the tallest, handsomest men in the whole army. In short, to gratify the present taste, our author is now adapting some words to the 'Grenadier March', which he intends to have performed tomorrow, if the lady who is to sing it should not happen 35 to be sick.°

This he concludes to be the surest way
To draw you hither, for you'll all obey
Soft music's call, though you should damn his play.

THE BEAUX' STRATAGEM

A Comedy

DRAMATIS PERSONAE

The play was first staged at the Queen's Theatre, Haymarket, on 8 March 1707, with the following cast:

[MEN]

Aimwell	*two gentlemen of broken fortunes, the first as master, and the*	Mr Mills
Archer	*second as servant*	Mr Wilks
Count Bellair,° *a French officer, prisoner at Lichfield*		Mr Bowman
Sullen, *a country blockhead, brutal to his wife*		Mr Verbruggen
Freeman, *a gentleman from London*		Mr Keen
Foigard,° *a priest, chaplain to the French officers*		Mr Bowen
Gibbet, *a highwayman*		Mr Cibber
Hounslow° Bagshot° } *his companions*		
Boniface,° *landlord of the inn*		Mr Bullock
Scrub,° *servant to Mr Sullen*		Mr Norris

[WOMEN]

Lady Bountiful,° *an old, civil, country gentlewoman, that cures all her neighbours of all distempers, and foolishly fond of her son, Sullen*	Mrs Powell
Dorinda, *Lady Bountiful's daughter*	Mrs Bradshaw
Mrs Sullen, *her daughter-in-law*	Mrs Oldfield
Gypsy, *maid to the ladies*	Mrs Mills
Cherry, *the landlord's daughter in the inn*	Mrs Bignal

SCENE

Lichfield

ADVERTISEMENT

The reader may find some faults in this play, which my illness°
prevented the amending of, but there is great amends made in the
representation, which cannot be matched, no more than the
friendly and indefatigable care of Mr Wilks,° to whom I chiefly
owe the success of the play.   5

George Farquhar.

Prologue

spoken by Mr Wilks

When strife disturbs or sloth corrupts an age,
Keen satire is the business of the stage.
When the Plain Dealer writ, he lashed those crimes
Which then infested most—the modish times.°
But now, when faction sleeps and sloth is fled, 5
And all our youth in active fields are bred;
When through GREAT BRITAIN's fair extensive round,
The trumps of fame the notes of UNION sound;°
When ANNA's sceptre points the laws their course,
And her example gives her precepts force:° 10
There scarce is room for satire—all our lays
Must be, or songs of triumph, or of praise.°
But as, in grounds best cultivated, tares
And poppies rise among the golden ears,°
Our products so, fit for the field or school, 15
Must mix with Nature's favourite plant—a fool.
A weed that has to twenty summers ran,
Shoots up in stalk, and vegetates to man.
Simpling our author goes from field to field,
And culls such fools, as may diversion yield;° 20
And, thanks to Nature, there's no want of those,
For rain, or shine, the thriving coxcomb grows.
Follies tonight we show ne'er lashed before,
Yet such as Nature shows you every hour;
Nor can the pictures give a just offence, 25
For fools are made for jests to men of sense.

1.1

Scene, an inn

Enter Boniface running

BONIFACE Chamberlain, maid, Cherry, daughter Cherry—all asleep,
all dead?

Enter Cherry running

CHERRY Here, here—why d'ye bawl so, father?—d'ye think we have
no ears?

BONIFACE You deserve to have none,° you young minx. The com-   5
pany of the Warrington° coach has stood in the hall this hour, and
nobody to show them to their chambers.

CHERRY And let 'em wait further; there's neither redcoat in the
coach, nor footman behind it.

BONIFACE But they threaten to go to another inn tonight.   10

CHERRY That they dare not, for fear the coachman should overturn
them tomorrow.°

[*Noises off*]

Coming, coming. Here's the London coach arrived.

*Enter several people with trunks, bandboxes, and other luggage,
and cross the stage*

BONIFACE Welcome, ladies.

CHERRY Very welcome, gentlemen. [*Calling off-stage*] Chamberlain,   15
show the Lion and the Rose.°

*Exit [Cherry] with the company. Enter Aimwell in riding habit,
Archer as footman carrying a portmantle*

BONIFACE This way, this way, gentlemen.

AIMWELL [*to Archer*] Set down the things, go to the stable, and see
my horses well rubbed.

ARCHER I shall, sir.   20

Exit [Archer]

AIMWELL You're my landlord, I suppose?

BONIFACE Yes, sir, I'm old Will Boniface, pretty well known upon
this road, as the saying is.°

AIMWELL [*bowing*] O Mr Boniface, your servant.

BONIFACE O sir. What will your honour please to drink, as the   25
saying is.

AIMWELL I have heard your town of Lichfield much famed for ale—I
think I'll taste that.

BONIFACE Sir, I have now in my cellar ten tun of the best ale in
   Staffordshire; 'tis smooth as oil, sweet as milk, clear as amber, and   30
   strong as brandy; and will be just fourteen year old the fifth day
   of next March old style.°
AIMWELL You're very exact, I find, in the age of your ale.
BONIFACE As punctual, sir, as I am in the age of my children. I'll
   show you such ale. [*Calling*] Here, tapster, broach number 1706,   35
   as the saying is. [*To Aimwell*] Sir, you shall taste my *Anno Domini*:°
   I have lived in Lichfield man and boy above eight and fifty years,
   and I believe have not consumed eight and fifty ounces of meat.
AIMWELL At a meal, you mean, if one may guess your sense by your
   bulk.   40
BONIFACE Not in my life, sir—I have fed purely upon ale; I have ate
   my ale, drank my ale, and I always sleep upon ale.
            Enter tapster with a bottle and glass[es]
   Now, sir, you shall see. (*Filling [them] out*) Your worship's health.
   [*Drinking*] Ha! delicious, delicious—fancy it burgundy, only fancy
   it, and 'tis worth ten shillings a quart.   45
            [*Exit tapster*]
AIMWELL (*drinks*) 'Tis confounded strong.
BONIFACE Strong! It must be so, or how should we be strong that
   drink it?
AIMWELL And have you lived long upon this ale, landlord?
BONIFACE Eight and fifty years upon my credit, sir; but it killed my   50
   wife, poor woman, as the saying is.
AIMWELL How came that to pass?
BONIFACE I don't know how, sir; she would not let the ale take its
   natural course, sir—she was for qualifying it every now and then
   with a dram,° as the saying is; and an honest gentleman that came   55
   this way from Ireland, made her a present of a dozen bottles of
   usquebaugh. But the poor woman was never well after. But howe'er,
   I was obliged to the gentleman, you know.
AIMWELL Why, was it the *usquebaugh* that killed her?
BONIFACE My Lady Bountiful said so. She, good lady, did what   60
   could be done—she cured her of three tympanies, but the fourth
   carried her off; but she's happy, and I'm contented, as the saying
   is.
AIMWELL Who's that Lady Bountiful you mentioned?
BONIFACE Ods my life, sir, we'll drink her health. (*Drinks*) My Lady   65
   Bountiful is one of the best of women. Her last husband, Sir
   Charles Bountiful, left her worth a thousand pound a year; and I

believe she lays out one half on't in charitable uses for the good of her neighbours; she cures rheumatisms, ruptures, and broken shins in men; green-sickness, obstructions, and fits of the mother in women; the king's evil,° chin-cough, and chilblains in children. In short, she has cured more people in and about Lichfield within ten years than the doctors have killed in twenty; and that's a bold word. 70

AIMWELL Has the lady been any other way useful in her generation? 75

BONIFACE Yes, sir—she has a daughter by Sir Charles, the finest woman in all our country, and the greatest fortune. She has a son too by her first husband, Squire Sullen, who married a fine lady from London t'other day; if you please, sir, we'll drink his health.

AIMWELL What sort of a man is he? 80

BONIFACE Why, sir, the man's well enough; says little, thinks less, and does—nothing at all, faith. But he's a man of a great estate, and values nobody.

AIMWELL A sportsman, I suppose.

BONIFACE Yes, sir, he's a man of pleasure—he plays at whisk, and 85
smokes his pipe eight and forty hours together sometimes.

AIMWELL And married, you say?

BONIFACE Ay, and to a curious° woman, sir. But he's a—he wants it, here, sir. (*Pointing to his forehead*)

AIMWELL He has it there, you mean?° 90

BONIFACE That's none of my business—he's my landlord, and so a man you know, would not—. But, ecod, he's no better than—sir, my humble service to you. (*Drinks*) Though I value not a farthing what he can do to me; I pay him his rent at quarter day,° I have a good running trade, I have but one daughter, and I can give 95
her—but no matter for that.

AIMWELL You're very happy, Mr Boniface—pray what other company have you in town?

BONIFACE A power of fine ladies, and then we have the French officers.° 100

AIMWELL O that's right, you have a good many of those gentlemen. Pray how do you like their company?

BONIFACE So well, as the saying is, that I could wish we had as many more of 'em—they're full of money, and pay double for everything they have; they know, sir, that we paid good round taxes for the 105
taking of 'em, and so they are willing to reimburse us a little; one of 'em lodges in my house.

  Enter Archer

ARCHER Landlord, there are some French gentlemen below that ask for you.

BONIFACE I'll wait on 'em. (*To Archer*) Does your master stay long in town, as the saying is?   110

ARCHER I can't tell, as the saying is.

BONIFACE Come from London?

ARCHER No.

BONIFACE Going to London, mayhap?   115

ARCHER No.

BONIFACE [*aside*] An odd fellow this. [*To Aimwell*] I beg your worship's pardon—I'll wait on you in half-a-minute.
> *Exit* [*Boniface*]

AIMWELL The coast's clear, I see. Now my dear Archer, welcome to Lichfield.   120

ARCHER I thank thee, my dear brother in iniquity.

AIMWELL Iniquity! prithee leave canting—you need not change your style with your dress.

ARCHER Don't mistake me, Aimwell, for 'tis still my maxim, that there is no scandal like rags, nor any crime so shameful as poverty.   125

AIMWELL The world confesses it every day in its practice, though men won't own it for their opinion. Who did that worthy lord, my brother, single out of the sidebox to sup with him t'other night?

ARCHER Jack Handicraft, a handsome, well-dressed, mannerly,   130 sharping rogue, who keeps the best company in Town.

AIMWELL Right, and pray who married my Lady Manslaughter t'other day, the great fortune?

ARCHER Why, Nick Marrabone, a professed pick-pocket, and a good bowler;° but he makes a handsome figure, and rides in his coach,   135 that he formerly used to ride behind.

AIMWELL But did you observe poor Jack Generous° in the Park° last week?

ARCHER Yes, with his autumnal periwig,° shading his melancholy face, his coat older than anything but its fashion, with one hand   140 idle in his pocket, and with the other picking his useless teeth; and though the Mall was crowded with company, yet was poor Jack as single and solitary as a lion in a desert.

AIMWELL And as much avoided, for no crime upon earth but the want of money.   145

ARCHER And that's enough. Men must not be poor—idleness is the root of all evil. The world's wide enough—let 'em bustle. Fortune has taken the weak under her protection, but men of sense are left to their industry.

AIMWELL Upon which topic we proceed, and I think luckily hither-to. Would not any man swear now that I am a man of quality, and you my servant,° when if our intrinsic value were known— 150

ARCHER Come, come, we are the men of intrinsic value, who can strike our fortunes out of ourselves, whose worth is independent of accidents in life, or revolutions in government; we have heads to get money, and hearts to spend it. 155

AIMWELL As to our hearts, I grant ye, they are as willing tits° as any within twenty degrees;° but I can have no great opinion of our heads from the service they have done us hitherto, unless it be that they have brought us from London hither to Lichfield, made me a lord, and you my servant. 160

ARCHER That's more than you could expect already. But what money have we left?

AIMWELL But two hundred pound.

ARCHER And our horses, clothes, rings, &c—why we have very good fortunes now for moderate people; and let me tell you, besides, that this two hundred pound, with the experience that we are now masters of, is a better estate than the ten thousand we have spent.° Our friends indeed began to suspect that our pockets were low; but we came off° with flying colours—showed no signs of want either in word or deed. 165, 170

AIMWELL Ay, and our going to Brussels was a good pretence enough for our sudden disappearing; and I warrant you, our friends imagine that we are gone a-volunteering.°

ARCHER Why faith, if this prospect fails, it must e'en come to that—I am for venturing one of the hundreds if you will upon this knight-errantry; but in case it should fail, we'll reserve the t'other to carry us to some counterscarp, where we may die as we lived in a blaze. 175

AIMWELL With all my heart; and we have lived justly, Archer—we can't say that we have spent our fortunes, but that we have enjoyed 'em. 180

ARCHER Right, so much pleasure for so much money—we have had our pennyworths, and had I millions, I would go to the same market again. O London, London! Well, we have had our share and let us be thankful. Past pleasures, for aught I know, are best, such as we are sure of—those to come may disappoint us. 185

AIMWELL It has often grieved the heart of me, to see how some
inhuman wretches murder their kind fortunes; those that by   190
sacrificing all to one appetite, shall starve all the rest. You shall
have some that live only in their palates, and in their sense of
tasting shall drown the other four. Others are only epicures in
appearances, such who shall starve their nights to make a figure
a-days, and famish their own° to feed the eyes of others. A   195
contrary sort confine their pleasures to the dark, and contract their
spacious acres to the circuit of a muff-string.

ARCHER Right; but they find the Indies in that spot where they
consume 'em, and I think your kind keepers° have much the best
on't; for they indulge the most senses by one expense—there's   200
the seeing, hearing, and feeling amply gratified; and some philosophers will tell you, that from such a commerce there arises a
sixth sense that gives infinitely more pleasure than the other five
put together.

AIMWELL And to pass to the other extremity, of all keepers, I think   205
those the worst that keep their money.

ARCHER Those are the most miserable wights in being—they destroy
the rights of nature, and disappoint the blessings of Providence.
Give me a man that keeps his five senses keen and bright as his
sword, that has 'em always drawn out in their just order and   210
strength, with his reason as commander at the head of 'em, that
detaches 'em by turns upon whatever party of pleasure agreeably
offers, and commands 'em to retreat upon the least appearance of
disadvantage or danger. For my part I can stick to my bottle, while
my wine, my company, and my reason holds good; I can be   215
charmed with Sappho's singing° without falling in love with her
face; I love hunting, but would not, like Actaeon,° be eaten up by
my own dogs; I love a fine house, but let another keep it; and just
so I love a fine woman.

AIMWELL In that last particular you have the better of me.   220

ARCHER Ay, you're such an amorous puppy, that I'm afraid you'll
spoil our sport; you can't counterfeit the passion without feeling
it.

AIMWELL Though the whining part be out of doors° in Town, 'tis
still in force with the country ladies. And let me tell you Frank,   225
the fool in that passion shall outdo the knave at any time.

ARCHER Well, I won't dispute it now—you command for the day,
and so I submit. At Nottingham you know I am to be master.

AIMWELL And at Lincoln I again.

ARCHER Then at Norwich° I mount, which, I think, shall be our last   230
    stage; for if we fail there, we'll embark for Holland, bid adieu to
    Venus, and welcome Mars.°

AIMWELL A match!°

    Enter Boniface

    Mum.

BONIFACE What will your worship please to have for supper?°   235

AIMWELL What have you got?

BONIFACE Sir, we have a delicate piece of beef in the pot, and a pig
    at the fire.

AIMWELL Good supper-meat, I must confess. I can't eat beef,
    landlord.   240

ARCHER And I hate pig.

AIMWELL Hold your prating, sirrah—do you know who you are?

BONIFACE Please to bespeak something else—I have everything in
    the house.

AIMWELL Have you any veal?   245

BONIFACE Veal! Sir, we had a delicate loin of veal on Wednesday
    last.

AIMWELL Have you got any fish or wildfowl?

BONIFACE As for fish, truly sir, we are an inland town, and
    indifferently provided with fish, that's the truth on't, and then for   250
    wildfowl—we have a delicate couple of rabbits.

AIMWELL Get me the rabbits fricasséd.

BONIFACE Fricasséd! Lard, sir, they'll eat much better smothered
    with onions.

ARCHER Pshaw! damn your onions.   255

AIMWELL Again, sirrah! Well, landlord, what you please; but hold—I
    have a small charge of money, and your house is so full of
    strangers, that I believe it may be safer in your custody than mine;
    for when this fellow of mine gets drunk, he minds nothing. [*To
    Archer*] Here, sirrah, reach me the strong box.   260

ARCHER Yes, sir. (*Aside*) This will give us a reputation.

    Brings the box

AIMWELL Here, landlord, the locks are sealed down both for your
    security and mine; it holds somewhat above two hundred pound;
    if you doubt it, I'll count it to you after supper; but be sure you
    lay it where I may have it at a minute's warning; for my affairs are   265
    a little dubious at present—perhaps I may be gone in half-an-hour,
    perhaps I may be your guest till the best part of that be spent; and
    pray order your ostler to keep my horses always saddled; but one

thing above the rest I must beg, that you would let this fellow
have none of your *Anno Domini*, as you call it. For he's the   270
most insufferable sot. [*To Archer*] Here, sirrah, light me to my
chamber.

    Exit [Aimwell], lighted by Archer

BONIFACE Cherry, daughter Cherry!

    Enter Cherry

CHERRY D'ye call, father?

BONIFACE Ay, child, you must lay by this box for the gentleman—   275
'tis full of money.

CHERRY Money! all that money! Why, sure father, the gentleman
comes to be chosen parliament-man.° Who is he?

BONIFACE I don't know what to make of him—he talks of keeping
his horses ready saddled, and of going perhaps at a minute's   280
warning, or of staying perhaps till the best part of this be spent.

CHERRY Ay, ten to one, father, he's a highwayman.

BONIFACE A highwayman! Upon my life, girl, you have hit it, and
this box is some new-purchased booty. Now could we find him
out, the money were ours.   285

CHERRY He don't belong to our gang.

BONIFACE What horses have they?

CHERRY The master rides upon a black.

BONIFACE A black! ten to one 'the man upon the black mare';° and
since he don't belong to our fraternity, we may betray him with a   290
safe conscience; I don't think it lawful to harbour any rogues but
my own. Look'ye, child, as the saying is, we must go cunningly to
work—proofs we must have. The gentleman's servant loves
drink—I'll ply him that way—and ten to one loves a wench—you
must work him t'other way.   295

CHERRY Father, would you have me give my secret for his?

BONIFACE Consider, child, there's two hundred pound to boot.°

    Ringing without

Coming, coming. Child, mind your business.

    [*Exit Boniface*]

CHERRY What a rogue is my father! My father! I deny it. My mother
was a good, generous, free-hearted woman, and I can't tell how far   300
her good nature might have extended for the good of her children.
This landlord of mine, for I think I can call him no more, would
betray his guest, and debauch his daughter into the bargain—by a
footman too!

    Enter Archer

ARCHER What footman, pray, mistress, is so happy as to be the   305
subject of your contemplation?

CHERRY Whoever he is, friend, he'll be but little the better for't.

ARCHER I hope so, for I'm sure you did not think of me.

CHERRY Suppose I had?

ARCHER Why then you're but even with me; for the minute I came   310
in, I was a-considering in what manner I should make love to you.

CHERRY Love to me, friend!

ARCHER Yes, child.

CHERRY Child! Manners; if you kept a little more distance, friend, it
would become you much better.   315

ARCHER Distance! good night, sauce-box. (*Going*)

CHERRY (*aside*) A pretty fellow! I like his pride.—Sir, pray, sir, you
see, sir—

Archer returns

I have the credit to be entrusted with your master's fortune here, which
sets me a degree above his footman; I hope, sir, you an't affronted.   320

ARCHER Let me look you full in the face, and I'll tell you whether
you can affront me or no. 'Sdeath, child, you have a pair of delicate
eyes, and you don't know what to do with 'em.

CHERRY Why, sir, don't I see everybody?

ARCHER Ay, but if some women had 'em, they would kill everybody.   325
Prithee, instruct me—I would fain make love to you, but I don't
know what to say.

CHERRY Why, did you never make love to anybody before?

ARCHER Never to a person of your figure, I can assure you,
madam—my addresses have been always confined to people within   330
my own sphere; I never aspired so high before. [*Sings*]

> But you look so bright
> And are dressed so tight,°
> That a man would swear you're right,
> As arm was e'er laid over.   335
> Such an air
> You freely wear
> To ensnare
> As makes each guest a lover!
>
> Since then, my dear, I'm your guest,   340
> Prithee give me of the best
> Of what is ready drest:
> Since then, my dear, &c.

CHERRY (*aside*) What can I think of this man?—Will you give me
that song, sir?   345

ARCHER Ay, my dear, take it while 'tis warm.
        Kisses her
Death and fire! her lips are honeycombs.

CHERRY And I wish there had been bees too, to have stung you for
your impudence.

ARCHER There's a swarm of cupids, my little Venus, that has done   350
the business much better.

CHERRY (*aside*) This fellow is misbegotten as well as I—What's your
name, sir.

ARCHER (*aside*) Name! Egad, I have forgot it. [*Aloud*] Oh! Martin.

CHERRY Where were you born?   355

ARCHER In St Martin's parish.°

CHERRY What was your father?

ARCHER St Martin's parish.

CHERRY Then, friend, goodnight.

ARCHER I hope not.   360

CHERRY You may depend upon't.

ARCHER Upon what?

CHERRY That you're very impudent.

ARCHER That you're very handsome.

CHERRY That you're a footman.   365

ARCHER That you're an angel.

CHERRY I shall be rude.

ARCHER So shall I.

CHERRY Let go my hand.

ARCHER Give me a kiss.   370
        Kisses her

[BONIFACE] (*without*) Cherry, Cherry.

CHERRY [*still kissing Archer*] I'mmm. [*Breaking free*] My father calls;
you plaguy devil, how durst you stop my breath so? Offer to follow
me one step, if you dare.
        [*Exit Cherry*]

ARCHER A fair challenge by this light; this is a pretty fair opening of an   375
adventure; but we are knight-errants, and so Fortune be our guide.
        Exit

2.[1]

Scene, a gallery in Lady Bountiful's house
Mrs Sullen and Dorinda meeting

DORINDA Morrow, my dear sister; are you for church this morning?

MRS SULLEN Anywhere to pray; for Heaven alone can help me. But, I think, Dorinda, there's no form of prayer in the liturgy against bad husbands.

DORINDA But there's a form of law in Doctors' Commons;° and   5
I swear, sister Sullen, rather than see you thus continually discontented, I would advise you to apply to that. For besides the part that I bear in your vexatious broils, as being sister to the husband, and friend to the wife, your example gives me such an impression of matrimony, that I shall be apt to condemn my   10
person to a long vacation° all its life. But supposing, madam, that you brought it to a case of separation, what can you urge against your husband? My brother is, first, the most constant man alive.°

MRS SULLEN The most constant husband, I grant ye.   15

DORINDA He never sleeps from you.

MRS SULLEN No, he always sleeps with me.

DORINDA He allows you a maintenance suitable to your quality.

MRS SULLEN A maintenance! do you take me, madam, for an hospital child,° that I must sit down, and bless my benefactors for   20
meat, drink, and clothes? As I take it, madam, I brought your brother ten thousand pounds, out of which I might expect some pretty things, called pleasures.

DORINDA You share in all the pleasures that the country affords.

MRS SULLEN Country pleasures! Racks and torments! Dost think,   25
child, that my limbs were made for leaping of ditches, and clambering over stiles; or that my parents wisely foreseeing my future happiness in country pleasures, had early instructed me in the rural accomplishments of drinking fat ale, playing at whisk, and smoking tobacco with my husband; or of spreading of plasters,   30
brewing of diet-drinks, and stilling rosemary°-water with the good old gentlewoman, my mother-in-law?

DORINDA I'm sorry, madam, that it is not more in our power to divert you; I could wish indeed that our entertainments were a little more polite, or your taste a little less refined. But, pray,   35

madam, how came the poets and philosophers that laboured so
much in hunting after pleasure, to place it at last in a country life?

MRS SULLEN Because they wanted money, child, to find out the
pleasures of the Town. Did you ever see a poet or philosopher
worth ten thousand pound? If you can show me such a man, I'll   40
lay you fifty pound you'll find him somewhere within the weekly
bills.° Not that I disapprove rural pleasures, as the poets have
painted them; in their landscape every Phillis has her Corydon,
every murmuring stream, and every flowery mead gives fresh
alarms to love.° Besides, you'll find, that their couples were never   45
married. [*Looking off-stage*] But yonder I see my Corydon, and a
sweet swain it is, Heaven knows. Come, Dorinda, don't be
angry—he's my husband, and your brother; and between both is
he not a sad brute?

DORINDA I have nothing to say to your part of him—you're the best   50
judge.

MRS SULLEN O sister, sister! if ever you marry, beware of a sullen,
silent sot, one that's always musing, but never thinks. There's
some diversion in a talking blockhead; and since a woman must
wear chains, I would have the pleasure of hearing 'em rattle a little.   55
Now you shall see—but take this by the way.° He came home this
morning at his usual hour of four, wakened me out of a sweet
dream of something else, by tumbling over the tea-table, which he
broke all to pieces; after his man and he had rolled about the room
like sick passengers in a storm, he comes flounce into bed, dead as   60
a salmon into a fishmonger's basket; his feet cold as ice, his breath
hot as a furnace, and his hands and his face as greasy as his flannel
nightcap. O matrimony! He tosses up the clothes with a barbarous
swing over his shoulders, disorders the whole economy of my bed,
leaves me half naked, and my whole night's comfort is the tuneable   65
serenade of that wakeful nightingale, his nose. O the pleasure of
counting the melancholy clock by a snoring husband! But now,
sister, you shall see how handsomely, being a well-bred man, he
will beg my pardon.

Enter Sullen

SULLEN My head aches consumedly.   70

MRS SULLEN Will you be pleased, my dear, to drink tea with us this
morning? It may do your head good.

SULLEN No.

DORINDA Coffee, brother?

SULLEN Pshaw.   75

MRS SULLEN Will you please to dress and go to church with me—the
　　air may help you.

SULLEN [*calls*] Scrub!
　　　　Enter Scrub

SCRUB Sir.

SULLEN What day o'th' week is this?   80

SCRUB Sunday, an't please your worship.

SULLEN Sunday! Bring me a dram, and d'ye hear, set out the
　　venison-pasty, and a tankard of strong beer upon the hall-table—
　　I'll go to breakfast. (*Going*)

DORINDA Stay, stay, brother, you shan't get off so; you were very   85
　　naught° last night, and must make your wife reparation; come,
　　come, brother, won't you ask pardon?

SULLEN For what?

DORINDA For being drunk last night.

SULLEN I can afford it, can't I?   90

MRS SULLEN But I can't, sir.

SULLEN Then you may let it alone.

MRS SULLEN But I must tell you, sir, that this is not to be borne.

SULLEN I'm glad on't.

MRS SULLEN What is the reason, sir, that you use me thus inhumanly?   95

SULLEN Scrub!

SCRUB Sir.

SULLEN Get the things ready to shave my head.°
　　　　[*Exeunt Sullen and Scrub*]

MRS SULLEN Have a care of coming near his temples, Scrub, for fear
　　you meet something there that may turn the edge of your razor.   100
　　Inveterate stupidity! Did you ever know so hard, so obstinate a
　　spleen as his? O sister, sister! I shall never ha' good of the beast
　　till I get him to Town; London, dear London is the place for
　　managing and breaking a husband.

DORINDA And has not a husband the same opportunities there for   105
　　humbling a wife?

MRS SULLEN No, no, child, 'tis a standing maxim in conjugal
　　discipline, that when a man would enslave his wife, he hurries her
　　into the country; and when a lady would be arbitrary with her
　　husband, she wheedles her booby up to Town. A man dare not   110
　　play the tyrant in London, because there are so many examples to
　　encourage the subject to rebel. O Dorinda, Dorinda! a fine woman
　　may do anything in London. O' my conscience, she may raise an
　　army of forty thousand men.

259

DORINDA I fancy, sister, you have a mind to be trying your power   115
that way here in Lichfield; you have drawn the French count to
your colours already.

MRS SULLEN The French are a people that can't live without their
gallantries.

DORINDA And some English that I know, sister, are not averse to   120
such amusements.

MRS SULLEN Well, sister, since the truth must out, it may do as well
now as hereafter; I think one way to rouse my lethargic sottish
husband—is—to give him a rival. Security begets negligence in all
people, and men must be alarmed to make 'em alert in their duty.   125
Women are like pictures—of no value in the hands of a fool, till
he hears men of sense bid high for the purchase.

DORINDA This might do, sister, if my brother's understanding were
to be convinced into a passion for you; but I fancy there's a natural
aversion of his side; and I fancy, sister, that you don't come much   130
behind him, if you dealt fairly.

MRS SULLEN I own it, we are united contradictions, fire and water.
But I could be contented, with a great many other wives, to
humour the censorious mob, and give the world an appearance of
living well with my husband, could I bring him but to dissemble   135
a little kindness to keep me in countenance.

DORINDA But how do you know, sister, but that instead of rousing
your husband by this artifice to a counterfeit kindness, he should
awake in a real fury?

MRS SULLEN Let him. If I can't entice him to the one, I would   140
provoke him to the other.

DORINDA But how must I behave myself between ye?

MRS SULLEN You must assist me.

DORINDA What, against my own brother!

MRS SULLEN He's but half a brother, and I'm your entire friend. If   145
I go a step beyond the bounds of honour, leave me; till then I
expect you should go along with me in everything—while I trust
my honour in your hands, you may trust your brother's in mine.
The count is to dine here today.

DORINDA 'Tis a strange thing, sister, that I can't like that man.   150

MRS SULLEN You like nothing—your time is not come; love and
death have their fatalities, and strike home one time or other.
You'll pay for all one day, I warrant ye. But, come, my lady's tea
is ready, and 'tis almost church time.

  Exeunt

[2.2]

Scene, the inn

Enter Aimwell dressed [for church], and Archer

AIMWELL And was she the daughter of the house?

ARCHER The landlord is so blind as to think so; but I dare swear she has better blood in her veins.

AIMWELL Why dost think so?

ARCHER Because the baggage has a pert *je ne sais quoi*°—she reads plays, keeps a monkey, and is troubled with vapours. 5

AIMWELL By which discoveries I guess that you know more of her.

ARCHER Not yet, faith, the lady gives herself airs, forsooth—nothing under a gentleman!

AIMWELL Let me take her in hand. 10

ARCHER Say one word more o'that, and I'll declare myself, spoil your sport there, and everywhere else; look ye, Aimwell, every man in his own sphere.

AIMWELL Right; and therefore you must pimp for your master.

ARCHER In the usual forms, good sir, after I have served myself. But 15
to our business. You are so well dressed, Tom, and make so handsome a figure, that I fancy you may do execution in a country church; the exterior part strikes first, and you're in the right to make that impression favourable.

AIMWELL There's something in that which may turn to advantage. 20
The appearance of a stranger in a country church draws as many gazers as a blazing star;° no sooner he comes into the cathedral,° but a train of whispers runs buzzing round the congregation in a moment: 'Who is he?' 'Whence comes he?' 'Do you know him?' Then I, sir, tips me the verger with half-a-crown; he pockets the 25
simony, and inducts me into the best pew in the church; I pull out my snuff-box, turn myself round, bow to the bishop, or the dean, if he be the commanding officer; single out a beauty, rivet both my eyes to hers, set my nose a-bleeding by the strength of imagination, and show the whole church my concern by my endeavouring to 30
hide it; after the sermon, the whole town gives me to her for a lover, and by persuading the lady that I am a-dying for her, the tables are turned, and she in good earnest falls in love with me.

ARCHER There's nothing in this, Tom, without a precedent; but instead of riveting your eyes to a beauty, try to fix 'em upon a 35
fortune—that's our business at present.

AIMWELL Pshaw, no woman can be a beauty without a fortune. Let me alone, for I am a marksman.

ARCHER Tom.

AIMWELL Ay.

ARCHER When were you at church before, pray?

AIMWELL Um—I was there at the coronation.°

ARCHER And how can you expect a blessing by going to church now?

AIMWELL Blessing! nay, Frank, I ask but for a wife.

    Exit [Aimwell]

ARCHER Truly the man is not very unreasonable in his demands.

    Exit [Archer] at the opposite door. Enter Boniface and Cherry

BONIFACE Well daughter, as the saying is, have you brought Martin to confess?

CHERRY Pray, father, don't put me upon getting anything out of a man; I'm but young you know, father, and I don't understand wheedling.

BONIFACE Young! why you jade, as the saying is, can any woman wheedle that is not young? Your mother was useless at five and twenty. Not wheedle! Would you make your mother a whore and me a cuckold, as the saying is? I tell you his silence confesses it, and his master spends his money so freely, and is so much a gentleman every manner of way that he must be a highwayman.

    Enter Gibbet in a cloak

GIBBET Landlord, landlord, is the coast clear?

BONIFACE O, Mr Gibbet, what's the news?

GIBBET No matter, ask no questions—all fair and honourable— here, my dear Cherry.

    Gives her a bag

Two hundred sterling pounds, as good as any that ever hanged or saved a rogue;° lay 'em by with the rest, and here, three wedding or mourning rings°—'tis much the same you know. Here, two silver-hilted swords; I took those from fellows that never show any part of their swords but the hilts. Here is a diamond necklace which the lady hid in the privatest place in the coach, but I found it out. This gold watch I took from a pawnbroker's wife; it was left in her hands by a person of quality—there's the arms° upon the case.

CHERRY But who had you the money from?

GIBBET Ah! poor woman! I pitied her. From a poor lady just eloped
from her husband—she had made up her cargo, and was bound for
Ireland, as hard as she could drive; she told me of her husband's   75
barbarous usage, and so I left her half-a-crown. But I had almost
forgot, my dear Cherry, I have a present for you.

CHERRY What is't?

GIBBET A pot of ceruse, my child, that I took out of a lady's
under-pocket.   80

CHERRY What, Mr Gibbet, do you think that I paint?°

GIBBET Why, you jade, your betters do; I'm sure the lady that I took
it from had a coronet upon her handkerchief. Here, take my cloak,
and go, secure the premises.°

CHERRY I will secure 'em.   85

    Exit [Cherry]

BONIFACE But, heark'ye, where's Hounslow and Bagshot?

GIBBET They'll be here tonight.

BONIFACE D'ye know of any other gentlemen o' the pad° on this
road?

GIBBET No.   90

BONIFACE I fancy that I have two that lodge in the house just now.

GIBBET The Devil! how d'ye smoke 'em?°

BONIFACE Why, the one is gone to church.

GIBBET That's suspicious, I must confess.

BONIFACE And the other is now in his master's chamber; he pretends   95
to be servant to the other—we'll call him out and pump him a little.

GIBBET With all my heart.

BONIFACE [*calls*] Mr Martin, Mr Martin!

    Enter [Archer] combing a periwig, and singing

GIBBET The roads are consumed deep; I'm as dirty as old Brentford
at Christmas.° [*Affecting to see Archer*] A good pretty fellow that.   100
Whose servant are you, friend?

ARCHER My master's.

GIBBET Really?

ARCHER Really.

GIBBET That's much. The fellow has been at the Bar by his   105
evasions.°—But, pray, sir, what is your master's name?

ARCHER (*sings and combs the periwig*) Tall, all dall. This is the most
obstinate curl.

GIBBET I ask you his name.

ARCHER Name, sir—Tall, all dall—I never asked him his name in my   110
life. Tall, all dall.

BONIFACE [*to Gibbet*] What think you now?

GIBBET Plain, plain—he talks now as if he were before a judge.
[*Aloud*] But, pray, friend, which way does your master travel?

ARCHER A-horseback.   115

GIBBET [*to Boniface*] Very well again, an old offender, right. [*Aloud*]
But I mean, does he go upwards or downwards?°

ARCHER Downwards, I fear, sir. Tall, all.

GIBBET I'm afraid my fate will be a contrary way.°

BONIFACE Ha, ha, ha! Mr Martin you're very arch. This gentleman   120
is only travelling towards Chester, and would be glad of your
company, that's all. [*To Gibbet*] Come, Captain, you'll stay tonight,
I suppose; I'll show you a chamber. Come, Captain.

GIBBET Farewell, friend.
            [*Exeunt Gibbet and Boniface*]

ARCHER Captain, your servant.—Captain! a pretty fellow; s'death, I   125
wonder that the officers of the army don't conspire to beat all
scoundrels in red, but their own.
            Enter Cherry

CHERRY (*aside*) Gone! and Martin here! I hope he did not listen; I
would have the merit of the discovery all my own, because I would
oblige him to love me. [*Aloud*] Mr Martin, who was that man with   130
my father?

ARCHER Some recruiting sergeant, or whipped-out trooper,° I suppose.

CHERRY (*aside*) All's safe, I find.

ARCHER Come, my dear, have you conned over the catechise° I
taught you last night?   135

CHERRY Come, question me.

ARCHER What is Love?

CHERRY Love is I know not what, it comes I know not how, and goes
I know not when.

ARCHER Very well, an apt scholar.   140
            Chucks her under the chin
Where does Love enter?

CHERRY Into the eyes.

ARCHER And where go out?

CHERRY I won't tell 'ye.

ARCHER What are objects of that passion?   145

CHERRY Youth, Beauty, and Clean Linen.

ARCHER The reason?

CHERRY The first two are fashionable in Nature, and the third at
Court.

ARCHER That's my dear. What are the signs and tokens of that   150
    passion?

CHERRY A stealing look, a stammering tongue, words improbable,
    designs impossible, and actions impracticable.

ARCHER That's my good child—kiss me. What must a lover do to
    obtain his mistress?   155

CHERRY He must adore the person that disdains him, he must bribe
    the chambermaid that betrays him, and court the footman that
    laughs at him. He must, he must—

ARCHER Nay, child, I must whip you if you don't mind your lesson;
    he must treat his—   160

CHERRY O, ay, he must treat his enemies with respect, his friends
    with indifference, and all the world with contempt; he must suffer
    much, and fear more; he must desire much, and hope little; in
    short, he must embrace his ruin, and throw himself away.

ARCHER Had ever man so hopeful a pupil as mine? Come, my dear,   165
    why is Love called a riddle?

CHERRY Because being blind, he leads those that see, and though a
    child, he governs a man.

ARCHER Mighty well. And why is Love pictured blind?°

CHERRY Because the painters out of the weakness or privilege of   170
    their art chose to hide those eyes that they could not draw.

ARCHER That's my dear little scholar—kiss me again. And why
    should Love, that's a child, govern a man?

CHERRY Because that a child is the end of Love.

ARCHER And so ends 'Love's Catechism'. And now, my dear, we'll   175
    go in, and make my master's bed.

CHERRY Hold, hold, Mr Martin—you have taken a great deal of
    pains to instruct me, and what d'ye think I have learned by it?

ARCHER What?

CHERRY That your discourse and your habit are contradictions, and   180
    it would be nonsense in me to believe you a footman any longer.

ARCHER 'Oons, what a witch it is!

CHERRY Depend upon this, sir, nothing in this garb° shall ever
    tempt me; for though I was born to servitude, I hate it. Own your
    condition, swear you love me, and then—   185

ARCHER And then we shall go make the bed.

CHERRY Yes.

ARCHER You must know then, that I am born a gentleman, my
    education was liberal; but I went to London a younger brother, fell
    into the hands of sharpers, who stripped me of my money, my   190

friends disowned me, and now my necessity brings me to what you see.

CHERRY Then take my hand—promise to marry me before you sleep, and I'll make you master of two thousand pound.

ARCHER How!   195

CHERRY Two thousand pound that I have this minute in my own custody; so throw off your livery this instant, and I'll go find a parson.

ARCHER What said you? A parson!

CHERRY What! do you scruple?   200

ARCHER Scruple! no, no, but—two thousand pound you say?

CHERRY And better.

ARCHER 'Sdeath, what shall I do?—but heark'ee, child, what need you make me master of your self and money, when you may have the same pleasure out of me, and still keep your fortune in your   205
hands?

CHERRY Then you won't marry me?

ARCHER I would marry you, but—

CHERRY O sweet—sir—I'm your humble servant—you're fairly caught. Would you persuade me that any gentleman who could   210
bear the scandal of wearing a livery, would refuse two thousand pound, let the condition be what it would—no, no, sir; but I hope you'll pardon the freedom I have taken, since it was only to inform myself of the respect that I ought to pay you. (*Going*)

ARCHER Fairly bit, by Jupiter—hold, hold, and have you actually two   215
thousand pound?

CHERRY Sir, I have my secrets as well as you—when you please to be more open, I shall be more free, and be assured that I have discoveries that will match yours, be what they will; in the meanwhile be satisfied that no discovery I make shall ever hurt   220
you, but beware of my father.

　　　Exit [*Cherry*]

ARCHER So—we're like to have as many adventures in our inn, as Don Quixote had in his.° Let me see—two thousand pound! If the wench would promise to die when the money were spent, egad, one would marry her, but the fortune may go off in a year or two,   225
and the wife may live—Lord knows how long! Then an inn-keeper's daughter; ay that's the Devil—there my pride brings me off.

　　　For whatsoe'er the sages charge on pride—
　　　The angels' fall, and twenty faults beside—   230

On earth I'm sure, 'mong us of mortal calling,
Pride saves man oft, and woman too, from falling.
Exit

3.[1]

Scene, [a gallery in] Lady Bountiful's house
Enter Mrs Sullen, Dorinda

MRS SULLEN Ha, ha, ha, my dear sister, let me embrace thee, now
we are friends indeed! for I shall have a secret of yours, as a pledge
for mine; now you'll be good for something—I shall have you
conversable in the subjects of the sex.°

DORINDA But do you think that I am so weak as to fall in love with   5
a fellow at first sight?

MRS SULLEN Pshaw! now you spoil all—why should not we be as
free in our friendships as the men? I warrant you the gentleman
has got to his confidant already, has avowed his passion, toasted
your health, called you ten thousand angels, has run over your lips,   10
eyes, neck, shape, air and everything, in a description that warms
their mirth to a second enjoyment.

DORINDA Your hand, sister, I an't well.

MRS SULLEN So, she's breeding already. Come child, up with it:
hem a little—so. Now tell me, don't you like the gentleman that   15
we saw at church just now?

DORINDA The man's well enough.

MRS SULLEN Well enough! is he not a demigod, a Narcissus,° a star,
the man i' the moon?

DORINDA O sister, I'm extremely ill.   20

MRS SULLEN Shall I send to your mother, child, for a little of her
cephalic plaster° to put to the soles of your feet, or shall I send to
the gentleman for something for you? Come, unlace your stays,
unbosom yourself; the man is perfectly a pretty fellow—I saw him
when he first came into church.   25

DORINDA I saw him too, sister, and with an air that shone, methought, like rays about his person.

MRS SULLEN Well said, up with it!

DORINDA No forward coquette behaviour, no airs to set him off, no
studied looks nor artful posture—but nature did it all—   30

MRS SULLEN Better and better. One touch more—come.

DORINDA But then his looks—did you observe his eyes?

MRS SULLEN Yes, yes, I did. His eyes—well, what of his eyes?

DORINDA Sprightly, but not wandering; they seemed to view, but
never gazed on anything but me—and then his looks so humble   35

were, and yet so noble, that they aimed to tell me that he could
with pride die at my feet, though he scorned slavery anywhere else.

MRS SULLEN The physic works purely. How d'ye find yourself now,
my dear?

DORINDA Hem! much better, my dear. O, here comes our Mercury!° 40
Enter Scrub
Well Scrub, what news of the gentleman?

SCRUB Madam, I have brought you a packet of news.

DORINDA Open it quickly, come.

SCRUB In the first place I inquired who the gentleman was—they told
me he was a stranger. Secondly, I asked what the gentleman   45
was—they answered and said, that they never saw him before.
Thirdly, I inquired what countryman he was°—they replied 'twas
more than they knew. Fourthly, I demanded whence he came—
their answer was, they could not tell. And fifthly, I asked whither
he went—and they replied they knew nothing of the matter—and 50
this is all I could learn.

MRS SULLEN But what do the people say—can't they guess?

SCRUB Why some think he's a spy, some guess he's a mountebank,
some say one thing, some another; but for my own part, I believe
he's a Jesuit.°   55

DORINDA A Jesuit! why a Jesuit?

SCRUB Because he keeps his horses always ready saddled and his
footman talks French.

MRS SULLEN His footman!

SCRUB Ay, he and the count's footman were jabbering French like 60
two intriguing ducks in a mill-pond, and I believe they talked of
me, for they laughed consumedly.

DORINDA What sort of livery has the footman?

SCRUB Livery! Lord, madam, I took him for a captain, he's so
bedizened with lace, and then he has tops to his shoes, up to his 65
mid-leg, a silver-headed cane dangling at his knuckles—he carries
his hands in his pockets just so (*walks in the French air*), and has
a fine long periwig tied up in a bag.° Lord, madam, he's clear
another sort of man than I.

MRS SULLEN That may easily be, but what shall we do now, sister? 70

DORINDA I have it; this fellow has a world of simplicity, and some
cunning—the first hides the latter by abundance.—Scrub.

SCRUB Madam.

DORINDA We have a great mind to know who this gentleman is, only
for our satisfaction.   75

SCRUB Yes, madam, it would be a satisfaction, no doubt.

DORINDA You must go and get acquainted with his footman, and invite him hither to drink a bottle of your ale, because you're butler today.

SCRUB Yes, madam, I am butler every Sunday.   80

MRS SULLEN O brave, sister—o' my conscience, you understand the mathematics already: 'tis the best plot in the world. Your mother, you know, will be gone to church, my spouse will be got to the ale-house with his scoundrels, and the house will be our own—so we drop in by accident and ask the fellow some questions   85 ourselves. In the country you know any stranger is company, and we're glad to take up with the butler in a country dance, and happy if he'll do us the favour.

SCRUB O! Madam, you wrong me—I never refused your ladyship the favour° in my life.   90

        Enter Gypsy

GYPSY Ladies, dinner's upon table.

DORINDA Scrub, we'll excuse your waiting—go where we ordered you.

SCRUB I shall.

        Exeunt

[3.2]

        Scene changes to the inn

        Enter Aimwell and Archer

ARCHER Well, Tom, I find you're a marksman.

AIMWELL A marksman! who so blind could be, as not discern a swan among the ravens?

ARCHER Well, but hark'ee, Aimwell.

AIMWELL Aimwell! call me Oroondates,° Cesario,° Amadis°—all   5 that romance can in a lover paint, and then I'll answer. O Archer, I read her thousands in her looks: she looked like Ceres° in her harvest—corn, wine and oil, milk and honey, gardens, groves and purling streams played on her plenteous face.

ARCHER Her face! her pocket, you mean; the corn, wine and oil lies   10 there. In short, she has ten thousand pound, that's the English on't.

AIMWELL Her eyes—

ARCHER Are demi-cannons to be sure, so I won't stand their battery. 15
    (*Going*)

AIMWELL Pray excuse me, my passion must have vent.

ARCHER Passion! what a plague, d'ee think these romantic airs will
    do our business? Were my temper as extravagant as yours, my
    adventures have something more romantic by half.

AIMWELL Your adventures! 20

ARCHER Yes,
    The nymph that with her twice ten hundred pounds
    With brazen engine hot, and quoif clear starched
    Can fire the guest in warming of the bed—
    There's a touch of sublime Milton° for you, and the subject but 25
    an inn-keeper's daughter; I can play with a girl as an angler does
    with his fish; he keeps it at the end of his line, runs it up the
    stream, and down the stream, till at last he brings it to hand, tickles
    the trout,° and so whips it into his basket.
        Enter Boniface

BONIFACE Mr Martin, as the saying is—yonder's an honest fellow 30
    below, my Lady Bountiful's butler, who begs the honour that you
    would go home with him and see his cellar.

ARCHER Do my baisemains to the gentleman, and tell him I will do
    myself the honour to wait on him immediately.
        Exit Boniface

AIMWELL What do I hear? Soft Orpheus° play, and fair Toftida° 35
    sing!

ARCHER Pshaw! damn your raptures, I tell you here's a pump
    going to be put into the vessel, and the ship will get into
    harbour, my life on't. You say there's another lady very handsome
    there. 40

AIMWELL Yes, faith.

ARCHER I'm in love with her already.

AIMWELL Can't you give me a bill upon Cherry° in the meantime?

ARCHER No, no, friend, all her corn, wine and oil is engrossed to my
    market.° And once more I warn you to keep your anchorage clear 45
    of mine, for if you fall foul of me, by this light you shall go to the
    bottom. What! make prize of my little frigate, while I am upon the
    cruise for you!

AIMWELL Well, well, I won't.
        Exit [Archer]. Enter Boniface
    Landlord, have you any tolerable company in the house? I don't 50
    care for dining alone.

BONIFACE Yes, sir, there's a captain below, as the saying is, that arrived about an hour ago.

AIMWELL Gentlemen of his coat are welcome everywhere: will you make him a compliment from me, and tell him I should be glad of his company.   55

BONIFACE Who shall I tell him, sir, would—?

AIMWELL [aside] Ha! that stroke was well thrown in. [Aloud] I'm only a traveller like himself, and would be glad of his company, that's all.   60

BONIFACE I obey your commands, as the saying is.

> *Exit [Boniface]. Enter Archer*

ARCHER 'Sdeath! I had forgot—what title will you give yourself?

AIMWELL My brother's to be sure—he would never give me anything else, so I'll make bold with his honour this bout. You know the rest of your cue.   65

ARCHER Ay, ay.

> *Exit [Archer]. Enter Gibbet*

GIBBET Sir, I'm yours.

AIMWELL 'Tis more than I deserve, sir, for I don't know you.

GIBBET I don't wonder at that, sir, for you never saw me before— (aside) I hope.   70

AIMWELL And pray, sir, how came I by the honour of seeing you now?

GIBBET Sir, I scorn to intrude upon any gentleman, but my landlord—

AIMWELL O, sir, I ask your pardon—you're the captain he told me of?   75

GIBBET At your service, sir.

AIMWELL What regiment, may I be so bold?

GIBBET A marching regiment, sir, an old corps.

AIMWELL (aside) Very old, if your coat be regimental.—You have served abroad, sir?   80

GIBBET Yes, sir, in the plantations—'twas my lot to be sent into the worst service;° I would have quitted it indeed, but a man of honour, you know. Besides 'twas for the good of my country that I should be abroad. Anything for the good of one's country—I'm a Roman for that.°   85

ARCHER (aside) One of the first,° I'll lay my life.—You found the West Indies very hot, sir?

GIBBET Ay, sir, too hot for me.

AIMWELL Pray, sir, han't I seen your face at Will's° coffee-house?   90

GIBBET Yes, sir, and at White's° too.

AIMWELL And where is your company now, Captain?

GIBBET They an't come yet.

AIMWELL Why, d'ye expect 'em here?

GIBBET They'll be here tonight, sir.   95

AIMWELL Which way do they march?

GIBBET Across the country. [*Aside*] The Devil's in't, if I han't said
   enough to encourage him to declare°—but I'm afraid he's not
   right; I must tack about.

AIMWELL Is your company to quarter in Lichfield?   100

GIBBET In this house, sir.

AIMWELL What! all?

GIBBET My company's but thin, ha, ha, ha—we are but three, ha, ha,
   ha.

AIMWELL You're merry, sir.   105

GIBBET Ay, sir, you must excuse me, sir—I understand the world,
   especially the art of travelling; I don't care, sir, for answering
   questions directly upon the road—for I generally ride with a
   charge about me.

AIMWELL (*aside*) Three or four, I believe.°   110

GIBBET I am credibly informed that there are highwaymen upon this
   quarter—not, sir, that I could suspect a gentleman of your figure.
   But truly, sir, I have got such a way of evasion upon the road, that
   I don't care for speaking truth to any man.

AIMWELL Your caution may be necessary. Then I presume you're no   115
   captain?

GIBBET Not I, sir—'Captain' is a good travelling name, and so I take
   it; it stops a great many foolish inquiries that are generally made
   about gentlemen that travel, it gives a man an air of something,
   and makes the drawers obedient. And thus far I am a captain, and   120
   no further.

AIMWELL And pray, sir, what is your true profession?

GIBBET O sir, you must excuse me—upon my word, sir, I don't
   think it safe to tell you.

AIMWELL Ha, ha, ha, upon my word, I commend you.   125
      Enter Boniface
   Well, Mr Boniface, what's the news?

BONIFACE There's another gentleman below, as the saying is, that
   hearing you were but two, would be glad to make the third man if
   you would give him leave.

AIMWELL What is he?   130

BONIFACE A clergyman, as the saying is.

AIMWELL A clergyman! Is he really a clergyman, or is it only his travelling name, as my friend the captain has it?

BONIFACE O, sir, he's a priest and chaplain to the French officers in town.   135

AIMWELL Is he a Frenchman?

BONIFACE Yes, sir, born at Brussels.

GIBBET A Frenchman, and a priest! I won't be seen in his company, sir; I have a value for my reputation, sir.

AIMWELL Nay, but Captain, since we are by ourselves—can he speak   140
English, landlord?

BONIFACE Very well, sir—you may know him, as the saying is, to be a foreigner by his accent, and that's all.

AIMWELL Then he has been in England before?

BONIFACE Never, sir, but he's a master of languages, as the saying   145
is—he talks Latin; it does me good to hear him talk Latin.

AIMWELL Then you understand Latin, Mr Boniface?

BONIFACE Not I, sir, as the saying is, but he talks it so very fast that I'm sure it must be good.

AIMWELL Pray desire him to walk up.   150

BONIFACE Here he is, as the saying is.

      Enter Foigard

FOIGARD Save you, gentlemens,° both.

AIMWELL [*aside*] A Frenchman!—Sir, your most humble servant.

FOIGARD Och, dear joy, I am your most faithful shervant, and yours alsho.   155

GIBBET Doctor, you talk very good English, but you have a mighty twang of the foreigner.

FOIGARD My English is very vel for the vords, but we foreigners you know cannot bring our tongues about the pronunciation so soon.   160

AIMWELL (*aside*) A foreigner! a downright Teague° by this light.—
Were you born in France, Doctor?

FOIGARD I was educated in France, but I was borned at Brussels—I am a subject of the King of Spain, joy.

GIBBET What King of Spain,° sir?—speak.   165

FOIGARD Upon my shoul joy, I cannot tell you as yet.

AIMWELL Nay, Captain, that was too hard upon the Doctor—he's a stranger.

FOIGARD O let him alone, dear joy—I am of a nation that is not easily put out of countenance.   170

AIMWELL Come, gentlemen, I'll end the dispute. Here, landlord, is dinner ready?

BONIFACE Upon the table, as the saying is.

AIMWELL [*gesturing*] Gentlemen—pray—that door.

FOIGARD No, no fait, the captain must lead.   175

AIMWELL No, Doctor, the Church is our guide.

GIBBET Ay, ay, so it is.

   Exit [Gibbet] foremost; they follow

[3.3]

Scene changes to a gallery in Lady Bountiful's house

Enter Archer and Scrub singing, and hugging one another, Scrub with a tankard in his hand, Gypsy listening at a distance

SCRUB Tall, all dall. Come, my dear boy, let's have that song once more.

ARCHER No, no, we shall disturb the family. But will you be sure to keep the secret?

SCRUB Pho! upon my honour, as I'm a gentleman.

ARCHER 'Tis enough. You must know then that my master is the   5
Lord Viscount Aimwell; he fought a duel t'other day in London, wounded his man so dangerously, that he thinks fit to withdraw till he hears whether the gentleman's wounds be mortal or not. He never was in this part of England before, so he chose to retire to this place, that's all.   10

GYPSY And that's enough for me.

   Exit [Gypsy]

SCRUB And where were you when your master fought?

ARCHER We never know of our masters' quarrels.

SCRUB No! If our masters in the country here receive a challenge, the first thing they do is to tell their wives; the wife tells the servants,   15
the servants alarm the tenants, and in half-an-hour you shall have the whole county in arms.

ARCHER To hinder two men from doing what they have no mind for. But if you should chance to talk now of my business?

SCRUB Talk! ay, sir, had I not learnt the knack of holding my tongue,   20
I had never lived so long in a great family.

ARCHER Ay, ay, to be sure there are secrets in all families.

SCRUB Secrets, ay. But I'll say no more. Come, sit down—we'll make an end of our tankard. Here—

ARCHER With all my heart; who knows but you and I may come to   25
be better acquainted, eh? Here's your ladies' healths; you have
three, I think, and to be sure there must be secrets among 'em.

SCRUB Secrets! Ay, friend; I wish I had a friend—

ARCHER Am not I your friend? Come, you and I will be sworn
brothers.   30

SCRUB Shall we?

ARCHER From this minute. Give me a kiss—and now brother
Scrub—

SCRUB And now, brother Martin, I will tell you a secret that will
make your hair stand on end. You must know, that I am   35
consumedly in love.

ARCHER That's a terrible secret, that's the truth on't.

SCRUB That jade, Gypsy, that was with us just now in the cellar, is
the arrantest whore that ever wore a petticoat; and I'm dying for
love of her.   40

ARCHER Ha, ha, ha. Are you in love with her person, or her virtue,
brother Scrub?

SCRUB I should like virtue best, because it is more durable than
beauty; for virtue holds good with some women long, and many a
day after they have lost it.   45

ARCHER In the country, I grant ye, where no woman's virtue is lost,
till a bastard be found.

SCRUB Ay, could I bring her to a bastard, I should have her all to
myself; but I dare not put it upon that lay,° for fear of being sent
for a soldier. Pray, brother, how do you gentlemen in London like   50
that same Pressing Act?°

ARCHER Very ill, brother Scrub. 'Tis the worst that ever was made
for us. Formerly I remember the good days, when we could dun
our masters for our wages, and if they refused to pay us, we could
have a warrant to carry 'em before a justice; but now if we talk of   55
eating, they have a warrant for us, and carry us before three justices.

SCRUB And to be sure we go, if we talk of eating; for the justices
won't give their own servants a bad example. Now this is my
misfortune: I dare not speak in the house, while that jade Gypsy
dings about like a Fury. Once I had the better end of the staff.°   60

ARCHER And how comes the change now?

SCRUB Why, the mother of all this mischief is a priest.

ARCHER A priest!

SCRUB Ay, a damned son of a whore of Babylon,° that came over
hither to say grace to the French officers, and eat up our   65

provisions. There's not a day goes over his head without dinner or supper in this house.

ARCHER How came he so familiar in the family?

SCRUB Because he speaks English as if he had lived here all his life; and tells lies as if he had been a traveller from his cradle. 70

ARCHER And this priest, I'm afraid has converted the affections of your Gypsy.

SCRUB Converted! ay, and perverted, my dear friend. For I'm afraid he has made her a whore and a papist. But this is not all; there's the French count and Mrs Sullen—they're in the confederacy, and 75 for some private ends of their own to be sure.

ARCHER A very hopeful family yours, brother Scrub; I suppose the maiden lady has her lover too.

SCRUB Not that I know. She's the best on 'em, that's the truth on't. But they take care to prevent my curiosity, by giving me so much 80 business, that I'm a perfect slave. What d'ye think is my place in this family?

ARCHER Butler, I suppose.

SCRUB Ah, Lord help you—I'll tell you. Of a Monday, I drive the coach; of a Tuesday, I drive the plough; on Wednesday, I follow 85 the hounds; o' Thursday, I dun the tenants; on Friday, I go to market; on Saturday, I draw warrants;° and o' Sunday, I draw beer.

ARCHER Ha, ha, ha! if variety be a pleasure in life, you have enough on't, my dear brother. [*Looking off-stage*] But what ladies are those?

SCRUB° Ours, ours; that upon the right hand is Mrs Sullen, and the 90 other is Mrs Dorinda. Don't mind 'em—sit still, man.

Enter Mrs Sullen, and Dorinda

MRS SULLEN I have heard my brother talk of my Lord Aimwell, but they say that his brother is the finer gentleman.

DORINDA That's impossible, sister.

MRS SULLEN He's vastly rich, but very close, they say. 95

DORINDA No matter for that; if I can creep into his heart, I'll open his breast, I warrant him. I have heard say, that people may be guessed at by the behaviour of their servants; I could wish we might talk to that fellow.

MRS SULLEN So do I; for, I think he's a very pretty fellow. Come 100 this way—I'll throw out a lure for him presently.

They walk a turn towards the opposite side of the stage

ARCHER [*aside*] Corn, wine, and oil, indeed. But, I think, the wife has the greatest plenty of flesh and blood; she should be my choice.

Mrs Sullen drops her glove

Aha, say you so.

Archer runs, takes it up, and gives it to her

Madam—your ladyship's glove.   105

MRS SULLEN O, sir, I thank you. [*To Dorinda*] What a handsome bow the fellow has.

DORINDA Bow! why I have known several footmen come down from London set up here for dancing-masters, and carry off the best fortunes in the country.   110

ARCHER (*aside*) That project, for aught I know, had been better than ours.—Brother Scrub, why don't you introduce me.

SCRUB Ladies, this is the strange gentleman's servant that you see at church today; I understood he came from London, and so I invited him to the cellar, that he might show me the newest flourish in   115 whetting my knives.

DORINDA And I hope you have made much of him?

ARCHER O yes, madam, but the strength of your ladyship's liquor is a little too potent for the constitution of your humble servant.   120

MRS SULLEN What, then you don't usually drink ale?

ARCHER No, madam, my constant drink is tea, or a little wine and water; 'tis prescribed me by the physician for a remedy against the spleen.

SCRUB O la, O la!—a footman have the spleen.   125

MRS SULLEN I thought that distemper had been only proper to people of quality.

ARCHER Madam, like all other fashions it wears out, and so descends to their servants; though in a great many of us, I believe it proceeds from some melancholy particles in the blood, occasioned by the   130 stagnation of wages.

DORINDA How affectedly the fellow talks. How long, pray, have you served your present master?

ARCHER Not long; my life has been mostly spent in the service of the ladies.   135

MRS SULLEN And pray, which service do you like best?

ARCHER Madam, the ladies pay best; the honour of serving them is sufficient wages; there is a charm in their looks that delivers a pleasure with their commands, and gives our duty the wings of inclination.   140

MRS SULLEN [*aside*] That flight was above the touch of a livery.— And, sir, would not you be satisfied to serve a lady again?

ARCHER As a groom of the chamber, madam, but not as a footman.

MRS SULLEN I suppose you served as footman before.

ARCHER For that reason I would not serve in that post again; for my   145
memory is too weak for the load of messages that the ladies lay
upon their servants in London; my Lady Howd'ye, the last
mistress I served, called me up one morning, and told me,
'Martin, go to my Lady Allnight with my humble service; tell her
I was to wait on her ladyship yesterday, and left word with Mrs   150
Rebecca, that the preliminaries of the affair she knows of are
stopped, till we know the concurrence of the person that I know
of, for which there are circumstances wanting which we shall
accommodate at the old place; but that in the meantime there
is a person about her ladyship, that from several hints and   155
surmises, was accessary at a certain time to the disappointments
that naturally attend things that to her knowledge are of more
importance . . .'

MRS SULLEN [and] DORINDA Ha, ha, ha! Where are you going,
sir?   160

ARCHER Why, I han't half done. The whole 'Howd'ye' was about
half-an-hour long; so I happened to misplace two syllables, and
was turned off, and rendered incapable.°

DORINDA The pleasantest fellow, sister, I ever saw.—But, friend, if
your master be married, I presume you still serve a lady.   165

ARCHER No, madam, I take care never to come into a married family;
the commands of the master and mistress are always so contrary,
that 'tis impossible to please both.

DORINDA (aside) There's a main point gained. My lord is not
married, I find.   170

MRS SULLEN But, I wonder, friend, that in so many good services,
you had not a better provision made for you.

ARCHER I don't know how, madam. I had a lieutenancy offered me
three or four times; but that is not bread, madam—I live much
better as I do.   175

SCRUB Madam, he sings rarely. I was thought to do pretty well here
in the country till he came; but alack-a-day, I'm nothing to my
brother Martin.

DORINDA Does he? Pray, sir, will you oblige us with a song?

ARCHER Are you for passion, or humour?   180

SCRUB O le! he has the purest ballad about a trifle—

MRS SULLEN A trifle! Pray, sir, let's have it.

ARCHER I'm ashamed to offer you a trifle, madam. But since you
command me.

Sings to the tune of 'Sir Simon the King'°

> A trifling song you shall hear,   185
> Begun with a trifle and ended;°
> All trifling people draw near,
> And I shall be nobly attended.

> Were it not for trifles, a few,
> That lately have come into play,   190
> The men would want something to do,
> And the women want something to say.

> What makes men trifle in dressing?
> Because the ladies, they know,
> Admire, by often possessing,   195
> That eminent trifle a beau.

> When the lover his moments has trifled,
> The trifle of trifles to gain,
> No sooner the virgin is rifled,
> But a trifle shall part 'em again.   200

> What mortal man would be able
> At White's half-an-hour to sit?
> Or who could bear a tea-table,
> Without talking of trifles for wit?

> The Court is from trifles secure—   205
> Gold keys are no trifles, we see;°
> White rods are no trifles, I'm sure,°
> Whatever their bearers may be.

> But if you will go to the place,
> Where trifles abundantly breed,   210
> The levée will show you his grace
> Makes promises trifles indeed.°

> A coach with six footmen behind,
> I count neither trifle nor sin;
> But, ye gods! how oft do we find   215
> A scandalous trifle within?

> A flask of champagne, people think it
> A trifle, or something as bad;
> But if you'll contrive how to drink it,
> You'll find it no trifle egad.   220

> A parson's a trifle at sea,
> A widow's a trifle in sorrow;
> A Peace is a trifle today—°
> Who knows what may happen tomorrow?

> A black coat, a trifle may cloak,   225
> Or to hide it, the red may endeavour;°
> But if once the army is broke,
> We shall have more trifles than ever.

> The stage is a trifle, they say;
> The reason, pray carry along: 230
> Because at every new play
> The house they with trifles so throng.

> But with people's malice to trifle,
> And to set us all on a foot,
> The author of this is a trifle,   235
> And his song is a trifle to boot.

MRS SULLEN Very well, sir, we're obliged to you. (*Offering him money*) Something for a pair of gloves.°

ARCHER I humbly beg leave to be excused.° My master, madam, pays me; nor dare I take money from any other hand without injuring his honour, and disobeying his commands.   240

   Exit [Archer]

DORINDA This is surprising. Did you ever see so pretty a well-bred fellow?

MRS SULLEN The Devil take him for wearing that livery.

DORINDA I fancy, sister, he may be some gentleman, a friend of my lord's, that his lordship has pitched upon for his courage, fidelity, and discretion, to bear him company in this dress, and who, ten to one, was his second too.   245

MRS SULLEN It is so, it must be so, and it shall be so—for I like him.

DORINDA What! better than the count?   250

MRS SULLEN The count happened to be the most agreeable man upon the place; and so I chose him to serve me in my design upon my husband. But I should like this fellow better in a design upon myself.

DORINDA But now, sister, for an interview with this lord, and this   255
gentleman; how shall we bring that about?

MRS SULLEN Patience! you country ladies give no quarter, if once you be entered.° Would you prevent their desires, and give the fellows no wishing-time? Look'ye, Dorinda, if my Lord Aimwell loves you or deserves you, he'll find a way to see you, and there   260
we must leave it. My business comes now upon the tapis°—have you prepared your brother?

DORINDA Yes, yes.

MRS SULLEN And how did he relish it?

DORINDA He said little, mumbled something to himself, promised to   265
be guided by me. But here he comes.

    Enter Sullen

SULLEN What singing was that I heard just now?

MRS SULLEN The singing in your head, my dear—you complained of it all day.

SULLEN You're impertinent.   270

MRS SULLEN I was ever so, since I became one flesh with you.

SULLEN One flesh! rather two carcasses joined unnaturally together.

MRS SULLEN Or rather a living soul coupled to a dead body.°

DORINDA So, this is fine encouragement for me.

SULLEN Yes, my wife shows you what you must do.   275

MRS SULLEN And my husband shows you what you must suffer.

SULLEN 'Sdeath, why can't you be silent?

MRS SULLEN 'Sdeath, why can't you talk?

SULLEN Do you talk to any purpose?

MRS SULLEN Do you think to any purpose?   280

SULLEN Sister, hark'ye.

    [He] whispers [to her, then speaks for his wife to hear]
I shan't be home till it be late.

    Exit [Sullen]

MRS SULLEN What did he whisper to ye?

DORINDA That he would go round the back way, come into the closet, and listen as I directed him. But let me beg you once more,   285
dear sister, to drop this project; for, as I told you before, instead of awaking him to kindness, you may provoke him to a rage; and then who knows how far his brutality may carry him?

MRS SULLEN I'm provided to receive him, I warrant you. But here
comes the count°—vanish.   290
          Exit Dorinda. Enter Count Bellair
     Don't you wonder, monsieur le count, that I was not at church this
     afternoon?

COUNT I more wonder, madam, that you go dere at all, or how you
     dare to lift those eyes to Heaven that are guilty of so much killing.

MRS SULLEN If Heaven, sir, has given to my eyes, with the power   295
     of killing, the virtue of making a cure, I hope the one may atone
     for the other.

COUNT O largely, madam, would your ladyship be as ready to apply
     the remedy as to give the wound. Consider, madam, I am doubly
     a prisoner; first to the arms of your general, then to your more   300
     conquering eyes. My first chains are easy—there a ransom may
     redeem me°—but from your fetters I never shall get free.

MRS SULLEN Alas, sir, why should you complain to me of your
     captivity, who am in chains myself? You know, sir, that I am
     bound, nay, must be tied up in that particular that might give you   305
     ease. I am like you, a prisoner of war—of war indeed. I have given
     my parole of honour. Would you break yours to gain your liberty?

COUNT Most certainly I would, were I a prisoner among the Turks;
     dis is your case; you're a slave, madam, slave to the worst of
     Turks, a husband.   310

MRS SULLEN There lies my foible, I confess; no fortifications, no
     courage, conduct, nor vigilancy can pretend to defend a place,
     where the cruelty of the governor forces the garrison to mutiny.

COUNT And where de besieger is resolved to die before de place.
     Here will I fix (*kneels*)—with tears, vows, and prayers assault your   315
     heart, and never rise till you surrender; or if I must storm: 'Love
     and St Michael!'°—and so [*rises*] I begin the attack.

MRS SULLEN Stand off! (*Aside*) Sure he hears me not°—and I could
     almost wish he—did not. The fellow makes love very prettily.
     [*Aloud*] But, sir, why should you put such a value upon my person,   320
     when you see it despised by one that knows it so much better?

COUNT He knows it not, though he possesses it; if he but knew the
     value of the jewel he is master of, he would always wear it next his
     heart, and sleep with it in his arms.

MRS SULLEN But since he throws me unregarded from him—   325

COUNT And one that knows your value well, comes by, and takes you
     up, is it not justice?
          Goes to lay hold on her. Enter Sullen with his sword drawn

SULLEN Hold, villain, hold.

MRS SULLEN (*presenting a pistol*) Do you hold.

SULLEN What! Murder your husband, to defend your bully.   330

MRS SULLEN Bully! for shame, Mr Sullen. Bullies wear long swords, the gentleman has none—he's a prisoner, you know. I was aware of your outrage, and prepared this to receive your violence, and, if occasion were, to preserve myself against the force of this other gentleman.   335

COUNT O madam, your eyes be bettre firearms than your pistol—they nevre miss.

SULLEN What! court my wife to my face!

MRS SULLEN Pray, Mr Sullen, put up—suspend your fury for a minute.   340

SULLEN To give you time to invent an excuse.

MRS SULLEN I need none.

SULLEN No, for I heard every syllable of your discourse.

COUNT Ay! and begar, I tink de dialogue was vera pretty.

MRS SULLEN Then I suppose, sir, you heard something of your own   345 barbarity.

SULLEN Barbarity! Oons, what does the woman call barbarity? Do I ever meddle with you?

MRS SULLEN No.

SULLEN As for you, sir, I shall take another time.   350

COUNT Ah, begar, and so must I.

SULLEN Look'ee, madam, don't think that my anger proceeds from any concern I have for your honour, but for my own, and if you can contrive any way of being a whore without making me a cuckold, do it and welcome.   355

MRS SULLEN Sir, I thank you kindly—you would allow me the sin but rob me of the pleasure. No, no, I'm resolved never to venture upon the crime without the satisfaction of seeing you punished for't.

SULLEN Then will you grant me this, my dear? Let anybody else do you the favour but that Frenchman, for I mortally hate his whole   360 generation.

Exit [Sullen]

COUNT Ah, sir, that be ungrateful—for, begar, I love some of yours, madam—(*approaching her*)

MRS SULLEN No, sir.

COUNT No, sir! Garzoon, madam, I am not your husband.   365

MRS SULLEN 'Tis time to undeceive you, sir. I believed your addresses to me were no more than an amusement, and I hope you

will think the same of my complaisance, and to convince you that
you ought, you must know, that I brought you hither only to make
you instrumental in setting me right with my husband, for he was   370
planted to listen by my appointment.

COUNT By your appointment?

MRS SULLEN Certainly.

COUNT And so, madam, while I was telling twenty stories to part you
from your husband, begar, I was bringing you together all the   375
while.

MRS SULLEN I ask your pardon, sir, but I hope this will give you a
taste of the virtue of the English ladies.

COUNT Begar, madam, your virtue be vera great, but garzoon your
honeste be vera little.   380
          Enter Dorinda

MRS SULLEN Nay, now you're angry, sir.

COUNT Angry! [*Singing*] '*Fair Dorinda . . .*'
          Sings 'Dorinda', the opera tune, and addresses to Dorinda
Madam, when your ladyship want a fool, send for me, fair
Dorinda. [*Sings*] '*Revenge*' &c°
          Exit [*Count Bellair*]

MRS SULLEN There goes the true humour of his nation—resentment   385
with good manners, and the height of anger in a song. Well sister,
you must be judge, for you have heard the trial.

DORINDA And I bring in my brother guilty.

MRS SULLEN But I must bear the punishment—'tis hard, sister.

DORINDA I own it—but you must have patience.   390

MRS SULLEN Patience! the cant of custom. Providence sends no evil
without a remedy. Should I lie groaning under a yoke I can shake
off, I were accessary to my ruin, and my patience were no better
than self-murder.°

DORINDA But how can you shake off the yoke? Your divisions don't   395
come within the reach of the law for a divorce.

MRS SULLEN Law! what law can search into the remote abyss of
nature, what evidence can prove the unaccountable disaffections of
wedlock? Can a jury sum up the endless aversions that are rooted
in our souls, or can a Bench give judgment upon antipathies?°   400

DORINDA They never pretended, sister—they never meddle but in
case of uncleanness.°

MRS SULLEN Uncleanness! O sister, casual violation is a transient
injury, and may possibly be repaired, but can radical hatreds be
ever reconciled? No, no, sister, Nature is the first lawgiver, and   405

when she has set tempers opposite, not all the golden links of wedlock, nor iron manacles of law can keep 'em fast.°

    Wedlock we own ordained by Heaven's decree,
    But such as Heaven ordained it first to be,
    Concurring tempers in the man and wife   410
    As mutual helps to draw the load of life.
    View all the works of Providence above—
    The stars with harmony and concord move;
    View all the works of Providence below—
    The fire, the water, earth, and air we know   415
    All in one plant agree to make it grow.
    Must man the chiefest work of art divine,
    Be doomed in endless discord to repine?
    No, we should injure Heaven by that surmise—
    Omnipotence is just, were man but wise.   420
    [*Exeunt*]

4.[1]

Scene [in the gallery of Lady Bountiful's house] continues

Enter Mrs Sullen

MRS SULLEN Were I born an humble Turk, where women have no soul nor property, there I must sit contented.° But in England, a country whose women are its glory, must women be abused?— where women rule, must women be enslaved,° nay, cheated into slavery, mocked by a promise of comfortable society into a wilderness of solitude? I dare not keep the thought about me. O, here comes something to divert me.

    Enter a countrywoman

WOMAN I come, an't please your ladyships—you're my Lady Bountiful, an't ye?

MRS SULLEN Well, good woman, go on.

WOMAN I come seventeen long mail to have a cure for my husband's sore leg.

MRS SULLEN Your husband! what woman, cure your husband!

WOMAN Ay, poor man, for his sore leg won't let him stir from home.

MRS SULLEN There, I confess, you have given me a reason. Well good woman, I'll tell you what you must do—you must lay your husband's leg upon a table, and with a chopping-knife, you must lay it open as broad as you can; then you must take out the bone, and beat the flesh soundly with a rolling-pin, then take salt, pepper, cloves, mace and ginger, some sweet herbs, and season it very well, then roll it up like brawn, and put it into the oven for two hours.

WOMAN Heavens reward your ladyship. I have two little babies too that are piteous bad with the graips,° an't please ye.

MRS SULLEN Put a little pepper and salt in their bellies, good woman.

    Enter Lady Bountiful

I beg your ladyship's pardon for taking your business out of your hands—I have been a-tampering here a little with one of your patients.

LADY BOUNTIFUL Come, good woman, don't mind this mad creature—I am the person that you want, I suppose. What would you have, woman?

MRS SULLEN She wants something for her husband's sore leg.

LADY BOUNTIFUL What's the matter with his leg, Goody?

WOMAN It come first as one might say with a sort of dizziness in his   35
foot, then he had a kind of a laziness in his joints, and then his leg
broke out, and then it swelled, and then it closed again, and then
it broke out again, and then it festered, and then it grew better,
and then it grew worse again.

MRS SULLEN Ha, ha, ha.   40

LADY BOUNTIFUL How can you be merry with the misfortunes of
other people?

MRS SULLEN Because my own make me sad, madam.

LADY BOUNTIFUL The worst reason in the world, daughter—your
own misfortunes should teach you to pity others.   45

MRS SULLEN But the woman's misfortunes and mine are nothing
alike—her husband is sick, and mine, alas, is in health.

LADY BOUNTIFUL What! would you wish your husband sick?

MRS SULLEN Not of a sore leg, of all things.

LADY BOUNTIFUL Well, good woman, go to the pantry, get your   50
bellyful of victuals, then I'll give you a receipt of diet-drink for
your husband. But d'ye hear, Goody, you must not let your
husband move too much.

WOMAN No, no, madam, the poor man's inclinable enough to lie
still.   55

Exit [countrywoman]

LADY BOUNTIFUL Well, daughter Sullen, though you laugh, I have
done miracles about the country here with my receipts.

MRS SULLEN Miracles, indeed, if they have cured anybody, but, I
believe, madam, the patient's faith goes further toward the miracle
than your prescription.   60

LADY BOUNTIFUL Fancy helps in some cases, but there's your
husband who has as little fancy as anybody—I brought him from
death's door.

MRS SULLEN I suppose, madam, you made him drink plentifully of
ass's milk.°   65

Enter Dorinda, runs to Mrs Sullen

DORINDA News, dear sister, news, news.

Enter Archer running

ARCHER Where, where is my Lady Bountiful? Pray which is the old
lady of you three?

LADY BOUNTIFUL I am.

ARCHER O, madam, the fame of your ladyship's charity, goodness,   70
benevolence, skill and ability have drawn me hither to implore

your ladyship's help in behalf of my unfortunate master, who is
this moment breathing his last.

LADY BOUNTIFUL Your master! Where is he?

ARCHER At your gate, madam, drawn by the appearance of your   75
handsome house to view it nearer, and walking up the avenue
within five paces of the courtyard, he was taken ill of a sudden with
a sort of I know not what, but down he fell, and there he lies.

LADY BOUNTIFUL [*calling off-stage*] Here, Scrub, Gypsy, all run, get
my easy chair downstairs, put the gentleman in it, and bring him   80
in quickly, quickly.

ARCHER Heaven will reward your ladyship for this charitable act.

LADY BOUNTIFUL Is your master used to these fits?

ARCHER O yes, madam, frequently—I have known him have five or
six of a night.   85

LADY BOUNTIFUL What's his name?

ARCHER Lord, madam, he's a-dying—a minute's care or neglect may
save or destroy his life.

LADY BOUNTIFUL Ah, poor gentleman! Come friend, show me the
way—I'll see him brought in myself.   90

> *Exit [Lady Bountiful] with Archer*

DORINDA O sister my heart flutters about strangely—I can hardly
forbear running to his assistance.

MRS SULLEN And I'll lay my life, he deserves your assistance more than
he wants it. Did not I tell you that my lord would find a way to come
at you? Love's his distemper, and you must be the physician; put on   95
all your charms, summon all your fire into your eyes, plant the whole
artillery of your looks against his breast, and down with him.

DORINDA O sister, I'm but a young gunner—I shall be afraid to
shoot, for fear the piece should recoil and hurt myself.

MRS SULLEN Never fear—you shall see me shoot before you, if you   100
will.

DORINDA No, no, dear sister, you have missed your mark so
unfortunately, that I shan't care for being instructed by you.

> *Enter Aimwell, in a chair carried by Archer and Scrub, [with]*
> *Lady Bountiful, [and] Gypsy, Aimwell counterfeiting a swoon*

LADY BOUNTIFUL Here, here, let's see the hartshorn drops. Gypsy,
a glass of fair water—his fit's very strong. Bless me, how his hands 105
are clinched.

ARCHER For shame, ladies, what d'ye do—why don't you help us?
(*To Dorinda*) Pray, madam, take his hand and open it if you can,
whilst I hold his head.

Dorinda takes his hand

DORINDA Poor gentleman—O—he has got my hand within his, and   110
squeezes it unmercifully.

LADY BOUNTIFUL 'Tis the violence of his convulsion, child.

ARCHER O, madam, he's perfectly possessed° in these cases—he'll
bite if you don't have a care.

DORINDA O, my hand, my hand.   115

LADY BOUNTIFUL What's the matter with the foolish girl? I have
got this hand open, you see, with a great deal of ease.

ARCHER Ay, but, madam, your daughter's hand is somewhat warmer
than your ladyship's, and the heat of it draws the force of the
spirits that way.   120

MRS SULLEN [*to Archer*] I find, friend, you're very learned in these
sorts of fits.

ARCHER 'Tis no wonder, madam, for I'm often troubled with them
myself—I find myself extremely ill at this minute. (*Looking hard
at Mrs Sullen*)   125

MRS SULLEN (*aside*) I fancy I could find a way to cure you.

LADY BOUNTIFUL His fit holds him very long.

ARCHER Longer than usual, madam. Pray, young lady, open his
breast, and give him air.

LADY BOUNTIFUL Where did his illness take him first, pray?   130

ARCHER Today at church, madam.

LADY BOUNTIFUL In what manner was he taken?

ARCHER Very strangely, my lady. He was of a sudden touched with
something in his eyes, which at the first he only felt, but could not
tell whether 'twas pain or pleasure.   135

LADY BOUNTIFUL Wind, nothing but wind.

ARCHER By soft degrees it grew and mounted to his brain—there his
fancy caught it; there formed it so beautiful, and dressed it up in
such gay pleasing colours, that his transported appetite seized the
fair idea, and straight conveyed it to his heart. That hospitable seat   140
of life sent all its sanguine spirits forth to meet, and opened all its
sluicy gates to take the stranger in.°

LADY BOUNTIFUL Your master should never go without a bottle to
smell to. O! He recovers—the lavender-water—some feathers to
burn under his nose—Hungary-water° to rub his temples. O, he   145
comes to himself. Hem a little, sir, hem—Gypsy, bring the
cordial-water.

Aimwell seems to awake in amaze

DORINDA How d'ye, sir?

AIMWELL (*rising*) Where am I?
   Sure I have passed the gulf of silent death,   150
   And now I land on the Elysian shore—
   Behold the goddess of those happy plains,
   Fair Prosperpine: let me adore thy bright divinity.°
     Kneels to Dorinda and kisses her hand

MRS SULLEN [*aside*] So, so, so, I knew where the fit would end.

AIMWELL Eurydice perhaps—   155
      How could thy Orpheus keep his word,
      And not look back upon thee?
      No treasure but thyself could sure have bribed him
      To look one minute off thee.

LADY BOUNTIFUL Delirious, poor gentleman.   160

ARCHER Very delirious, madam, very delirious.

AIMWELL Martin's voice, I think.

ARCHER Yes, my lord—how does your lordship?

LADY BOUNTIFUL 'Lord!'—did you mind that, girls?

AIMWELL Where am I?   165

ARCHER In very good hands, sir. You were taken just now with one
of your old fits under the trees just by this good lady's house; her
ladyship had you taken in, and has miraculously brought you to
yourself, as you see.

AIMWELL I am so confounded with shame, madam, that I can now   170
only beg pardon—and refer my acknowledgements for your ladyship's care, till an opportunity offers of making some amends. I
dare be no longer troublesome. Martin, give two guineas to the
servants. (*Going*)

DORINDA Sir, you may catch cold by going so soon into the air—you   175
don't look, sir, as if you were perfectly recovered.
     Here Archer talks to Lady Bountiful in dumb show

AIMWELL That I shall never be, madam—my present illness is so
rooted, that I must expect to carry it to my grave.

MRS SULLEN Don't despair, sir—I have known several in your
distemper shake it off, with a fortnight's physic.   180

LADY BOUNTIFUL Come, sir, your servant has been telling me that
you're apt to relapse if you go into the air. Your good manners
shan't get the better of ours. You shall sit down again, sir. Come,
sir, we don't mind: ceremonies in the country. Here, sir—'My
service t'ye'°—you shall taste my water; 'tis a cordial I can assure   185
you, and of my own making—drink it off, sir.
     Aimwell drinks

And how d'ye find yourself now, sir?

AIMWELL Somewhat better—though very faint still.

LADY BOUNTIFUL Ay, ay, people are always faint after these fits. Come girls, you shall show the gentleman the house—'tis but an   190
old family building, sir, but you had better walk about and cool by degrees than venture immediately into the air. You'll find some tolerable pictures—Dorinda, show the gentleman the way. I must go to the poor woman below.

   Exit [Lady Bountiful]

DORINDA This way, sir.   195

AIMWELL Ladies, shall I beg leave for my servant to wait on you, for he understands pictures very well.

MRS SULLEN Sir, we understand originals,° as well as he does pictures, so he may come along.

   Exeunt [all but Scrub]. Aimwell leads Dorinda. Enter Foigard

FOIGARD Save you, Master Scrub.   200

SCRUB Sir, I won't be saved your way—I hate a priest, I abhor the French, and I defy the Devil. Sir, I'm a bold Briton, and will spill the last drop of my blood to keep out popery and slavery.

FOIGARD Master Scrub, you would put me down in politics, and so I would be speaking with Mrs Shypsy.   205

SCRUB Good Mr Priest, you can't speak with her—she's sick, sir—she's gone abroad, sir—she's—dead two months ago, sir.

   Enter Gypsy

GYPSY How now, impudence; how dare you talk so saucily to the doctor? Pray, sir, don't take it ill; for the common people of England are not so civil to strangers, as—   210

SCRUB You lie, you lie—'tis the common people that are civilest to strangers.

GYPSY Sirrah, I have a good mind to—get you out, I say.

SCRUB I won't.

GYPSY You won't, sauce-box! Pray, Doctor, what is the captain's   215
name that came to your inn last night?

SCRUB The captain! Ah, the Devil—there she hampers me again. The captain has me on one side, and the priest on t'other. So between the gown and the sword, I have a fine time on't. But *cedunt arma togae.*° (*Going*)   220

GYPSY What, sirrah, won't you march?

SCRUB No, my dear, I won't march—but I'll walk. [*Aside*] And I'll make bold to listen a little too.

   Goes behind the side-scene° and listens

GYPSY Indeed, Doctor, the count has been barbarously treated, that's
the truth on't.   225

FOIGARD Ah, Mrs Gypsy, upon my shoul, now, gra, his complain-
ings would mollify the marrow in your bones, and move the bowels
of your commiseration; he veeps, and he dances, and he fistles, and
he swears, and he laughs, and he stamps, and he sings. In
conclusion, joy, he's afflicted, *à la française*,° and a stranger would   230
not know whider to cry, or to laugh with him.

GYPSY What would you have me do, Doctor?

FOIGARD Noting, joy, but only hide the count in Mrs Sullen's closet
when it is dark.

GYPSY Nothing! Is that nothing? It would be both a sin and a shame,   235
Doctor.

FOIGARD Here is twenty *louis d'ors*,° joy, for your shame; and I will
give you an absolution for the shin.°

GYPSY But won't that money look like a bribe?

FOIGARD Dat is according as you shall tauk it. If you receive the   240
money beforehand, 'twill be *logicé* a bribe: but if you stay till
afterwards, 'twill be only a gratification.

GYPSY Well, Doctor, I'll take it *logicé*. But what must I do with my
conscience, sir?

FOIGARD Leave dat wid me, joy; I am your priest, gra; and your   245
conscience is under my hands.

GYPSY But should I put the count into the closet?

FOIGARD Vel, is dere any shin for a man's being in a closhet? One
may go to prayers in a closhet.

GYPSY But if the lady should come into her chamber, and go to bed?   250

FOIGARD Vel, and is dere any shin in going to bed, joy?

GYPSY Ay, but if the parties should meet, Doctor?

FOIGARD Vel den—the parties must be responsible. Do you be
after putting the count in the closet; and leave the shins wid
themselves. I will come with the count to instruct you in your   255
chamber.

GYPSY Well, Doctor, your religion is so pure—methinks I'm so
easy after an absolution, and can sin afresh with so much
security, that I'm resolved to die a martyr to't. Here's the key of
the garden door—come in the back way when 'tis late; I'll be   260
ready to receive you, but don't so much as whisper, only take
hold of my hand—I'll lead you, and do you lead the count, and
follow me.
                    Exeunt [Gypsy and Foigard. Scrub comes forward]

SCRUB   What witchcraft now have these two imps of the Devil been
a-hatching here? There's twenty *louis d'ors*, I heard that, and saw   265
the purse. But I must give room to my betters.
>   [*Exit Scrub.*] *Enter Aimwell leading Dorinda, and making love
>   in dumb show, Mrs Sullen and Archer*

MRS SULLEN (*to Archer*) Pray, sir, how d'ye like that piece?
>   [*She points to a painting*]

ARCHER   O, 'tis Leda. You find, madam, how Jupiter comes disguised
to make love.°

MRS SULLEN [*looking at a second painting*] But what think you there   270
of Alexander's battles?°

ARCHER   We want only a Le Brun,° madam, to draw greater battles,
and a greater general° of our own. The Danube,° madam, would
make a greater figure in a picture than the Granicus;° and we have
our Ramillies° to match their Arbela.°   275

MRS SULLEN [*looking at a third painting*] Pray, sir, what head is that
in the corner there?

ARCHER   O, madam, 'tis poor Ovid in his exile.°

MRS SULLEN   What was he banished for?

ARCHER   (*bowing*) His ambitious love, madam. His misfortune   280
touches me.

MRS SULLEN   Was he successful in his amours?

ARCHER   There he has left us in the dark. He was too much a
gentleman to tell.

MRS SULLEN   If he were secret,° I pity him.   285

ARCHER   And if he were successful, I envy him.

MRS SULLEN [*looking at a fourth painting*] How d'ye like that Venus
over the chimney?

ARCHER   Venus! I protest, madam, I took it for your picture; but now
I look again, 'tis not handsome enough.   290

MRS SULLEN   Oh, what a charm is flattery! If you would see my
picture, there it is, over that cabinet. How d'ye like it?

ARCHER   I must admire anything, madam, that has the least resem-
blance of you. But, methinks, madam—
>   *He looks at the picture and Mrs Sullen three or four times, by
>   turns*

Pray, madam, who drew it?   295

MRS SULLEN   A famous hand, sir.
>   *Here Aimwell and Dorinda go off*

ARCHER   A famous hand, madam? Your eyes, indeed, are featured
there; but where's the sparkling moisture, shining fluid, in which

they swim? The picture indeed has your dimples; but where's the
swarm of killing cupids° that should ambush there? The lips too   300
are figured out; but where's the carnation dew, the pouting
ripeness that tempts the taste in the original?

MRS SULLEN [aside] Had it been my lot to have matched with such
a man!

ARCHER Your breasts too—presumptuous man! What! paint Heaven!   305
Apropos, madam, in the very next picture is Salmoneus, that was
struck dead with lightning, for offering to imitate Jove's thunder;°
I hope you served the painter so, madam?

MRS SULLEN Had my eyes the power of thunder, they should
employ their lightning better.   310

ARCHER [looking into a room off the gallery] There's the finest bed in
that room, madam—I suppose 'tis your ladyship's bedchamber.

MRS SULLEN And what then, sir?

ARCHER I think the quilt is the richest that ever I saw. I can't at this
distance, madam, distinguish the figures of the embroidery. Will   315
you give me leave, madam—?

MRS SULLEN [aside] The Devil take his impudence. Sure if I gave
him an opportunity, he durst not offer it. I have a great mind to
try. (Going) 'Sdeath, what am I doing? (Returns) And alone too.
Sister, sister!   320

    [Mrs Sullen] runs out

ARCHER I'll follow her close—
    For where a Frenchman durst attempt to storm,
    A Briton sure may well the work perform. (Going)
        Enter Scrub

SCRUB Martin, brother Martin.

ARCHER O, brother Scrub, I beg your pardon, I was not a-going;   325
here's a guinea, my master ordered you.

    [Gives it to him]

SCRUB A guinea, hee, hee, hee, a guinea! Eh—[looks at it] by this
light it is a guinea; but I suppose you expect one and twenty
shillings in change.

ARCHER Not at all; I have another for Gypsy.   330

SCRUB A guinea for her! Faggot and fire for the witch. Sir, give me
that guinea, and I'll discover a plot.

ARCHER A plot!

SCRUB Ay, sir, a plot, and a horrid plot. First, it must be a plot
because there's a woman in't; secondly, it must be a plot because   335
there's a priest in't; thirdly, it must be a plot because there's

French gold in't;° and fourthly, it must be a plot, because I don't know what to make on't.

ARCHER Nor anybody else, I'm afraid, brother Scrub.

SCRUB Truly I'm afraid so too; for where there's a priest and a   340
woman, there's always a mystery and a riddle. This I know, that here has been the doctor with a temptation in one hand, and an absolution in the other; and Gypsy has sold herself to the Devil; I saw the price paid down, my eyes shall take their oath on't.

ARCHER And is all this bustle about Gypsy?   345

SCRUB That's not all. I could hear but a word here and there; but I remember they mentioned a count, a closet, a back door, and a key.

ARCHER The count! Did you hear nothing of Mrs Sullen?

SCRUB I did hear some word that sounded that way; but whether it was 'Sullen' or 'Dorinda', I could not distinguish.   350

ARCHER You have told this matter to nobody, brother?

SCRUB Told! No, sir, I thank you for that; I'm resolved never to speak one word pro nor con, till we have a peace.

ARCHER You're i'th' right, brother Scrub; here's a treaty afoot between the count and the lady. The priest and the chambermaid   355
are the plenipotentiaries. It shall go hard but I find a way to be included in the treaty. Where's the doctor now?

SCRUB He and Gypsy are this moment devouring my lady's marmalade in the closet.

AIMWELL (*from without*) Martin, Martin.   360

ARCHER I come, sir, I come.

SCRUB But you forget the other guinea, brother Martin.

ARCHER Here, I give it with all my heart.

SCRUB And I take it with all my soul.

[*Exit Archer*]

Ecod, I'll spoil your plotting, Mrs Gypsy; and if you should set   365
the captain upon me, these two guineas will buy me off.

Exit [*Scrub by a different way*]. *Enter Mrs Sullen and Dorinda, meeting*

MRS SULLEN Well, sister.

DORINDA And well, sister.

MRS SULLEN What's become of my lord?

DORINDA What's become of his servant?   370

MRS SULLEN Servant! he's a prettier fellow, and a finer gentleman by fifty degrees than his master.

DORINDA O' my conscience, I fancy you could beg that fellow at the gallows-foot.°

MRS SULLEN O' my conscience, I could, provided I could put a   375
friend of yours in his room.°

DORINDA You desired me, sister, to leave you, when you transgressed the bounds of honour.

MRS SULLEN Thou dear censorious country girl—what dost mean?
You can't think of the man without the bedfellow, I find.   380

DORINDA I don't find anything unnatural in that thought—while the
mind is conversant with flesh and blood, it must conform to the
humours of the company.

MRS SULLEN How a little love and good company improves a
woman; why, child, you begin to live—you never spoke before.   385

DORINDA Because I was never spoke to. My lord has told me that I
have more wit and beauty than any of my sex; and truly I begin
to think the man is sincere.

MRS SULLEN You're in the right, Dorinda—pride is the life of a
woman, and flattery is our daily bread; and she's a fool that won't   390
believe a man there, as much as she that believes him in anything
else. But I'll lay you a guinea, that I had finer things said to me
than you had.

DORINDA Done. What did your fellow say t'ye?

MRS SULLEN My fellow took the picture of Venus for mine.   395

DORINDA But my lover took me for Venus herself.

MRS SULLEN Common cant! Had my spark called me a Venus
directly, I should have believed him a footman in good earnest.

DORINDA But my lover was upon his knees to me.

MRS SULLEN And mine was upon his tiptoes to me.   400

DORINDA Mine vowed to die for me.

MRS SULLEN Mine swore to die with me.°

DORINDA Mine spoke the softest moving things.

MRS SULLEN Mine had his moving things too.

DORINDA Mine kissed my hand ten thousand times.   405

MRS SULLEN Mine has all that pleasure to come.

DORINDA Mine offered marriage.

MRS SULLEN O lard! D'ye call that a moving thing?

DORINDA The sharpest arrow in his quiver, my dear sister—why, my
ten thousand pounds may lie brooding here this seven years, and   410
hatch nothing at last but some ill-natured clown like yours.
Whereas, if I marry my Lord Aimwell, there will be title, place
and precedence, the Park, the play and the Drawing Room,°
splendour, equipage, noise and flambeaux—'Hey, my Lady Aimwell's servants there!', 'Lights, lights to the stairs!', 'My Lady   415

Aimwell's coach put forward!', 'Stand by, make room for her ladyship!'. Are not these things moving? What! melancholy of a sudden?

MRS SULLEN Happy, happy sister! Your angel has been watchful for your happiness, whilst mine has slept regardless of his charge. 420 Long smiling years of circling joys for you, but not one hour for me.

Weeps

DORINDA Come, my dear, we'll talk of something else.

MRS SULLEN O Dorinda, I own myself a woman, full of my sex, a gentle, generous soul—easy and yielding to soft desires; a spacious 425 heart, where Love and all his train might lodge. And must the fair apartment of my breast be made a stable for a brute to lie in?

DORINDA Meaning your husband, I suppose.

MRS SULLEN Husband! No. Even husband is too soft a name for him. But, come, I expect my brother here tonight or tomorrow; he 430 was abroad when my father married me; perhaps he'll find a way to make me easy.

DORINDA Will you promise not to make yourself easy in the meantime with my lord's friend?

MRS SULLEN You mistake me, sister. It happens with us, as among 435 the men, the greatest talkers are the greatest cowards; and there's a reason for it; those spirits evaporate in prattle, which might do more mischief if they took another course. Though to confess the truth, I do love that fellow. And if I met him dressed as he should be, and I undressed as I should be—look'ye, sister, I have no 440 supernatural gifts; I can't swear I could resist the temptation, though I can safely promise to avoid it; and that's as much as the best of us can do.

Exeunt

[4.2]

[Scene, the inn]

Enter Aimwell and Archer laughing

ARCHER And the awkward kindness of the good motherly old gentlewoman—

AIMWELL And the coming easiness of the young one—'sdeath, 'tis pity to deceive her.

ARCHER Nay, if you adhere to those principles, stop where you are. 5

AIMWELL I can't stop; for I love her to distraction.

ARCHER 'Sdeath, if you love her a hair's breadth beyond discretion, you must go no further.

AIMWELL Well, well, anything to deliver us from sauntering away our idle evenings at White's, Tom's,° or Will's, and be stinted to 10
bear looking at our old acquaintance, the cards, because our impotent pockets can't afford us a guinea for the mercenary drabs.

ARCHER Or be obliged to some purse-proud coxcomb for a scandalous bottle, where we must not pretend to our share of the discourse, because we can't pay our club o'th' reckoning.° Damn 15
it, I had rather sponge upon Morris,° and sup upon a dish of bohea scored behind the door.

AIMWELL And there expose our want of sense by talking criticisms, as we should our want of money by railing at the government.

ARCHER Or be obliged to sneak into the sidebox, and between both 20
houses steal two acts of a play, and because we han't money to see the other three,° we come away discontented, and damn the whole five.

AIMWELL And ten thousand such rascally tricks, had we outlived our fortunes among our acquaintance. But now— 25

ARCHER Ay, now is the time to prevent all this. Strike while the iron is hot. This priest is the luckiest part of our adventure; he shall marry you,° and pimp for me.

AIMWELL But I should not like a woman that can be so fond of a Frenchman. 30

ARCHER Alas, sir, necessity has no law; the lady may be in distress; perhaps she has a confounded husband, and her revenge may carry her further than her love. Egad, I have so good an opinion of her, and of myself, that I begin to fancy strange things; and we must say this for the honour of our women, and indeed of ourselves, that 35
they do stick to their men, as they do to their *Magna Carta*.° If the plot lies as I suspect—I must put on the gentleman.°

    [*Looks off-stage*]

But here comes the doctor. I shall be ready.

    Exit [*Archer*]. *Enter Foigard*

FOIGARD Sauve you, noble Friend.

AIMWELL O sir, your servant; pray Doctor, may I crave your name? 40

FOIGARD Fat naam is upon me? My naam is Foigard, joy.

AIMWELL Foigard—a very good name for a clergyman. Pray, Doctor Foigard, were you ever in Ireland?

FOIGARD   Ireland! No joy. Fat sort of plaace is dat saam Ireland? Dey
say de people are catcht dere° when dey are young.   45

AIMWELL   And some of 'em when they're old—as for example.
       Takes Foigard by the shoulder
Sir, I arrest you as a traitor against the government; you're a
subject of England, and this morning showed me a commission, by
which you served as chaplain in the French army. This is death
by our law, and your reverence must hang for't.°   50

FOIGARD   Upon my shoul, noble friend, dis is strange news you tell
me—Fader Foigard a subject of England, de son of a burgomaster
of Brussels, a subject of England! Ubooboo—

AIMWELL   The son of a bogtrotter in Ireland; sir, your tongue will
condemn you before any Bench in the kingdom.   55

FOIGARD   And is my tongue all your evidensh, joy?

AIMWELL   That's enough.

FOIGARD   No, no, joy, for I vill never spake English no more.

AIMWELL   Sir, I have other evidence—[*calls*] here, Martin, you know
this fellow.   60
       Enter Archer

ARCHER   (*in a brogue*)°   Saave you, my dear cussen, how does your
health?

FOIGARD   (*aside*)   Ah! upon my shoul dere is my countryman, and his
brogue will hang mine. [*Aloud*] Mynheer, Ick wet neat watt hey
zacht—Ick universton ewe neat, sacramant.°   65

AIMWELL   Altering your language won't do, sir—this fellow knows
your person, and will swear to your face.

FOIGARD   Faace! fay, is dear a brogue upon my faash, too?

ARCHER   Upon my soulvation dere ish, joy; but cussen MacShane, vil
you not put a remembrance upon me?   70

FOIGARD   (*aside*)   MacShane! By St Paatrick, dat is naame,° shure
enough.

AIMWELL   [*aside to Archer*]   I fancy Archer, you have it.

FOIGARD   The Devil hang you, joy—by fat acquaintance are you my
cussen?   75

ARCHER   O, de Devil hang yourself, joy—you know we were
little boys togeder upon de school, and your foster moder's son
was married upon my nurse's chister, joy, and so we are Irish
cussens.°

FOIGARD   De Devil taake the relation! Vel, joy, and fat school was it?   80

ARCHER   I tinks it vas—aay—'twas Tipperary.

FOIGARD   No, no, joy, it vas Kilkenny.°

AIMWELL That's enough for us—self-confession. Come, sir, we must deliver you into the hands of the next magistrate.

ARCHER He sends you to gaol, you're tried next assizes, and away you go swing into Purgatory.° 85

FOIGARD And is it so wid you, cussen?

ARCHER It vill be sho wid you, cussen, if you don't immediately confess the secret between you and Mrs Gypsy. Look'ee, sir, the gallows or the secret, take your choice. 90

FOIGARD The gallows! upon my shoul I hate that saam gallow, for it is a diseash dat is fatal to our family. Vel den, dere is nothing, shentlemens, but Mrs Shullen would spaak wid the count in her chamber at midnight, and dere is no haarm joy, for I am to conduct the count to the plash, myshelf. 95

ARCHER As I guessed. Have you communicated the matter to the count?

FOIGARD I have not sheen him since.

ARCHER Right again. Why then, Doctor—you shall conduct me to the lady instead of the count.

FOIGARD Fat, my cussen to the lady! Upon my shoul, gra, dat is too much upon the brogue. 100

ARCHER Come, come, Doctor, consider we have got a rope about your neck, and if you offer to squeak, we'll stop your windpipe, most certainly—we shall have another job for you in a day or two, I hope.

AIMWELL Here's company coming this way—let's into my chamber, and there concert our affair further. 105

ARCHER Come, my dear cussen, come along.
Exeunt [Aimwell, Archer and Foigard]. Enter Boniface, Hounslow and Bagshot at one door, Gibbet at the opposite

GIBBET Well, gentlemen, 'tis a fine night for our enterprise.

HOUNSLOW Dark as Hell.

BAGSHOT And blows like the Devil; our landlord here has showed us the window where we must break in, and tells us the plate stands in the wainscot cupboard in the parlour. 110

BONIFACE Ay, ay, Mr Bagshot, as the saying is, knives and forks, and cups, and cans, and tumblers, and tankards. There's one tankard, as the saying is, that's near upon as big as me—it was a present to the squire from his godmother, and smells of nutmeg and toast like an East India ship.° 115

HOUNSLOW Then you say we must divide at the stairhead?

BONIFACE Yes, Mr Hounslow, as the saying is—at one end of that gallery lies my Lady Bountiful and her daughter, and at the other Mrs Sullen. As for the squire— 120

GIBBET He's safe enough—I have fairly entered° him, and he's more
than half seas over° already. But such a parcel of scoundrels are
got about him now, that egad I was ashamed to be seen in their
company.   125

BONIFACE 'Tis now twelve, as the saying is—gentlemen, you must
set out at one.

GIBBET Hounslow, do you and Bagshot see our arms fixed, and I'll
come to you presently.

HOUNSLOW and BAGSHOT We will.   130
      Exeunt [Hounslow and Bagshot]

GIBBET Well, my dear Bonny, you assure me that Scrub is a coward.

BONIFACE A chicken, as the saying is—you'll have no creature to
deal with but the ladies.

GIBBET And I can assure you, friend, there's a great deal of address
and good manners in robbing a lady—I am the most a gentleman   135
that way that ever travelled the road. But, my dear Bonny, this
prize will be a galleon, a Vigo business°—I warrant you we shall
bring off three or four thousand pound.

BONIFACE In plate, jewels and money, as the saying is, you may.

GIBBET Why then, Tyburn,° I defy thee—I'll get up to Town, sell   140
off my horse and arms, buy myself some pretty employment in the
Household,° and be as snug, and as honest as any courtier of 'em
all.

BONIFACE And what think you then of my daughter Cherry for a
wife?   145

GIBBET Look'ee, my dear Bonny—Cherry 'is the goddess I adore',°
as the song goes; but it is a maxim that man and wife should never
have it in their power to hang one another, for if they should, the
Lord have mercy on 'em both.
      Exeunt

5.[1]

Scene continues

Knocking without. Enter Boniface

BONIFACE Coming, coming. A coach and six foaming horses at this
time o'night! Some great man, as the saying is, for he scorns to
travel with other people.

Enter Sir Charles Freeman

SIR CHARLES What, fellow! a public house, and a-bed when other
people sleep.   5

BONIFACE Sir, I an't a-bed, as the saying is.

SIR CHARLES Is Mr Sullen's family a-bed, think'e?

BONIFACE All but the squire himself, sir, as the saying is—he's in
the house.

SIR CHARLES What company has he?   10

BONIFACE Why, sir, there's the constable, Mr Guage the exciseman,
the hunch-backed barber, and two or three other gentlemen.

SIR CHARLES I find my sister's letters gave me the true picture of
her spouse.

Enter Sullen drunk

BONIFACE Sir, here's the squire.   15

SULLEN The puppies left me asleep. [*Seeing Sir Charles*]—Sir.

SIR CHARLES Well, sir.

SULLEN Sir, I'm an unfortunate man—I have three thousand pound
a year, and I can't get a man to drink a cup of ale with me.

SIR CHARLES That's very hard.   20

SULLEN Ay, sir—and unless you have pity upon me, and smoke one
pipe with me, I must e'en go home to my wife, and I had rather
go to the° Devil by half.

SIR CHARLES But, I presume, sir, you won't see your wife tonight—
she'll be gone to bed. You don't use to lie with your wife in that   25
pickle!

SULLEN What! not lie with my wife! Why, sir, do you take me for
an atheist or a rake?

SIR CHARLES If you hate her, sir, I think you had better lie from her.

SULLEN I think so too, friend—but I'm a justice of peace, and must   30
do nothing against the law.

SIR CHARLES Law! as I take it, Mr Justice, nobody observes law for
law's sake, only for the good of those for whom it was made.

303

SULLEN But if the law orders me to send you to gaol, you must lie there, my friend.   35

SIR CHARLES Not unless I commit a crime to deserve it.

SULLEN A crime! Oons, an't I married?

SIR CHARLES Nay, sir, if you call marriage a crime, you must disown it for a law.

SULLEN Eh! I must be acquainted with you, sir. But, sir, I should be very glad to know the truth of this matter.   40

SIR CHARLES Truth, sir, is a profound sea, and few there be that dare wade deep enough to find out the bottom on't. Besides, sir, I'm afraid the line of your understanding mayn't be long enough.

SULLEN Look'ee, sir, I have nothing to say to your sea of truth, but if a good parcel of land can entitle a man to a little truth, I have as much as any he in the country.   45

BONIFACE I never heard your worship, as the saying is, talk so much before.

SULLEN Because I never met with a man that I liked before.   50

BONIFACE [to Sir Charles] Pray, sir, as the saying is, let me ask you one question—are not man and wife one flesh?

SIR CHARLES You and your wife, Mr Guts, may be one flesh, because ye are nothing else—but rational creatures have minds that must be united.   55

SULLEN Minds.

SIR CHARLES Ay, minds, sir—don't you think that the mind takes place of the body?°

SULLEN In some people.

SIR CHARLES Then the interest of the master must be consulted before that of his servant.   60

SULLEN Sir, you shall dine with me tomorrow. Oons, I always thought that we were naturally one.°

SIR CHARLES Sir, I know that my two hands are naturally one, because they love one another, kiss one another, help one another in all the actions of life, but I could not say so much, if they were always at cuffs.   65

SULLEN Then 'tis plain that we are two.

SIR CHARLES Why don't you part with her, sir?

SULLEN Will you take her, sir?   70

SIR CHARLES With all my heart.

SULLEN You shall have her tomorrow morning, and a venison pasty into the bargain.

SIR CHARLES You'll let me have her fortune too?

SULLEN Fortune! Why, sir, I have no quarrel at her fortune—I only   75
hate the woman, sir, and none but the woman shall go.

SIR CHARLES But her fortune, sir—

SULLEN Can you play at whisk, sir?

SIR CHARLES No, truly, sir.

SULLEN Nor at all-fours?   80

SIR CHARLES Neither!

SULLEN (aside) Oons! where was this man bred?—Burn me, sir, I
can't go home—'tis but two o'clock.

SIR CHARLES For half-an-hour, sir, if you please—but you must
consider 'tis late.   85

SULLEN Late! that's the reason I can't go to bed. Come, sir.
     Exeunt [Sir Charles and Sullen]. Enter Cherry, runs across the
     stage and knocks at Aimwell's chamber door. Enter Aimwell in
     his nightcap and gown

AIMWELL What's the matter? You tremble, child, you're frighted.

CHERRY No wonder, sir—but in short, sir, this very minute a gang
of rogues are gone to rob my Lady Bountiful's house.

AIMWELL How!   90

CHERRY I dogged 'em to the very door, and left 'em breaking in.

AIMWELL Have you alarmed anybody else with the news?

CHERRY No, no, sir—I wanted to have discovered the whole plot,
and twenty other things to your man Martin; but I have searched
the whole house and can't find him. Where is he?   95

AIMWELL No matter, child—will you guide me immediately to the
house?

CHERRY With all my heart, sir—my Lady Bountiful is my godmother; and I love Mrs Dorinda so well—

AIMWELL Dorinda! The name inspires me—the glory and the danger   100
shall be all my own. Come my life, let me but get my sword.
     Exeunt

[5.2]

Scene changes to a bedchamber in Lady Bountiful's house

Enter Mrs Sullen, Dorinda undressed; a table and lights

DORINDA 'Tis very late, sister—no news of your spouse yet?

MRS SULLEN No, I'm condemned to be alone till towards four, and
then perhaps I may be executed with his company.

DORINDA Well, my dear, I'll leave you to your rest; you'll go directly
    to bed, I suppose.   5
MRS SULLEN I don't know what to do. Hey-ho.
DORINDA That's a desiring sigh, sister.
MRS SULLEN This is a languishing hour, sister.
DORINDA And might prove a critical minute, if the pretty fellow
    were here.   10
MRS SULLEN Here! what, in my bedchamber, at two o'clock o'th'
    morning, I undressed, the family asleep, my hated husband abroad,
    and my lovely fellow at my feet—O gad, sister!
DORINDA Thoughts are free, sister, and them I allow you—so, my
    dear, goodnight.   15
MRS SULLEN A good rest to my dear Dorinda.
        [*Exit Dorinda*]
    Thoughts free! are they so? Why then suppose him here, dressed
    like a youthful, gay and burning bridegroom—
        Here Archer steals out of the closet
    with tongue enchanting, eyes bewitching, knees imploring.
        Turns a little o' one side, and sees Archer in the posture she describes
    Ah!   20
        Shrieks, and runs to the other side of the stage
    Have my thoughts raised a spirit? What are you, sir, a man or a devil?
ARCHER (*rising*) A man, a man, madam.
MRS SULLEN How shall I be sure of it?
ARCHER Madam, I'll give you demonstration this minute.
        Takes her hand
MRS SULLEN What, sir! do you intend to be rude?   25
ARCHER Yes, madam, if you please.
MRS SULLEN In the name of wonder, whence came ye?
ARCHER From the skies, madam—I'm a Jupiter in love, and you shall
    be my Alcmena.°
MRS SULLEN How came you in?   30
ARCHER I flew in at the window, madam—your cousin Cupid lent
    me his wings, and your sister Venus opened the casement.
MRS SULLEN I'm struck dumb with admiration.
ARCHER And I with wonder.
        Looks passionately at her
MRS SULLEN What will become of me?   35
ARCHER How beautiful she looks—the teeming jolly spring smiles in
    her blooming face, and when she was conceived, her mother smelt
    to° roses, looked on lillies:

Lillies unfold their white, their fragrant charms,
When the warm sun thus darts into their arms.

  Runs to her

MRS SULLEN (*shrieks*) Ah!

ARCHER Oons, madam, what d'ye mean? You'll raise the house.

MRS SULLEN Sir, I'll wake the dead before I bear this. What! approach me with the freedoms of a keeper; I'm glad on't—your impudence has cured me.

ARCHER If this be impudence (*kneels*) I leave to your partial self; no panting pilgrim after tedious, painful voyage, e'er bowed before his saint with more devotion.

MRS SULLEN (*aside*) Now, now, I'm ruined, if he kneels! Rise thou prostrate engineer—not all thy undermining skill shall reach my heart.° Rise, and know, I am a woman without my sex°—I can love to all the tenderness of wishes, sighs and tears— but go no further. Still to convince you that I'm more than woman, I can speak my frailty, confess my weakness even for you—but—

ARCHER For me! (*Going to lay hold on her*)

MRS SULLEN Hold, sir, build not upon that, for my most mortal hatred follows if you disobey what I command you now—leave me this minute. (*Aside*) If he denies, I'm lost.

ARCHER Then you'll promise—

MRS SULLEN Anything another time.

ARCHER When shall I come?

MRS SULLEN Tomorrow when you will.

ARCHER Your lips must seal the promise.

MRS SULLEN Pshaw!

ARCHER They must, they must.

  Kisses her

Raptures and paradise! and why not now, my angel? The time, the place, silence and secrecy, all conspire—and the now conscious stars have preordained this moment for my happiness.

  Takes her in his arms

MRS SULLEN You will not, cannot sure.

ARCHER If the sun rides fast, and disappoints not mortals of tomorrow's dawn, this night shall crown my joys.

MRS SULLEN My sex's pride assist me.

ARCHER My sex's strength help me.

MRS SULLEN You shall kill me first.

ARCHER I'll die with you. (*Carrying her off*)

MRS SULLEN Thieves, thieves, murder—
>   *Enter Scrub in his breeches, and one shoe*

SCRUB Thieves, thieves, murder, popery.

ARCHER Ha! the very timorous stag will kill in rutting time.
>   *Draws and offers to stab Scrub*

SCRUB (*kneeling*) O, pray, sir, spare all I have and take my life.   80

MRS SULLEN (*holding Archer's hand*) What does the fellow mean?

SCRUB O, madam, down upon your knees, your marrow bones—he's one of 'um.

ARCHER Of whom.

SCRUB One of the rogues—I beg your pardon, sir, one of the honest   85
gentlemen that just now are broke into the house.

ARCHER How!

MRS SULLEN I hope, you did not come to rob me?

ARCHER Indeed I did, madam, but I would have taken nothing but
what you might ha' spared, but your crying 'Thieves' has waked   90
this dreaming fool, and so he takes 'em for granted.

SCRUB Granted! 'tis granted, sir—take all we have.

MRS SULLEN The fellow looks as if he were broke out of Bedlam.°

SCRUB Oons, madam, they're broke into the house with fire and
sword—I saw them, heard them, they'll be here this minute.   95

ARCHER What, thieves!

SCRUB Under favour, sir, I think so.

MRS SULLEN What shall we do, sir?

ARCHER Madam, I wish your ladyship a goodnight.

MRS SULLEN Will you leave me?   100

ARCHER Leave you! Lord, madam, did not you command me to be
gone just now upon pain of your immortal hatred?

MRS SULLEN Nay, but pray, sir—
>   *Takes hold of him*

ARCHER Ha, ha, ha, now comes my turn to be ravished. You see now,
madam, you must use men one way or other; but take this by the   105
way, good madam—that none but a fool will give you the benefit
of his courage, unless you'll take his love along with it. [*To Scrub*]
How are they armed, friend?

SCRUB With sword and pistol, sir.

ARCHER Hush—I see a dark lantern° coming through the gallery.   110
Madam, be assured I will protect you, or lose my life.

MRS SULLEN Your life!—no, sir, they can rob me of nothing that I
value half so much; therefore, now, sir, let me entreat you to be
gone.

ARCHER No, madam, I'll consult my own safety for the sake of   115
yours—I'll work by stratagem. Have you courage enough to stand
the appearance of 'em?

MRS SULLEN Yes, yes, since I have scaped your hands, I can face
anything.

ARCHER Come hither, brother Scrub—don't you know me?   120

SCRUB Eh! my dear brother, let me kiss thee.

     Kisses Archer

ARCHER This way—here.

     *Archer and Scrub hide behind the bed. Enter Gibbet with a dark
lantern in one hand and a pistol in t'other*

GIBBET Ay, ay, this is the chamber, and the lady alone.

MRS SULLEN Who are you, sir? What would you have? D'ye come
to rob me?   125

GIBBET Rob you! alack-a-day, madam, I'm only a younger brother,°
madam; and so, madam, if you make a noise, I'll shoot you
through the head; but don't be afraid, madam. (*Laying his
lantern and pistol upon the table*) These rings, madam—don't
be concerned, madam—I have a profound respect for you,   130
madam. Your keys, madam—don't be frighted, madam—I'm the
most of a gentleman. (*Searching her pockets*) This necklace,
madam—I never was rude to a lady—I have a veneration—for this
necklace—

     *Here Archer having come round and seized the pistols, takes
Gibbet by the collar, trips up his heels, and claps the pistol to his
breast*

ARCHER Hold, profane villain, and take the reward of thy sacrilege.   135

GIBBET O! Pray, sir, don't kill me; I an't prepared.

ARCHER How many is there of 'em, Scrub?

SCRUB Five and forty, sir.

ARCHER Then I must kill the villain to have him out of the way.

GIBBET Hold, hold, sir—we are but three, upon my honour.   140

ARCHER Scrub, will you undertake to secure him?

SCRUB Not I, sir; kill him, kill him.

ARCHER Run to Gypsy's chamber—there you'll find the doctor;
bring him hither presently.

     Exit Scrub running

Come, rogue, if you have a short prayer, say it.   145

GIBBET Sir, I have no prayer at all; the government has provided a
chaplain to say prayers for us on these occasions.°

MRS SULLEN Pray, sir, don't kill him. You fright me as much as him.

ARCHER The dog shall die, madam, for being the occasion of my
disappointment. [*To Gibbet*] Sirrah, this moment is your last.   150
GIBBET Sir, I'll give you two hundred pound to spare my life.
ARCHER Have you no more rascal?
GIBBET Yes, sir, I can command four hundred; but I must reserve
two of 'em to save my life at the sessions.°
    Enter Scrub and Foigard
ARCHER Here, Doctor, I suppose Scrub and you between you may   155
manage him. Lay hold of him, Doctor.
    Foigard lays hold of Gibbet
GIBBET What! turned over to the priest already. Look'ye, Doctor,
you come before your time; I an't condemned yet, I thank'ye.
FOIGARD Come, my dear joy, I vill secure your body and your shoul
too; I vill make you a good Catholic, and give you an absolution.   160
GIBBET Absolution! can you procure me a pardon, Doctor.
FOIGARD No, joy.
GIBBET Then you and your absolution may go to the Devil.
ARCHER Convey him into the cellar—there bind him. Take the
pistol, and if he offers to resist, shoot him through the head, and   165
come back to us with all the speed you can.
SCRUB Ay, ay, come, Doctor—do you hold him fast, and I'll guard
him.
    Takes the pistol
MRS SULLEN But how came the doctor?
ARCHER In short, madam—(*Shrieking without*) 'Sdeath! the rogues   170
are at work with the other ladies. I'm vexed I parted with the
pistol; but I must fly to their assistance. Will you stay here,
madam, or venture yourself with me?
MRS SULLEN O, with you, dear sir, with you.
    Takes him by the arm and exeunt

[5.3]

Scene changes to another apartment in the same house

Enter Hounslow dragging in Lady Bountiful, and Bagshot
hauling in Dorinda; the rogues with swords drawn
HOUNSLOW Come, come, your jewels, mistress.
BAGSHOT Your keys, your keys, old gentlewoman.°
    Enter Aimwell and Cherry

AIMWELL Turn this way, villains; I durst engage an army in such a
cause.
>   *He engages 'em both*
DORINDA O, madam, had I but a sword to help the brave man!   5
LADY BOUNTIFUL There's three or four hanging up in the hall; but
they won't draw.° I'll go fetch one however.
>   *Exit [Lady Bountiful]. Enter Archer and Mrs Sullen*
ARCHER Hold, hold, my lord—every man his bird,° pray.
>   *They engage man to man; the rogues are thrown and disarmed*
CHERRY [*aside*] What! The rogues taken!—then they'll impeach my
father; I must give him timely notice.   10
>   *[Cherry] runs out*
ARCHER Shall we kill the rogues?
AIMWELL No, no, we'll bind them.
ARCHER Ay, ay. (*To Mrs Sullen who stands by him*) Here, madam,
lend me your garter!
MRS SULLEN [*aside*] The Devil's in this fellow. He fights, loves and   15
banters, all in a breath. [*Aloud*] Here's a cord that the rogues
brought with 'em, I suppose.
ARCHER Right, right, the rogue's destiny—a rope to hang himself. [*To
Aimwell*] Come, my lord, (*binding the rogues together*) this is but a
scandalous sort of an office, if our adventures should end in this sort   20
of hangman-work; but I hope there is something in prospect that—
>   *Enter Scrub*
Well, Scrub, have you secured your Tartar?
SCRUB Yes, sir—I left the priest and him disputing about religion.
AIMWELL And pray carry these gentlemen to reap the benefit of the
controversy.   25
>   *Delivers the prisoners to Scrub, who leads 'em out*
MRS SULLEN Pray, sister, how came my lord here?
DORINDA And pray, how came the gentleman here?
MRS SULLEN I'll tell you the greatest piece of villainy—
>   *They talk in dumb show*
AIMWELL I fancy, Archer, you have been more successful in your
adventures than the house-breakers.   30
ARCHER No matter for my adventure, yours is the principal. Press
her this minute to marry you—now while she's hurried between
the palpitation of her fear and the joy of her deliverance, now while
the tide of her spirits are at high flood. Throw yourself at her feet;
speak some romantic nonsense or other. Address her like Alex-   35
ander in the height of his victory,° confound her senses, bear down

her reason, and away with her—the priest is now in the cellar, and
dare not refuse to do the work.

> *Enter Lady Bountiful*

AIMWELL But how shall I get off without being observed?

ARCHER You a lover, and not find a way to get off! Let me see.   40

AIMWELL You bleed, Archer.

ARCHER 'Sdeath, I'm glad on't; this wound will do the business—I'll
amuse the old lady and Mrs Sullen about dressing my wound,
while you carry off Dorinda.

LADY BOUNTIFUL Gentlemen, could we understand how you would   45
be gratified for the services—

ARCHER Come, come, my lady, this is no time for compliments—I'm
wounded, madam.

LADY BOUNTIFUL and MRS SULLEN How! Wounded!

DORINDA [*to Aimwell*] I hope, sir, you have received no hurt?   50

AIMWELL None but what you may cure.

> *Makes love in dumb show*

LADY BOUNTIFUL Let me see your arm, sir. I must have some
powder-sugar to stop the blood. O me! an ugly gash upon my
word, sir—you must go into bed.

ARCHER Ay, my lady, a bed would do very well. (*To Mrs Sullen*)   55
Madam will you do me the favour to conduct me to a chamber?

LADY BOUNTIFUL Do, do, daughter—while I get the lint and the
probe and the plaster ready.

> *Runs out one way; Aimwell carries off Dorinda another*

ARCHER Come, madam, why don't you obey your mother's commands?

MRS SULLEN How can you, after what is past, have the confidence   60
to ask me?

ARCHER And if you go to that, how can you, after what is past, have
the confidence to deny me? Was not this blood shed in your
defence, and my life exposed for your protection? Look'ye,
madam, I'm none of your romantic fools, that fight giants and   65
monsters for nothing; my valour is downright Swiss;° I'm a soldier
of fortune and must be paid.

MRS SULLEN 'Tis ungenerous in you, sir, to upbraid me with your
services.

ARCHER 'Tis ungenerous in you, madam, not to reward 'em.   70

MRS SULLEN How! At the expense of my honour.

ARCHER Honour! Can honour consist with ingratitude? If you would
deal like a woman of honour, do like a man of honour—d'ye think
I would deny you in such a case?

Enter a servant

SERVANT Madam, my lady ordered me to tell you that your brother   75
is below at the gate.

MRS SULLEN My brother? Heavens be praised. [*To Archer*] Sir, he
shall thank you for your services—he has it in his power.

ARCHER Who is your brother, madam?

MRS SULLEN Sir Charles Freeman. You'll excuse me, sir; I must go   80
and receive him.
          [*Exit Mrs Sullen*]

ARCHER Sir Charles Freeman! 'Sdeath and Hell!—my old acquaintance. Now unless Aimwell has made good use of his time,
all our fair machine goes souse into the sea like the Eddystone.°   85
          Exit

[5.4]

Scene changes to the gallery in the same house

Enter Aimwell and Dorinda

DORINDA Well, well, my lord, you have conquered; your late
generous action will, I hope, plead for my easy yielding, though I
must own your lordship had a friend in the fort before.

AIMWELL The sweets of Hybla° dwell upon her tongue.

          Enter Foigard with a book

Here, Doctor—   5

FOIGARD Are you prepared boat?

DORINDA I'm ready. But first, my lord, one word. I have a frightful
example of a hasty marriage in my own family; when I reflect
upon't, it shocks me. Pray, my lord, consider a little—

AIMWELL Consider! Do you doubt my honour or my love?   10

DORINDA Neither. I do believe you equally just as brave. And were
your whole sex drawn out for me to choose, I should not cast a
look upon the multitude if you were absent. But my lord, I'm a
woman; colours, concealments may hide a thousand faults in me.
Therefore know me better first; I hardly dare affirm I know myself   15
in anything except my love.

AIMWELL (*aside*) Such goodness who could injure? I find myself
unequal to the task of villain; she has gained my soul, and made it
honest like her own—I cannot, cannot hurt her—Doctor, retire.

          Exit Foigard

Madam, behold your lover and your proselyte, and judge of my 20
passion by my conversion. I'm all a lie, nor dare I give a fiction to
your arms; I'm all counterfeit except my passion.

DORINDA Forbid it Heaven! a counterfeit!

AIMWELL I am no lord, but a poor needy man, come with a mean,
a scandalous design to prey upon your fortune. But the beauties of 25
your mind and person have so won me from myself, that like a
trusty servant, I prefer the interest of my mistress to my own.

DORINDA Sure I have had the dream of some poor mariner, a sleepy
image of a welcome port, and wake involved in storms. Pray, sir,
who are you?   30

AIMWELL Brother to the man whose title I usurped, but stranger to
his honour or his fortune.

DORINDA Matchless honesty—once I was proud, sir, of your wealth
and title, but now am prouder that you want it. Now I can show
my love was justly levelled, and had no aim but love. Doctor, 35
come in.

> Enter Foigard at one door, Gypsy at another, who whispers [to]
> Dorinda

[To Foigard] Your pardon, sir, we sha'not want you now. [To
Aimwell] Sir, you must excuse me—I'll wait on you presently.

> Exit [Dorinda] with Gypsy

FOIGARD Upon my shoul, now, dis is foolish.

> Exit [Foigard]

AIMWELL Gone! and bid the priest depart. It has an ominous look. 40

> Enter Archer

ARCHER Courage, Tom—shall I wish you joy?

AIMWELL No.

ARCHER Oons, man, what ha' you been doing?

AIMWELL O, Archer, my honesty, I fear, has ruined me.

ARCHER How!   45

AIMWELL I have discovered myself.

ARCHER Discovered! and without my consent? What! Have I embarked my small remains in the same bottom with yours, and you
dispose of all without my partnership?

AIMWELL O, Archer, I own my fault.   50

ARCHER After conviction—'tis then too late for pardon. You may
remember, Mr Aimwell, that you proposed this folly. As you
begun, so end it. Henceforth I'll hunt my fortune single. So
farewell.

AIMWELL Stay, my dear Archer, but a minute.   55

ARCHER Stay! What—to be despised, exposed and laughed at? No, I
would sooner change conditions with the worst of the rogues we
just now bound, than bear one scornful smile from the proud
knight that once I treated as my equal.

AIMWELL What knight?   60

ARCHER Sir Charles Freeman, brother to the lady that I had
almost—but no matter for that, 'tis a cursed night's work, and so
I leave you to make your best on't. (*Going*)

AIMWELL Freeman! One word, Archer. Still I have hopes; methought she received my confession with pleasure.   65

ARCHER 'Sdeath! who doubts it?

AIMWELL She consented after to the match; and still I dare believe
she will be just.

ARCHER To herself, I warrant her, as you should have been.

AIMWELL [*looking off-stage*] By all my hopes, she comes, and smiling   70
comes.

> *Enter Dorinda mighty gay*

DORINDA Come, my dear lord, I fly with impatience to your arms.
The minutes of my absence was a tedious year. Where's this
tedious priest?

> *Enter Foigard*

ARCHER Oons! a brave girl!   75

DORINDA I suppose, my lord, this gentleman is privy to our affairs.

ARCHER Yes, yes madam—I'm to be your father.°

DORINDA Come, priest, do your office.

ARCHER Make haste, make haste—couple 'em any way.

> *Takes Aimwell's hand*

Come, madam, I'm to give you—   80

DORINDA My mind's altered, I won't.

ARCHER Eh—

AIMWELL I'm confounded.

FOIGARD Upon my shoul, and sho is myshelf.

ARCHER What's the matter now, madam?   85

DORINDA Look'ye sir, one generous action deserves another. This
gentleman's honour obliged him to hide nothing from me; my
justice engages me to conceal nothing from him. In short, sir, you
are the person that you thought you counterfeited; you are the true
Lord Viscount Aimwell; and I wish your lordship joy. Now, priest,   90
you may be gone; if my lord is pleased now with the match, let his
lordship marry me in the face of the world.

AIMWELL and ARCHER What does she mean?

DORINDA Here's a witness for my truth.
    Enter Sir Charles and Mrs Sullen
SIR CHARLES My dear Lord Aimwell, I wish you joy.   95
AIMWELL Of what?
SIR CHARLES Of your honour and estate. Your brother died the day
    before I left London; and all your friends have writ after you to
    Brussels; among the rest I did myself the honour.
ARCHER Hark ye, sir knight, don't you banter now?   100
SIR CHARLES 'Tis truth upon my honour.
AIMWELL Thanks to the pregnant stars that formed this accident.
ARCHER Thanks to the womb of time that brought it forth; away
    with it.
AIMWELL Thanks to my guardian angel that led me to the prize.   105
    (*Taking Dorinda's hand*)
ARCHER And double thanks to the noble Sir Charles Freeman. My
    lord, I wish you joy. My lady I wish you joy. Egad, Sir Freeman,°
    you're the honestest fellow living. 'Sdeath, I'm grown strange airy
    upon this matter. My lord, how d'ye?—a word, my lord. Don't   110
    you remember something of a previous agreement, that entitles me
    to the moiety of this lady's fortune, which, I think will amount to
    five thousand pound?
AIMWELL Not a penny, Archer. You would ha' cut my throat just
    now, because I would not deceive this lady.   115
ARCHER Ay, and I'll cut your throat again, if you should deceive her now.
AIMWELL That's what I expected; and to end the dispute, the lady's
    fortune is ten thousand pound; we'll divide stakes; take the ten
    thousand pound, or the lady.
DORINDA How! is your lordship so indifferent?   120
ARCHER No, no, no, madam, his lordship knows very well, that I'll
    take the money; I leave you to his lordship, and so we're both
    provided for.
    Enter Count Bellair[1]
COUNT *Mesdames, et messieurs*,° I am your servant trice humble. I
    hear you be rob here.   125

---

[1] *In the 1728 edition ll. 124–34 read as follows*:

    Enter Foigard
FOIGARD Arrah, fait, de people do say you be all robbed, joy.
AIMWELL The ladies have been in some danger, sir, as you saw.   125
FOIGARD Upon my shoul, our inn be rob too.

AIMWELL The ladies have been in some danger, sir.

COUNT And begar, our inn be rob too.

AIMWELL Our inn! By whom?

COUNT By the landlord, begar—garzoon he has rob himself and run away.   130

ARCHER Robbed himself!

COUNT Ay, begar, and me too of a hundre pound.

ARCHER A hundred pound.

COUNT Yes, that I owed him.

AIMWELL Our money's gone, Frank.   135

ARCHER Rot the money, my wench is gone. *Savez-vous quelquechose de mademoiselle Cherry?*°

    Enter a fellow with a strong box and a letter

FELLOW Is there one Martin here?

ARCHER Ay, ay—who wants him?

FELLOW I have a box here and letter for him.   140

ARCHER (*taking the box*) Ha, ha, ha, what's here? Legerdemain! by this light, my lord, our money again; but this unfolds the riddle. (*Opening the letter, reads*) Hum, hum, hum—O, 'tis for the public good, and must be communicated to the company. [*Reading aloud*] 'Mr Martin—my father being afraid of an impeachment by the   145
rogues that are taken tonight is gone off, but if you can procure him a pardon he will make great discoveries that may be useful to the country. Could I have met you instead of your master tonight, I would have delivered myself into your hands with a sum that much exceeds that in your strong box, which I have sent you, with   150
an assurance to my dear Martin, that I shall ever be his most faithful friend till death, Cherry Boniface.' There's a billet-doux for you. As for the father, I think he ought to be encouraged, and for the daughter—pray, my lord, persuade your bride to take her into her service instead of Gypsy.   155

AIMWELL Our inn! By whom?

FOIGARD Upon my shalwation, our landlord has robbed himself and run away wid da money.

ARCHER Robbed himself!   130

FOIGARD Ay, fait, and me too of a hundred pounds!

ARCHER Robbed you of a hundred pound!

FOIGARD Yes, fait, honey, that I did owe to him.

AIMWELL I can assure you, madam, your deliverance was owing to her discovery.

DORINDA Your command, my lord, will do without the obligation. I'll take care of her.

SIR CHARLES This good company meets opportunely in favour of a 160 design I have in behalf of my unfortunate sister—I intend to part her from her husband. Gentlemen, will you assist me?

ARCHER Assist you! 'Sdeath, who would not?

COUNT Assist! Garzoon, we all assest.[1]

Enter Sullen

SULLEN What's all this? They tell me, spouse, that you had like to 165 have been robbed.

MRS SULLEN Truly, spouse, I was pretty near it, had not these two gentlemen interposed.

SULLEN How came these gentlemen here?

MRS SULLEN That's his way of returning thanks, you must know. 170

COUNT Garzoon, the question be apropos for all dat.[2]

SIR CHARLES You promised last night, sir, that you would deliver your lady to me this morning.

SULLEN Humph.

ARCHER Humph. What do you mean by 'Humph'? Sir, you shall 175 deliver her. In short, sir, we have saved you and your family, and if you are not civil we'll unbind the rogues, join with 'em and set fire to your house. What does the man mean? Not part with his wife!

COUNT Ay, garzoon, de man no understan common justice.[3]

MRS SULLEN Hold, gentlemen—all things here must move by 180 consent. Compulsion would spoil us: let my dear and I talk the matter over, and you shall judge it between us.

---

[1] *1728:*

FOIGARD Ay, upon my shoul, we'll all ashist.

[2] *1728:*

FOIGARD Ay, but upon my conshience, de question be apropos for all dat.

[3] *1728:*

FOIGARD Arrah, not part wid your wife! Upon my shoul, de man dosh not understand common shivility.

SULLEN Let me know first who are to be our judges. Pray, sir, who are you?

SIR CHARLES I am Sir Charles Freeman, come to take away your wife.   185

SULLEN And you, good sir?

AIMWELL Charles Viscount Aimwell, come to take away your sister.

SULLEN And you, pray sir?

ARCHER Francis Archer, Esquire; come—

SULLEN To take away my mother, I hope. Gentlemen, you're   190
heartily welcome—I never met with three more obliging people
since I was born. And now my dear, if you please, you shall have
the first word.

ARCHER [aside] And the last for five pound.

MRS SULLEN Spouse.   195

SULLEN Rib.°

MRS SULLEN How long have we been married?

SULLEN By the almanac fourteen months—but by my account
fourteen years.

MRS SULLEN 'Tis thereabout by my reckoning.   200

COUNT Garzoon, their account will agree.[1]

MRS SULLEN Pray, spouse, what did you marry for?

SULLEN To get an heir to my estate.

SIR CHARLES And have you succeeded?

SULLEN No.   205

ARCHER The condition fails of his side. Pray, madam, what did you
marry for?

MRS SULLEN To support the weakness of my sex by the strength of
his, and to enjoy the pleasures of an agreeable society.

SIR CHARLES Are your expectations answered?   210

MRS SULLEN No.

COUNT A clear case, a clear case.[2]

SIR CHARLES What are the bars to your mutual contentment?

MRS SULLEN In the first place I can't drink ale with him.

SULLEN Nor can I drink tea with her.   215

---

[1] 1728:

FOIGARD Upon my conshience, dere accounts vill agree.

[2] 1728:

FOIGARD Arrah, honeys, a clear caase, a clear caase!

MRS SULLEN I can't hunt with you.

SULLEN Nor can I dance with you.

MRS SULLEN I hate cocking and racing.

SULLEN And I abhor ombre and piquet.

MRS SULLEN Your silence is intolerable.   220

SULLEN Your prating is worse.

MRS SULLEN Have we not been a perpetual offence to each other—a gnawing vulture at the heart?

SULLEN A frightful goblin to the sight.

MRS SULLEN A porcupine to the feeling.   225

SULLEN Perpetual wormwood to the taste.

MRS SULLEN Is there on earth a thing we could agree in?

SULLEN Yes—to part.

MRS SULLEN With all my heart.

SULLEN Your hand.   230

MRS SULLEN Here.

SULLEN These hands joined us, these shall part us—away.

MRS SULLEN North.

SULLEN South.

MRS SULLEN East.   235

SULLEN West—far as the poles asunder.

COUNT Begar the ceremony be vera pretty.[1]

SIR CHARLES Now, Mr Sullen, there wants only my sister's fortune to make us easy.

SULLEN Sir Charles, you love your sister, and I love her fortune;   240
everyone to his fancy.

ARCHER Then you won't refund?

SULLEN Not a stiver.

ARCHER Then I find, madam, you must e'en go to your prison again.

COUNT What is the portion?[2]   245

---

[1] *1728:*

FOIGARD Upon my shoul, a pretty sheremony.

[2] *1728 replaces ll. 245–54 as follows:*

ARCHER What is her portion?

SIR CHARLES Ten thousand pound, sir.

ARCHER I'll pay it. My lord, I thank him, has enabled me, and if the lady pleases, she shall go home with me. This night's adventure has proved . . .

SIR CHARLES Ten thousand pound, sir.

COUNT Garzoon I'll pay it, and she shall go home wid me.

ARCHER Ha, ha, ha—French all over. Do you know, sir, what ten thousand pound English is?

COUNT No, begar, not *justement*.°   250

ARCHER Why, sir, 'tis a hundred thousand *livres*.°

COUNT A hundred tousand livres! Ah, garzoon, me canno' do't. Your beauties and their fortunes are both too much for me.

ARCHER Then I will. This night's adventure has proved strangely lucky to us all, for Captain Gibbet in his walk had made bold, Mr   255
Sullen, with your study and escritoire, and had taken out all the writings of your estate, all the articles of marriage with your lady,° bills, bonds, leases, receipts to an infinite value; I took 'em from him, and I deliver them to Sir Charles.

    Gives him a parcel of papers and parchments

SULLEN How my writings! My head aches consumedly. Well,   260
gentlemen, you shall have her fortune, but I can't talk. If you have a mind, Sir Charles, to be merry, and celebrate my sister's wedding, and my divorce, you may command my house. But my head aches consumedly—Scrub, bring me a dram.

ARCHER (*to Mrs Sullen*) Madam, there's a country dance to the trifle   265
that I sung today; your hand, and we'll lead it up.

    Here a dance.

'Twould be hard to guess which of these parties is the better pleased, the couple joined, or the couple parted—the one rejoicing in hopes of an untasted happiness, and the other in their deliverance from an experienced misery.   270

       Both happy in their several states we find,
       Those parted by consent, and those conjoined.
       Consent, if mutual, saves the lawyer's fee;
       Consent is law enough to set you free.

An Epilogue

designed to be spoke in *The Beaux' Stratagem*°

If to our play your judgment can't be kind,
Let its expiring author pity find.
Survey his mournful case with melting eyes,
Nor let the bard be damned before he dies.
Forbear you fair on his last scene to frown,   5
But his true exit with a plaudit crown;
Then shall the dying poet cease to fear
The dreadful knell, while your applause he hears.
At Leuctra so, the conquering Theban died,°
Claimed his friends' praises, but their tears denied: 10
Pleased in the pangs of death he greatly thought
Conquest with loss of life but cheaply bought.
The difference this, the Greek was one would fight—
As brave, though not so gay, as Sergeant Kite.°
Ye Sons of Will's, what's that to those who write?   15
To Thebes alone the Grecian owed his bays;
You may the bard above the hero raise,
Since yours is greater than Athenian praise.°

EXPLANATORY NOTES

References in these Notes to the views of earlier editors are indicated as follows:

Archer   George Farquhar [*Four Plays*], ed. William Archer (1906)
Cordner   *The Beaux' Stratagem*, ed. Michael Cordner (1976; rev. 1990)
Dixon   *The Recruiting Officer*, ed. Peter Dixon (1986)
Fifer   *The Beaux' Stratagem*, ed. Charles Fifer (1978)
Hunt   *The Dramatic Works of Wycherley, Congreve, Vanbrugh, and Farquhar*, ed. Leigh Hunt (1840)
Jeffares *The Recruiting Officer*, ed. A. Norman Jeffares (1972).
Kenny   *The Works of George Farquhar*, ed. Shirley Strum Kenny (2 vols., 1988).
Ross   *The Recruiting Officer*, ed. John Ross (1973; rev. 1991)
Shugrue   *The Recruiting Officer*, ed. Michael Shugrue (1966)
Stonehill *The Complete Works of George Farquhar*, ed. Charles Stonehill (2 vols., 1930)
Strauss   *A Discourse upon Comedy, The Recruiting Officer and The Beaux' Stratagem*, ed. Louis A. Strauss (1914)

The Constant Couple

Title-page
   Sive favore . . . ago: whether I have this reputation by favour or on account of the work itself, it is right, kind reader, to give you my thanks (Latin). Ovid (43 BC–AD 18) was regarded as one of the more libertine of the Roman poets. See Notes *BS* 4.1.278.

Dramatis Personae
   disbanded: in December 1698, William III's fourth Parliament passed an Act disbanding land forces in England by the following May. William, greatly offended, threatened to retire to Holland. Farquhar supports the views of William and his Whig ministers. See Introduction pp. viii, xx. For a Tory view (isolationist, pro-navy, anti-army), see Dryden's 'To My Honoured Kinsman', 142–70.

   VIZARD: a person wearing a mask.

   SMUGGLER: see Notes 1.1.39–40 below.

   CLINCHER: a maker of puns.

Dedication

    Sir Roger Mostyn: (1675–1739), a Tory and not therefore a natural patron for Farquhar. The latter does not appear to have been helped by this dedication.

7 *too young an author*: see Introduction p. xiii.

14–15 *a senator*: Sir Roger was not elected to Parliament until 1701. Farquhar's flattery is thus undisguised.

16 *the Ancient Briton*: a literary way of referring to Sir Roger's Welshness. He was supposed to be possibly even more flattered to be called English.

20–1 *The play . . . representation*: the play has been honoured by the appearance in the audience of many distinguished people while it was being performed.

24 *Materia superabit Opus*: the matter will excel the workmanship (Latin), i.e. Sir Roger's career will be more splendid than the play introduced by his name. The wording reverses Ovid's description of the doors of the palace of the sun—*Materiam superabit opus* ('The workmanship excelled the material'—*Metamorphoses* ii. 5).

Preface to the Reader

5 *third night*: the first of the author's benefit nights, of which Farquhar enjoyed a total of four in the play's successful first run.

10 *the Town*: I retain the initial capital when the sense implies fashionable London Society, centred on the Court. I do the same for the City, i.e. the City of London, and its banking and mercantile institutions. The rivalry and interdependence of the two is one of the principal themes of comedy between 1660 and 1780.

13 *to make a party for the play*: to fill the auditorium with his friends by giving them free tickets.

19 *smut and profaneness*: a reference to the controversy caused by *A Short View of the Immorality and Profaneness of the English Stage* (1698) by Jeremy Collier (1675–1739), which attacked Dryden, Congreve, and Vanbrugh among others for indecency and blasphemy. Congreve and Vanbrugh defended themselves but altered their plays. Though he had got away with the indecencies of *Love and a Bottle*, Farquhar injected a note of rectitude into the characterizations of Standard and Angelica in *The Constant Couple*, and reverted to the more relaxed libertinism of comedy before 1675, thus avoiding the harsher eroticism of later Restoration plays. See also Introduction pp. vii, xii.

20 *the beauties of action*: the attractions of performance.

24 *Mr Wilks's*: Robert Wilks (1665–1732), an Anglo-Irish actor. See Introduction pp. vii, viii, and Notes *BS* Advertisement 4 and 4.2.61.

28 *the Jubilee*: Jubilee years are celebrated by the Catholic Church in Rome every fifty years, attracting many besides Catholics to the city. However

the Peace of Ryswick (1697) had only just ended the War of the Treaty of Augsburg with Catholic France, and the English throne was still claimed by the exiled James II (reigned 1685–9) who was a Catholic. His claim, and that of his son, James Francis Edward (1688–1756), 'The Old Pretender', were to remain on the political agenda until the death of James's second daughter, Queen Anne (reigned 1702–14). James's nephew and son-in-law, William III (reigned 1689–1702) accordingly forbade people from travelling to the Jubilee. See Introduction pp. vii, xix.

29 *a misnomer*: because no trip to Rome takes place.

30 *trips in the play*: technical violations of neoclassical norms of correctness, for which Farquhar was often attacked. In 'A Discourse upon Comedy', he argues that comedy ought to please audiences and not merely follow the rules sanctioned by traditional criticism. See Introduction p. xviii and Notes *TR* Preface 10–15.

Prologue

by a Friend: the Friend is probably a device of Farquhar's to assist his self-presentation. The poor quality of the versification suggests this.

3 *Our spark*: Farquhar himself.

what medley's come: what a mixed audience has turned up.

7 *great wig*: voluminous wigs for men were currently in fashion.

14 *double entendre*: indecent pun, Anglicized to rhyme with 'slander'.

15 *a spark just come from France*: Sir Harry Wildair.

17 *Like coin . . . thence*: unlike Sir Harry, travellers to France usually returned with less money and sense than when they set out.

18 *There's yet a*: there's still another.

19 *elbow-shaking*: dice-throwing.

21 *scours a way*: all early editions read 'scours away', but this leaves a transitive verb without a specifiable object.

24 *he*: Farquhar, not the elbow-shaking fool.

27 *bulky 'mother'*: large brothel-madam, conventionally a formidable middle-aged woman.

28 *the bubble gallery*: the middle gallery, where prostitutes could be picked up, and naïve members of the public ('bubbles') gulled.

29 *mounted friends*: footmen, coachmen, etc., in the galleries about the side-boxes. They had free admission.

30 *side-box tricks*: occupiers of boxes could avoid payment by leaving at the end of the second act when fees were collected in the boxes. See *BS* 4.2.20–2.

31 *with your love*: i.e. not with cash.

32 *Dorset Garden House*: i.e. the Queen's (originally the Duke's) Theatre, Dorset Street; it was not much used for plays after 1697. It was let in 1699 to the Kentish strongman, William Joy.

35 *That strong dog . . . heads*: Joy has destroyed the Queen's Theatre as Samson destroyed the Philistines' temple. See Judg. 6: 23–31.

37 *will one day hold him*: by the neck, on the scaffold.

39 *pull his prizes down*: possibly a reference to heavily weighted levers (prizes) which Joy could depress, and members of the public could not. There may also be a pun on 'prices'.

A New Prologue

First published in the third edition, 1700, having been written for Farquhar's final benefit night on 13 July.

In answer . . . at the new: John Oldmixon (?1673–1742) was once a friend of Farquhar's. Farquhar wrote an epilogue for Oldmixon's *The Grove* (1700), but the play failed, as Oldmixon's *Amyntas* (1698) had done. To 'curry favour' with the rival company at Lincoln's Inn Fields, Oldmixon added a prologue to *The Grove* attacking Farquhar.

5–7 *He touch'd . . . sour debate*: B——re is probably Sir Richard Blackmore (d. 1729), court physician and translator of Virgil (70–19 BC). Dryden attacked him in 'To my Honoured Kinsman' (1700) as Maurus who 'sweeps whole parishes and peoples every grave' (83). In an earlier couplet, Dryden punned on the word 'Bill': 'So lived our sires, ere doctors learned to kill | And multiply with theirs the weekly Bill' (71–2)—i.e. doctors' fees and the Bills of Mortality published weekly by the London Company of Parish Clerks. Dryden held court at Will's Coffee House, Covent Garden until his death in May 1700. Farquhar claims that unlike either Dryden or Blackmore he has avoided making slighting references to other writers and so maintained good relations with both Dryden and Dryden's enemies.

8 *Brisco's fate*: Sam Briscoe, publisher and friend of Farquhar's, was bankrupted by his enemies, but rescued by prominent writers, including Dryden and Wycherley.

10 *He's none . . . t'other house*: the ruinous competition between the Theatre Royal, Drury Lane, and Lincoln's Inn Fields tilted in the former's favour with the success of *The Constant Couple*, which the latter's supporters then attacked. Farquhar disclaims any responsibility for the financial difficulties of the rival theatre on the grounds that no play of his has been produced there. See Introduction p. viii and Notes *RO* 5.4.21.

17 *purpose to starve the players*: Oldmixon claimed the public praised the plays at Lincoln's Inn Fields but let the players starve.

21 *Our plays are farce*: another of Oldmixon's accusations.

23 *Because we . . . tools*: this indecent pun contrasts notably with the claim made in the earlier Prologue (14).

25 *true blue*: the colour of loyalty; the Protestant colour.

26 *And, men . . . to you*: and by the 'respects' they pay, men of breeding, to you [in calling you fools]. Other editors have deleted the comma after 'And', making the sense 'they call themselves men of breeding by virtue of the respect they show to you.'

28 *old Shakespeare's ghost*: Oldmixon's epilogue was spoken by an actor playing Shakespeare's ghost.

1.1 S.D. *the Park*: St James's Park.

7 *conversation*: familiar social intercourse.

23 *pious ejaculations*: short prayers said spontaneously throughout the day.

24 *Hobbes*: Thomas Hobbes (1588–1679), the philosopher notorious for the strong if implicit atheism of his works. See Introduction p. xviii and Notes *TR* 2.5.65–7.

37 *St Sebastian's*: San Sebastian (Donostia), the northern Spanish seaport.

39–40 *upon the statute*: trade with France was illegal under Acts of Parliament of 1689 and 1692. However, 'smuggling, conducted on a large scale' nullified the effects of the blockade. English wool was traded for 'French silks, wine, and brandy' either directly or through Scotland and the Netherlands. England's ally Spain 'lent a hand in facilitating the sale of French textiles in the Spanish possessions; she also "doctored" large quantities of French wine [in San Sebastian] which was then conveyed to England, mainly through Portuguese ports' (David Ogg, *England in the Reigns of James II and William III* (1969 edn.), 302–3).

41–2 *than the war did*: the Peace of Ryswick was signed in September 1696, but see Notes 1.1.74 below.

42 *privateers*: both France and England authorized privateers (in effect pirates) to prey on each other's shipping. They were not always scrupulous about whose ships they seized. See Ogg, *England in the Reigns*, 303 and Notes *RO* 5.4.21.

43 *a red coat and feather*: soldiers wore red coats, officers feathers.

48 *broke*: deprived of his commission as an officer.

51 *grazed*: first edn. 'gazed', an obvious misprint corrected in the second edn. a few weeks later.

54 *the Monument*: a memorial, 202 feet high, to the outbreak of the Great Fire of London in 1666.

61 *Actaeon*: a young huntsman in Greek legend, who was turned into a deer and killed by his own hounds after seeing Artemis, Greek goddess of the moon and of hunting, naked. An old Actaeon is an ageing husband with

horns like a deer in accordance with the tradition that a man with an unfaithful wife grew horns on his forehead.

62–3 *free quarter*: billeted by compulsion and without payment. The cuckolding of citizens in such circumstances was deemed normal in comedies of the period.

72 *the Rummer*: a popular tavern between Whitehall and Charing Cross.

74 *Hungary*: Hungary, ruled by the Habsburgs, who like the English and the Dutch were traditionally enemies of France, was still at war with the Turks, traditional *de facto* allies of the French. See Notes *RO* 3.1.156–7.

77 *colours in Westminster Hall*: the flags of disbanded regiments were laid up in Westminster Hall, the seat of the law courts, where they slowly decayed.

86 *between Ludgate and Charing Cross*: from the centre of the City to Whitehall.

87 *Buda*: capital of Hungary.

98 *Mars and Venus*: the Roman gods of War and Love. Their affair symbolizes the success of soldiers with women. This may be a friendly allusion to an afterpiece called *The Loves of Mars and Venus*, by Peter Motteux (1663–1718), played at Lincoln's Inn Fields in 1696. Motteux almost certainly collaborated with Farquhar in writing *The Stage-Coach* and supplied prologues for *The Inconstant* and *The Twin Rivals*.

113–14 *a campaign in Flanders*: French forces were almost entirely successful in this theatre of war in the 1690s. See also Notes *BS* 1.1.174.

116 *behaved himself very bravely*: i.e. in spite of his unmilitary bearing.

127 *out of the rubric*: disobeying (as Dissenters often did) the Order of Service in the Prayer Book; Sir Harry is surprised Vizard has not conformed and embarked on a career as a Church of England clergyman.

137 *We are all so reformed*: reformation of manners was the object of many religious societies founded during the 1690s. Attempts were made to suppress gaming houses. In 1697 William III declared 'one of the greatest advantages of the Peace' was that he would 'now have leisure . . . to discourage profanenes and debauchery' (Ogg, *England in the Reigns*, 240). See also 2.4.27–33 below, Introduction p. xii, and Notes *BS* Prologue 10.

139 *À la mode de Paris*: in the fashion of Paris (French).

140 *between Ludgate and Aldgate*: in the confines of the City.

146 *the Groom-porter's*: a licensed gambling establishment.

147 *Newmarket*: the headquarters of horse-racing in England.

148 *Doctors' Commons*: the law courts which issued marriage licences and dealt with ecclesiastical, probate, and matrimonial law. Divorce and

alimony proceedings were notoriously humiliating for litigants and entertaining for scandal-mongers.

150 *the Bath*: Bath, Somerset, the most fashionable spa town in England, 'the resort of the sound, rather than the sick; the bathing is made more a sport and diversion, than a physical prescription for health; and the town is taken up in raffling, gaming, visiting, and in a word, all sorts of gallantry and levity' (Daniel Defoe, *A Tour through the Whole Island of Great Britain* [1724–6], Letter 6).

coach: first edn. 'watch'.

the Ring: a circle in Hyde Park where the fashionable promenaded, exercised their horses, and rode in carriages.

156 *Landen*: the Battle of Landen was won by the French in 1693. See *RO* 3.1.219–20. Standard recalls Sir Harry being in Flanders 'three or four years ago' (1.1.114). This suggests the date of the action should be 1697, which would coincide with the Peace of Ryswick and the earliest disbanding of land forces, but not with the Jubilee and the further demobilization of 1699.

157 *a Swiss musket*: the musket of a Swiss mercenary soldier.

159 *in statu quo*: as I was when I started (Latin).

166 *Louis le Grand*: Louis the Great (French), i.e. Louis XIV of France (reigned 1643–1715), whose aggressive policies made him the enemy of William of Orange, later William III.

178–80 SIR HARRY . . . *say you?*: omitted in later editions.

179 *St James's*: the area around St James's Square, between Jermyn Street and Pall Mall, a very fashionable district.

188 *breast*: later edns. 'breasts'.

190 *quality*: 'rank or station'.

227 *a Middlesex jury*: a Middlesex jury of 'cits' and tradesmen was likely to be unsympathetic towards duelling gallants.

228 *cast*: of the dice; relying on an acquittal would be a gamble.

240 *piercing a new pipe*: broaching a half-tun cask of wine. See Notes *RO* 1.1.283.

257 *your honour*: Sir Harry's baronetcy.

262–3 *twenty or thirty pieces*: twenty or thirty pounds in modern currency, then a considerable sum. The value of gold pieces issued in the reign of Charles II increased by about 20 per cent in the twenty years following his death.

263–4 *ensure her sound*: guarantee her free of infection. The exchange is notably brutal.

269 *I'll walk across the Park too*: it is not clear whether Clincher Senior is addressing his own footman or pretending to do so. In either case the

business must be conducted so that the audience understands the situation.

290–1 *like Olivia's . . . of Thames Street*: Manly, the hero of Wycherley's *The Plain Dealer* (1676), hears his mistress, Olivia, speak of him in these terms (2.1). The Customs House and numerous warehouses were in Thames Street.

292 *the Princess's chocolate-house*: in the Strand.

293 *Allons*: let us go (French).

1.2.14 *a second Eve*: Eve, the first woman, was also the first temptress. See Gen. 3: 6–17.

16–17 *The Practice of Piety*: by Lewis Bayley (d. 1632), the most popular devotional work in the seventeenth century.

27 *if she secures the main chance*: if she acts successfully in her own interests.

39–40 *who would take our post*: whoever wishes to relieve us of our duty.

48 *This commission*: Standard's commission as a colonel.

69 *nor coat a coward*: the 'coat' of a soldier was scarlet, that of a clergyman black. Lady Lurewell could have been deceived by either into an alliance with a coward.

98 *office-broker*: the sale of public offices was customary and less scandalous than now, but to make a business of brokering such sales was neither manly nor gentlemanly. See Notes *BS* 4.2.141–2.

127 *by Act of Parliament*: see Notes Dramatis Personae above.

2.1.14 *five hundred surgeons*: surgeons (rather than physicians) usually treated venereal disease. See Notes *RO* 4.2.167.

s.d. *Pointing*: either off-stage, or more probably at a woman in the audience.

20 *Jupiter Ammon*: Jupiter, the king of the Roman gods, was worshipped in the form of a ram under this title in Libya. Swearing by Jupiter (or Jove, his other name) came into practice in consequence of laws against blaspheming the Christian religion. Clincher Junior's recondite oath is an effective catchphrase.

21 *A gentlewoman! . . . whores in Town, sir*: this unobtrusively introduces a major theme of the play, the interchangeability (or at any rate the confusion) of ladies and gentlemen with whores and their clients. See Introduction p. xi.

31 *impertinent*: irrelevant, pointless.

34 *extravagant*: given to excess in behaviour, dress, etc., as well as 'free-spending'. Sir Harry is the authentic 'extravagant heir' in the play.

41–2 *Why the Jubilee . . . in the City*: the grand procession by land and water following the installation of a new Lord Mayor of London was notoriously vulgar.

45–6 *in Amsterdam to study poetry*: Dutch was regarded as an unpoetical language. Dryden complained that the Teutonic languages consisted 'mostly in monosyllables, and those encumbered with consonants' (*Of Dramatick Poesie and Other Critical Essays*, ed. George Watson (1962), ii. 38).

47–8 *through Muscovy to learn fashions*: the notorious visit to London of Tsar Peter the Great of Russia (reigned 1682–1725) in 1698 may have earned the Russians their reputation for not having much fashion sense.

2.2.1–2 *Like light . . . the coming day*: quoted from *Sophonisba*, i. 240–1 (1675) by Nathaniel Lee.

3 *this paper-kite*: Vizard's letter. The sense of a kite as a bird of prey is still strong.

5 *by the courtesy*: the children of peers above the rank of baron used nominal or 'courtesy' titles—a further conflation of Society and the sexual underworld.

15–16 *Ay, her 'cousin' . . . right procuress again*: 'cousin' was a typical brothel-madam's euphemism for one of her clients.

26 *my daughter*: a madam's (or 'mother's') term for one of her whores.

27 *bawd of Babylon*: Babylon (a coded name for imperial Rome) is personified in the New Testament as a woman robed in scarlet and 'the mother of the harlots' (Rev. 17: 5).

36 *character of*: reputation for.

50 *Business to impart!*: 'business' was a cant term for 'sexual intercourse'.

51–4 *singing birds . . . chirped in a cage*: Angelica naturally fails to appreciate that Sir Harry is referring to 'gold finches' in the sense of 'guineas' not 'birds'.

56 *What then, sir?*: Sir Harry assumes that this expression of puzzlement is a request for additional payment.

85 s.d. *Exeunt as into the house*: The normal entrances and exits in theatres of the period were through four doors, two on each side of the stage in front of the proscenium arch, and opening on to the forestage which projected about twenty feet into the pit and was the main acting area. By 1699 the forestage in the Drury Lane theatre had been reduced and there were only two entrance doors, one on each side of the stage. In this scene it is probable that the door on one side of the stage was understood to lead out of the house, and that on the other into it.

2.3.32 *in an honourable way . . . for me*: telling untruths did not compromise a lady's honour as sharing a bed with a man did.

42 *Sibyl's Leaves*: the sibyllae were prophetesses in the ancient world. The prophecies of the Cumaean Sibyl were inscribed on leaves, one collection

NOTES TO PAGES 25-9

of which was kept in Rome and was consulted only at the command of the Senate.

58 *'Let her wander', &c.*: I have been unable to identify the song. Presumably it is in the libertine tradition which took a relaxed attitude towards women's infidelities. Sir Harry sings it out of bravado.

59-60 *You are jilted ... that's all*: Standard insists that the song only increases Sir Harry's discomfort and implies that the latter has sung out of tune.

72 *Pall Mall*: a fashionable street running along the northern side of St James's Park.

the Holy Lamb: an inn.

92 *briskness*: keenness.

92-3 *the loves of ... different shapes*: Jove had the habit of seeking sexual partners in disguise (bull, swan, shower of gold) in the vain hope of deceiving his wife, Juno. See Notes *BS* 4.1.268-9.

93-5 *A legerdemain mistress ... your arms again*: a sleight-of-hand mistress, who disappears at the cry of 'presto' and a pass of the hand, and then is back again in your arms in an instant. See Introduction p. xvii.

97 *a broken voyage by your card*: a failed voyage because of the inadequacy of your compass-card, i.e. Vizard's letter of introduction at Lady Darling's.

2.4.5 *pretend*: profess, claim.

8 *the writings*: Lady Lurewell's contracts, title-deeds, securities, etc. From the 1690s the possession of such documents plays a key part in many comedies, notably *The Way of the World* (1700) by Congreve. See also *BS* 5.4.58-9.

13 *is reduced very low*: has very low reserves.

21 *a course*: of action in the courts.

31 *cut and long tail*: of every kind (literally 'docked and undocked', as of dogs and horses).

32-3 *I voted ... down the playhouse*: the societies for the reformation of manners tried to close the playhouses.

50 *Buss and guinea*: Smuggler proposes to pay for a kiss by passing a guinea from his mouth to Lady Lurewell's.

62 *Egad so, cod so*: 'egad' and 'cod' were disguised forms of 'God'. Such mild oaths are as frequent in Farquhar's dialogue as they were in contemporary speech.

66 *the next room*: see Notes 2.2.85 above.

68-9 *My life ... death to live*: to indicate their familiarity, Sir Harry and Lady Lurewell habitually greet one another in couplets as here.

72 *Machiavel*: schemer—after Niccolò Machiavelli (1469–1527) whose treatise, *The Prince* (1531) was interpreted as justifying unprincipled political intrigue.

78 *Ah! c'est . . . monde*: ah! it's the loveliest country in the world (French).

80 *Madame, vous . . . partout*: Madam, you see I follow you everywhere (French).

81 *O monsieur . . . obligée*: Sir, I'm very obliged to you (French).

82–3 *the Court . . . Marli, madam*: the French court moved frequently to Marli-le-roi, ten miles west of Paris.

85 *Notre Dame*: Our Lady (French)—the most celebrated church in Paris.

91 *En cavalier*: in the manner of a gallant (French).

93 *the beau monde*: fashionable society (French).

98 *as our army did Namur*: English and Dutch forces recaptured Namur from the French in 1695.

100 *forced to capitulate*: forced to seek a formal agreement. The term did not imply surrender.

102 *Montrez-moi votre chambre*: show me your bedroom (French).

103 *Attende, attende, un peu*: wait, wait a bit (French).

106 *treaties made in France are never kept*: by the First Partition Treaty (1698), Louis XIV surrendered the claim of the Dauphin to the throne of Spain on the death of the Spanish king, Charles II (reigned 1665–1700) who was childless. Spain denied the validity of this treaty, and it was widely understood that France would not be bound by it. By the same token no one in France was supposed to believe that a lover's promises were binding.

108 *Le mariage . . . mal*: marriage is a great evil (French).

118–19 *bills of exchange*: written instructions ordering a debtor to pay to the bearer the money owed to the drafter of the bill; an early form of bank note or traveller's cheque but without official or institutional backing.

129 *Royal Exchange*: the centre of business life in the City, situated between Threadneedle Street and Cornhill.

run the gauntlet: a military punishment; the man being punished ran between two lines of soldiers, and was beaten by them with ropes or sticks.

130 *brushed beavers and formal cravats*: Well-brushed beaver-hide hats and formal neckties—correct attire in the City.

140–1 *pestered next term . . . and attorneys*: when the law courts next sit, Sir Harry will be pestered by civil and criminal suits for damages and costs, and by solicitors and attorneys.

2.5 S.D. *Scene changes to another room in the same house.* Scenery, consisting of a series of shutters on each side of the stage to the rear of the proscenium arch, led the eye to the back of the stage area where the shutters came together to terminate the stage picture. These could be rolled back to reveal another in position behind them. See Colin Visser, 'Scenery and Technical Design', *London Theatre World, 1660–1800*, ed. Robert D. Hume (1980), 73.

33–4 *Pardon sir . . . a gentleman*: Smuggler is surprised by the apology, knowing Sir Harry does not consider him a gentleman.

48 *Signor*: Sir (Italian).

49 *Frappez, frappez*: hit him, hit him (French).

51–2 *Frappez plus rudement, frappez*: hit him harder, hit him (French).

71–2 *Let scholars . . . fools commence*: let scholars trouble their brains by working out the mood and tense of verbs and graduate ['commence'] as fools by the sheer force of their reason.

74 *summum bonum*: supreme good (Latin), a term in scholastic philosophy.

3.1.15 *property*: 'a mere means to an end; an instrument, a tool, a catspaw' (*OED*).

25 *plies at the Blue Posts*: carries on his trade at the Blue Posts inn.

30 *prevent us*: stop us [duelling].

36 *People call me so*: Tom Errand is a working name—his wife calls him Timothy (4.1.61).

59–62 *bought this lace . . . deal boards*: Flanders lace was particularly fine, but its import was forbidden. As in his references to Dutch poetry and Muscovite fashions (2.1.45–8), Sir Harry teases Clincher Senior with the idea that in timber-rich Norway lace is made from the shavings of pine wood.

70 *swimming girdle*: early form of life-jacket or water-wings, made of cork and/or bladders.

73 *goes me, I*: I go; an obsolete, vulgar usage—the so-called ethical dative.

74 *bear-baiting*: a sport in which dogs were tested for courage by being set on a chained bear.

75 *bona roba*: courtesan; a good piece of stuff (Italian).

77 *Seigniour Angle . . . Seigniora*: Mr Englishman . . . madam—Clincher Senior's inept attempts at Italian.

78–9 *Russell Street*: near Covent Garden, where prostitutes plied their trade.

80 *bravo*: pimp (Italian).

83 *bull-dog*: slang term for a firearm.

85–6 *a beau behind the scenes*: a beau who has slipped back-stage to meet the actresses.

88–9 *Only a brace . . . seven Italians a week*: a possible obscenity, according to Kenny, 'bullets' being another word for 'balls', and 'shoot' for 'have sex with'. Clincher Senior, whether he knows it or not, is proposing to kill a pimp and have sex with his whore on a daily basis.

91 *Zauns*: 'Zouns' is only us'd by the disbanded Officers and Bullies: but 'Zauns' is the beaux' pronunciation (*Love and a Bottle*, 2.2.27–8).

96–7 *cast away*: wrecked or stranded.

98 *whips*: first edn. 'whip', but all other verbs in this sentence are in the colloquial form.

104 *Civita Vecchia*: a port, some forty miles from Rome.

107 *before he goes abroad*: the grand tour was often said to turn young men into accomplished asses. See Prologue 17.

3.2.1–7 *Unhappy state . . . our conversation*: an important protest against the constraints laid on women's utterances, in life as well as in the theatre. The freedom of witty innuendo enjoyed, for example, by the women characters in Wycherley's *The Country Wife* (1675) was no longer possible in the post-Collier climate. See Introduction p. xii.

6 *be*. Omitted in first edn.

19 *You may march, sir*: you may take yourself off, sir.

47 *gallantry*: from the 1670s 'gallantry' had had the sense 'amorous intrigue'. The rhetoric of gallantry in the older sense—'courtliness or polite attention to ladies' (*OED*)—which Sir Harry is resorting to is thus as debased as the slang terms of brothel life.

86 *Je vous remercie*: thank you (French).

102 *the Piazza of Covent Garden*: the arcade, designed by Inigo Jones, running along the northern and eastern sides of Covent Garden was incorrectly called a piazza—properly 'a square' (Italian). The two scenes that follow are based on *The Adventures of Covent Garden*. See Introduction p. viii.

106 *No fair play I can assure you*: either 'No, Sir Harry—I will not play foul with the lady, I will play fair', or 'I can assure you, Sir Harry, I will not play fair.' It is for the actor to voice this ambiguity if he can.

3.3 S.D. *the balcony*: each of the four entrance doors in front of the proscenium arch had a balcony above it. When the stage area at Drury Lane was reduced (see Notes 2.2.85 above), two of these balconies became boxes. The other remained available for balcony scenes such as this.

1–4 *that daring reason . . . woman's eyes!*: that over-ambitious reason which claims a right to question the works of God, but yields to our weakest passions, gives to foolish love the kind of unqualified faith which is due only to God, and devotes itself with blind religious fervour to the eyes of faithless woman! It is unclear how ironical the rather solemn Standard is being in thus misapplying the vocabulary of religion.

11 S.D. [*Standard*] *goes . . . with Clincher Senior*: Standard exits by the door beneath the balcony as Lady Lurewell and Clincher come down from the balcony off-stage.

3.4 S.D. *The scene changes . . . dining-room*: it was an accepted convention that actors could exit as from the street through a door, and then return on stage by the same door as if entering the house (and vice versa). In this case, however, a pulling back of shutters behind the proscenium arch to reveal an interior scene is indicated (see Notes 2.5. S.D. above), and Standard's entrance is delayed. Nevertheless, Kenny does not count this as a change of scene.

32 *one look belies another*: one exchange of glances contradicts another.

46 *O woman in perfection*: how typical of a woman!

85 *in labour of horns*: labouring to bring forth [cuckold's] horns.

113 *Fort bon*: excellent (French). 1704 edn. 'forthoon' which Kenny glosses as 'forth on, onwards, forwards'.

117–18 *a collar of bandoleers*: a broad belt worn over the chest and shoulder containing changes of powder for a musket.

136 *managed*: see Note to l. 238 below.

137–9 *Thus the . . . expense*: the quotation is from 'A Letter from Artemezia in the Towne to Chloe in the Countrey', 224–5, *The Poems of John Wilmot, Earl of Rochester*, ed. Keith Walker (1984) 89. See Introduction p. xviii.

146 *mankind*: the male sex.

170–1 *a heavy, pedantic . . . in their behaviour*: a reflection on Farquhar's experiences at Trinity College, Dublin?

185 *Cassandra*: a French romance in ten volumes, published 1642–5, by Gautier de Coste, Seigneur de la Calprenède (1610?–1663). In such romances, love is inseparable from high-flown notions of honour.

209–10 *sole heiress . . . pounds a year*: a considerable fortune; see *RO* 2.2.14–15. As sole executrice of her father's will, Lady Lurewell almost has the legal standing of a man.

214 *done some execution*: an expression often used of a soldier killing a number of the enemy in hand-to-hand fighting.

222 *manage*: 'to cause (persons, animals, etc.) to submit to one's control' (*OED*). The word was frequently used of putting a horse through its paces; Lady Lurewell uses it with some relish (226).

238 *hansel*: initiate auspiciously—even though Smuggler has implied that he has put his female garments to good use on other occasions.

240–2 *Fortune . . . brain*: Fortuna, the Roman goddess of Fortune controlled human destinies by turning her wheel.

4.1.29–30 *understand the languages*: Latin, French, and possibly Greek and Italian.

57–8 *some means . . . your satisfaction*: the first hint of the plot against Lady Lurewell. See 4.2.55–6.

61 *Timothy*: see Notes 3.1.36 above.

74 S.D. *constable*: parish constables were not members of a regular force and were traditionally represented, like Dull in Shakespeare's *Love's Labour's Lost* and Dogberry in *Much Ado About Nothing*, as self-important and stupid.

78–9 *Murder and robbery . . . be abused*: street violence was common and the subject of much complaint in pamphlets from the societies for the reformation of manners, but their complaints, like the constable's, were directed more at the poor than at the upper-class rakes, who usually got away with their thuggery.

96 *Gemini*: the Twins (Latin), the modern 'jiminy', a mild oath. The Twins, Castor and Pollux, were sons of Leda by Jupiter who came to her in the form of a swan. They were gods of hunting, boxing, and horsemanship.

102 *Newgate*: a prison in the City.

103 *to the Jubilee now indeed*: probably a reference to the large, merrymaking crowds that assembled to watch public executions.

109–11 *You shall sa, sa . . . to be damned*: 'sa, sa'—from '*ça, ça*' ('here, here' [French])—was a cry used by fencers when delivering a thrust; a '*coupée*' was a dance-step often incorporated into an elaborate bow. Sir Harry uses technical terms from fencing and dancing to set up a contrast between himself and Standard. 'Dancing being that which gives graceful Motions all the life, and above all Manliness . . . cannot be learn'd too early . . . Fencing . . . [is] looked upon as so necessary [a part] of Breeding, that it would be thought a great omission to neglect [it]' (John Locke, *Some Thoughts concerning Education* (1693), paragraphs 184, 186).

118 *Penelope*: the wife of Odysseus, who was faithful to him during his twenty-year absence from home. See Notes *RO* Prologue 1.

127 *but his honesty . . . his knavery*: his honesty has only to be mistrusted and his knavery is spoiled.

129–30 *which, if I . . . of their security*: if I doubted your word and honour, that very distrust would cancel the obligations to me which they put upon you.

133 *a certain project*: completing his design upon Angelica.

138 *Probatum est*: it has been proved (Latin).

147 *the Pope*: as reputed Antichrist, a figure of fear and horror in the popular Protestant imagination.

151 *he looks like a Jesuit already*: the Jesuits had a reputation for diabolical cunning and deceit. See Notes *BS* 3.1.55.

153 *cross the Garden*: move to the south side of Covent Garden.

154 *pretty secure*: either because he could then take refuge in the Savoy, once a place of sanctuary, later a hang-out for thieves and debtors (see also Notes *RO* 3.1.126); or because, as the presence of his wife and neighbours suggests, he would then be on home territory.

157 *parliament man*: Member of Parliament.

167 *O crimini*: 'a vulgar expression of astonishment' (*OED*).

168–9 *I'm heir though. Speak sirrah*: first edn. 'I'm heir. Tho' speak sirrah.' I have followed Archer. The alternative is to read 'tho'' in the archaic sense of 'then', but in that sense the word is always an adverb of time, and never means 'in that case', the sense in which 'Then' is used in Clincher Junior's next speech.

187 *compos mentis*: of sound mind (Latin). Clincher Junior knows that the phrase has something to do with the laws of inheritance; it refers, of course, to the state of mind of a testator making a will.

4.2.11 *family*: household, including the servants.

12 *closet*: a small room, not a cupboard.

14 *clown*: 'a countryman, or peasant; a boor . . . an ignorant, uncouth, ill-bred man' (*OED*).

15 S.D. *sings*: on the evidence of broadsheet versions of this song, Kenny suggests that the singer in the first run was not Wilks. The song was set to music for the first performance by Daniel Purcell (1660–1714). For a later production in Dublin, it was reset by Richard Leveridge (1670?–1758).

25 *'No'*: I have punctuated the second set of 'No's as Damon's refusal to consider Celia's virginity, but this is speculative.

29 *key*: pronounced 'kay'. See Notes Epilogue 18 below.

43–5 *As pure and . . . beauty fires*: see Notes 2.4.68–9 above.

48 *mistresses'*: the first edn. has no apostrophe and may be read as 'mistress's'.

53 *industrious in your profuseness*: work so hard at being lavish and wasteful.

55–6 *To design . . . will succeed*: first edn. makes the whole speech an aside, but the first half is clearly addressed to Lady Lurewell. This is the second hint of Sir Harry's plot.

61 *free*: Lady Lurewell uses the word in the sense of 'open', Sir Harry in a sexual sense.

74 *couple of shillings*: nominally the equivalent of two five-pence pieces in modern coinage.

76–7 *What are you . . . my pockets for?*: Parly is of course planting the spoons on his person.

79 S.D. *Puts him into the closet*: i.e. the stage door opposite the one by which he and Vizard enter.

88–9 *like the Persian . . . of the world*: it was a capital offence to approach Ahasuerus, King of the Medes and Persians, without a royal summons. See Esther 4: 11.

99 *as an actor possessed with a poet*: as an actor is in effect possessed by the poet whose words he has to speak. Anti-stage propaganda freely used the language of demonic possession to describe stage performance.

112 *tuneful nose*: the nasal singing of hymns and recitation of prayers was associated with Dissenters.

131–2 *warm the statue . . . of an Epicure*: the Stoics, a school of philosophers, founded by Zeno (*c*.300 BC), believed in the pursuit of virtue independently of pleasure and were popularly thought of as grimly self-denying. Epicureans, following the apparently atheistical atomism of Democritus (*c*.460 BC), believed in pleasure as the only value and were reputedly unabashed hedonists.

138 *interest*: i.e. self-interest.

143 *died of a gout*: gout was thought to be a consequence of over-indulgence, particularly at table.

154 *purchase*: to procure (in any way); to take possession of.

156–7 *I'll cozen . . . deed of conveyance*: I'll trick the old miser into making over his capital and conveying his real estate to me.

177 *City Liberties*: a 'liberty' was 'a district within the limits of a county, but exempt from the jurisdiction of the sheriff, and having a separate commission of the peace' (*OED*), or 'a district beyond the bounds of the city, which [was] subject to the control of the municipal authority' (*OED*). Gaining access to either would ensure that Smuggler would not have to face legal authorities unsympathetic to an alderman such as himself. See 5.2.11–13.

S.D. *close*: in hiding.

182–3 *the cunning-man*: a fortune-teller, such as Kite pretends to be (*RO* 4.2). The butler's reliance on such help is consistent with his fear of witches.

191 *a midwife*: midwives frequently operated as procuresses as Mrs Mandrake does in *The Twin Rivals*.

204–5 *some Covent Garden . . . James's devil*: the 'devil' was either a rogue from Covent Garden or a person of honour from St James's.

226 *him!*: either Lady Lurewell or Farquhar forgets that the servants do not know Smuggler's real sex.

5.1.4 *without reproach to your modesty*: 'young women are seldom permitted to make their own Choice; their Friends Care and Experience are thought safer Guides to them, than their own Fancies; and their Modesty often forbiddeth them to refuse when their Parents recommend' ('The Lady's New Year's Gift: or, Advice to a Daughter', *The Complete Works of George Savile, First Marquess of Halifax*, ed. Walter Raleigh (1912), 7–8).

38–9 *swallowed cupids like loaches*: cupids were mischievous winged boys, frequently depicted as attendants on Cupid, the god of love. Loaches were eaten to generate a thirst.

53 *quarter my coat-of-arms with yours*: combine the coats-of-arms of our respective families. If Sir Harry thought Angelica was a woman of honour this would be a proposal of marriage. As it is, he is simply expressing his determination to go to bed with her.

56–7 *'Burgundy's' the word . . . will ensue*: the battle-cry is 'Burgundy' and the killing will follow.

63 S.D. *pelting*: hitting vigorously.

64 *charmed the dragon*: in classical mythology, the golden apples of the Hesperides were guarded by the dragon, Ladon, slain by Atlas at the request of the hero, Hercules. Sir Harry's gold has put Angelica's protectors to sleep.

69 *conjure*: solemnly appeal to.

81 *generous*: 'gallant, magnanimous' (*OED*)—gentlemanly in the best sense.

97 *alarmed*: stirred the fighting spirit in.

101–4 *Your surprising conduct . . . part, my soul*: the run of subordinate clauses requires an 'and' either before or after 'disdaining common fuel'.

118–19 *But since I can't . . . at a stroke*: only the conqueror of Asia was supposed to be able to untie the Gordian Knot. Before his Asian campaign Alexander the Great cut it open with his sword.

128 *scruple no price*: not to be niggardly in the price offered.

172–3 *and virtue . . . purer mind*: virtue purifies and intensifies the pleasures of love, so as to feast a refined sensibility. The sexual inexperience of a bride was commonly thought to increase her attractiveness to her experienced but (of course) reformed husband.

Revised text

See Introduction p. xiv.

83 *Tall ti . . . didum*: Sir Harry mocks Angelica's high-flown iambics.

85 *The Rival Queens*: *The Rival Queens; or, The Death of Alexander the Great* (1677) by Lee was the first heroic play in blank verse, though it retained the ranting rhetoric of its rhymed predecessors. The queens were the gentle Statira and the violent Roxana.

86 *O my Statira! . . . eyes on me*: *The Rival Queens* 3.1.272–3; 'thy' should read 'thine', a correction made in later editions, though as Sir Harry is quoting from memory the lapse is understandable.

87 *beau in buskins*: a beau assuming the high tragic manner. 'Buskins' were the footwear worn in tragedy.

97–104 *but pray, madam . . . woman with virtue?*: Rothstein (69) notes that this speech is reminiscent of Falstaff's soliloquy on honour in Shakespeare's *1 Henry IV*, 5.1.

101–2 *hire you . . . a church?*: enclosed benches in churches and chapels were available for hire and were thus a sign of the social standing of an individual or a family. Church-going was the occasion of much social display. See *BS* 2.2.21–33.

114–15 *a rich escritoir . . . Prayer Book*: a possible source of Pope's description of Belinda's dressing-table, *The Rape of the Lock*, i. 138. See Introduction n. 15.

121–3 *but these women . . . their extortion*: but these women will force me to become a Member of Parliament in spite of my distaste for the place, so that I can introduce a Bill prohibiting their extortionate prices.

126 *make my markets*: do my bargaining.

131 *will you take it?*: the emphasis evidently falls on 'you'.

141 *double entendie*: an Anglicized form of the absolute *double entente*, indelicate pun (French).

147 *minuet*: 'a slow, stately dance, in triple measure, for two dancers' (*OED*). The sexual implication is obvious.

155 *sent him on*: first and later edns. 'sent him of'.

162–3 *à la mode . . . votre occupation*: in the French way—[*aloud*] I judge your employment (French).

165 *à la mode Londres*: in the London way (French).

168 *presenting friends*: friends who give presents, especially money, i.e. generous patrons of Lady Darling's 'house'.

168–9 *imperial tea*: tea of an officially approved quality.

188 *stand to 't*: be bound by it.

221 *the Old Bailey?*: the criminal court near Newgate prison. Both were replaced in 1902 by the Central Criminal Court.

5.2.1–8 *How severe . . . a halfpenny apiece*: there was a considerable market for the confessions of criminals and for ballads about their crimes, particularly among the crowds that came to witness their executions.

29 *full-bottom wig*: a shoulder-length wig or longer, worn only by gentlemen.

31–2 *to swing in masquerade*: to be hanged in fancy dress.

341

48 *a hard taking*: a difficult thing to accept. There may be a reference to the obsolete sense of 'taking' as 'receipt, wage'.

49 *say grace to the gallows*: say 'Grace' before being hanged—instead of before a meal.

49–51 *swung handsomely . . . ungenteel*: noblemen had the right to be hanged by a rope made of silk, rather than the rough hemp with which lowborn criminals were throttled.

59 *a commonwealth*: a republic. See Introduction p. xx.

65–6 *I'm twenty thousand strong*: I have the strength of twenty thousand pounds to support me.

5.3.10 *like the sun, grow warmer by reflection*: the heat of the rays of the sun were thought to grow warmer by reflection.

17–18 *the general composition*: the occasion at the beginning of the world when atoms joined together to form bodies of all sorts. This atheistical or Epicurean account of the creation in general, and of women in particular, aligns Sir Harry with the sceptical libertinism of writers and rakes such as Rochester.

19 *with ecstasy she*: all early authorities, as well as Stonehill and Kenny, read 'with ecstasy. The'. I follow Archer's sensible emendation.

63–4 *if you should . . . the sheets*: grossly insulting. Clincher Junior envisages Angelica suffering the irrational appetites of pregnancy, or, Kenny suggests, of adolescent anaemia.

68 *Send for the dean and chapter*: senior clergymen who could exorcize his brother's ghost.

85 *the bear-garden*: where bears were baited.

170 *Manly*: I see no good reason for accepting Archer's suggestion that Lady Lurewell was based on the playwright and novelist, Mary de la Riviere Manly (1663–1724).

245–6 *Would you be thought*: if you wish to be thought of as.

Epilogue

3 *Hippolito's*: a tavern in Covent Garden.

4 *th' Rose*: the Rose Tavern, Russell Street, close to the Drury Lane Theatre.

6 *in number three*: in a side-room, where a couple might eat, drink, and enjoy each other's company undisturbed.

7 *if Phillis aught gainsays*: if Phillis resists in any way—either sexually or in his judgement of the play. Phillis was a name common in pastoral poetry. The use of the name in this context is mildly ironic.

8 *murders Bays*: tears the work of the playwright to pieces. 'Bays' was a common name for a writer.

10 *Locket's*: a tavern close to the Rummer.

14 *Monteith*: a punchbowl with a scalloped brim.

18 *tea*: pronounced 'tay'. See Notes 4.2.29 above and Pope's *The Rape of the Lock*, iii. 7–8: 'Here thou, great Anna, whom three Realms obey | Dost sometimes Counsel take, and sometimes Tea.'

22–4 *too well . . . steal the play*: a jibe already made in the Prologue.

26 *Among our . . . Cheapside*: merchants and clerks in the City.

28 *world*: Archer suggests that Farquhar pronounced this word with two syllables—'worruld'.

33 *censure*: judgement (without any implication of disapproval).

42 *Flatter us here*: by applauding.

The Twin Rivals

Title page
Sic vos non vobis: thus you [labour] but not for yourself (Latin).

Dramatis Personae

BALDERDASH: crude cocktail of incompatible liquors.

TEAGUE: Anglicized spelling of the Irish name Tadgh; a mildly contemptuous name for any Irishman. See Introduction p. xv and Notes 3.2.16–17 below.

AURELIA: Chrysalis (Latin).

MANDRAKE: Kenny argues that this character 'was called "Midnight" on stage . . . even during the first run' (i. 490), a possible prompt-book copy in the Folger Library having this emendation written-in in hand. Certainly 'Midnight' was the name used in all authoritative texts of the *Works* from 1728. It is also an appropriate name for a midwife and bawd. A mandrake is any plant in the genus mandragora, the roots of such plants being in roughly human shape, and as Kenny points out, the citations in *OED* 'tie the word to men'. However, the part was played by a man in the first production, and mandrake lore is less male-centred than Kenny suggests. Thus in *The Herbal or General History of Plants* (1597) by John Gerard (1545–1612) mandrakes are said to grow under the gallows 'where the matter that hath fallen from the dead body, hath given it the shape of a man: and the matter of a woman, the substance of a female plant' (l. 281). In 'Goe, and catch a falling star', Donne writes of getting 'with child a mandrake roote' (l. 2). On balance, I have chosen to keep the name printed in the first edition, for even if the Folger copy is indeed a prompt-book copy, it does not follow that the name 'Mandrake' in the first edition did not represent Farquhar's original intention. Here may be another example of the fluidity of his text. Certainly the oddity of the name is consistent with a highly original idea brilliantly executed. See Introduction pp. ix, x, xxiii.

Dedication

Henry Bret: (d. 1724), a witty man-about-town, a devotee of the theatre and briefly a lieutenant-colonel of foot (1705). He had the Drury Lane patent from 1707 and was a member of the Whiggish literary circle around Addison, a sympathetic and useful patron for Farquhar to cultivate.

1–3 *by your place . . . the subject*: as an MP (first elected 1701), Bret was required to receive petitions from the public and seek to redress their grievances.

5–6 *dedications . . . of the world*: only the published text of a play had a dedicatee.

9–10 *Books, like . . . and current*: like metals which only acquire value as current coin when stamped with the face of a sovereign, so books need to be stamped with the effigy of a patron.

Preface

2–3 *Mr Collier's Short View*: see Notes *CC* Preface 19.

11 *poetical justice*: the judicious distribution of rewards and punishments to good and evil characters at the end of a play. The term was probably introduced into English by Thomas Rymer (1641–1713).

11–15 *the greater share . . . of the subject*: 'poetic licence' allowed writers to depart from strict adherence to scientific or historical truth, and the confining and morally conservative 'rules' of neoclassical criticism. English playwrights were less strict than the French in these matters, who, Dryden wrote, 'follow the Ancients too servilely in the mechanic rules, and we assume too much licence to ourselves' (Watson, *Of Dramatick Poesie*, ii. 163). The Whiggish Farquhar links this alleged licence (a shade facetiously perhaps) with 'the liberty of the subject'. See also Introduction p. xviii.

26 *to that end of the Town*: out of the City to the West End.

30 *a midwife*: Mandrake. See Notes *CC* 4.2.191.

40 *I made her only nominal*: Clelia is named by the other characters but does not appear on stage.

46–7 *he was no sooner . . . his mind*: see Introduction p. xv.

47 *in statu quo*: in her original [unmarried] state (Latin).

48–51 *'tis application . . . happen to fit*: a person becomes an ass when the name is applied to him and its appropriateness is recognized; characters in plays are not based on specific originals; they are like second-hand clothes waiting to be tried on. In effect, if the cap fits wear it. Long Lane between Smithfield and Aldergate contained many second-hand clothes dealers.

50 *those*: first edn. 'that'.

57–8 *too high . . . for the buskin*: too exalted [morally and socially] for comedy, but not serious enough for tragedy. Low-life characters were deemed appropriate for farce; tragedy was expected to present the actions of kings, queens, and people of exalted rank.

71 *start*: outburst.

85 *Mr Longueville*: Archer identifies Longueville as William Longueville (1639–1721) whom Stonehill represents as an Irish fencing master.

90 *foreign assistance*: outside help. Farquhar had been accused of plagiarism. He is not referring to texts in foreign languages.

Prologue

Mr Motteux: see Notes CC 1.1.98. In lines addressed 'To my Friend, the Author' in *Beauty in Distress* (1698), a tragedy by Motteux, Dryden responded to the attacks of Collier and his associates, and praised Motteux for not being 'thinly regular' like the French.

Mr Wilks: see Notes CC Preface 24.

1 *this warring age*: the King of Spain died in October 1700, leaving all his realms to Philip, Duke of Anjou, grandson of Louis XIV of France, rather than to the Habsburg claimant, Charles. The Dauphin, whose claim by strict primogeniture was stronger than Anjou's, was also excluded as the will expressly prohibited the union of the thrones of Spain and France. It also, quite properly, rejected the Partition Treaties (see Notes CC 2.4.106), by which the powers had proposed to carve up the Spanish dominions. In contravention of the latter, Louis not only accepted the will but also reneged on undertakings at Ryswick not to recognize the claims of James, Prince of Wales, to the Scottish, English, and Irish thrones. The War of Spanish Succession was thus about to break out when William III died in 1702. It lasted until 1713. Philip became King of Spain, and France finally abandoned the Stuarts.

3–4 *New plays . . . they fear*: before they are acted, new plays are like towns surrounded by an army and afraid of a siege.

5 *'forlorn hope'*: 'a picked body of men, detached to the front, to begin an attack' (*OED*).

13 *snip-snap*: 'sharp repartee' (*OED*).

15 *The next*: the second act of the play; so 'the third' (17), 'the fourth' (20), and 'the last' (23) refer to the third, fourth, and fifth acts.

17–19 *feints, mines . . . confound*: the play and its critics engage in false troop movements to deceive each other, and dig tunnels under each other's defences. The critics, however, manage to get under the play and blow it up.

22 *insult our counterscarp*: assault the outer wall supporting the covering over our defensive ditch.

24 *poet-governor*: the author is represented as the governor of the town under siege.

27 *Don and Monsieur*: i.e. Spaniard and Frenchman. Unlike the earlier war, Spain and France were now allies.

28 *Venlo*: a fort on the Meuse, captured by British forces in 1702.

Liège: an important citadel captured by British forces in 1702; the pronunciation is Anglicized to make good the rhyme.

29 *Viva Spagnia*: long live Spain (Spanish).

Vive France: long live France (French).

30 *Quartier . . . Senor*: quarter! Sir! Quarter! Ah! Sir! (French and Spanish).

37 *generous terms*: when they are defeated by the critics.

40 *the third . . . the sixth*: the author's benefit nights. Audiences at *The Twin Rivals* were poor. See Introduction p. viii.

1.1.4 *Were I an honest brute*: recalls the opening of Rochester's 'Satire', 'Were I (who to my cost already am | One of those strange prodigious Creatures Man) | A Spirit free, to choose for my own share, | What Case of Flesh, and Blood, I pleas'd to weare, | I'd be a Dog, a Monkey, or a Bear, | Or any thing but that vain Animal, | Who is so proud of being rational' (Walker (ed.), *Poems of John Wilmot*, 91–2). See Notes *CC* 3.4.137–9 and Introduction pp. xvii–xviii

12 *stoicism*: see Notes *CC* 4.2.131–2.

17 *something else*: i.e. venereal disease.

21 *break her windows*: rakes frequently broke the windows of brothels, sometimes in revenge for contracting venereal disease from their occupants, sometimes as a form of gentlemanly amusement. See *RO* 3.1.40–1.

24 *are*: a common grammatical error.

25 *Vin te koop*: wine for sale (Flemish).

26 *bush*: the traditional sign of a tavern.

a decoy to trade: a device for attracting passers-by, as a decoy draws down birds it is painted to look like.

28 *put up an affront*: put up with an injury or insult.

31 *Flying Post*: a newspaper started in 1695.

31–2 *physical advertisements?*: advertisements for medicines or other cures (particularly for venereal disease).

34 *pit-masks*: prostitutes working the theatres.

hedge-taverns: down-market taverns.

35 *the Ring*: see Notes *CC* 1.1.150.

Pawlet's: probably Pawlett's Great Dancing Room near Rowgate (Archer followed by Kenny) but Stonehill thinks 'this would not have been mentioned in the same breath with the Ring, the Court and the Park' and suggests Pawlet or Powlet House (i.e. Winchester House, Old Broad Street).

35–6 *the Park*: see Notes *CC* 1.1.

50–1 *Doctor Chamberlain*: Hugh Chamberlain (1664–1728), 'the man midwife ... known for his achievements in two unconnected spheres, finance and obstetrics' (Ogg, *England in the Reigns*, 431).

54 *communicate*: an ironic use of the word, which frequently implied the imparting of confidential information.

55 *Gazette*: a twice-weekly official journal; a news-sheet.

72 *Covent Garden*: see Notes *CC* 3.1.78–9.

76–7 *like a branch . . . grow so crooked*: Young Wouldbe is like a cutting grafted on to the Wouldbe family tree and growing crookedly in consequence.

94 *Because he thinks . . . should be so*: either 'Because he thinks it reasonable that he should know how I feel about him', or 'Because he thinks, that, in reason, someone in my position would inevitably feel the way I do'.

100–1 *by drinking him up to his dignity*: by inducing him to consume lordly quantities of alcohol.

112 *my sisters' fortunes*: the dowries due to his sisters under their parents' marriage settlement and his father's will. Early editions all read 'sister's'. See Notes *BS* 2.1.12–14.

129 *turned the pad upon*: became a thief so as to rob.

138–9 *an equality*: i.e. of rank and wealth.

143 *club of friendship*: equal share in the expenses of friendship.

147 *second*: chief supporter in a duel.

157 *copious look*: fat—in more ways than one.

165 *pledge you*: a pun, 'pledge' meaning both 'drink to the health of' and 'guarantee future payment with a pledge or deposit'. Young Wouldbe may raise his glass at this point.

174 *of*: omitted in first edn.

201 *I have an honour for*: I have respect for.

221–2 *pit-partridges*: whores in the pit of a theatre.

225 *Thou sophisticated tun of iniquity*: you adulterated wine-barrel of wickedness. Recalls Prince Hal's speech to Falstaff in Shakespeare's *1 Henry IV*, 2.5.

238 *conjure down*: back into Hell, the reverse of 'conjure up'.

243 *Broad*: Jacob Broad, a well-known bailiff.

1.2.8–9 *the first of April*: Sir James had sex with his adulterously pregnant wife on All Fools' Day. The play's first performance was 14 December; Farquhar's obstetrics are accurate.

14 *oblige mankind*: a pun on 'mankind' in the sense of 'humankind' and 'the male sex'.

40–2 *Are not you . . . upon your head?*: the room where Richmore and Clelia made love.

48 *sad*: a usually jocular way of saying 'deplorable'.

61–4 *I think she . . . at an easy rate*: having only a modest dowry, Aurelia has her virtue to give her value to a suitor. Once she loses it, she will become available cheaply.

72 *young Templer*: student of law in chambers in the Temple.

81–2 *had she made . . . yielded sooner*: had she regarded the action as a meritorious (and not a shameful) one, she would have gone to bed with me sooner.

91–4 *making over . . . when you will*: Richmore will be like a landlord who denies himself unrestricted use of his property when he lets it, but still has right of occasional access.

114 *distracts me*: drives me mad.

120–1 *any living in my gift*: parishes and other offices in the Church of England were known as 'livings', those who held them as 'incumbents'; the income which attached to them varied considerably. Colleges, noblemen, and various gentlemen, as well as the Crown, had the right to nominate appointees to vacant livings, which could be sold to the highest bidder or presented gratis to a favoured candidate.

121–2 *like the cure . . . there before?*: enjoy the living the less because he had a predecessor? The root meaning of 'incumbent' is 'that which lies on top of, or presses down upon'.

127 *'mother'*: see Notes *CC* Prologue 27 and *CC* 2.2.26.

135–6 *dear of*: expensive at.

2.1. S.D. *the Park*: see Notes *CC* 1.1.

34 *wars with heaven like the giants of old*: Jupiter, having killed his father, Cronus, and established himself as king of the gods, had to fight with most of his father's surviving brothers, the Titans, or 'giants of old'. He won.

42 *clean well-furnished*: smart, well-presented.

61 *disappears all the . . . like a woodcock*: wars could be fought only in the summer. The woodcock only winters in England.

78 *put in*: get a word in.

82 *wounding a man in the Park*: it was forbidden to draw swords in St James's Park.

83–4 *a Vigo business ... at once*: James Butler, second Duke of Ormonde (1665–1745) and Admiral Sir George Rooke (1650–1709) captured a Spanish treasure fleet in Vigo Bay, 1702, by breaking the boom protecting it.

84–7 *Sir, if you ... I beseech you, sir*: sir, if you are only bantering, let my cousin have her share in your wit. If, however, you are addressing me in particular, please be more respectful—less plain speaking, I beg you, sir.

2.2.28 *Be a lord to choose*: choose to be a lord, so that you can make what other choices you will.

55 *this potent inspiration*: i.e. her bottle.

85 *a' course*: as a matter of course.

104 *this trick*: this trifle, i.e. Clelia's letter to Richmore.

2.3.12 *Jermyn Street*: running parallel with Piccadilly, Jermyn Street was very fashionable. Lord Gouty's steward has bought himself into Society in grand style.

42 *ability*: power—as the heir.

58 *October 10, new style*: since 1582, European countries had used a calendar which corrected an error in the Julian or imperial Roman calendar. This had overestimated the length of a year by 11 minutes, or 1 day in every 126 years. This 'new style' of dating was adopted in Britain in 1751.

124–5 *a cargo of witnesses and usquebaugh*: giving false evidence for mercenary or other motives was common in the late seventeenth and early eighteenth centuries. See Introduction pp. xiv–xx. Poor Irish immigrants were particularly easy to persuade into this way of making money. The Irish invented usquebaugh ('the water of life'—Irish), or whiskey.

2.4.9 *so high a gamester?*: a gambler who plays for such high stakes, the word 'gamester' having sexual connotations like those now attaching to the word 'tramp' (cf. the modern usage 'on the game').

17 *a standing army upon us*: in peacetime the mere existence of an army had long been deemed 'Dang'rous to Liberty, and desir'd alone | By Kings, who seek an Arbitrary Throne' (Dryden, 'Sigismonda and Guiscardo' (1700), 600–1). See also Notes *CC* Dramatis Personae

39 *Marshal Boufflers*: Louis François, duc de Boufflers, Marshal of France (1644–1711) had been forced to retreat before Marlborough's troops throughout the 1702 campaign. See Notes Prologue 28 above.

41 *capitulations*: see Notes *CC* 2.4.100 and *RO* 1.1.174–5.

50 *You han't five hundred pounds to give?*: the exact sum for which Melissa was apparently prepared to surrender to Worthy before she came into her money. See *RO* 1.1.175–7.

51–2 *she dwindles to a perfect basset-bank*: she will have become as accessible as a gambling house where basset is played.

56 *in the presence*: of the sovereign.

2.5.11 *intervals*: of lucidity.

38–9 *a dead hand holds fastest*: lands held *mortmain* (literally 'by a dead hand'—Norman French) were inalienable. Subtleman's pun is brutal and legally exact.

52 S.D. *Subscribes*: appends his signature.

59–60 *these foreign evidences . . . since the wars*: these independent witnesses have gone up in price like everything else in wartime—possibly because so many likely candidates for such employment are now in the forces.

60–1 *if mine escape . . . head of 'em*: Subtleman collects potential witnesses as a matter of professional routine and expects to make £200 profit on each, but is always in danger of finding that amateur witness-recruiters—'privateers' (see Notes *CC* 1.1.42 and *RO* 5.4.21)—have got in ahead of him. Or alternatively that the ships carrying his witnesses have literally been seized by real privateers.

65–7 *The world has broke . . . knew a father*: ingeniously and disingenuously, Young Wouldbe declares himself an outlaw. Society has broken its contract ('civilities') with him. He is not even subject to paternal authority; and since fathers are 'the natural and original governments in the world' (Temple, *An Essay*, 67), he is in a state of nature, like the 'noble savage' in Dryden's *The First Part of The Conquest of Granada* (1670), 'as free as nature first made man, | Ere the base laws of servitude began' (1.1). Except that he is not noble: his state is rather that described by Hobbes in which all pre-social human beings are at war with one another. See Introduction pp. xvii–xviii and Notes *CC* 1.1.24.

71 *We are all . . . were enemies*: as descendants of Adam all men are brothers; but Adam's eldest son, Cain, murdered his brother, Abel. See Gen. 4: 1–8.

3.1.5 *the Commissioners*: a permanently constituted government board. As a member of the House of Lords Young Wouldbe would have considerable influence in official circles.

7 *your Board*: possibly the Board of Directors of a joint stock company, thus illustrating Young Wouldbe's influence in commerce as well as government.

15 *In utrumque paratus*: in readiness for either (Latin).

21–2 *a-rehearsing . . . and a half*: a hit at Lincoln's Inn Fields which 'suffered the ill effects of management by a committee of prima donna actors' (Robert D. Hume, *The Development of English Drama in the Late Seventeenth Century*, 433). There may also be a reference to *Courtship à la Mode* (1700) by David Crauford, which was withdrawn from Lincoln's Inn and played successfully at Drury Lane.

23–6 *a great deal . . . plot for't*: since 'business' was a term for sexual intercourse, one of Comic's plays lacks love-interest, the other a story-line.

27–8 *read the Italian, and Spanish plays*: in order to plagiarize them, a common practice.

34–5 *that vacant commission*: army commissions could be granted or purchased. Experience, or the capacity to raise recruits from among one's tenantry, were grounds for the granting of a commission, but influence was more important than either. The dedication of *Sir Harry Wildair* to the Earl of Albemarle (1669–1719), who returned to Holland after the death of William III, did not gain Farquhar military advancement, but the support of the Boyle family proved helpful later. See Kenny, i. 641 and Notes *RO* Dedication 54–5.

47 *the House*: the House of Lords.

62–3 *trainbands*: part-time soldiers recruited in the City and some large towns, the equivalent of the militia in the countryside. See *RO* 5.5.10. Both forces were regarded with contempt by professional soldiers.

70–1 *upon the Rhine*: the Rhine valley was defended against the French until 1707.

78 *the Round House*: a lock-up for drunks in St Martin's Lane.

91 *my glove*: leaving money in a glove was a conventional method of bribery.

113 *looks so like a challenge*: throwing down a glove (or gauntlet) was a traditional way of challenging a man to a duel.

114 *between you and I*: a common bit of slovenly grammar.

121–3 *But, my lord . . . soliciting sometimes*: the alderman refers to the patent insincerity of Young Wouldbe's earlier promises and now seeks real commitment. If the whole of Young Wouldbe's reply is an aside, the alderman's efforts have again proved useless.

131 *made up my liveries*: the cut and colour of servants' dress identified them as working for different employers.

136–7 *debt of honour*: a gambling debt, legally unenforceable and for that reason taking precedence over the other debts of 'a person of honour'.

155 *White's*: a fashionable chocolate house in St James's Street from 1693. It became a Tory club famous for gambling and is still operating.

3.2.1 *Monday the . . . 1702*: the 1728 edition reads 'Monday the 14th of December, 1702', the date, as Kenny notes, of the play's first night. 'The manuscript must have omitted the date because the opening had not been scheduled' (Kenny, i. 489). Whether the date changed with each performance is unclear. This strongly reinforces Kenny's belief that the 1728 edition was indebted to a Drury Lane prompt-book dating from the play's first run.

7 *Through all the . . . that I have run*: through all the varied countries (i.e. climates) that I have travelled in.

11 *Circe's*: sister of Aeetes, King of Colchis, and an enchantress, who transformed the companions of Odysseus into swine because of their greed. On this occasion at least Homer's much-travelled hero resisted temptation, and Elder Wouldbe claims to have followed his example. See Introduction pp. xiv–xv.

16-17 *Be me shoul . . . I tire him*: Teague speaks the language of the conventional stage-Irishman, presumably in an Antrim accent: 'by' becomes 'be', 'my' 'me'; he tends to pronounce 's' as 'sh', and 'th' as 't'. The characterization clearly derives from that of the Irish servant, Teg or Teague, in *The Committee* (1662) by Sir Robert Howard (1626-98), a hugely popular part.

20 *Fet*: faith.

joy: an endearment which came to be associated with the Irish. It is used constantly by Foigard in *The Beaux' Stratagem*.

21 *Carrickfergus*: a small town on the Antrim coast in what is now Northern Ireland.

26-7 *cormorant*: a sea-bird with a voracious appetite.

28 *Deel tauk*: devil take.

28-9 *a great deal . . . twelve a'clock*: the first of Teague's many so-called 'Irishisms'.

39 *fat naam*: what name.

43 *bred and born*: Teague reverses the logical order, like Lady Lurewell's butler (*CC* 4.2.206-7).

45 *would know it*: wishes to know it.

50 *fere vil*: where will.

64 *hone*: alas (Irish).

76 *take no care*: don't worry.

77 *the Friars*: Whitefriars had been a place of sanctuary for debtors until 1622 and remained so customarily throughout the seventeenth century. It was a hang-out for petty criminals, paid perjurers among them.

81 *my countryman*: a man of the nationality I am looking for. 1728 edn. 'one for my purpose'.

87 *an Irish poet*: the English were amused by the tendency of quite humble Irish people to claim descent from kings and poets, but both were commoner in traditional Irish society than outsiders could readily

recognize, and their descendants were among the thousands of Irish people rendered destitute by Jacobean, Cromwellian, and Williamite confiscations of Irish land.

102–3 *vith King Jamish into France*: after his defeat at the Battle of the Boyne in 1690, James II spent the rest of his life in exile in France.

106 *Je ne sais pas*: I don't know (French).

108 *Oui, monsieur*: yes, sir (French).

109–11 *dat will excuse . . . excuse the rest*: another 'Irishism' laced with the commonplace misreading of the Catholic doctrines of absolution (forgiveness of sin) and indulgences (remission of the penalties attaching to sins already forgiven).

123–5 *That Providence . . . I am just*: a facile identification of Providence with poetic justice. See Notes Preface 11 above and Introduction p. xvii.

127 *honest Mr Fairbank! my father's goldsmith*: goldsmiths functioned as bankers. See Introduction p. xiv.

139 *my eyes that question should resolve*: because he is in tears. The inverted syntax adds to the scene's awkwardness.

168 *scandalum magnatum*: a statute of 1378 made the malicious utterance of reports (true or false) against persons holding positions of dignity in the realm punishable by the infliction of heavy damages. It was scandalously revived by Charles II and James II to suppress their political opponents, and William III's ministers found it useful in their turn to keep it on the Statute Book.

188–9 *I pay the . . . of the nation*: in 1698 the Aid or Land Tax was assessed at the equivalent of 15 per cent of the value of property. This was raised to 20 per cent in Queen Anne's reign. See Ogg, *England in the Reigns*, 402–3.

189 *Swiss slave*: Switzerland provided the armies of Europe with mercenary soldiers, who often subsequently became personal bodyguards.

207–8 *an herald*: heralds regulate the use of coats of arms.

3.3.1 *Heaven's*: first edn. 'Heaven''.

10–11 *no formal . . . on my bed*: for a month after a bereavement women of fashion remained in seclusion and received visits of condolence on a day-bed.

24 *waxwork, perfect waxwork*: as perfect as if it were modelled in wax. It is a comment on Young Wouldbe's deformity that Mandrake speaks of the loveliness of his ears.

25 *His nurse*: upper-class women often had their babies breast-fed by women whose own babies had been weaned or had died.

46 S.D. *a picture*: obviously a miniature.

53 *officious*: dutiful, solicitous—not 'overzealous'.

71   *my sex has bounds*: as a woman, I must control my actions.

97–8   *a piece*: popular term for the sovereign or guinea coin.

4.1.38–9   *Mr Moabite . . . in Lombard Street*: Lombard Street, near the Exchange in the City, was inhabited by goldsmiths, bankers, and merchants. Although Ruth, the ancestress of King David, was a Moabite, the name is insulting to Jews. The Moabites were thought to be descendants of Lot's incestuous union with his eldest daughter (Gen. 19: 30–7) and were enemies of Israel. ('Judah is my law-giver, Moab is my wash-pot'—Ps. 108.)

42   *Weekly Preparation*: presumably a work of devotion. I have been unable to identify it.

43–4   *what hears me I*: see Notes *CC* 3.1.73.

45–6   *chair, the windows close drawn*: a sedan chair with the curtains drawn.

53   *made a Jew on't*: i.e. had the child circumcised. If Mandrake were as familiar with Scripture as she apparently is with the *Weekly Preparation* she would have known that circumcision takes place eight days after birth. (See Gen. 17: 12, Luke 2: 21.)

55   *a good Christian*: the anti-Judaism in the account of Subtleman's birth is somewhat deflected by this conclusion.

65–6   *valet de chambre*: personal manservant (French).

68   *a manteau-maker*: a dress-maker; the incorrect 'mantua-maker' replaced this form.

73   *this closet*: see Notes *CC* 4.2.79 S.D.

91   *follow the tipstaff*: be led into court by a sheriff's officer.

100–1   *retort your cunning to your infamy*: respond to your cunning in a way that will redound to your infamy.

113   *signatum et sigillatum*: signed and sealed (Latin).

116   *Clifford's Inn*: one of the Inns of Court where barristers are trained and practise.

119   *that produced thee*: since ancient times it had been believed that worms and maggots did not reproduce sexually but were generated spontaneously from rotting matter.

157–8   *ask him no cross questions*: not to cross-examine him.

167   *My brother's servant*: it is not clear when Young Wouldbe met Teague who has never been in London before.

171   *maake swear*: take an oath.

177   *taaking*: talking.

178   *unlucky*: fated to bring ill-luck on others.

231   *a King at Arms*: one of the three chief heralds of the College of Arms by whom the granting and bearing of coats of arms are regulated.

236–7 *Master in Chancery*: the Lord Chancellor was assisted by twelve Masters.

261 *vi et armis*: by force and arms (Latin).

267 *Croon Offish*: Crown Office.

273 *sibyl*: see Notes *CC* 2.3.42.

287 *rent-charge*: 'a rent forming a charge upon lands, etc., granted or reserved by deed to one who is not the owner' (*OED*).

4.2.4 *bail*: first edn., 'fail'.

9–10 *know me agen*: 1728 edn. adds 'now I am a prishoner'.

19 *Bashtile*: Teague's pronunciation of *Bastille*, the prison-fortress in Paris which symbolized French absolutism.

22 *iron glash window*: barred window.

25 *grash*: grace. The religious implications of the word are ironically inconsistent with Teague's proposal.

25–6 *her word would go for two*: as a pregnant woman she would be the equivalent of the two witnesses as to character required to secure the release of Teague and his master.

4.3.1 *The Tower*: the Tower of London where the nobility were imprisoned.

5–6 *Virgil, though . . . splenetic tale*: apart (possibly) from the tragedy of Dido in Book IV, it is hard to see why the *Aeneid* should be represented as neurotic or peevish.

7–8 *Cervantes revels . . . in a gaol*: Cervantes, author of *Don Quixote* (1605; 1615) was the captive of Algerian pirates from 1575 to 1580. This song is evidence that Elder Wouldbe is not mad but plays his game with the constable in a spirit of bitter facetiousness.

10 *the Lieutenant of the Tower*: the officer commanding the Tower on behalf of the sovereign.

19 *damask*: fine linen with a patterned weave. Elder Wouldbe is being ironic.

19–20 *the flowers are so bold*: a comment on the stains on the sheets.

20–1 *the headwork! Point de Venise*: Venetian lace was very expensive. 'Headwork' is presumably the edging of the bedspread.

22 *Kidderminster*: a two-ply carpet manufactured in the Worcestershire town of Kidderminster; a bit of old carpet is apparently serving as a bedspread.

25 *Indian pieces*: carvings from the East Indies.

49 *Tree, be me shoul*: three, by my soul. Teague's claims to friendship with Elder Wouldbe may be due to his absurd self-importance (see his ambition to be a justice of the peace—5.4.148–9). On the other hand, his master's failure to include him among his friends may be a reflection on Elder Wouldbe.

53 *golden fetters*: Constance hopes Trueman is marrying a wealthy woman, i.e. Aurelia, who has a fortune of fifteen hundred pounds (2.4.19).

54–5 *four thousand . . . the purse*: Trueman puns on the pound weight and the pound sterling; the 'purse' refers to the lady as a 'container' of so much wealth and pleasure.

66 *confine a peer of the realm*: as Members of Parliament, peers enjoyed freedom from arrest for debt or misdemeanours. They could only be tried by their fellow-peers.

67 *you may give good words though*: you may speak politely none the less.

86 *staff*: staff of office as a constable.

89–90 *his worship's . . . your grace*: in his confusion the constable refers to Elder Wouldbe below his rank ('your worship'), and above it ('your grace').

102 *iron grates*: iron bars on the windows.

4.4.15 *your sufficiency*: Richmore's wealth.

5.1.1 *stoic*: see Notes *CC* 4.2.131–2.

5 *epicurean*: see Notes, *CC* 4.2.131–2.

14 *the passage at the old playhouse*: as Kenny notes, the passage leading to the Drury Lane Theatre, where *The Twin Rivals* was playing, was notorious as the haunt of prostitutes.

15 *Rosamond's Pond*: a small lake in St James's Park, now filled in.

16 *the Chequer ale-house in Holborn*: an 'unfashionable posting-house' (Stonehill).

35 *Coup de grace, ciel gramerci*: the final blow, thank heaven (French).

53 *Le coup d'éclat*: the stroke meriting applause (French).

53–4 *like the noblest Roman of 'em all*: an echo of Antony's final tribute to Brutus in Shakespeare's *Julius Caesar*, 5.5.

88 *non compos*: not of sound [mind] (Latin). A suicide could be given a decent burial after such a verdict.

111 *Elysian fields*: the abode of the noble dead in Hades, the underworld of classical mythology.

119–20 *my sultana . . . may possess 'em*: Young Wouldbe, as sultan, has promoted Constance to the rank of sultana. He leaves his concubines to his courtiers.

5.2.5 *sign*: inn-sign.

5–6 *St Alban's Tavern!*: in St Alban's Street, Pall Mall.

7 *St James's Square . . . Soho*: Trueman has been fairly inattentive himself—he has been led more than half a mile out of his way. Teague, of course, is unfamiliar with London.

16 *the King's name*: a slip either by Trueman or Farquhar—Queen Anne had been on the throne some months. See Notes Epilogue 24 below.

31 S.D. *the balcony*: see Notes *CC* 3.3 S.D.

5.3 S.D. *Scene changes . . . and mob*: see Notes *CC* 2.5 S.D. and *CC* 3.4 S.D. *Proserpine*: the lovely wife of Pluto and so Queen of Hades. Mandrake is a grotesque parody of the Queen of the underworld.

18–19 *A cart, Bridewell*: see *CC* 2.4.31. Bridewell was a prison near St Bride's Church in the City, to which prostitutes were committed after their whipping.

23–4 *Dere is a joak for you*: possibly addressed directly to the audience. See Introduction p. xv.

41 *a monster*: a cuckold, with a cuckold's horns. See Notes *CC* 1.1.61.

52–3 *commission of the peace*: like almost all landowners of standing, Richmore is a magistrate.

56–7 *use to make . . . before company*: usually sort out this kind of business in public.

74–5 *taken up . . . justice of peace*: paternity suits were decided by magistrates, often arbitrarily. It was virtually impossible for a poor woman to pursue a paternity claim against a gentleman.

76–7 *bring me off*: get me off.

80–2 *I am for liberty . . . of the subject*: another example of a subversive parodying of radical political slogans. See Introduction p. xx.

104 *Don John*: the principal character in *The Libertine* (1675) by Shadwell; the name is an Anglicized version of Don Juan.

162 S.D. *Exit [Richmore]*: see, however, Preface 46.

5.4.9–10 *I never admitted . . . command me*: I never allowed anyone to serve me as a professed lover without my intending to obey him as a husband.

21–32 *it is better . . . than a rebel*: the whole of this exchange is couched in the language of politics. Constance's position is the conventional one, that the laws of marriage are like the English constitution as understood in the Settlement of 1689, allowing for the limited exercise of husbandly (or monarchic) power. She compares marriage vows to the oaths of loyalty to William and Mary in 1689 and to William as sole monarch in 1701. Young Wouldbe—in contrast to the radically libertarian pose adopted by Trueman in the previous scene (5.3.80–2)—affects to offer Constance the arbitrary powers of absolute monarchy such as prevailed not only in France but in Sweden, Denmark, and Russia also. In practice, absolute power was vested in the rich man rather than the beautiful mistress or dutiful wife, as his own and Richmore's behaviour indicates. See Introduction p. xx.

43-4 *Not angels . . . innocence*: a blasphemous allusion to the Annunciation (Luke 1: 26-38).

50-1 *I have read somewhere these lines*: I have been unable to locate them.

53 *Since Fate has*: since then, Fate has.

62 *stanza*: pronounced to rhyme with 'man saw'.

94 *Mandrake in custody*: Archer suggests this speech would come more naturally from the villainous Young Wouldbe.

100 *as he was still esteemed*: as he was always thought to be.

127 *déshabillé*: undressed; in a state of casual or negligent undress (French).

139 *maishter Fuller*: William Fuller (1670-1714) was pilloried three times and was currently in prison for perjury.

150 *Yesh*: all early edns. 'Yest'. I have accepted Archer's sensible emendation.

151-2 *a great rogue for my clark*: as amateur judges, justices of the peace were advised by better qualified, though often ignorant and villainous clerks. The spelling 'clark' indicates that the received pronunciation of 'clerk' was the same as in modern American English.

156 *Fortune must . . . act like me*: a facile assertion in view of the sheer chance, brought openly to our attention in the text (5.3.38-41), which prevents Trueman from marrying Clelia, but entirely in line with Elder Would-be's other comments on this theme. See Introduction p. xvii.

Epilogue

3 *bring him off with quarter*: allow him to escape with his life (like a soldier given quarter in battle).

7 *a hard struggling part*: as Aurelia.

13 *You like . . . best defence*: you men prefer women who put up the best show of resistance.

16 *the wits of Athens and of Rome*: the acute critics of classical times.

20 *He*: our poet—Farquhar.

24 *this female reign*: Queen Anne was proclaimed Queen in March 1702. See also Notes *BS* 4.1.2-4.

The Recruiting Officer

Title-page

Captique . . . coacti: captured by tricks and compelled by gifts (Latin), a misquotation (deliberate or not) of '*captique dolis, lacrimisque coactis*' ('captured by tricks and by forced tears'), *Aeneid* ii. 196, Virgil's reference being to the Greeks' deception of the Trojans. Attempts to read political significance into the change are not convincing.

Dramatis Personae

> *SCRUPLE*: a tiny unit of weight (1/4 of an ounce); hence a minute point of conscience. The names of the three justices all relate to the scales traditionally held (along with a sword) by the blindfolded goddess of Justice.
>
> *BRAZEN*: shameless, impudent. See also 1 Cor. 13: 1—'I am become sounding brass'.
>
> *COSTAR PEARMAIN*: the 'costar' or 'costard' was a large-sized variety of apple (as in costermonger), 'pearmain' a variety of apple or pear.

Dedication

> *To all . . . The Wrekin*: a famous Shropshire toast (Dixon). The Wrekin, an isolated hill in the middle of the county, is a prominent local landmark.

4 *the favours you have already conferred*: a reference to the entertainment Farquhar received as a recruiting officer in the area, possibly in 1704. See Introduction pp. viii, xv.

10 *Salop*: an alternative name for Shropshire, a county on the Welsh borders, of which Shrewsbury is the county town.

11 *recruiting the army*: recruiting for the army.

19–20 *Some little . . . this comedy*: the extent to which Farquhar drew on personal experience for this play is uncertain. There was much speculation about the identities of his originals in the eighteenth century. See Stonehill, vol. i, p. xxvi.

25–6 *puris naturabilis*: natural state (Latin).

26 *apprehensive*: ready to seize an opportunity offered.

28–9 *and of as . . . short of his own*: how the play is read greatly depends on the extent to which Farquhar endorses the attitudes and values of Balance. He is not on oath in Dedications and Prefaces. See *TR* Preface 46–7.

31 *Mr Rich*: Christopher Rich (d. 1714), manager of Drury Lane, a ruthless operator, may not have been as guiltless of sharp practice as Farquhar maintains.

34 *Mr Durfey's third night*: see Notes *CC* Preface 5. Thomas Durfey (1653–1723) had to close his comic extravaganza, *Wonders of the Sun, or The Kingdom of the Birds. A Comic Opera* after six nights at the Haymarket, which had been specially built for the staging of operas. See Introduction p. viii.

35–6 *Be it known . . . act and deed*: let this document certify that the decision was mine. The style parodies legal documents.

37–42 *He brought down . . . in the sun*: Farquhar ironically represents himself as capable of offering only Kite, Plume, and Brazen to compete with the entire Kingdom of Birds in the fifth act of Durfey's play.

45 *all commanded to their posts abroad*: the battle of Ramillies was fought just six weeks after the first night of the play. The war (see Notes *TR* Prologue 1) had lasted four years and was not popular.

47–8 *his woodcocks . . . is over*: see Notes *TR* 2.1.61. Woodcock are proverbially stupid.

50 *posted*: the culminating pun on the two senses of the verb 'to post'—'to assign soldiers to their duties' and 'to advertise with posters'.

54 *The Duke of Ormonde*: see Notes *TR* 2.1.83–4 and *BS* 3.3.211–12, and Introduction p. viii. Ormonde, a commander of the allied forces in Spain, was Farquhar's general.

54–5 *the Earl of Orrery*: Charles Boyle, Earl of Orrery (1676–1731) in whose regiment Farquhar was a lieutenant. See Notes *TR* 3.1.34–5 and Introduction p. viii.

56 *pass muster*: be present and correct on parade.

60 *the wearing*: the passage of time.

Prologue

1–2 *when Helen's . . . to arms*: the Greek expedition against Troy under the command of Agamemnon, King of Argos, followed the abduction of his sister-in-law, Helen, wife of Menelaus, by Paris, son of Priam, the Trojan king.

11 *Ulysses well could talk*: Achilles was hidden by his mother, Thetis, among her handmaidens, because his death in the war had been foretold. He was tricked, by the wily Odysseus (Ulysses) disguised as a pedlar, into disclosing his sex when he siezed a weapon from among the ornaments being offered by Odysseus for sale.

warms: first edn. 'warns'.

13 *fine laced coats*: the facetious mingling of classical and modern images of military life was common at the time, as in Dryden's references to a 'troop of cut-throat guards' (l. 25) and a thieving 'red-coat' (l. 32) in his translation of *The Tenth Satire of Juvenal* (1693).

16 *Hector*: Prince of Troy and leader of the Trojans, killed in battle by Ulysses.

1.1. S.D. *'Grenadier March'*: according to Ross, a tune first published in *A Collection of the Newest and Choicest Songs* (1683).

1 *gentlemen-soldiers*: see *CC* 1.1.113–14 and Notes *BS* 1.1.174.

2 *her Majesty*: Queen Anne.

5–6 *the Raven*: an inn in Castle Street, Shrewsbury.

7 *relief and entertainment*: unless his listeners are careful they will be offered 'relief' in the sense of payment of recruitment money, and not just rest and recreation; 'entertainment' was similarly ambiguous (Dixon).

11 *grenadiers*: 'a company attached to every regiment equipped with hand grenades; later a company of the finest, tallest men in the regiment' (*OED*).

12 *this cap*: the military cap of the period had high points front and rear.

17 *[MAN]*: all early edns. read 'MOB'. Speeches so marked may be distributed among several individuals. The 1728 edn. assigns them all to Costar [Pearmain], but as Dixon points out there is no sign in subsequent scenes of Costar's being married.

20 *conjuration*: see Glossary. The theme of magic is introduced here remarkably early and inconspicuously. It is picked up in Plume's question and Kite's answer below (125–9) and more casually in Plume's address to Worthy (137). See also 2:2. 30 and Introduction p. xvii.

20–1 *gunpowder plot*: the original gunpowder plot was a conspiracy of Catholics to blow up the King and Parliament in November 1605. It became the focus of extravagant anti-Catholic propaganda in the late seventeenth century and made a powerful impact on the popular imagination. See Notes *BS* 4.1.334–7.

26 *'The Crown, or the Bed of Honour'*: the badge of the Grenadier Guards was a crown above the royal cipher (the sovereign's initials reversed), but as Ross notes this was not the regimental motto, nor that of any other regiment. Plume subsequently makes it clear that the Bed of Honour is the grave.

28–9 *the great bed of Ware*: a famous bed, 12 feet square, kept in the Crown Inn, Ware, Hertfordshire.

41 *at this present writing*: at the time of writing this, i.e. at present.

62 S.D. *Enter*: Stonehill starts a new scene here.

74 *the strong man of Kent*: see Notes *CC* Prologue 35.

the king of the gypsies: the leader of a band of Gypsies was conventionally called a king.

75 *a Welsh parson*: Wales was notoriously neglected by the Church of England throughout the seventeenth and eighteenth centuries; Welsh parsons were quite likely to be disreputable.

93 *the Castle*: Shrewsbury Castle where there was rented accommodation.

97 *And so*: in that case.

99 *they*: first edn. 'she'.

106 *Sheely Snikereyes*: literally 'Sheila Giggle-eyes'.

108 *the Horseguard*: headquarters of the Household Cavalry, in Whitehall.

109–10 *'Mademoiselle Van-Bottomflat'—at the Buss*: literally 'Miss Broadbeam'—at the [Hertogen]bosch, or [Duke's] Wood', in Northern Brabant. 'Buss' also means 'kiss'. The Dutch commonly built broadbottomed boats.

110 *'Jenny Oakum'*: oakum—the fibres of old rope used for caulking ships' seams—was frequently picked, laboriously and painfully, in prisons and workhouses. Jenny's name may allude to this as well as to her 'husband's' profession.

117–19 *Then set the . . . his subsistence*: Stonehill (following J. Hill Burton, *The Reign of Queen Anne* (1880), i. 205) notes that the granting of an ensign's commission to a child was an officially sanctioned device for supporting a mother and her child. Plume's proposal, however, is obviously the sort of cheerfully corrupt practice common in all armies in all ages.

122–3 *German doctor's habit*: Dixon notes the widespread association of magic with learned Germans in consequence of the Faustus legend.

125 *famous*: second edn. 'faithful'.

127 *trusty*: second edn. 'faithful'.

128 *confided*: second edn. 'trusted'.

134 *the vapours in his ears*: up to his ears in gloom.

141 *nor nose*: the loss of one's nose was a common effect of syphilis.

142 *sympathies nor antipathies*: a sympathy between different organs of the body was thought to result in the disorder of one communicating itself to the other, an antipathy between organs to cause their mutual malfunctioning.

151 *turning Quaker*: members of the Society of Friends (Quakers) were often derided for their pacifism, piety, and rectitude.

157 *you*: second edn. 'thou', possibly parodying Quaker usage (Dixon).

163 *pickle*: second edn. 'condition'.

164 *miraculous*: second edn. 'wonderful'.

174–5 *Why she began . . . upon honourable terms*: see Notes *CC* 2.4.100. Melinda was about to agree to a financial arrangement to become Worthy's mistress. The terms would, of course, have redounded to Worthy's honour as a gallant, not to hers as a woman. See 5.3.34.

180 *turn my siege into a blockade*: having abandoned hope of using Melinda's poverty to induce her to surrender, Worthy took up the more troublesome task of cutting her off from contact with the outside world—i.e. other men.

188 *died upon the breach*: see Introduction p. xx.

199 *Would you bring her*: if you wish to bring her.

214 *your best blood*: semen was thought to contain or to derive from blood.

245 *makes love to you*: makes advances to you, not has sex with you.

248–9 *give a fig for*: second edn. 'value'.

278–9 *lose an inch . . . that way*: Dixon points to the erotic sense of 'lose an inch'. See *CC* 5.1.144 (revised text).

283 *Horton*: Dixon suggests this may be Edward Haughton who kept an inn in Castle Ward, Shrewsbury in 1704.

   a fresh pipe of choice Barcelona: see Notes *CC* 1.1.240. Wine was still imported from Spain though not from France, even though Britain was at war with both countries.

286 *the lady*: Silvia.

1.2.1 S.D. *salute*: embrace, kiss.

  3 *heads of shires*: county towns.

  4–6 *here we have . . . is intolerable*: such complaints were usually made about London. A metropolitan audience would find Melinda's protest ridiculous and affected.

12–15 *airs in conversation . . . impudent airs*: omitted in second edn.

24 *our noses drop*: second edn. 'our fingers ache'.

29 *salts*: medicinal salts. First edn. 'salt'.

32 *shoot flying*: shoot birds on the wing (*OED*). The expression probably has an obscene sense also—see Notes *CC* 3.1.88–9 and 5.5.60–1 below. In the sexual act, women do not 'shoot'. See also Introduction p. xii.

40–1 *And there's a . . . madmen know*: Dryden, *The Spanish Fryar* (1680), 2.2—a play frequently revived in the 1700s. Farquhar wrote an Epilogue for one such performance in 1706. The play is strongly anti-Catholic and anti-Nonconformist and its plot concerns a disputed succession to the throne of Spain.

42 *Quixote*: see Notes *TR* 4.3.7–8. Don Quixote acts out a daydream of knight-errantry and foolish romanticism.

45 *corner*: second edn. 'part'.

53 *an appendix to our sex*: her virginity.

67 *expect satisfaction*: as when a challenge to a duel is issued—a further appropriation of men's language.

89 *advised*: second edn. 'persuaded'.

2.1.5 *'prison bars'*: a country game in which one player attempts to 'imprison' others (Dixon).

  6–7 *colours, and standards*: captured from the French.

  7–8 *another Marshal of France*: Camile d'Hostun, duc de Tallard (1652–1709), Marshal of France and former French ambassador to William III, was taken prisoner after the great allied victory at Blenheim in August 1704, under the command of John Churchill, Earl (later Duke) of Marlborough (1650–1722), a battle which completely changed the balance of power in Europe. See Notes *TR* 2.4.39.

10 *to*: compared with.

12 *the battle of Hockstadt*: another name for the battle of Blenheim. The French troops were garrisoned in Hockstadt.

15 *our general*: first edn. 'generals', but the subsequent pronoun is 'he'.

20 *war is*: second edn. 'victory is'.

41–2 *at her own disposal*: Silvia's fortune, probably inherited from her mother as part of her parents' marriage settlement, is hers absolutely—she cannot be disinherited even if she marries against her father's wishes. However the sum in question, though substantial, is not sufficient to maintain her in the style to which she is accustomed. Nevertheless, like Millamant in Congreve's *The Way of the World* (1700), and unlike the only recently enriched Melinda, she has grown up in the expectation of this relative independence, which may help to explain her remarkable self-assurance.

51 *give you fair quarter*: spare your life on reasonable terms. See *TR* Epilogue 3.

54 *die*: climax sexually.

55 *to make your will*: marriage makes existing wills invalid. Making a new one was an essential part of a marriage settlement.

55–6 *leave me something*: this may have further sexual connotations.

59 *before the battle of Blenheim*: Marlborough's army was heavily outnumbered at Blenheim. Plume may not have made his will in a spirit of facile romanticism, but he has brought it with him on this occasion with an eye to the main chance.

Revised text

48 *are indebted to me*: do indeed owe me.

51 *soldiers were sincere*: included among the neo-classical rules of decorum (see Notes *TR* Preface 11–15) was the principle that characters should conform to type. According to Rymer soldiers were 'open-hearted, frank [and] plain-dealing' ('A Short View of Tragedy' (1692), *The Critical Works of Thomas Rymer*, ed. with an introduction and notes by Curt A. Zimansky (1956), 135). But see also Notes 3.2.46–7 below.

53 *insurance*: assurance.

80 *do either*: second edn. 'endanger either'.

2.2.5 *Owen*: a Welsh name. The Balances may in fact be Welsh. See Notes 3.1.227 below.

14–15 *which three . . . pound per annum*: second edn. 'which you know is about twelve hundred pounds a year'.

15–16 *fair claim to quality and a title*: see Notes *CC* 3.4.209–10.

24–5 *A captain . . . a year!*: an infantry captain's pay was of the order of £100 a year; a captain in the cavalry was paid £173 a year (Stonehill).

26 *woods upon my estate*: selling up all the timber on an estate indicated poor land management, a disregard for the amenities of the hunt, and the imprudent transfer of a major long-term asset into disposable funds.

32 *maggotty new-fashioned . . . upon the Thames*: a countryman's view of the expansion of London. Wren had designed the new Chelsea Hospital and Twickenham, where Pope and Horace Walpole (1717–97) were to build their celebrated houses. New domestic architecture often strikes established landowners as vulgarly decorated and eccentrically designed ('maggotty').

33–4 *habeas corpus*: a writ of habeas corpus—'you hold the person' (Latin)—requires an official to produce a prisoner before a court.

34 *terra firma*: solid ground (Latin).

39–40 *Prince Prettyman*: a character in *The Rehearsal* (1671) by Buckingham which satirizes the high-flown heroic plays of Dryden. Actually it is Prince Volsci who has to decide between love and honour, an error Farquhar repeats in *Love and Business* (Kenny, ii. 337).

43–4 *take it*: first edn. 'take'.

45 *an ass*: i.e. for a husband. Halifax (see Notes *CC* 5.1.4) advises his daughter not to worry in such a case: 'you must be very undextrous,' he tells her, 'if when your husband should resolve to be an ass, you do not take care he may be your ass' (17). Silvia has the wit to manage an ass and, like Dorinda (*BS* 4.1.412–17), she knows the attractions of high social standing, but she has other priorities.

86–7 *a hat and feather*: see Notes *CC* 1.1.43.

93 *advices*: second edn. 'letters'.

114 *a hank upon*: second edn. 'a power over'.

122 *BALANCE . . . I am satisfied*: omitted in second edn.

132 *with*: as.

144 *to us. Afterwards*: both early edns. 'to us afterwards'. The emendation appears in 1728 and is followed by Archer and later editors. Dixon defends the original reading, interpreting Balance's final sentence as meaning, 'Meanwhile you may drink my health, and remember me in your cups.' The fact that Balance seems to regard mourning for his son as a mere social duty is disconcerting.

2.3.1–10 *Our prentice Tom . . . Over the hills, &c.*: Ross reprints the whole of this famous recruiting song ('The Recruiting Officer; or, The Merry Volunteer' from Thomas Durfey's *Wit and Mirth; or, Pills to Purge Melancholy* (1719–20), v) of which these are the tenth and twelfth stanzas. The lyricist and composer are unknown. The tune was printed in 1706, by Durfey. See Introduction p. xii.

15 *COSTAR*: all early edns. '1ST MOB'.

19–20 *this Pressing Act . . . under the sun*: the Mutiny and Impressment Acts of 1703, 1704, and 1705 empowered justices of the peace to conscript able-bodied men into the army who were without lawful calling or visible means of support. Thus in Costar's view a justice exercised powers in his locality more arbitrary than those of the much derided absolute monarchs of Europe. (See Notes *TR* 5.4.21–32.) Radicals who had passionately supported the Revolution shared his opinion of parliamentary sovereignty. 'We can never be thoroughly ruin'd but by a Parliament', wrote Charles Blount (1654–93) in *Oracles of Reason* (1695), 177. 'They may cut the throats of us and our posterity by a law.' Under the laws in question the normal sentence for desertion (i.e. being found a mile from their garrison or camp without leave) was for the (usually impressed) deserter 'to be shot to death at the head of his regiment', and there 'was a large variety of corporal punishments . . . Lashing was very common' (Major R. E. Scouller, *The Armies of Queen Anne* (1966), 294–5 and 262).

22 *a rum duke*: a slang term for 'a jolly handsom Man' (*A New Dictionary of the Terms Ancient and Modern of the Canting Crew* (1699)).

23 *THOMAS*: all early edns. '2ND MOB'.

33 S.D. *broad pieces*: see Notes *CC* 1.1.262–3.

37 *written about?*: engraved around the edges.

38 '*Ca-ro-lus*': Charles (Latin), i.e. Charles II.

40 *scollard*: scholar.

41 *if it come . . . of a crawn*: if it costs no more than a crown (a coin worth 25 pence, or 5 shillings).

44 *Put them up*: put them away.

49 *hills*: first edn. 'hill'.

50 *away with it*: sing up.

55 *lieutenant-captains*: Thomas appears to think wrongly that a lieutenant-captain has a higher rank than a captain.

56 *nab*: hat.

58 *my vether's a freeholder*: most farmers were tenants, but Costar's father holds his land for life and may have a vote.

76–7 *St Mary's . . . St Chad's*: two fine churches in Shrewsbury.

110 *Mayar*: second edn. 'Mayor'.

115 [*THOMAS*]: this speech is wrongly assigned to Costar (1st Mob) in the first edn.

115–16 *you soldiers have more liberty of conscience*: Thomas (perhaps deliberately) confuses liberty of conscience (the right to hold one's own religious convictions and to worship accordingly) with lack of conscientious scruple. See Introduction p. xx.

NOTES TO PAGES 185-9

128 *etc.*: an invitation to the actor to improvise, a skill more richly developed in Italian than in English theatre.

132 *I have a month's mind*: I am quite determined (deriving from the Catholic practice of saying a Mass a month after a death).

134 *pretty*: second edn. 'honest'.

136 *a kidnapper . . . slaves*: the fate of children and disgruntled servants who were tricked into sailing for the Plantations (Dixon).

139-40 *carried a musket*: served as a common soldier.

157 *duna*: do not.

164 *command*: second edn. 'command it'.

172-4 *[THOMAS] . . . Pearmain*: first edn. wrongly assigns Thomas and Costar's speeches to '1st Mob' and '2nd Mob' respectively.

176 *Herefordshire*: the county on Shropshire's southern border.

3.1.7-8 *a couple . . . melancholy monsters*. Ross suggests that this is a reference to Caliban and Sycorax in *The Tempest* (1667) adapted by Davenant and Dryden from Shakespeare's play.

18 *in her smock*: literally 'in her nightdress', i.e. without rank or fortune. Dixon notes a parallel passage in *The Committee*. See Notes *TR* 3.2.16-17.

21-38 *Come, fair one . . . drink water-gruel*: omitted in all later edns.

38 *drink water-gruel*: as part of the treatment for venereal disease.

40-1 *break her windows*: see Notes *TR* 1.1.21.

48 S.D. *crying chickens*: calling out that she has chickens for sale.

57 *sarvice*: second edn. 'service'—there are numerous such changes out of dialect in later edns.

62 *put in your hand, feel, sir*: the sexual play here is obvious, but it is not clear from the text how conscious Rose is of the implications of what she says. The same applies to Bullock (see Notes 4.1.7-9 below). The former may well be more knowing than the latter.

69 *keep this market*: sell goods at this market whenever it is held.

71 *hast ye, we . . . liate a-whome*: hurry, we'll be late home.

75 *stracke o'*: strike of—an unofficial dry measure, usually a bushel but varying from one district to another.

77 *commodity*: an unintentional pun; the word can mean 'female genitalia', usually of a prostitute.

78-9 *as much out . . . out of fourpence*: as much out of a four-pence piece as you can get out of four pennies.

85-6 *by—you . . . the chickens*: second edn. 'by, chicken'.

86 *make change there*: the expression is sexually suggestive.

109 *born a gypsy*: the Romany people were thought to come from Egypt; Kite's mother is accordingly named after Cleopatra.

114 *brandy*: second edn. 'ratifia', a much more ladylike tipple, but the Queen preferred brandy, and Dixon thinks this may explain the change.

114–15 *bailliff's follower*: debt-collector and writ-server's assistant, or 'heavy'.

122–3 *hopes of a truncheon*: hopes of earning a marshal's baton—a ludicrously inflated ambition.

126 *a garret in the Savoy*: a converted barracks in the Strand. Scouller (*The Armies*, 105) cites a contemporary description of recruits being conducted 'as prisoners . . . pinioned or handcuffed, or with the buttons of their breeches cut off . . . and [secured] in that Epitome of Hell, the Savoy, more dreadful to the newly listed Soldier than all the Dangers and Hardships of the War.'

129 *take it again*: Kite plays on the double sense of garrison—a place for quartering troops and a fortified frontier post.

138 *an't*: if it.

141 *safe*: a pun. Rose is neither in danger nor diseased. She has also been secured by Plume.

154 *to smell powder*: to get to the bottom of the matter.

156–7 *a great fight . . . and the Irish*: the Hungarians naturally supported the Habsburg claimant to the Spanish throne: After James II's defeat in 1690, his Irish soldiers were permitted by the Articles of Limerick (1691) to take service with the French. Ross (*Notes and Queries* (1981), 218–19) thinks Bullock may be referring to an attack on 'Hanoverians' by Irish troops at Blenheim. Dixon cites the successful defence of Cremona by Irish units.

157–9 *and so, sir . . . the baggage*: assigned cleverly but without authority to Kite in later eighteenth-century edns.

159 *baggage*: a pun, the word meaning both 'portable military equipment' and 'a loose, often pert young woman'.

161 *and I*: second edn. 'and'.

170 *much*: second edn. 'just'.

176 *had*: first edn. 'has'.

177–8 *Venus has been . . . her cripple Vulcan*: Vulcan, the god of the forge and husband of Venus, was lame, one of the reasons for his spouse's infidelity with Mars.

186 *veni, vidi, vici*: I came, I saw, I conquered (Latin)—Julius Caesar's laconic description of his victory over Pharnaces at the battle of Zela in 47 BC.

196 *unimportant*: first and subsequent edns. 'important'. The emendation is Strauss's, strongly supported by Dixon.

200 *miles, leagues or hours*: the mile was a standarized unit of distance, the league (about three miles) less so, and the 'hour' as a measure of distance useful but variable.

203 S.D. *Enter Brazen*: the introduction of a virtuoso comic part at this point in a comedy is quite usual. See, for example, Sir Fopling Flutter's entrance in Act 3 of Etherege's *The Man of Mode* (1676).

208 *Mort de ma vie*: death of my life! (French).

216 *battle of Landen*: see Notes *CC* 1.1.156.

220 *are you a Jacobite*: Brazen thinks any suggestion that the French might attack the allies disloyal. In fact the French mounted 'a great onslaught' at Landen (Ogg, *England in the Reigns*, 385).

224-5 *two and twenty . . . that day*: Brazen is caught out in this lie later. See 5.6.5.

227 *my countryman*: Ross (*Notes and Queries* (1981), 220) suggests that this may be a reference to an equestrian acrobat named Evans who performed in London between 1703 and 1705; this seems to confirm that the Balance family is of Welsh extraction.

231 *chevaux de frise*: defensive line of spiked spars (French).

238-9 *Many, many . . . to fist*: we have emptied many, many bottles dry, man to man.

240 *India Company*: probably the old East India Company which was replaced by a new Company in 1698, though its affairs were not wound up until 1708.

241 *Tonguepad*: 'a smooth, glib-tongued, insinuating fellow' (*A New Diction- ary of the Terms of . . . the Canting Crew*).

Master in Chancery: see Notes *TR* 4.1.236-7.

245-6 *twenty thousand pounder*: Brazen refers to Melinda's fortune with an expression that would be more suited to declaring the weight of a ship, possibly a privateer. Worthy later calls her a frigate (3.2.89). See also 5.4.20-36.

255 S.D. *what she pleases*: anything Rose (or the actress) likes.

257 *a star*: a mark on the forehead.

258 *the tombs . . . and the Queen*: the tombs in Westminster Abbey, the lions in the Tower of London, and the Sovereign had become tourist attractions.

262 *Mechlin*: a Belgian town, famous for fine lace. See Notes *CC* 3.1.59-62.

266 *turkey shell*: Rose means 'tortoise-shell'.

267 *manageree*: Rose means 'orangeree', an expensive snuff.

268 *learned me*: taught me.

277 *withal*: as well.

279 *familiarity*: 1728 edn. 'fam-mam-mill-yar-rality'—i.e. Rose sneezes un-
controllably.

281–5 ROSE *But I . . . their companies*: omitted in second edn. Archer points
out that Rose must come back on stage with Plume, though there is no
stage-direction in the first edition, and suggests that it was found more
effective for Rose to remain on stage, and for Plume to enter and
embrace her before noticing Balance. Dixon suggests that she runs to the
back of the stage. Kenny believes that Balance's lines were deleted to
assuage stage reformers.

283–4 *with this gentleman*: as this gentleman.

286–90 *But it is . . . milking pail*: Ross (133–4) identifies this as the refrain
from a song written by Martin Parker in 1634 and reworked by Thomas
Durfey in 1694, with new music by John Eccles. In Durfey's version the
last two lines read 'With cheeks that glow | And carry the milking-pail'.

3.2.5 *pinners*: coifs with flaps hanging down, worn by women of rank.

8–9 *cheat the Queen of her duty*: see Notes CC 1.1.40.

19 *tied on his back*: second edn. 'tied upon his back'. Either 'trussed up and
lying on his [own] back', or 'tied on Worthy's back'.

36 *True to the touch*: true when tested. Second edn. 'Truth'.

36–41 *I'll draw . . . Severn side*: omitted in second edn.

44 *a pretty, melancholy amusement*: an elegant, enjoyably moody amusement.

46–7 *I have served . . . the Moors*: as the typically boastful soldier, Brazen
claims to have been in all the major campaigns since the reign of Charles
II—Tangiers before 1683, the War of the Treaty of Augsburg, 1686–97,
and the campaign against the Turks, 1697–9. He is thus in his
mid-forties, for the time in late middle age, and has not had much to do
with recent fighting.

58 *her stove disgusted me*: Dutch and German houses were heated with
stoves. Jeffares notes that 'Goldsmith writes later of Dutch women who
place small stoves under their skirts' and Kenny that 'a sexual double
entendre' is intended.

60–1 *she offered . . . escape with me*: this corresponds to the sub-plot of
Dryden's *Don Sebastian* (1689), from which Brazen may have got this
particular fabrication.

77 *The March beer at the Raven*: March beer was strong and rough. There
was no inn called the Raven in Shrewsbury.

78 *excise*: tax on beer and spirits.

85 *As fit . . . in a pit*: there may have been a touch of impudence in
prostitutes wearing pinners.

86–7 *that Tangerine*: a pirate vessel from Tangiers, an allusion to Brazen's
service there twenty-three years earlier.

89 *the frigate*: second edn. 'she'.

99–100 *I'll kneel . . . platooning*: infantry men fired kneeling or standing or stooping beside supports of some kind for their weapons. 'Platooning' is apparently a neologism of Farquhar's.

102 *I must*: second edn. 'must I'.

126 *be out*: get the words wrong.

137 *'your man'*: Plume deliberately takes Brazen's 'my man' in the sense of 'my servant'.

140 *my enemies thousands of lives*: second edn. 'me twenty pistoles in France, and my enemies thousands of lives in Flanders'. Ross suggests a pun on *livres*, the equivalent in French of 'pounds'. See Notes *BS* 5.4.251.

150 *the country*: second edn. 'this country', i.e. 'locally'.

151 *where I should*: second edn. 'where I stand'.

157 *shall have*: second edn. 'has'.

161 *You shall lie with me*: sharing beds was commonplace and respectable among relatives, masters or mistresses and their servants (of the same sex), and even strangers (in inns). It was the rule for common soldiers (Scouller, *The Armies*, 167).

S.D. *Kisses her*: among civilians it was regarded as foppish and French for men to kiss, but it was acceptable in the army.

163 *field officer*: an officer above the rank of captain, and under that of a general.

180 *here*: omitted in second edn.

182–3 *Hector of Holborn*: ' "Hectors" were swaggering ruffians, who infested the London streets and taverns' (Ross). Holborn runs into the City of London.

184 *forbid the banns*: formally object to an announced forthcoming marriage.

195 *Hold, hold*: omitted in second edn.

207 *and superscription*: omitted in second edn.

211 *C fa ut flat*: the musical key of C minor; second edn. 'Effa ut flat', the key of F minor. The correction is more effective in making the point that 'Jack Wilful' differs from 'Charles' only in the matter of 'his' noticeably higher voice.

234 S.D. *sounds . . . his mouth*: imitates the bugle call 'To arms'.

4.1.5 *great club*: William Bullock made this stage prop famous (Dixon).

7–9 *I fear . . . of followers*: I fear someone will 'look big' (i.e. either 'too big for their boots' or 'pregnant') rather more quickly than they expect. These smart airs are never introduced into country life without inducing a train of young men to go court the same woman. There is also an obvious pun on 'breeding', but whether the double meanings are deliberate or not depends on how the part of Bullock is acted. There are precedents for the country clown being played either as cunning and coarse or as stupid and innocent. See Notes 3.1.62 above.

17 *a commission*: the Queen's commission as an officer in the army—a reflection, perhaps, on another difference between the sexes that most ranting fellows value themselves upon.

19 *a rakish toss . . . cock*: a rakish toss of the head and a fashionably set hat. Bedford detects smutty punning here (153).

33 *you*: omitted in first edn.

47 *though there . . . and sparagus*: omitted in second edn. 'A popular, bawdy, late seventeenth-century ballad, The Three Jovial Companions, or The Three Merry Travellers . . . printed in *Wit and Mirth; or, Pills to Purge Melancholy*, v (1714), 17–19' (Dixon). Chickens have the same bawdy meaning in the song as in the play.

55 *bloody*: bloodthirsty.

57–66 PLUME *Entendez . . . prenez donc*: PLUME Do you understand French, my lad? SILVIA Yes. PLUME If you enlist in my company, the girl will be yours. SILVIA Have you slept with her? PLUME No. SILVIA Honestly? PLUME On my honour. SILVIA I'm satisfied. I will be your soldier. PLUME All right, have her. See Introduction p. xvi.

Revised text

68 *six before . . . behind*: six horses in front and six footmen behind.

68 *use to sell*: are accustomed to selling. Rose is afraid that like a male recruit she will be sold to another recruiting officer in the way Plume sells his recruits to Brazen, 5.7.145–7.

69–70 *send Ruose . . . Indies*: this could happen in two ways, if Rose were transported for prostitution or shipped out as a camp-follower. See *BS* 3.2.82–8.

95 *vestal*: i.e. a virgin. The shrine of Vesta in Rome was tended by six virgins.

106 *mistresses*: second edn. 'mistress'.

107 *their*: second edn. 'the'.

140–1 *of my own head*: by my own choice.

155 S.D. *Enter Melinda and Lucy*: Hunt and Archer begin a new scene here.

175 *set me upon the foot of*: put me in the position of. It was not uncommon for a lady's maid to come of relatively good family.

177 *the great design*: it is, alas, a sadly confused one. See Introduction p. xvi.

181 *the day of my*: second edn. 'upon my day of'.

212 *slave*: second edn. 'use'.

220 *late*: second edn. 'lately', matching the same word in Melinda's reply.

228 *as free . . . madam, and*: omitted in later edns.

234–5 *No, no . . . her fingers' ends.* Melinda's blow temporarily blinds Brazen who initially does not see Worthy. When he does so, he assumes the blow was meant to deceive his rival and is delighted by the thought of having a witty mistress.

257 *conduct*: sound management.

4.2.1–4 *By the position . . . sergeant of grenadiers*: the night sky was mapped on to a celestial globe. In Kite's facetious astrology, Luna, 'the Moon' (Latin), as controller of the tides, is a customs officer, and Sol, 'the Sun' (Latin), traditionally represented as surveying the whole earth, a land-valuer. Mercury, the messenger of the gods and the god of thieves, stole the cattle of Apollo as a child. Those born under Saturn were 'saturnine'—slow and humourless. See also *CC* 1.1.38 and Notes *CC* 1.1.98 and 2.1.20.

7–8 *a shoemaker . . . of dragoons*: Dixon notes that shoemakers and tailors, traditionally small and gentle, are inappropriate recruits for such tough and brutal corps.

9 *manage*: see Notes *CC* 3.4.222.

15–16 *break Melinda's windows*: see 3.1.40–1 above. Seconde edn. omits 'Melinda's' presumably, as Dixon notes, because Plume already knows about the letter. See 3.1.9.

18 *Tycho*: omitted in second edn. Kite calls his servant after Tycho Brahe (1546–1601), the celebrated Danish astronomer.

20 *Copernicus*: He names himself after the even more distinguished Polish astronomer, Nicholas Copernicus (1473–1543), who first suggested that the earth was a planet moving round the sun.

21 *Coppernose*: 'a red nose caused by disease, intemperance' (*OED*). Omitted in second edn.

31 *under Forceps*: there is no such zodiacal sign. Forceps are tongs used by blacksmiths.

33–4 *there's Leo, Sagittarius . . . Namur, Brussels, Charleroy*: only Leo 'the Lion' (Latin) and Sagittarius 'the Archer' (Latin) are authentic zodiacal signs. They have patriotic and military connotations. The other items (apart from 'Forceps') are fortresses or towns in Flanders which were won and/or lost in War of the Treaty of Augsburg. See Notes *CC* Preface 28.

41–8 *of your arrears . . . a fortnight's advance*: soldiers on active service received subsistence pay and arrears, or back pay, which the government was slow to dispense, and much of which disappeared into the pockets of officers and others. Money-lending by government agents was notorious. See Scouller, *The Armies*, 127–8. It was a capital offence under the Articles of War for soldiers to demand the pay due to them.

50 *So am I, sir*: second edn. 'Sir, I am above 'em.'

51–2 *Captain of ... Artillery*: a fictitious military title.

60 *cheapening a pen'worth*: haggling over a pennyworth.

60–1 *a cane hanging upon his button*: it was fashionable to carry canes hanging from the button of a sleeve.

69–70 *a collector of ... captain of grenadiers*: the list is absurdly varied. A collector of excise was a low-class tax official (see *BS* 5.1.11); a plenipotentiary was an ambassador with full powers to act on behalf of his sovereign.

73 *Right*: omitted in second edn.

75 *Tom o' Lincoln*: '[Protagonist] of *The Most Pleasant History of Tom a Lincoln*, by Richard Johnson (1599, 1607) of which a new edition appeared in 1705' (Ross). There is a bell of this name in Lincoln Cathedral.

75–6 *Tom–tit*: a common name for the blue titmouse.

76 *Tom Telltroth*: a proverbially truthful person (cf. Tom All-Thumbs and Tom Trifler).

Tom o' Bedlam: a wandering lunatic licensed to beg. See Edgar in Shakespeare's *King Lear* and Notes 5.5.148 below.

Tom Fool: a half-wit, one who acts the part of a fool (esp. in a group of morris dancers).

85 *Pluck*: 'the heart, liver, and lungs (sometimes with other viscera) of a beast used for food' (*OED*).

133 *a mercer*: 'in Country Towns one that Trades in all sorts of Linen, Wool, Silk and Grocery Wares' (cited *OED*); and also offering the kind of early banking service provided in the City by goldsmiths. See Notes *TR* 3.2.127.

154 *the*: omitted in second edn.

167 *guineas for claps*: army and navy surgeons received additional payment for every case of venereal disease they treated. According to Scouller (*The Armies*, 236), Surgeons-General received about half the sum Kite promises, but made money on the side by supplying medicines. Surgeons had low social and professional standing compared with physicians. They were generally without formal medical qualifications.

182 *make what money you can*: turn your assets into cash.

186–7 *he needs must ... the Devil drives*: anyone driven by the Devil has no choice but to go.

225 *Cacodemon del fuego*: Demon from Hell (Spanish). Second edn. substitutes the impudently nonsensical '*Cacodemon del Plumo*', 'Demon from Plume'.

234–43 *Here, Tre, Tre . . . the blood comes*: omitted in second edn. 'Tre' was
a common name for a dog.

257–8 *the word demonstration . . . father of lies*: 'demonstration' in fact derives
from the Latin *monstrare*, 'to show'. Satan is the father of lies. See John
8: 44.

287–93 *Ay, you may . . . for a wit*: omitted in second edn. in consequence of
the omission of 234–43.

296–7 *ever I . . . my life*: first edn. 'you ever made in your life'.

298 *the chops of the Channel*: the entrance to the English Channel from the
Atlantic. As channel also meant 'vagina', Kite is really telling Worthy
that he will remain in Shrewsbury with Melinda.

303 *familiar*: a devil ready to act as servant to a witch or magician, often in
the form of a domestic or pet animal.

307 *force my lines*: break through my defensive lines. Kite implies that his
magic circle is more dangerous than the defensive lines Brazen would
force professionally.

325–6 *billets-doux are like bank bills?*: before the introduction of paper money,
bank bills were individually drawn up, signed, and dated, like modern
bank-cheques.

358–9 *I once intended . . . to better advantage*: wisely omitted in second edn.
The plot is decidedly confused at this point. See Notes 5.4.47 below and
Introduction p. xvi.

375 *efforts*: accented on the second syllable.

5.1 s.d. *Scene*: this scene is entirely omitted in second edn.

17–18 *the duck and . . . in the decoy*: the duck and the wild drake in the trap
together.

27 *Mr Bridewell*: see Notes *TR* 5.3.18–19.

5.2.16 *the other spark*: Brazen.

18–19 *the very act, re infecta*: an absurd contradiction but the truth: *re infecta*
is legal Latin for 'a deed undone'; the constable should have said *in
flagrante delicto*—'caught in the heat of the act'.

30 *Goosecap*: sign of a fool or dolt (Kenny).

35–6 *danced, threw . . . by their bedside*: traditional rites at a wedding party.
The bridal pair were seen to bed by their friends to much ribald
comment. It was customary for men to stand with their backs to the
groom and throw his stockings at him blind. Women did the same with
the bride. Whoever hit their targets would be the next to marry.

44 *a sacrament*: the Roman Catholic view. Considerable uncertainty, both
theological and legal, existed about what constituted a marriage and how
and when it became binding. See also Introduction p. xxii and Lawrence
Stone, *Uncertain Unions: Marriages in England 1660–1753* (1992).

45–9 *among soldiers . . . is concise*: this ceremony is described in Francis Grose, *A Classical Dictionary of the Vulgar Tongue*, ed. Francis Partridge (1931), 217.

54 *exercise*: perform the standard movements of drill.

59 *a hat bien troussé*: a hat well set [on the head] (French). First edn. omits 'a hat'.

  a martial twist in my cravat: Kenny suggests that this is a reference to a style of neckwear first created at the Battle of Steinkirk or Steenkirk, 24 July 1692.

59–60 *a fierce knot in my periwig*: on campaign, wigs were worn knotted at each side (Kenny).

60 *a cane upon my button*: see Notes 4.2.60–1 above.

63 *'Captain Pinch'*: Silvia calls herself Wilful elsewhere (3.2.146). Her use of an obvious nickname here is splendidly insolent. 'Captain' is too high a rank for a mere youth, and 'Pinch' implies both poverty and rakish style. She knows that Plume will put the court right at the proper time. Balance uses the name Wilful later (5.7.54).

5.3.24 *Seven years' servitude*: an allusion to the two seven-year periods which Jacob served Laban in return for marrying his daughters, Leah and Rachel. Gen. 29: 20–8.

36 *begin upon a new score*: open a new account.

37 *till Lent be over*: in Catholic countries marriages could not be publicly celebrated during the six and a half weeks of Lent. The custom of waiting until Easter before marrying survived in post-Reformation England.

47 *your own horses*: on a long journey it made sense for those who could afford it to ride two horses alternately.

5.4.1–2 *the first colony . . . at Virginia*: at Jamestown in 1607.

 9–10 *he has . . . a turkey*: see Notes 1.1.74 above. Gypsies were notorious as poachers of fowl.

12 *the canonical hour*: marriages could only be celebrated in English churches between the hours of 8 a.m. and noon.

18 *a thousand pound*: all early edns. read 'twenty thousand pound'. But Brazen could not have spent £400,000 in the service, i.e. a third of the annual cost of the civil administration in the reign of William III (Ogg, *England in the Reigns*, 407). Ross's emendation, on the supposition that ' "twenty" is clearly caught from the line below', is eminently sensible.

20 *architecture*: the term covers the design of ships as well as that of buildings.

21 *a privateer or a playhouse*: Kenny suggests that the absurd dialogue arising from this 'odd question' makes satirical allusion to the appalling

acoustics at the Queen's Theatre in the Haymarket, which opened in 1705. Designed by Sir John Vanbrugh (1664–1726), playwright and architect, it was poorly managed ('ill-manned'), had financial problems (ran 'upon the shallows'), and its profits were skimmed by its leading actors (it sprang a 'leak'). See Notes Dedication 34 above and Epilogue 14–15 below.

37–8 *in specie*: in actual coin.

47 *her own hand*: as Robert L. Hough noted (*Notes and Queries* (1954), 474), Lucy has already sent two letters to Brazen (4.2.318–19) and had no need to rely on Melinda's real signature, though the plot requires the deception of Worthy. The entire Lucy–Brazen–Melinda–Worthy sub-plot is underdeveloped. See Introduction p. xvi.

55 *mount*: the sexual connotations of this word were commonly understood.

65 *ferried over to the Elysian Fields*: in classical mythology, the souls of the dead were ferried across the Acheron for judgement, the just going subsequently to the Elysian Fields. See Notes *TR* 5.1.111.

5.5.6 S.D. *saluting*: embracing, greeting—but not with a military salute.

9 *staff-officers*: officers acting as advisers to a general. Kite, however, is alluding to the fact that he and the constable used their staffs to control the unfortunates in their power.

10 *the militia*: locally raised part-time soldiers. See Notes *TR* 3.1.62–3.

20 *with a witness*: 'and no mistake' (*OED*).

28 S.D. *Plume ascends and sits upon the Bench*: Stonehill, following J. H. Burton, points out that under the Mutiny and Impressment Acts (see Notes 2.3.19–20 above), it was unlawful for officers to act as justices. However it was the custom in all courts for distinguished observers to sit on the bench with the justices or the judge, and this is all Plume does. The collusive relationship between the army and the magistracy is, however, obvious enough.

35 *SCRUPLE*: second edn. 'SCALE'.

41 *Counsel for the Queen*: Kite is ranking himself high in the legal profession. Queen's (or King's) Counsel were senior barristers. Another group of senior barristers were known as Serjeants at Law.

46 *five foot ten inches high*: for the times a tall man.

46–7 *the Cheshire Round*: a country dance.

50 *best-natured, painstaking*: second edn. 'best-naturedest, painstakingest'.

52–3 *A wife and . . . and five children?*: only unmarried men could be lawfully impressed.

57–8 *They live upon . . . five miles round*: Archer suggests that this speech ought to be Kite's, but all edns. assign it to Plume, who thus openly aligns himself with the country gentlemen in their war against the poachers—one of the great grievances of the poor against the rich in the countryside from the seventeenth century onwards. Under military law, the heaviest monetary penalty was for 'disobeying the provisions for the protection of game' (Scouller, *The Armies*, 268). The army knew better than to offend the gentry.

60–1 *he shoots flying*: see Notes 1.2.32 above. In its sexual sense, the pun refers to the man's many children. The phrase also implies that the French armies will be put to flight.

68–9 *that fellow upon ... at a birth*: such a well-fed, vigorous fellow may father twins or triplets. Multiple births were taken as evidence of exceptional paternal virility, while rude health among the poor was regarded as evidence of a secret source of income of which the gentry had a right to be suspicious.

73 *the house of correction*: a local place of detention and punishment of offenders, including women of low repute.

75 s.d. *Takes the man down*: leads the man away from in front of the bench.

93 *do more service in a siege*: the importance of mining skills in military operations is indicated in the Prologue to *TR*. Ogg (*England in the Reigns*, 84) notes the anomalous position of miners. They 'did not fit into any of the recognised [social] categories ... [They] lived strange, dangerous lives; they had their own vocabulary; their distinctive appearance marked them off from other men. The miner was further degraded by the black substance which he handled; moreover, he usually lived in a separate community. He earned good wages ... but he had to suffer ostracism.'

132 *PLUME (reads) 'Articles ... mutiny and desertion'*: early edns. print these words as a stage direction, but I agree with Archer and his eighteenth-century predecessor that it makes no sense to have Plume in the background droning this ritual of initiation for newly impressed recruits while the main dialogue proceeds. Silvia evidently interrupts Plume before he can embark on his task, and Balance has to repeat his request below.

136–8 *build a horse ... in your life*: the horse was a military punishment. With his feet heavily weighted and his hands tied, the prisoner was seated across acutely angled planks for hours at a time. See Scouller, *The Armies*, 268.

139 *Huffcap*: arrogant swashbuckler.

148 *Bedlam*: the Hospital of St Mary of Bethlehem for the insane in London.

155 *levy-money*: payment made on enlistment.

164–5 *the act allows him but ten*: up to 10 shillings (50 pence) was payable for each recruit produced by a constable.

182–3 *lay down your . . . done before you?*: dismissed officers of state were required to surrender their staffs or wands of office. Marshals surrendered their batons when taken prisoner.

5.6.5 *a foot officer*: as Dixon notes this contradicts Brazen's claim to have been in the cavalry at Landen (3.1.224–5). He is, however, within his rights to claim choice of weapon.

16–19 *how many paces . . . sure of you*: Worthy rejects the proposal that they step out a number of paces and fire together. He will let Brazen fire first, so that he can take a steady aim at him afterwards.

22 *fight upon a cloak*: at such close quarters, duels were dangerous indeed, and Worthy would have little chance of getting his own shot in. Brazen gets the better of this exchange.

32 *Rose Tavern, Covent Garden*: see Notes *CC* Epilogue 4.

33 *napkins*: probably a term for whores (Strauss).

5.7 S.D. *Scene*: all early edns. continue without a scene-change at this point. See Introduction pp. xvi–xvii.

81 *BALANCE*: second edn. 'SILVIA'.

113–14 *the Leeward Islands*: Antigua, Monserrat, Nevis, and St Christopher's (St Kitts) in the West Indies.

117 *fireship*: a crewless vessel deliberately set on fire and sent adrift into an enemy fleet. Slang for a prostitute with venereal disease. In neither sense is Brazen's account a compliment to Balance's supposed kinsman.

123–5 *to have been . . . a French picaroon*: he was nearly tricked by Lucy who was herself operating like a privateer and was possibly 'French'—i.e. diseased. See Notes 5.4.21 above and *CC* 1.1.42.

154 *lasting*: second edn. 'endless'.

Epilogue

1–4 *All ladies and . . . be kindly entertained*: see Kite's opening speech 1.1.1–8. Escourt, in the role of Kite, obviously spoke the Epilogue.

12–13 *'An Overture to a Battle'*: that was not its name; see Notes 1.1 S.D. above.

14–15 *the great operas . . . Schellenberg, and Blenheim*: see Notes *TR* 2.1.83–4 and 2.1.7–8 above. In representing these allied victories over the French as 'operas', Farquhar is alluding to the competition between the theatre companies in the staging of opera, a 'war' the Drury Lane company won, in spite of the opening of the Queen's Theatre.

17 *delicatesse*: fine sensibility (French).

22–3 *soft as Bononcini's . . . in the world*: Camilla, an English language version of the opera *Il Trionfo di Camilla, Regina del Volsci* by Giovanni Bononcini (1672–1750) was sung at Drury Lane to great acclaim nine days before *The Recruiting Officer* opened. Camilla was performed by the first English stage soprano, Toftida (Katherine Tofts (1685–1756)). See Notes *BS* 3.2.35.

29 *subscription*: i.e. it was paid for in advance by patrons and not by the sale of tickets. This may be why Farquhar felt free to write about it so contemptuously (Archer).

30 *Grand Alliance*: the Alliance signed on 7 September 1701 between William III, the Holy Roman Emperor, Leopold III, and the States-General of the Netherlands to resist the threat of a French Prince succeeding to the throne of Spain. See Notes *TR* Prologue 1.

35–6 *if the lady . . . to be sick*: Katherine Tofts was notoriously temperamental. She eventually lost her reason.

The Beaux' Stratagem

Dramatis Personae

    BELLAIR: handsome manner (French).

    FOIGARD: shield of faith (French).

    HOUNSLOW: Hounslow Heath was infested with highwaymen.

    BAGSHOT: Bagshot, Surrey, was also dangerous for travellers.

    BONIFACE: deriving from the Latin *bonum facere*, 'to do good', the name clearly alludes to the inn-keeper's appearance and may also be ironic.

    SCRUB: a drudge (*OED*).

    LADY BOUNTIFUL: see Introduction p. xvi.

Advertisement

1 *my illness*: the play was commissioned on 27 January 1707. Its first performance was on 8 March. Farquhar died approximately six weeks later, in late April.

4 *care of Mr Wilks*: see Notes *CC* Preface 24. Wilks's talent for friendship, and for giving life to parts written for him, are both beyond question.

Prologue

3–4 *When the Plain . . . the modish times*: an allusion to Wycherley's last play, *The Plain Dealer* (1677), a fiercely satirical work, whose eponymous hero was identified with its author. See Notes *CC* 1.1.290–1.

8 *UNION*: the Act of Union uniting the Kingdoms of Scotland and England received Royal Assent two days before the play's first night.

10 *her precepts*: 'One of the first of Queen Anne's proclamations was not merely for the punishment of vice and immorality, but for "the promotion of piety and virtue"; with her royal example . . . debauchery became less fashionable' (Ogg, *England in the Reigns*, 532). Nevertheless,

NOTES TO PAGES 246–50

though taken quite seriously at one level, there was often an undercurrent of facetiousness in literary celebrations of Queen Anne's reign. See Notes *CC* Epilogue 18.

12 *or*: either.

13–14 *tares . . . the golden ears*: an allusion to the parable of the wheat and the tares. See Matt. 13: 24–30.

19–20 *Simpling our author . . . may diversion yield*: our author goes from field to field gathering medicinable herbs and selecting such fools as may make for laughs. 'Simpling' puns on the word 'simple' in the senses of 'idiot' and 'cull'. See Glossary.

1.1.5 *deserve to have none*: cropping of ears was a common punishment in the seventeenth century.

6 *Warrington*: a town in Cheshire, about 60 miles north-west of Lichfield.

11–12 *overturn them tomorrow*: topple the coach, either from tiredness or (Cordner suggests) in revenge for not patronizing an inn where he and the landlord have an understanding.

16 *the Lion and the Rose*: the names of rooms in the inn.

23 *as the saying is*: Boniface's catchphrase.

32 *old style*: see Notes *TR* 2.3.58.

36 *Anno Domini*: in the year of the Lord (Latin). The phrase implies that the ale is very old and very good.

55 *a dram*: she ruined her constitution by drinking 'drams', i.e. measures of spirits, instead of sticking sensibly to ale.

71 *the king's evil*: scrofula, a disease which was thought to be curable by the touch of the English sovereign. See *Macbeth*, 4.3. Sam Johnson (1709–84), a sufferer from scrofula and a native of Lichfield, was 'touched' by Queen Anne. See Glossary for other diseases mentioned.

88 *curious*: 'difficult to satisfy, particular, nice, fastidious' (*OED*).

90 *He has it there, you mean*: an allusion to cuckold's horns. See Notes *CC* 1.1.61. Being stupid Sullen is more likely to have an unfaithful wife.

94 *quarter day*: rents fell due at three-monthly intervals on 25 March, 25 June, 29 September, and 25 December.

99–100 *French officers*: prisoners of war. Officers, being gentlemen, could be relied on to keep their word (parole) and not escape if released from confinement.

134–5 *Why, Nick Marrabone . . . a good bowler*: Marrabone, or Marylebone, was the site of celebrated Gardens, which included a bowling green and was a venue for pickpockets. Fifer notes that Archer's phrase is an ironical twist on the proverbial 'an honest man and a good bowler'.

137 *Generous*: 'high-born . . . gallant . . . magnanimous' (*OED*).

137 *the Park*: see Notes *CC* 1.1.

139 *autumnal periwig*: Jack's wig was balding, like a tree in autumn.

151–2 *I am a man . . . you my servant*: Kenny notes that this device was used in *The Lying Lover* (1703) by Richard Steele (1672–1729), a depressingly moral play which according to its author was 'damn'd for its piety' (quoted Hume, *Development of English Drama*, 468). See Introduction pp. xiv–xv.

157 *tits*: small horses, nags.

158 *twenty degrees*: of latitude or longitude—a wide area.

166–8 *and let me tell . . . we have spent*: the first edn. reads 'and let me tell you, besides thousand, that this two hundred pound, with the experience that we are now masters of, is a better estate than the ten we have spent.' I have accepted Archer's and Stonehill's suggestion that 'thousand' was misplaced, probably by the typesetter.

170 *came off*: left the scene—i.e. London.

174 *gone a-volunteering*: joined the allied armies in the Low Countries as volunteer gentlemen-rankers, a course of action which Sir Harry Wildair may have followed when he made 'a campaign in Flanders' (*CC* 1.1.113–14). Such volunteers were unpaid and not subject to the degrading discipline of the Mutiny Act (Scouller, *The Armies*, 259–60).

195 *famish their own*: starve their own eyes.

199 *kind keepers*: men who kept mistresses. See Dryden's play, *The Kind Keeper* (1679), for an alternative view of such pleasures.

216 *Sappho's singing*: Sappho was a Greek poet, who wrote passionate love lyrics, often addressed to women. She was born on the island of Lesbos in the seventh century BC.

217 *Actaeon*: see Notes *CC* 1.1.61.

224 *out of doors*: out of fashion.

228–30 *At Nottingham . . . at Norwich*: this journey would take them eastwards across England towards the North Sea and the Netherlands.

232 *Venus . . . Mars*: see Notes *CC* 1.1.98.

233 *A match!*: 'a compact, bargain' (*OED*).

235 *What will your worship please to have for supper?*: Kenny, following Richard Hindry Barker, points out that the ensuing dialogue is highly reminiscent of a scene in *She Wou'd and She Wou'd Not* (1702) by Colley Cibber (1671–1757).

278 *chosen parliament-man*: see Notes *CC* 4.1.157. Parliamentary candidates were expected to 'treat' the population at large (even the disenfranchised). Bribery was also commonplace.

289 *'the man upon the black mare'*: presumably a notorious but unidentified highwayman.

297 *to boot*: as well.

332–3 *But you look . . . dressed so tight*: only these lines are printed in the first edn. The text of the entire song is from the 1728 edn.

356 *St Martin's parish*: the parish of St Martin's-in-the-Fields, Charing Cross, where Farquhar was buried.

2.1.5 *Doctors' Commons*: see Notes *CC* 1.1.148.

11 *long vacation*: London was socially dead during the summer months when the law courts were not sitting.

12–14 *a case of . . . constant man alive*: the greatest obstacle to separation by mutual consent without divorce was the law of property in marriage. On marriage a husband became the owner of his wife's property. The effects of this could be modified by pre-marriage settlements, which might, for example, secure a proportion of the income from her former property on the wife, an adequate jointure for her widowhood, or a guarantee that some or all of their mother's fortune would be available for the dowries of any daughters of the marriage. Evidently Mrs Sullen enjoys considerable rights under her pre-marriage contract with Sullen, but as long as he holds 'all the articles of marriage with my lady, bills, bonds, leases and receipts' (5.4.256–8) she cannot exercise them. Nor can she obtain a separation from him against his will unless he commits repeated and flagrant infidelities, or his beatings are judged to be excessive. See Notes *TR* 1.1.112.

19–20 *an hospital child*: a child raised in a home for foundlings.

31 *rosemary*: 'an evergreen shrub . . . the leaves of which have an agreeable fragrance, and are used in perfumery, cookery and to some extent medicine' (*OED*).

41–2 *within the weekly bills*: see Notes *CC* A New Prologue 5–7.

43–5 *every Phillis has . . . alarms to love*: Corydon, like Phillis, is a name traditionally used in pastoral poetry, the flowery language of which Mrs Sullen parodies. See Notes *CC* Epilogue 7.

56 *by the way*: meanwhile.

86 *naught*: ill-behaved.

98 *shave my head*: a common and sensible practice when wigs were fashionable.

2.2.5 *je ne sais quoi*: literally, 'I don't know what' (French)—an indefinable quality.

22 *a blazing star*: a comet.

the cathedral: Lichfield is a cathedral city.

42 *at the coronation*: Queen Anne was crowned in April 1702. The action of the play takes place in 1707.

63–4 *that ever hanged or saved a rogue*: see Gibbet's remarks on this topic 5.2.153–4.

65 *mourning rings*: rings distributed to mourners at a funeral, sometimes paid for out of the estate.

70 *arms*: a coat of arms.

81 *paint?*: use make-up?

84 *premises*: either 'the aforementioned items' or 'the building'—both legal terms.

88 *gentlemen o' the pad*: gentlemen of the road—highwaymen.

92 *smoke 'em?*: suspect them?—i.e. get them to reveal themselves, like bees smoked out of a hive.

99–100 *old Brentford at Christmas*: a town to the west of London referred to in *The Castle of Indolence* (1748) by James Thomson (1700–48) as 'a town of mud'.

105–6 *has been at the Bar by his evasions*: seems to have been tried in a court of law if the evasiveness of his answers is anything to go by.

117 *upwards or downwards?*: towards or away from London.

119 *a contrary way*: i.e. upwards—Gibbet expects to be hanged.

132 *whipped-out trooper*: a common soldier who had been flogged prior to dismissal from the army.

134 *catechise*: more commonly 'catechism'—a fixed set of questions, usually on religious doctrine and practice, the answers to which had to be learned by heart.

169 *Love pictured blind?*: Cupid was frequently depicted blindfold, to represent the randomness of love's effects and the blindness of lovers.

183 *this garb*: Archer's servingman's livery. See Notes *TR* 3.1.131.

223 *Don Quixote had in his*: see Notes *TR* 4.3.7–8 and *RO* 1.2.42.

3.1.4 *conversable in the subjects of the sex*: able to talk about men.

18 *Narcissus*: in classical mythology the beautiful son of a river god, who fell in love with his own reflection in a pool.

22 *cephalic plaster*: a plaster for the head. Mrs Sullen's suggestion is deliberately ludicrous.

40 *Mercury!*: see Notes *RO* 4.2.1–4. The name was commonly used of human messengers, but applied to Scrub is evidently ridiculous.

47 *what countryman he was*: what part of the country he was from.

55 *a Jesuit*: see Notes *CC* 4.1.151. Jesuits were believed to be masters of disguise.

68 *a bag*: wigs with the back hair enclosed in a silken pouch were known as bagwigs.

89–90 *the favour*: Cordner suggests that Scrub gives these words an insolently sexual turn.

3.2.5 *Oroondates*: the hero of La Calprenède's *Cassandre* (10 vols., 1644–50). See Notes *CC* 3.4.185.

Cesario: the son of Cléopâtre and Julius Cæsar in La Calprenède's *Cléopâtre* (10 vols., 1647–56) which was published in England in 1687.

Amadis: the eponymous hero of *Amadis de Gaul*, a sixteenth-century romance of unknown Portuguese and/or Spanish authorship, translated into English in 1693.

7 *Ceres*: Roman goddess of vegetation who abandoned her care for the harvest when her daughter Persephone or Proserpina was abducted by Pluto, king of the underworld; Ceres was thought to resume her divine duties only during her daughter's six-monthly furloughs from Hades. See Notes *TR* 5.3.16.

22–5 *The nymph that . . . of sublime Milton*: except that they are in blank verse, these lines are not at all like the poetry of John Milton (1608–74). The reference to Cherry warming the bed with a warming pan ('brazen engine') is an obvious sexual innuendo. As Larson pointed out in his celebrated article (see Introduction n. 30.), Farquhar makes much better use of Milton's prose pamphlets on divorce than on his verse. See Notes 3.3.272–3, 397–400, 403–8, and 5.1.52–63 below.

28–9 *tickles the trout*: trout can be caught by hand if they are caressed gently from below.

35 *Orpheus*: son of Apollo, god of the sun and music in classical mythology, and of Calliope, muse of epic poetry, Orpheus was a superb musician, whose playing persuaded Dis (Pluto) to release Orpheus' wife, Eurydice, from Hades. By looking at her before she reached the upper world, however, Orpheus lost her forever. See Notes *TR* 5.3.16.

Toftida: see Notes *RO* Epilogue 22–3 and 35–6. Katherine Tofts was currently singing at Drury Lane.

43 *a bill upon Cherry*: a bill of credit from a bank authorized a named person to draw money on loan from other banks, etc. Aimwell wants to borrow Cherry while he pursues Dorinda.

44–5 *all her corn . . . to my market*: Cherry is Archer's Ceres; he has a monopoly on her goods (has 'engrossed' them).

82–3 *in the plantations . . . the worst service*: military service in the plantations (the West Indies) was unpopular because very dangerous to health. Gibbet, however, is covertly admitting that he was transported there as a criminal in expectation of Aimwell's making similarly coded admissions of a comparably criminal history. See Notes *RO* 4.1.69–70 (revised text).

86 *a Roman for that*: as courageous and self-sacrificing as an ancient Roman patriot.

87 *One of the first*: Strauss points out that the early followers of Romulus, founder of Rome, were a rabble.

90 *Will's*: see Notes *CC* A New Prologue 5–7.

91 *White's*: see Notes *TR* 3.1.155.

98 *encourage him to declare*: see Notes 82–3 above.

108–10 *a charge . . . four, I believe*: Fifer suggests a threefold pun here, a charge being a sum of money, a quantity of gunpowder, and an accusation in court. Gibbet clearly intends the first, Aimwell the second and third.

152 *gentlemens*: Foigard's Irish accent is at once detectable. See Notes *TR* 3.2.16–17 and Introduction pp. xv–xvi.

161 *Teague*: see Notes *TR* Dramatis Personae.

165 *What King of Spain*: see Notes *TR* Prologue 1.

3.3.49 *put it upon that lay*: take that course.

51 *that same Pressing Act?*: see Notes *RO* 2.3.19–20 and Introduction p. xvi.

60 *better end of the staff*: the advantage of a bargain or contract.

64 *son of a whore of Babylon*: the great whore of Revelation (see Notes *CC* 2.2.27) was identified by Protestants with Rome and the papacy; Foigard is accordingly called her son.

87 *draw warrants*: draft orders of various kinds. Warrants could be legal authorizations to make and receive payments, or receipts for payments made. Poor Scrub seems to function as Sullen's steward and as an unofficial justice's clerk. See Notes *TR* 5.4.151–2.

90 SCRUB: 1728 edn.; first edn. 'ARCHER'.

163 *turned off, and rendered incapable*: sacked, and denied any prospect of further employment—by being given no reference.

184 S.D. *'Sir Simon the King'*: a popular ballad.

185–6 *A trifling song . . . trifle and ended*: only these lines were printed in the first edn. The text of the entire song is from the 1728 edn.

206 *Gold keys*: the insignia of the Lord Chamberlain.

207 *White rods*: staffs of office. See Notes *RO* 5.5.182–3.

211–12 *The levée will . . . trifles indeed*: 'Your grace' being the proper form of address to a duke, these lines are a possible allusion to the failures of the Duke of Ormonde as a patron. See Introduction p. ix and Notes *TR* 3.1.34–5 and *RO* Dedication 54. On the other hand, the levée was a standard satirical target in the eighteenth century, which Farquhar had already tackled. See *TR* 3.1.

223 *A Peace*: attempts were made to end the war in 1706.

225–6 *A black coat . . . red may endeavour*: see Notes *CC* 1.2.69.

238 *Something for a pair of gloves*: a conventional expression for a gratuity. See Notes *TR* 3.1.91.

239 *excused*: a gentleman may marry for money, but he may not accept a tip.

257–8 *give no quarter . . . you be entered*: show no mercy once you have been entered—for a tournament or competition. Fifer suggests a sexual innuendo here. See Mrs Sullen's remark 3.1.3–4.

261 *upon the tapis*: upon the tablecloth, i.e. up for discussion.

272–3 *One flesh! . . . to a dead body*: Larson cites the following Miltonic parallel; 'nay instead of beeing one flesh, they will be rather two carkasses chain'd unnaturally together; or as it may happ'n, a living soule bound to a dead corps' (*Complete Prose Works of John Milton* (1959), ii. 326).

289–90 *But here comes the count*: a note in the 1728 edn. reports that Farquhar cut the scene from this point after the first night to exclude Bellair's involvement in it, but Sullen's whispering to Dorinda and the subsequent dialogue between Mrs Sullen and Dorinda would have had to have been cut also. Their dialogue could resume at 386–7—'Well sister, you must be judge'. See Introduction p. xvi and Note on the Texts.

301–2 *a ransom may redeem me*: Kenny notes that a prisoner of war could purchase his liberty for the equivalent of one month's pay, 'although the British preferred a higher sum'.

316–17 *'Love and St Michael!'*: Bellair invents a battle-cry. St Michael, 'Prince of the Heavenly Host', was the patron of soldiers.

318 *he hears me not*: as this whole scene is designed to make the concealed Sullen jealous, 'he' could refer either to Sullen or to Bellair.

382–4 *'Fair Dorinda' . . . 'Revenge' &c.*: in Bononcini's *Camilla* (see Notes *RO* Epilogue 22–3) the heroine takes the name Dorinda for most of the action. Stonehill identifies the Count's song as 'Fair Dorinda, happy happy', though this is not sung by the heroine, but to her, by the Baroness disguised as Lavinia. Fifer points out that in the third act Camilla/Dorinda does sing another song which includes the words 'Revenge! Revenge! I summon! Revenge is all my Care; | Revenge! I summon: yet no', and suggests that Bellair 'sings or hums bits of both songs'. It would make sense for him to begin by singing the first in ironic praise of Mrs Sullen, and to end his speech by threatening her with revenge.

392–4 *Should I lie . . . than self-murder*: Fifer rightly draws attention to parallels in J. Milton, *Complete Prose Works*, ii (1959), 274, 605, on the general theme of self-destructive acts, but there are no specific verbal echoes.

397–400 *Law! what law . . . upon antipathies*: Cordner and Fifer draw attention to the following Miltonic parallels: 'Christ so left it, preaching only to the conscience, and not authorizing a judiciall Court to tosse about and divulge the unaccountable and secret reasons of disaffection between man & wife, as a thing most improperly answerable to any such kind of trial' (*Milton* (1959), 343); and 'oftimes the causes of seeking divorce reside so deeply in the radical and innocent affections of nature, as is not within the diocese of Law to tamper with' (ibid. 345).

402 *case of uncleanness*: case involving adultery.

403–7 *Uncleanness! O sister . . . keep 'em fast*: Cordner and Fifer draw attention to the following Miltonic parallels: 'natural hatred whenever it arises, is a greater evil in mariage, then the accident of adultery, a greater defrauding, a greater injustice' (*Milton* (1959), 332); 'men . . . would be juster in their balancing between natural hatred and casuall adultery; this being but a transient injury, and soon amended . . . but that other being an unspeakable and unremitting sorrow and offence' (ibid. 333); 'to forbid dislike against the guiltles instinct of nature, is not within the province of any law to reach' (ibid. 346); and 'To couple hatred therefore though wedlock try all her golden links, and borrow to her aid all the iron manacles and fetters of Law, it does but seek to twist a rope of sand' (ibid. 345).

4.1.1–2 *Were I born . . . must sit contented*: it was a commonly held but erroneous view that in the teaching of Islam women had no souls or rights in law. The property rights of married women were in fact stronger in Islamic countries than those prevailing in England at the time.

2–4 *England, a country . . . women be enslaved*: an allusion not only to the fact that since 1689 there had been two English queens-regnant, but also to the view that, in spite of their legal disadvantages, women 'really' were more powerful than men. 'You have it in your power,' Halifax advised his daughter (see Notes *CC* 5.1.4), 'not only to free your selves, but to subdue your Masters, and without violence throw both their Natural and Legal Authority at your feet' (8). Mrs Sullen's freedom, however, will only be achieved by the violent appropriation of legal authority in the final scene of the play.

24 *graips*: gripes, colic pains.

65 *ass's milk*: a frequently prescribed restorative diet.

113 *perfectly possessed*: epilepsy was anciently attributed to diabolic possession; Archer's hidden meaning is that the image of Dorinda has gained possession of Aimwell's soul.

140–2 *That hospitable seat . . . the stranger in*: Aimwell's heart receives the image of Dorinda and promptly floods his body with desire in the form of 'sanguine spirits', i.e. the essence of blood understood (according to traditional medical theory) as one of the four humours—the others being phlegm, bile, and choler—and generating when dominant 'a courageous, hopeful and amorous disposition' (*OED*).

144–5 *feathers to burn ... Hungary-water*: the pungent smoke from burning feathers, and the application of Hungary water ('as distilled water, made of rosemary flowers infused in rectified spirits of wine'—*OED*) were common cures for fainting.

150–3 *Sure I have ... bright divinity*: see Notes *TR* 5.1.111 and *TR* 5.3.16.

184–5 *'My service t'ye'*: Lady Bountiful jokingly toasts Aimwell, possibly miming as she does so.

198 *we understand originals*: a pun on the two senses of 'original'—'an original portrait' (*OED*), not a copy, and 'a singular, odd, or eccentric person' (*OED*).

220 *cedunt arma togae*: arms yield to the gown (Latin). A misquotation from Cicero's *De Officiis*, i. 22, 77. The original reads 'Let arms yield (cedant) to the gown, the laurel give place to honest worth' ('concedat laurea laudi'). Scrub's learning would have been deemed absurd in a servant.

223 s.d. *the side-scene*: one of the shutters on each side of the stage behind the proscenium arch. See Notes *CC* 2.5 s.d.

230 *à la française*: in the French manner (French).

237 *louis d'ors*: gold louis (French)—gold coins engraved with the head of the French king.

238 *give you an absolution for the shin*: as priest, Foigard proposes to hear Gypsy's Confession and absolve her of her sins, a commonplace view among Protestants of the uses to which Catholic priests put the confessional.

268–9 *O, 'tis Leda ... to make love*: see Notes *CC* 4.1.96. As well as Castor and Pollux, Leda gave birth to Helen of Troy and Clytaemnestra, wife and murderer of Agamemnon.

271 *Alexander's battles?*: between 336 and 323 BC, Alexander the Great conquered Greece, Egypt, and the Persian Empire, before advancing towards the Indus.

272 *Le Brun*: Charles Le Brun (1619–90), court painter to Louis XIV. Le Brun's series of large historical canvasses depicting the career of Alexander drew a parallel between Alexander and Louis who was the model for Alexander in at least one of the paintings.

273 *a greater general*: the Duke of Marlborough. See Notes *RO* 2.1.7–8; 12.
The Danube: Blenheim was fought in the Danube valley.

274 *Granicus*: Alexander won a great victory over the Persians by the river Granicus in 334 BC.

275 *Ramillies*: see Notes *RO* Dedication 45.
Arbela: Alexander defeated Darius, King of the Persians at Arbela in Assyria in 331 BC.

278 *Ovid in his exile*: Ovid was banished by the emperor Augustus to Tomi on the Black Sea in AD 8. Ovid reports that his poem *Ars Amatoria* (*The Art of Love*) was judged subversive and that he was involved in a scandal. This was rumoured to involve the Emperor's granddaughter Julia. See also Notes *CC* Title-page.

285 *If he were secret*: if he protected the lady's honour by keeping quiet— as, it would seem, Ovid did, whether or not his love was success- ful.

300 *cupids*: see Notes *CC* 5.1.38-9.

306-7 *Salmoneus . . . Jove's thunder*: Salmoneus was a mythical king who emulated Jupiter by driving his chariot over a brazen bridge to imitate thunder, hurling lighted torches like thunderbolts at his subjects; and it was with a thunderbolt that Jupiter destroyed him.

334-7 *First, it must . . . gold in't*: as well as describing a plot in the sense of a love-intrigue, Scrub alludes to the various 'horrid plots' against the state from the 'Gunpowder Plot' (1605) (see Notes *RO* 1.1.20-1) to the 'Popish Plot' (1678) which had been laid at the door of Catholics. Women (the Catholic queens of Charles I, Charles II, and James II), priests and French gold were the alleged ingredients.

373-4 *beg that fellow at the gallows-foot*: on occasion a woman could save the life of a man about to be hanged by begging for his release on condition of his marrying her.

375-6 *a friend of yours in his room*: have Sullen hanged instead.

402 *die with me*: climax sexually. The sexual innuendo in this dialogue is particularly uninhibited.

413 *the Drawing Room*: at Court. See Introduction p. xxii.

4.2.10 *Tom's*: Tom's coffeehouse, named after Captain Thomas West, was in Russell Street between Covent Garden Market and the theatre in Drury Lane.

15 *club o'th' reckoning*: equal share in the cost of the entertainment.

16 *Morris*: generally taken to be the owner of Morris's coffeehouse, in Essex Street, the Strand.

20-2 *sneak into the . . . the other three*: see Notes *CC* Prologue 30.

27-8 *he shall marry you*: marriages conducted by Catholic priests were valid and binding in law, but it was none the less illegal to conduct them, and participants were subject to a fine of £100.

36 *as they do to their Magna Carta*: as the latter [men] stick to their Magna Carta, i.e. to their legally enshrined rights. *Magna Carta* ('Great Charter' [Latin]), signed by King John in 1215, was regarded as the legal foundation of the subject's rights against the Crown.

37 *put on the gentleman*: take up the role of gentleman.

45 *catcht dere*: caught there, probably in the sense of tricked or deceived—
by priests like himself.

48–50 *subject of England . . . hang for't*: technically Foigard is a subject of
Ireland. However, by an Act of the Irish Parliament in 1697, even those
Irish soldiers who had lawfully taken service with the French were
prohibited from returning to Ireland. The Kingdom of Ireland, more-
over, was 'subordinate' to the Kingdom of England (later the United
Kingdom of Great Britain) where penal laws against Catholics were still
on the statute book though rarely enforced. Aimwell could easily make
Foigard's life uncomfortable to say the least.

61 S.D. *in a brogue*: English people remain perversely confident of their
ability to imitate Irish accents, but with his Irish background Wilks
would have been up to it.

64–5 *Mynheer, Ick wet . . . neat, sacramant*: sir, I do not know what he says.
I do not understand you, I swear. Farquhar's Flemish (or Foigard's) is
not good.

71 *dat is naame*: Foigard's real name is Macshane. Even if this were as
common a name in Ireland as Murphy, or Smith in England, the odds
against Archer's getting it right would be unconvincingly high. See
Introduction pp. xv–xvi.

78–9 *Irish cussens*: the English had great difficulty in understanding, never
mind respecting, the kinship systems of the Scottish, Welsh, and Irish,
and of their other subject peoples.

81–2 *Tipperary . . . Kilkenny*: Cordner notes that there were excellent
schools in both towns. If this is relevant, it only adds to the difficulties
of Foigard's entrapment.

86 *Purgatory*: a mocking reference to the Catholic teaching, much disliked
by Protestants, that after death the souls of the saved may have to
undergo a punitive purgation before being admitted to the sight of God
in Heaven.

116–17 *smells of nutmeg . . . East India ship*: toast, heavily spiced, was floated
in wine to flavour it. Sullen's christening cup has been used so often for
this purpose that it smells as fragrant as a ship from the East Indies.

122 *fairly entered*: thoroughly disordered.

123 *half seas over*: drunk.

137 *a Vigo business*: see Notes *TR* 2.1.83–4.

140 *Tyburn*: the place of public execution in London.

141–2 *buy myself . . . in the Household*: like commissions in the navy and the
army, offices in the Royal Household could be purchased. See Notes *CC*
1.2.98.

146 *'is the goddess I adore'*: I have been unable to identify Gibbet's song.

5.1.23 *to the*: first edn., 'to'.

52–8 *are not man . . . of the body?*: Larson draws attention to the following Miltonic parallels: 'there is no true marriage between them, who agree not in true consent of mind' (Milton, *Complete Prose*, ii., 445); 'the solace and satisfaction of the minde is regarded and provided for before the sensitive pleasing of the body' (ibid. 246); 'This is that rationall burning that mariage is to remedy' (ibid. 270); 'what can be a fouler incongruity, a greater violence to the reverend secret of nature, then to force a mixture of minds that cannot unite . . . ?' (ibid. 251); 'mariage is a human society, and . . . must proceed from the mind . . . if the mind therefore cannot have that due company by mariage, that it may reasonably and humanly desire that mariage can be no human society but a certaine formalitie . . . little better then a brutish congresse' (ibid. 275); and 'the greatest breach thereof . . . [is] unfitness of mind' (ibid. 276).

63 *naturally one*: united by an unbreakable natural bond.

5.2.28–9 *I'm a Jupiter . . . my Alcmena*: in the case of Alcmena Jupiter disguised himself as the woman's husband, Amphitryon. Dryden's play *Amphitryon* (1690) treats this seduction as an elegant comedy.

37–8 *smelt to*: inhaled.

50–1 *prostrate engineer . . . reach my heart*: see Notes *TR* Prologue 17–19.

51–2 *without my sex*: outside the general run of my sex.

93 *Bedlam*: see Notes *RO* 5.5.148.

110 *a dark lantern*: a lantern lit but muffled.

126 *a younger brother*: Gibbet's excuse—that he is in the traditionally impoverished state of the younger brother—points up the parallel between the robbers and the beaux.

146–7 *the government has . . . on these occasions*: a clergyman was required to be in attendance at an execution.

154 *to save my life at the sessions*: bribery of jurors was common.

5.3.1–2 *Come, come . . . old gentlewoman*: recent editors agree with Strauss that each of the rogues should address their respective prisoners. It is no less effective, however, for one actor to threaten another at a slight distance and the business could easily be managed to facilitate this.

7 *won't draw*: cannot be pulled (from their sheaths).

8 *every man his bird*: it was improper at shooting parties to shoot a bird that someone else was aiming at.

35–6 *like Alexander in the height of his victory*: in Lee's *The Rival Queens*, the victorious Alexander exclaims 'O, I shall burst | Unless you give me leave to rave awhile' (Act 3).

66 *downright Swiss*: see Notes *TR* 3.2.189.

84–5 *Eddystone*: the first Eddystone lighthouse, off the Cornish coast, built between 1696 and 1699, collapsed in the sea in the great storm of 1703.

5.4.4 *The sweets of Hybla*: Hybla, on the east coast of Sicily, near Syracuse, was famous for its honey.

77 *be your father*: take the role of the bride's father and 'give her away' to the groom at the wedding service.

108 *Sir Freeman*: Kenny corrects this to the proper form 'Sir Charles', but the solecism may be a deliberate piece of insolence on Archer's part.

124 *Mesdames, et messieurs*: ladies and gentlemen (French).

136–7 *Savez-vous . . . mademoiselle Cherry?*: do you know anything of Miss Cherry (French).

196 *Rib*: wife—Eve being formed by God from the rib of her future husband Adam. See Gen. 2: 22–4, a scriptural passage heavily emphasizing the strength of the marriage bond.

250 *justement*: exactly (French).

251 *a hundred thousand livres*: the literal translation of the English word 'pound' into French is *livre*, but the French coin was worth only a tenth of a pound sterling. See Introduction p. xvi.

257 *your lady*: first edn. 'his lady' (obviously a misprint) and the second and third edns. 'this lady', which is inconsistent with the run of pronouns. I follow Kenny in accepting the emendation in the 1711 edn.

An Epilogue . . . *Stratagem*
This is attributed to Edmund Smith (1672–1710) in the *Dramatick Works* (1736). Smith's *Phaedra and Hypolitus* was in production at the same time as *The Beaux' Stratagem*.

9 *At Leuctra . . . Theban died*: Epaminondas (418?–362 BC) died fighting for Thebes against Sparta at Maninea nine years after the battle of Leuctra between the same armies.

14 *Sergeant Kite*: Kenny notes that *The Recruiting Officer* played immediately before and during the run of *The Beaux' Stratagem*.

16–18 *To Thebes alone . . . Athenian praise*: Thebes and Athens were the centres of Greek culture, but the reputation of Will's is greater than either—and Farquhar's standing accordingly higher than that of Epaminondas. (Successful poets and generals in the ancient world were honoured with crowns of bay leaves.)

GLOSSARY

action acting

admiring viewing with wonder or surprise

adso a mild oath (God's soul)

advices sources of information

affected disposed, inclined

airy sprightly

alarm a call to arms by means of noise or music

alaw exclamation of surprise (not cited in *OED*)

all-fours game of cards for two

appearances performances

apprehensive anxious, insecure

arrah Irish expression of emotion

aspect face, visage

assizes sittings of the county courts before a visiting judge

attach arrest

bailiff sheriff's officer

baisemains respects

bandbox lightly constructed case for collars, hats, etc.

bandoleer a soldier's shoulder-belt for carrying cartridges

barrack-master soldier with authority in military barracks

bashaw Turkish grandee

basilisk fabulous reptile hatched by a serpent from a cock's egg

basset card game

beat up disturb game, drive animals or birds into the open

beaver hat made of beaver's fur

bedizened vulgarly bedecked

begar a mild oath (by God)

bespeak engage

blazoned bedecked with heraldic devices

bodkin short pointed weapon; hairpin

bogtrotter Irishman (derog.)

bohea fine black tea

bordel brothel

bottom ship, boat

brace pair (usually of dogs or game)

bravo desperado, thug, hooligan

brawn boned piece of lean meat

brevet document conferring nominal military rank without corresponding pay

brimstone sulpher

bring in find, deliver a verdict on

brisk smart; hence 'briskness', smartness

broach (of a cask) pierce to draw off liquor for the first time

broke (of the military) disbanded

bubble (adj.) worthless, frivolous

buff-coats soldiers (from their leather-jackets)

bull-dog firearm (slang)

bully lover, pimp

bum-bailiff sheriff's officer of the lowest grade

buskin high boot worn by actors in tragedy, cf. sock

buss kiss

cambric fine white Flemish linen

canting (1) jargon of thieves and beggars; (2) hypocritical religious whining

capitulate come to an agreement under various heads; hence capitulation, an agreement.

careful of concerned for

carnation flesh-coloured

carpet tablecloth

carriage conduct, style of life

carrier driver of heavy cart for transporting goods

cast (noun) throw (of dice), gamble.

catechise catechism; set questions and answers on religious doctrine

ceruse cosmetic made of white lead

chair sedan carried on poles

chapman haggler, customer

character public reputation

charge (noun) heavy package

charge (verb) load (a gun)

cheapening asking the price of, bidding for

chin-cough whooping cough

chop about change direction suddenly

chopping big, strapping

chuck gently pinch

circumstance particular, matter of fact

cit citizen (derog.)

clinched clasped tight

close (adj.) miserly

clown countryman, peasant, boor

cock (verb) pull back the spring hammer of a gun

cocket a forward or wanton person, later confined to women and spelt coquette

cocking cock-fighting

collegian student

colour regimental standard

commence formally graduate

commerce interaction

commons the population at large excluding the nobility

complaisance obligingness, courtesy, politeness

composure musical composition

concert (verb) arrange

concerted agreed to

condition high standing

conjuration conspiracy

copious substantial, weighty

cordial strong drink, spirits

cornice horizontal projection on building or interior wall

counter token for keeping count in games of chance

counterscarp outer wall supporting cover of fortified ditch

coupee dance step incorporated into elaborate bow

covey brood (of partridges)

coxcomb conceited fool

cozened tricked, deceived

cross (adj.) obstructive, awkward

cruiser cruising ship, usually a privateer

cuffs blows

cull (of plants) gather; (of animals) select for elimination or exclusion

cully (1) man, mate; (2) dupe, hence 'cully-squire'

cure parish, ecclesiastical or pastoral office

decorums characterizations appropriate to the rank and occupations of characters in a play

deep (of ground or roadways) muddy

delicate choice, requiring careful handling

demi-cannon gun with $6\frac{1}{2}$-inch bore

deuce bad luck; an exclamation of incredulous surprise—the Devil!

diet-drink drink specially prepared for invalids

ding dash

discovered revealed (on stage when a scene opens)

distemper illness

divert entertain, distract

douse blow

drab whore

drawer tapster or barman in a tavern

drum-major non-commissioned officer in command of drummers

dun press repeatedly for payment

earnest (noun) foretaste, sample

elder senior Presbyterian layman

engines tricks, plans, plots

engross buy up wholesale, monopolize

equipage retinue

escritoire writing-desk, bureau

evidence witness

excise duty payable on wines and spirits

familiar a demon in the service of a wizard or witch

family household, including servants

farthing a quarter of an old penny

fat (of ale) full-bodied

favours gifts, love-tokens

fee-simple absolute possession in law

figure social prominence

firelock gunlock in which the fuse is ignited by sparks

first-rate highest rated (of war ships)

flambeau flame-torch

florid in the bloom of health

foreign outside, coming from an external source

form customary formality

fraught loaded

furbelow flounce or pleated border on a garment

furnish supply

gabbering chattering, jabbering

gall harass

garzoon mild oath (God's wounds)

Goody form of address to married woman of humble station

goosecap booby, numbskull

gra Irish term of endearment

gramercy thank you

grass-plot ornamental lawn

gratification tip

green-sickness anaemia esp. in adolescent girls

gripe grip

groat silver coin worth four-pence (less than 2p)

groom-porter officer in charge of gaming at Court; professional gambler

guinea coin nominally worth £1.05 or 21 shillings

habit clothes

halberd sergeant's staff, with blade and spearhead

hale drag, pull; hence 'haling', dragging

hand handwriting

hank hold, restraining power

hansel inaugurate with some ceremony (often used ironically); test, prove

hartshorn ammonia (extracted from the antlers of deer)

he (noun) man

heroics high-flown bombast in a heroic play

higgle bargain over trifles

House (1) theatre; (2) one of the Houses of Parliament

huff look or talk big

humming (of liquor) strong, frothy

idle worthless, useless

impertinent irrelevant; hence 'impertinencies', irrelevancies

imprimis firstly

incumbent parish priest, holder of an ecclesiastical office

indentures contract by which an apprentice is bound to his master

ingenuity high birth, liberal education, intellectual capacity

insurance reliable evidence

interline insert

invest besiege

jade low, unreliable woman (usually jocular)

joy term of endearment which became common in Ireland

justice (of persons) justice of the peace, non-stipendiary magistrate

keeper man who has a kept mistress

knot bow or ribbon; an embossed ornament or stud

laudanum a medicine, principally of opium

leading-staff staff for directing army drill; an early version of the drum-major's mace

leash set of three (used with reference to hounds, hawks, etc.)

legerdemain sleight of hand

levee morning assembly in the sleeping-quarters of a prince or nobleman

levelled aimed

lighten outwards shine forth

list (verb) enlist in the army; hence listed, listing

litter straw bedding

loach small, edible freshwater fish

loadstone magnet

logice in logic

lubberly loutish, clumsy

maggot capricious fancy; hence 'maggotty', fanciful, whimsical

main (noun) sea

main (adj.) major, chief

mainly forcefully, mightily

mankind the male sex; the human race

mantua-maker dressmaker

market (verb) shop around

maw stomach

mayhap perhaps

mechanic (adj.) vulgar, characteristic of manual work, intellectually undemanding

memorandum reminder (euphemism for a bribe)

mercer a dealer in expensive fabrics

miss kept mistress

mother (1) brothel madam; (2) hysteria

mountebank itinerant quack

mum hush!

nab hat

Nantes French town which gave its name to brandy

naught (adj.) ill-behaved

neat (noun) ox, cow, heiffer, bullock

nice fastidious, sensitive

oakam fibre unpicked from old rope

obstructions constipation; internal blockages

obviate dispose of

ombre card-game for three played with forty-card pack

orangery snuff scented with extract from orange flower

orange water alcoholic cordial, or orange-flower water

ostler stableman at an inn

ouns mild oath ((God's) wounds)

overprice excessive payment

own (verb) acknowledge, admit

pad (1) highway robber; (2) slow-paced horse

palisado defensive row of stakes

parts (of persons) talents

pelf wealth

pendant hanging ornament attached to a bracelet or necklace

physic medicine

physical medicinal

picaroon pirate

pinners women's headwear with flaps pinned on each side

piquet card-game for two, played with thirty-two card pack

pistole Spanish coin worth rather less than a pound sterling

pith central part or portion

plate gold and silver utensils

platoon squad of soldiers organized to fire a volley

plodding solemn and dull

pocket-book booklike case with compartments for memoranda, bank-notes, etc.

point-heads head-dress of point lace

policy practical or political sagacity

portal stately doorway or entrance

portion dowry

portmantle portmanteau, travelling bag

post (adv.) urgently

posted advertised (literally by notices on posts)

posy motto, typically inscribed inside a ring

powder-sugar powdered sugar used as a coagulant

power of numerous

precise ostentatiously scrupulous

prefer promote; hence 'preferment', promotion, advancement

presently at once

press large, shelved clothes-cupboard

pretence cause, explanation

pretend presume, lay claim to

pretension claim to title or honour

prevent anticipate

prinking smart dressing

privateer armed vessel, manned by private individuals, and licensed to attack hostile shipping

projecting planning, plotting

proselyte convert

pulvil scented powder

punctual scrupulous, exact

punctually accurately

punk prostitute, tart

purchase procure, take possession of

quality social standing

rakehelly wild, debauched

raree-show peep-show

ratafia alcoholic cordial flavoured with the kernels of almonds, peaches, etc.

ravelin angled outwork in a fortification

receipt recipe

relation story

resenting revenging; hence 'resentment', revenge

rodomontado extravagant, boastful gesture or saying

rosa solis alcoholic cordial made from the sundew plant or with a brandy base

rubs inconveniences

ruelle bedroom suitable for fashionable morning reception

ruff vibrating drum-beat quieter than a roll

sack sherry-type wine from Spain or the Canaries

sally attack from a defended position

sa sa exclamation of fencer delivering a thrust (from the French *ça ça*)

sash window-frame

savour smell

scored noted on a tally

scour roister around, usually at night

scrape bow with the foot drawn backwards over the ground

scrivener notary

'sdeath mild oath (God's death)

second chief supporter of one of the principals in a duel

sentinal common soldier, soldier on guard-duty

seraglio harem

sessions assizes, local sittings of the higher law-courts

setting-dog setter

severally separately

sharper cheat, swindler, trickster

sharping cheating (at cards)

sharps a fight with unbated swords, not fencing

sheer off turn aside, alter direction (of ships)

shift manage

shoulder-knot knot of ribbon or lace worn by gentlemen

side-box enclosed seat or seat at the side of a theatre auditorium

simony immoral payment for religious favours, objects or office

simpling gathering herbal remedies

'slife mild oath ([God]'s life)

small-shot ammunition made of small lead pellets

smith blacksmith; forger of iron horse-shoes and tools

smock shift, chemise

smoke (verb) uncover a plot, become suspicious of

snush snuff

sock a light shoe worn by actors in comedy (cf. buskin)

sophisticated adulterated

souse suddenly, violently

sparagus asparagus

spark smart, fashionable young man (often derog.)

spleen peevish, depressed, or violent temper

sponging-house house kept by bailiff for preliminary confinement of debtors

squibs fireworks

stays corset

stick (verb) hesitate, hold back from (doing something)

still (adv.) always

stilling distilling

stiver Dutch coin, originally silver, of low value

stomach appetite

succubus a female devil who has sexual intercourse with sleeping men

sultana wife or concubine of a sultan

surenderies persons to whom an estate is legally surrendered

surveyor customs official in charge of tide-waiters

swinge beat, chastise, pay back

swingeing swinging, large

sword-knot ribbon or tassel tied to the hilt of a sword

tabor drum

tack about change the direction of a vessel by sailing against the wind

tapster bartender, innkeeper

tares weeds

term time when law-courts are sitting

tide waiter junior customs officer

tight (of persons) smart, lively, able (often used ironically)

tilting duelling, quarreling

tit hussy, minx

toilet dressing-table

tops turned-over brims of riding boots

toy trifle

traffic do business

train retinue

trainbands volunteer, part-time soldiers, recruited in London and a few large towns

transport delight

traverse sideways movement in fencing

truckles yields

tun cask (of wine, ale or beer)

tuneable melodic

turned off dismissed, sacked

tympany swelling

ububoo exclamation of terror

uncase strip

under-pocket pocket in petticoat or other underclothing

undressed in night clothes

usquebaugh whiskey, 'water of life' (Irish)

vapours depression, hysteria, or other nervous disorder

vintner wine-merchant

wafer small seal for letters

wait on attend on, give attention to

want (noun) lack, deficiency

wash (noun) liquid cosmetic

wauns mild oath ([God's] wounds)

whetting-glass drinking-glass

whisk whist, the card-game

wight person (often derog.)

winter-quarters places occupied by troops on campaign during the winter

wormwood bitterness

woundy considerable, very great

writings legal documents, agreements, deeds, etc.

zauns, zoons, zounds forms of the same oath ([God']s wounds)

OXFORD

MORE OXFORD PAPERBACKS

This book is just one of nearly 1000 Oxford Paperbacks currently in print. If you would like details of other Oxford Paperbacks, including titles in the World's Classics, Oxford References, Oxford Books, OPUS, Past Masters, Oxford Authors, and Oxford Shakespeare series, please write to:

UK and Europe: Oxford Paperbacks Publicity Manager, Arts and Reference Publicity Department, Oxford University Press, Walton Street, Oxford OX2 6DP.

Customers in UK and Europe will find Oxford Paperbacks available in all good bookshops. But in case of difficulty please send orders to the Cash-with-Order Department, Oxford University Press Distribution Services, Saxon Way West, Corby, Northants NN18 9ES. Tel: 01536 741519; Fax: 01536 746337. Please send a cheque for the total cost of the books, plus £1.75 postage and packing for orders under £20; £2.75 for orders over £20. Customers outside the UK should add 10% of the cost of the books for postage and packing.

USA: Oxford Paperbacks Marketing Manager, Oxford University Press. Inc., 198 Madison Avenue, New York, N.Y. 10016.

Canada: Trade Department, Oxford University Press, 70 Wynford Drive, Don Mills, Ontario M3C 1J9.

Australia: Trade Marketing Manager, Oxford University Press, G.P.O. Box 2784Y, Melbourne 3001, Victoria.

South Africa: Oxford University Press, P.O. Box 1141, Cape Town 8000.

WORLD'S CLASSICS
Seventeenth-century texts

APHRA BEHN
OROONOKO AND OTHER WRITINGS
Edited with an Introduction by Paul Salzman

*The Fair Jilt, Memoirs of the Court of the King Bantam,
The History of the Nun, The Adventure of the Black Lady,*
and *The Unfortunate Bride* are complemented by a
generous selection of Behn's poetry, ranging from public
political verse to lyrics and witty conversation poems.

APHRA BEHN
THE ROVER AND OTHER PLAYS
Edited with an Introduction by Jane Spencer

Contains *The Rover; The Feigned Courtesans; The Lucky
Chance; The Emperor of the Moon.*

(*Forthcoming November 1995*)

JOHN BUNYAN
THE PILGRIM'S PROGRESS
Edited with an Introduction by N. H. Keeble

JOHN FORD
'TIS PITY SHE'S A WHORE
AND OTHER PLAYS
Edited with an Introduction by Marion Lomax

Contains *The Lover's Melancholy; The Broken Heart;
'Tis Pity She's a Whore; Perkin Warbeck.*